FAILURE TO COMMUNICATE

The #1 Reason Teams Fail — and How to Fix It

Adriane "Ace" Crabtree

LSSBB | PROSCI | CAPM

Failure to Communicate: The #1 Reason Teams Fail — and How to Fix It

First Edition

Printed in the United States of America

ISBN 979-8-9956659-0-8

Published by **From the Floor Press**
fromthefloorpress.com

TABLE OF CONTENTS

THE COMMUNICATION PLAYBOOK — Frameworks, Scripts, and Use Cases

APPENDICES

Find Your Situation

How to Use This Book

This book is designed to be read straight through — but it's also built to be grabbed off your desk when you need it most.

Here's where to go based on what you're facing right now.

If Your Team Has Gone Quiet...

Start with Chapter 1 (p. 21) to understand the **Silent Spiral™,** then jump to **Chapter 7 (p. 154)** to rebuild trust and psychological safety. The silence is a symptom — these chapters show you the root cause.

If You Have a Tough Conversation Coming...

Go directly to the **Use Cases — What to Say in the Moment in the Playbook (p. 405).** Twenty-one scripts for escalation, feedback, bad news, accountability, and more — with exact language you can adapt to your situation. Then **read Chapter 9 (p. 183) for the Situation/Impact/Ask (SIA) framework** that structures every difficult conversation.

If Your Team Communicates But Nothing Changes...

Chapter 11 (p. 223) on closing the loop and accountability without blame. The problem isn't that people aren't talking — it's that nothing happens after they do.

If You're Dealing with Silos and Cross-Functional Chaos...

Chapter 12 (p. 237) on connecting silos, plus the Templates and Tools (p. 466) in Appendix B — stakeholder mapping and cross-functional meeting templates.

If You're Leading Through a Major Change...

Chapter 13 (p. 256) on leading through communication, and Chapter 14 (p. 271) on communicating through change — scope discovery, the change

communication framework, and what happens when leaders go silent during transitions.

If Your Remote or Hybrid Team Is Struggling...

Chapter 15 (p. 295) addresses every communication challenge unique to distributed teams — from meeting fatigue to the loneliness spiral.

If You Need a Framework Right Now...

The Communication Playbook (p. 370) contains 15+ frameworks, twenty-one scripts, five templates, and three quick-reference cards. **Designed to be used** this week, not studied for a semester.

If You Want to Assess Where Your Team Stands...

Appendix A (p. 460) has the 25-question Communication Self-Assessment with scoring. Take it alone or run it with your team. It will tell you which stage of the Silent Spiral™ you're in — and which chapters to prioritize.

If Everything Has Already Fallen Apart...

Chapter 17 (p. 346) — recovery, triage, and resilience. Then the Conclusion (p. 359) for the seven words that change everything.

Note from *Ace*

- ☑ **You don't need anyone's permission to start fixing communication.**
- ☑ You need **one honest conversation** and the **willingness** to have it.
- ☑ It **doesn't require** a **conference room**, a **mandate**, or a **reorganization**.
- ☑ It **requires one person** who decides that the next time **something isn't clear**, they'll **say so directly**, **respectfully**, and **without waiting for someone else to go first.**

Start wherever you are.

The next conversation is the one that matters.

Author's Note & Introduction

I did not set out to write a book about communication. I set out to fix a problem — and after twenty years across healthcare, government, for-profit education, and supply chain and logistics, I finally understood that the problem had a name.

In every environment — corporate conference rooms, state agency offices, warehouse floors — I kept seeing a version of the same pattern. Strong teams were capable of excellent work, and many delivered under pressure. But when they struggled, it was rarely because people were incompetent or unwilling.

More often, somewhere along the way, **people stopped talking to each other.** Or they were talking, *but not to the right people.* Or **they *assumed silence meant agreement.*** Or they knew exactly what was going wrong and ***did not feel safe enough to say it.***

So, I learned to stop asking only, "How did this happen?" and start asking the more useful question: "Where did the communication break down?" More often than not, the answer led back to a specific moment.

- *A handoff that was not made.*
- *An assumption that was not tested.*
- *A role nobody owned.*
- *A concern someone saw but did not feel safe enough to raise.*

That pattern followed me across industries, roles, and systems — and over time, I learned to see it through more than one lens.

I am a Lean Six Sigma Black Belt (LSSBB), a Prosci Certified Change Practitioner, and a Certified Associate in Project Management (CAPM). I have a master's degree in public relations from Ball State University and a bachelor's degree in Public Relations and Professional Journalism from Indiana State University.

I have spent two decades working in for-profit education, healthcare operations, government services, and high-volume warehouse and distribution environments — places where communication failures do not just slow things down. They cost *real safety, real money, real trust, and real momentum.*

This book exists because I have lived and worked through enough **communication breakdowns to know they are not simply personality problems.** They **are system problems.** And system problems require system solutions.

But the goal is not just to *recognize breakdowns after they happen.* Recognition is only the starting point. **The real goal is to stop treating communication as something we repair after failure and start treating it as a proactive, purposeful, intentional part of how work gets done.**

Communication belongs in the planning, the handoff, the decision, the escalation, the follow-up, and the recovery. Not after the fact. Not only when something goes wrong. Every time.

What this book is not: *A blame game.*

This book **is not about finding the "difficult personality,"** pointing at **one person,** and declaring the problem solved. I have seen that approach. *The person leaves. The pattern stays.* Why? Because the *system that produced the dysfunction was never addressed.*

Who this book is for:

- The project manager who wants to get ahead of the breakdown before it starts
- The team lead who senses something is off in the communication rhythm but cannot name it yet
- The individual contributor who has been burned by role confusion and unclear expectations
- The operations supervisor trying to build a culture where people speak up instead of quietly working around problems until they become crises

You do not need a certification. You **do not need to be a manager.** You **do not need to work in a specific industry.**

If you have ever thought, *"How did this not surface sooner?"* or *"Where did the handoff break?"* or *"We all saw the problem — so what kept us from naming it?"* this book is for you.

I have tried to write it the way some of my best mentors wish someone had talked to me twenty years ago: directly, honestly, practically, and from real experience.

The examples are real in spirit, even when they are general in name. **That familiarity is the point.**

You've already seen this. Now let's do something about it.

— *Ace*

Introduction: "What we've got here is failure to communicate."

A Line Born on a Real Chain Gang

Before this line became one of the most quoted in American cinema, it came from something real.

In 1949, a merchant seaman turned safecracker named Donn Pearce was arrested for burglary and sentenced to two years at Raiford State Prison in central Florida. He worked hard labor on a road gang — tarring highways, clearing brush with sling blades under the Florida sun, sleeping in cramped bunks, and answering to armed guards who enforced compliance with billy clubs and a solitary-confinement "punishment box" barely large enough to stand in. At night, he wrote about what he witnessed and the stories other inmates told him.

After his release, Pearce turned those notes into a novel. He later said about a third of *Cool Hand Luke* was his own story, a third was based on stories he heard at Raiford, and another third was pure fiction. The novel was published in 1965, and Warner Bros. bought the film rights for $80,000.

What matters here is the writing choice behind the line. Pearce originally thought "What we've got here is failure to communicate" sounded too intellectual for the Captain — the soft-spoken but sadistic prison warden.

So he invented a backstory: the Captain had picked up the phrase in penology courses he was required to take for the job. A man parroting academic language he barely understood, *dressing up brute force as reason.*

That detail alone tells you almost everything about how the line works — and why it matters far beyond the movie.

The Scene That Made It Iconic

Cool Hand Luke, the 1967 film directed by Stuart Rosenberg, arrived at a moment when Hollywood was channeling the anti-authority energy of the counterculture. *Bonnie and Clyde* and *The Graduate* were released that same year, each taking a hard look at institutions and the people who refuse to submit to them. *Cool Hand Luke* fit right in.

Paul Newman plays Lucas "Luke" Jackson, a decorated war veteran sentenced to a Florida chain gang for the absurd crime of drunkenly cutting the heads off parking meters. From his first day in camp, Luke doesn't follow the rules. He cannot help it. It is in his nature.

When Luke mocks the Captain's fatherly patience one time too many, the Captain — played with unsettling warmth by Strother Martin — beats him with a billy club in front of the other prisoners. Then he straightens himself, composes his face into something between a smile and a warning, and delivers the line:

"What we've got here is failure to communicate. Some men, you just can't reach. So, you get what we had here last week — which is the way he wants it. Well, he gets it. And I don't like it any more than you men."

The American Film Institute ranked it No. 11 on its list of the 100 greatest movie quotes of all time. But the genius of the line — and its relevance to everything this book is about — isn't in its delivery. **It's in what it reveals about how power corrupts communication.**

The Failure Isn't What You Think It Is

At first glance, the Captain's words sound almost reasonable. Measured, even. Like a disappointed father explaining that he tried his best but the boy just would not listen.

But that is the mask.

Look closer. The Captain has just beaten a man to the ground. He is standing over Luke in the dirt. *And now he is reframing that act of violence as a communication problem* — and one that belongs entirely to Luke. The Captain communicated perfectly well, thank you very much. The failure, in his telling, lies with the man who would not comply.

As one analysis of the film puts it, the "failure to communicate" is really **"the failure to understand the one-way nature of communication between the powerful and the powerless."** Communication is supposed to be two-way, but the Captain has no interest in that. His words are a velvet lining on *iron-fist violence dressed up as dialogue, compliance framed as understanding.*

That instinct to locate communication failure in the other person is exactly how most organizations think about this problem. And it is exactly why they never solve it.

I have watched managers deliver directives and call it "alignment." I have watched leaders say, "My door is always open," while every signal in the room says otherwise. I have watched teams sit through status updates where the words of communication are present, but the act of communication is completely absent. The Captain's speech could be delivered, almost word for word, in a conference room — and no one would flinch.

The Reversal That Changes Everything

At the end of the film, Luke is cornered. Police surround the church where he is hiding. He knows what is coming. He steps to the window, looks out, and repeats the Captain's line back to him: "What we've got here is failure to communicate" — with that *Luke* smile on his face. Moments later, he is shot.

The line that was used as a weapon of authority becomes, in Luke's mouth, an act of resistance. He is saying: *You never listened. You never intended to. And I see that now.*

That reversal is the arc of this book:

- **Part I** shows how organizations use the language of communication as a tool of control — where assumptions go unchecked, silence gets mistaken for agreement, and frustration becomes a workaround.
- **Part II** breaks down what's actually happening underneath — the silent spiral that turns small misalignments into systemic failures, and the moments where leaders can interrupt it.
- **Part III** hands the words back to the people on the floor and says: here is how you actually build a team that communicates.

The quote endures — on coffee mugs, in boardrooms, in dozens of films and songs — because it compresses institutional power into eight deceptively polite words. This book is about what happens after you see through those words. When you stop accepting one-way communication disguised as two-way. When you stop blaming the person in the dirt and start examining the system that put them there.

Communication is **not something you do *to* people.** It is something **that happens — or fails to happen — *between* them.** The moment you accept that framing, everything changes. The question stops being, *Why won't people just listen?* and starts being, *What is getting in the way of information moving the way it needs to?* That is the question this book is built to answer.

The Data Behind the Obvious

The **Project Management Institute (PMI)** has been tracking root causes of project failure for years, and the findings are consistent: poor communication is not a contributing factor to project failure — **it is *the* primary contributor.**

The numbers are stark. PMI research shows that **56 percent of project failures** are caused by poor communication. Organizations risk roughly **$135 million for every $1 billion** spent on projects, with **$75 million**

of that risk tied directly to ineffective communication. U.S. companies collectively lose an estimated **$1.2 trillion annually** due to poor workplace communication. And **86 percent of employees and executives** cite **lack of effective collaboration and communication as the primary cause of workplace failures.**

These aren't soft numbers. They're structural. **More than half of project failures trace back not to bad scope, underfunding, technical complexity, or market shifts — but to communication**.

We have the frameworks. We have the certifications. We have project management software, status dashboards, weekly standups, and communication plans sitting in SharePoint that no one has opened since kickoff. **And still. *This is not a coincidence. And it is not a mystery.***

What the Cost Actually Looks Like

We tend to talk about project failure in financial terms because money is easy to quantify. But the true cost of communication failure is much larger, and most of it doesn't show up in a budget variance report.

The Financial Cost:

- A miscommunicated **scope change extends the timeline by six weeks and blows the budget by a third**
- A **failed system implementation requires a multi-year recovery effort**
- Organizations risk roughly $135M for every $1B spent on projects, with $75M of that **risk tied directly to ineffective communication** (PMI)
- U.S. companies collectively lose an estimated $1.2 trillion annually **due to poor workplace communication**

The Human Cost:

- Team members who **burned out filling gaps** nobody acknowledged existed

- Project managers **who knew the project was in trouble six months before it was officially "in trouble"** — but didn't have the psychological safety to say so clearly enough to matter
- **Trust that doesn't rebuild after a major communication breakdown**
- Working relationships that become **transactional and cold**
- Talented people who leave not because the work was bad, but because the **communication environment made it impossible to do the work well**
- **Institutional knowledge that walks out the door with them**

Communication failure costs organizations money, yes. But it also costs people their confidence, their credibility, their engagement, and sometimes their careers. It costs teams their cohesion. It costs projects their soul.

How This Book Is Organized

This book follows a deliberate sequence: **diagnose the problem, prevent the failure, make it stick.**

Part	Focus	Best For
Part I: The Problem — Why Teams Stop Talking — The Silent Spiral™	The mechanics of communication failure, including the five-stage Silent Spiral™ (Assumption → Silence → Frustration → Workaround → Failure)	Understanding the patterns before you can prevent them
Part II: The Framework — How to Prevent the Failure — Breaking the Spiral™	The Breaking the Spiral™ framework (Test the Assumption → Break the Silence → Make It Safe → Close the Loop → Name It), plus the working tools: communication styles, trust and psychological safety, rules of engagement, saying what you mean,	Hands-on application — each chapter stands alone

Part	Focus	Best For
	listening, accountability, breaking down silos, leading through communication, change, and remote/hybrid	
Part III: Sustaining It — Making Good Communication the Culture	Embedding practices into daily operations, building communication culture that holds under pressure, recovering when something breaks	Leaders building lasting culture change
The Communication Playbook	Quick-reference frameworks, situation-specific scripts, diagnostic tools, and templates	When you're in the middle of something right now
Reader Exercises	Reflection questions and practical application prompts that help readers connect each concept to their own team, project, or workplace	Readers who want to apply the material as they go, use it for team discussion, or turn the book into a working development tool
Appendices (A, B, C)	Communication Self-Assessment, templates and tools, recommended reading	Ongoing use — designed to be adapted and reused

How to Use This Book

Cover-To-Cover: Read front-to-back if you want the full picture.

- **The progression is intentional:**
  - Diagnosis first,
  - Prevention next,
  - Then practical tools and templates to help sustain better communication over time.

Dip in directly: If you're in the middle of something right now:

- Dealing with role confusion? **Find that chapter in Part II.**
- Escalation failing? **Go to the Playbook.**
- Team gone silent? **Start with Part I on the Silent Spiral™,** then go directly to the **Breaking the Spiral™** chapter in Part II.

Every problem identified in the Silent Spiral™ has a direct counterpart in the Breaking the Spiral™ framework. This book is designed so that the diagnosis and the solution are always in conversation with each other — not in separate chapters you might never connect.

Use The Appendices:

- The **templates are ready to adapt** — pick them up and use them this week — **take what you need and leave the rest.** They're written as working documents, not theoretical ideals
- **With your team:** Consider reading this together.
    - The conversations that come out of working through these concepts — naming the patterns you've experienced, identifying your team's specific gaps — are often *worth more than the book itself.*

Where We Go from Here

At some point in every communication breakdown I've witnessed, there was a moment when the outcome could have been different. Not because someone needed to be smarter or more technically skilled — but because if someone had said the right thing, to the right person, at the right time, the whole trajectory would have changed.

That's what this book is about: building the kind of teams and environments where that moment doesn't get missed. Where the information flows before the crisis. Where the person who sees the problem can say so. Where the loop gets closed, the handoff gets made, the concern gets raised, and the work gets done — together, clearly, with everyone who needs to know actually knowing.

You've seen what it looks like when *that doesn't happen.* **Most of us have. Let's talk about what it looks like** *when it does.*

PART I

THE PROBLEM

The Silent Spiral™

Why Teams Stop Talking

This is where communication failure begins:
*In the **assumptions, silences, frustrations, and workarounds** that happen **long before the breakdown becomes visible.***

THE SILENT SPIRAL™

HOW SMALL COMMUNICATION BREAKDOWNS BECOME BIG PROBLEMS

It rarely starts with failure. It starts small — and spirals when we don't speak up, ask questions, or confirm what matters.

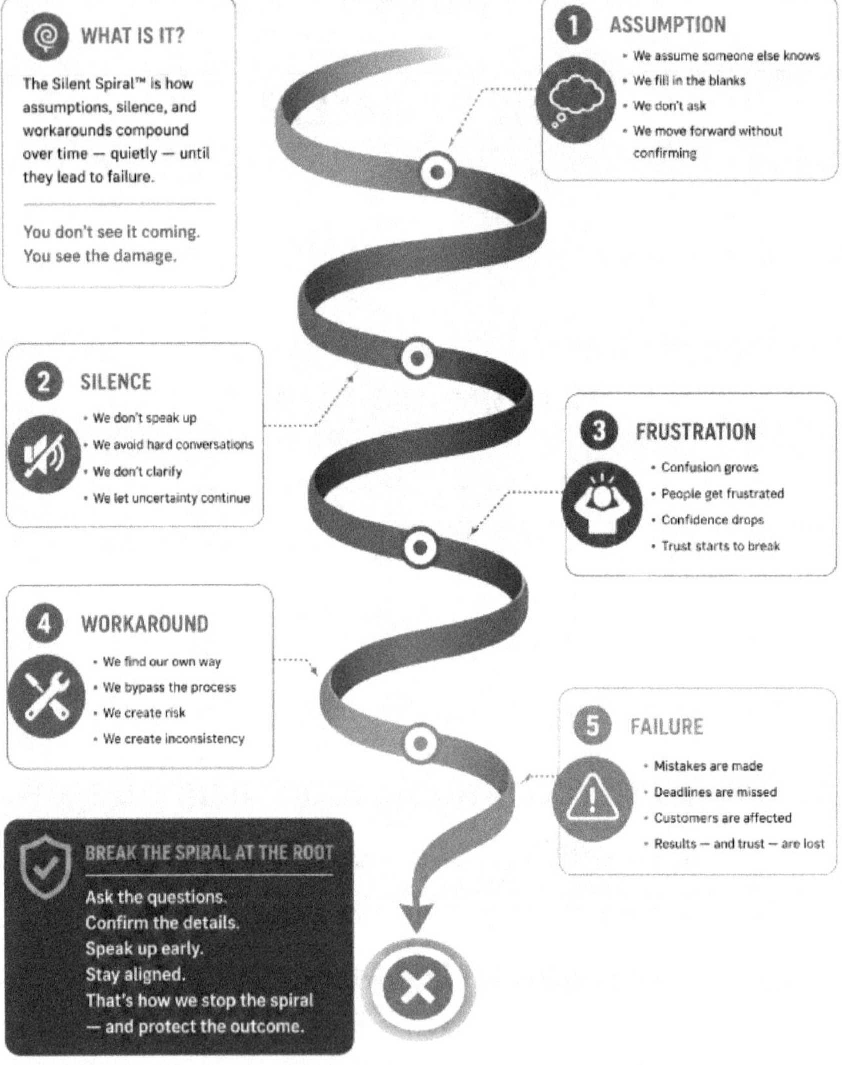

PART I: THE PROBLEM

If you've ever sat in a meeting where everyone nodded, walked out, and then did something completely different — **welcome to the illusion.**

Communication breakdown is rarely dramatic. **By the time something explodes visibly, the real breakdown happened weeks or months earlier** — in a silence nobody filled, a question nobody asked, an assumption nobody challenged.

In the chapters that follow, we'll pull back the curtain on how communication actually fails: the anatomy of a breakdown, the specific communication failures that accelerate it, the human psychology that enables it, and the organizational structures that institutionalize it. *Before we can fix something, we have to see it clearly.*

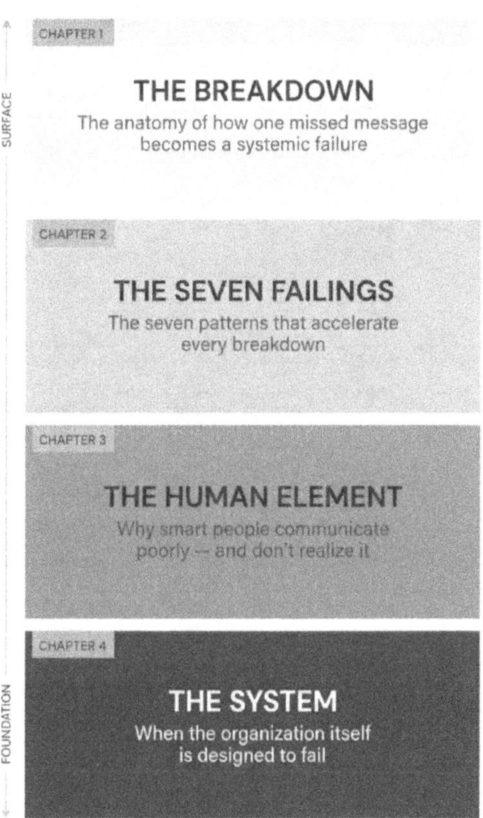

"By the time it's visible, the failure is already four layers deep."

And once you see it, you'll start seeing it everywhere.

THE SILENT SPIRAL™ THE ANATOMY OF A COMMUNICATION BREAKDOWN

Breakdowns don't happen all at once—they happen in stages.

The **Silent Spiral™** shows how small communication failures compound into system-wide breakdowns—unless they are interrupted.

THE SILENT SPIRAL™ THE STAGES	WHAT IT LOOKS LIKE	BREAKING THE SPIRAL™ WHERE TO INTERVENE
  **SIGNAL MISSED** *The Silent Spiral™ begins.* The message is not seen, heard, or noticed. The signal never enters the system.	• Email overlooked or buried • Update missed in a thread or meeting • Important information not shared	 **MAKE THE SIGNAL VISIBLE** Share intentionally. Use the right channels. Confirm receipt.
  **MEANING DISTORTED** *People think they understand—but don't.* The message is received, but misunderstood. Different meaning. Different results.	• Different definitions of the same word • Jargon or unclear language • Assumptions fill in the gaps	 **CLARIFY AND PARAPHRASE** Check understanding. Use plain language. Ask, "What does this mean to you?"
  **CONTEXT LOST** *Decisions are made on partial truth.* The message is vague, incomplete, or missing key context. Missing the "why" leads to the wrong "what."	• Missing "why" or background • Vague requests or goals • Key details, dates, or constraints left out	 **ADD CONTEXT AND PURPOSE** Explain the why. Share the full picture. Connect it to the goal.
  **RESPONSE DELAYED** *Momentum breaks.* The message is understood, but action is delayed, filtered, or altered along the way. Timing slips. Ownership blurs.	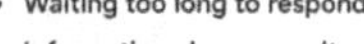 • Waiting too long to respond • Information changes as it moves • Unclear ownership or accountability	 **RESPOND QUICKLY AND CLEARLY** Acknowledge. Decide. Act. Communicate next steps.
 **FRICTION CREATED** *Energy shifts from progress to recovery.* The breakdown causes confusion, rework, debate, and frustration. We spend more time talking about the work than doing the work.	• People talk past each other • Duplicate work or rework • Time wasted and deadlines missed	 **NAME OWNERSHIP EXPLICITLY** Assign the who. Clarify the what. Set expectations.
  **TRUST ERODES** *People protect themselves instead of the work.* Repeated breakdowns signal inconsistency, unreliability, or disrespect. Silence grows. Collaboration shrinks.	• Promises not kept • People stop speaking up • Cynicism replaces collaboration	 **CREATE PSYCHOLOGICAL SAFETY** Invite voices. Listen well. Thank people for speaking up.
  **SYSTEM FAILURE** *The Spiral is now the system.* Breakdown becomes the norm—productivity, quality, and culture all suffer. Silos deepen. Results decline. The Spiral continues.	• Silos deepen • Blame culture takes over • Results decline across the board	 **CLOSE THE LOOP EVERY TIME** Follow through. Share outcomes. Build a system of reliability.

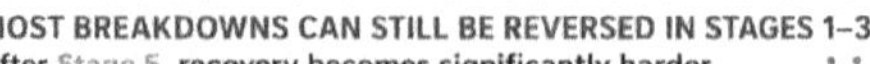

MOST BREAKDOWNS CAN STILL BE REVERSED IN STAGES 1–3.
After Stage 5, recovery becomes significantly harder.

THE SILENT SPIRAL™ DOESN'T START WITH FAILURE. IT STARTS WITH A MISSED SIGNAL.
BREAKING THE SPIRAL™ STARTS BY CATCHING IT EARLY—AND CLOSING THE LOOP.

Chapter 1: The Anatomy of a Communication Breakdown

There is a particular kind of meeting most people recognize: everyone's in the room, the agenda exists, notes are taken, action items assigned. Three weeks later, nothing has moved — or things have moved in exactly the wrong direction, with everyone believing they were following the plan.

That meeting is the visible surface. What you don't see is the fault line running beneath it.

Communication breakdown almost never announces itself. It creeps in through a meeting invite with no context, a SharePoint message someone forgot to answer, a hallway decision that never made it back to the team. **By the time the failure becomes visible, the accumulation is months deep.**

I've watched this happen in hospitals, for-profit education systems, government agencies, and warehouses the size of multiple football fields. Industry doesn't matter. Headcount doesn't matter. The failure mode is startlingly consistent. This is **The Silent Spiral™** — five predictable stages, each one making the next harder to escape.

The Five Stages of The Silent Spiral™

Stage 1: Assumption

Stage	What You'll Hear	What's Really Happening	Warning Sign
Assumption	"I emailed them — they know."	Message sent; receipt and understanding unconfirmed	No one asks follow-up questions
	"We aligned on that in the meeting."	Agreement was performative, not actual	Same decision relitigated next meeting
	"They have the context — they'll figure it out."	Critical "why" was never transmitted	Execution diverges from intent

The assumption stage is quiet. Nothing has gone wrong visibly yet. The cracks are there, invisible, waiting.

The Silent Spiral™

Stage 1: Assumption

The breakdown starts when people confuse sending with understanding.

Assumption

1. WHAT IT LOOKS LIKE
- A message goes out
- Heads nod in the room
- No one checks for clarity

2. WHAT'S ACTUALLY HAPPENING
- Meaning is being guessed
- Context is incomplete
- Agreement is assumed, not verified

3. WHAT IT LEADS TO
- Different people act on different interpretations
- Work drifts from the original intent
- The same issue resurfaces later

BREAK THE SPIRAL EARLY

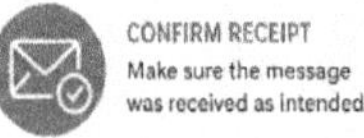

EXPLAIN THE WHY
Share the purpose and desired outcome.

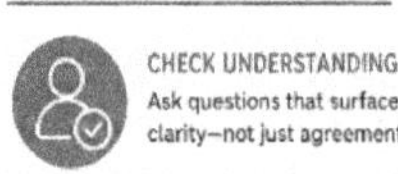

Assumption feels efficient in the moment. It becomes expensive later.

The subtler dimension: **we assume not only that the message was received, but that the receiver has all the context needed to interpret it correctly** — the history behind the decision, the constraints that shaped it, the priority level. We transmit the conclusion without transmitting the reasoning.

Stage 2: Silence

Stage	What You'll Hear	What's Really Happening	Warning Sign
Silence	"No questions? Great, we're all set."	People are confused but won't say so	Zero pushback in meetings
	(Nothing — the message sits unacknowledged)	Fear or overwhelm preventing response	Emails go unanswered for days
	"I didn't want to bother anyone."	Culture has signaled that asking questions costs you	Questions arrive too late to change anything

Silence is almost never what it looks like. It doesn't mean, "everything is fine." It means "nobody asked, so nobody said anything."

Why silence takes root:

- People believe they understand, when they actually understand their *own interpretation* of what was said
- Fear of looking confused or incompetent
- The culture has signaled that asking questions is career suicide
- Everyone assumes someone else will break the silence first — so nobody does

Silence is especially dangerous in cross-functional environments, where teams have different vocabularies, different priorities, and different assumptions about ownership. A silence on one end of a hand-off can mean something entirely different on the other end — and the gap between them is where projects go to die.

The compounding effect: The longer silence persists, the harder it is to break. The person who didn't ask for clarification on Day 1 is even less likely to ask on Day 10 — now they also have to explain why they waited. The silence grows heavier the longer it sits.

Stage 3: Frustration

Stage	What You'll Hear	What's Really Happening	Warning Sign
Frustration	"Why does nobody ever tell me anything?"	Information isn't reaching the people who need it	Same surprises happening repeatedly
	"She's just difficult to work with."	A systemic failure is being misread as a personality problem	Leader focusing on individuals instead of the process
	"I'm just going to handle it myself."	Trust in official channels has eroded	Team members making unilateral decisions

Eventually, the silence becomes expensive.

What triggers frustration:

- Deadlines missed because assumptions were wrong
- Work duplicated because teams weren't connected
- Someone finds out at the last minute about a decision affecting their work
- A deliverable comes back wrong — different version of the requirements
- A team member feels invisible

The misdiagnosis trap: Frustration wears the costume of interpersonal drama. *She's difficult. He doesn't listen. They're territorial.* This is one of the most expensive mistakes a leader can make — it trains the spotlight on individuals rather than systems. The system keeps churning out the same failures with different people.

Frustration also rewires future communication. *A team member blindsided multiple times becomes guarded.* They start making decisions independently — not because they want to go rogue, but because they've learned that waiting for information puts them behind.

Stage 4: Workaround

Stage	What You'll Hear	What's Really Happening	Warning Sign
Workaround	"I know a guy — I'll just go through him."	Official channels have failed; informal ones are running in parallel	Decisions being made outside normal process
	"Don't bother filing it in the system, just text me."	Shadow infrastructure has replaced official infrastructure	Institutional knowledge is invisible and fragile
	"Oh, we stopped using that tracker months ago."	The official process exists on paper only	New team members have no idea what's actually happening

When official channels fail, <u>people build unofficial ones</u>.

Official channel	Workaround that replaces it
Team email list	Text thread with one trusted person
Weekly status meeting	Parallel "real" conversation elsewhere
Escalation to manager	Going around them directly
Official tracking system	Shadow spreadsheet someone built themselves
Approval process	Hand-walking approvals to a specific director

Workarounds *feel* like solutions. They're pragmatic. They often work short-term. But every workaround:

- Is a symptom of a broken system
- Makes the dysfunction survivable enough that nobody fixes the root cause

- Creates shadow structures invisible to the organization
- Collapses when the person who built it leaves

Stage 5: Failure

Stage	What You'll Hear	What's Really Happening	Warning Sign
Failure	"How did we not catch this sooner?"	The problem was visible for months — it just wasn't safe to say so	Post-mortem reveals multiple people knew
	"This wasn't in the report."	Reporting captured comfortable information, not accurate information	Green dashboard on a red project
	"We need to do a lessons-learned."	Lessons are documented; root cause is not traced back far enough	Same failure pattern recurs 12 months later

Stage 5 is what everyone points to.

What failure looks like:

- The project that derailed
- The audit finding
- The client who didn't renew
- The employee who resigned and said in their exit interview they "didn't feel heard"
- The mistake that got made because the right people weren't at the table — and weren't even told the table existed

Failure gets analyzed, post-mortem'd, documented. *But if that report doesn't trace the failure all the way back to Stage 1 — to the original assumptions, the sustained silences — the lessons haven't actually been learned.* ***They've just been archived.***

Breaking the Spiral™ is the direct antidote to everything described in these five stages. Part II introduces the full framework — but the essential idea is this: **for every stage of the Silent Spiral™ there is a corresponding Breaking the Spiral™ intervention.** Stage 1 (Assumption) is met by "Test the Assumption"; Stage 2 (Silence) is met by "Break the Silence"; and so on through "Name It" at Stage 5.

The Silent Spiral™ is not about dramatic blowups. It is the **slow, polite collapse of communication that happens when people stop talking and start assuming** — and nobody notices until the damage is already done.

The Silent Spiral™

WHAT WE NOTICE

Failure

WHAT HAPPENED FIRST

Assumption
We assume understanding without checking.

Silence
We stay quiet when clarity is needed.

Frustration
Tension builds as the problem grows.

Workaround
We adapt in the moment instead of addressing the root cause.

The visible failure is usually the last stage, not the first sign.

The spiral is predictable — and so is the way out.

Inside the Spiral: What It Looks Like

Each stage has its own texture — its own language, its own Monday morning meeting, its own way of leaving evidence on the floor. The five sections that follow walk through each stage from the inside: what is actually happening, how it sounds, what it costs, and **the one question that interrupts it.**

STAGE 1: ASSUMPTION

Communication Confused with Transmission

What the Stage Is Really About

Stage 1 is where the spiral begins, and it begins quietly. Nothing blows up. Nobody storms out of a meeting. From the outside, Stage 1 looks like everything is working fine.

The **breakdown at Stage 1 is this: the person sending information believes that sending it is the same as communicating it.** An email goes out, a memo gets posted, a manager says something during a shift change—**and in their mind, the work is done. Message delivered. Box checked.**

What they did not account for is whether **anyone received it, understood it,** or **knew what to do with it.** They transmitted. They did not communicate.

There is a meaningful difference between those two things, and most organizations never teach it. Communication requires a sender, a receiver, a shared understanding of what was meant, and confirmation that the loop is closed. Transmission is just noise traveling through a channel. You can transmit all day long and communicate nothing.

The assumption embedded in Stage 1 is simple and almost universally held: if I said it, they heard it; if they heard it, they understood it; if they understood it, they will act on it correctly.

That chain of logic feels reasonable. It is also wrong about half the time, and the consequences pile up silently while everyone involved believes communication happened.

What This Looks Like in Your Monday Morning Meeting

1. **The manager reads through last week's updates from a printed sheet, makes no eye contact, and wraps up in four minutes.** Nobody asks questions. The manager takes this as confirmation that everyone is aligned.
2. **A new process is announced verbally during the meeting. No documentation follows.** By Wednesday, three people are doing it three different ways.
3. **Someone says, "we already covered this in the email" when an operator asks a clarifying question** — *as if the email's existence is the same as its comprehension.*
4. **Attendees nod along not because they understand but because nodding is the social expectation in that room.** Nobody wants to be the one who "didn't get it."
5. **The manager leaves the meeting feeling confident.** *The team leaves the meeting and immediately whispers to each other to figure out what was actually just decided.*
6. **Action items are mentioned but not assigned, not written down, and not tied to deadlines.** Whoever is most conscientious on the team quietly picks them up. Everyone else waits to be told again.
7. **A policy change is communicated to shift supervisors but not verified to have been passed to floor-level operators.** The supervisors assume that sharing is someone else's job, or that the operators will figure it out.

A Story From the Floor

A regional distribution center rolled out a new inbound receiving protocol over the course of a single week. The logistics coordinator put together a one-page summary, sent it to all shift leads via company email, and posted a printed copy on the bulletin board near the dock doors.

Two weeks later, inbound accuracy numbers started sliding. Pallets were being logged in old categories. Discrepancy reports were stacking up. A floor audit caught three different receiving workflows running simultaneously

— one by the book, one halfway updated, and one that was a complete holdover from a process that had been deprecated eighteen months earlier.

When the coordinator pulled the team together, the question came up immediately: **"Didn't you all get the email?"**

They had. Every single one of them had received it. Several had opened it. Two or three had read it start to finish. **But "reading it" and "knowing what to do differently starting Monday at 6 a.m." turned out to be very different things.**

The email described the new protocol in general terms. It did not walk through specific scenarios. It did not clarify which part of the old process was being replaced versus retained. **It did not confirm that everyone had read it, let alone understood it.**

The coordinator had done everything right by the old standard: write it up, send it out, post it up. *What he had not done was close the loop — verify receipt, walk through the change in person, allow questions, or confirm that the message he intended to send was the message people actually received.*

The email had been transmitted.
The communication had never happened.

The Language of This Stage

These are real phrases that signal Stage 1 is in play. You may recognize them. You may have said them yourself.

1. *"I already sent that out."*
2. *"That was covered in the morning meeting."*
3. *"They know — we talked about it last week."*
4. *"It's on the board."*
5. *"I don't know why they keep asking — it's all in the SOP."*
6. *"If they had questions, they would have said something."*
7. *"I told my leads. It's their job to pass it down."*

Every one of these phrases has something in common: **the speaker is pointing to the act of sending and treating it as evidence of successful communication.** None of them *indicate that* ***understanding was confirmed*** *on the other end.*

What It Costs

The organizational damage at Stage 1 is invisible at first, *which is part of what makes it dangerous*. Nothing catastrophic happens immediately. The costs accumulate in the background:

1. **Inconsistent execution.** When people fill gaps in their understanding with their own best guesses, you get a dozen variations of the same process running in parallel. None of them may be catastrophically wrong, but none of them are right either — and the drift compounds over time.
2. **Repeated rework.** Work gets done wrong not because employees are careless but because they were working from incomplete information. That work has to be redone. The time, labor, and materials tied up in rework are real costs that never show up on a communication audit because nobody identifies the root cause as a communication failure.
3. **Credibility erosion.** When people receive information that turns out to be incomplete or contradictory, they stop trusting the information channel. After enough of these cycles, announcements and memos get ignored not out of defiance but out of experience. “It’ll change again anyway” becomes the operating assumption.
4. **Decision lag.** Operators who are unclear on direction do one of two things: they wait for clarification that may never come, or they make their best guess and move. Either way, the organization loses response time.
5. **Manager time drain.** The manager who assumed communication happened now spends time in one-on-ones and corridor conversations correcting misunderstandings that a fifteen-minute clarifying conversation could have prevented.

STOP AND CHECK

Before you leave your next team meeting or send your next all-staff update, ask yourself this one question: *How do I actually know they understood it?* **Not, *"did I say it?"* Not, *"did I send it?"* Not, *"did they nod?"***

How do you know? If you cannot answer that question with something more concrete than "I assume so," you are at Stage 1. That is not a character flaw. It is a communication design problem — and ***you can fix it before it goes further.***

STAGE 2: SILENCE

Absence of Feedback Misread as Agreement

What the Stage Is Really About

If Stage 1 is where the wrong belief gets planted, Stage 2 is where it gets watered. Once someone has transmitted information and assumed the communication is complete, they watch for signals that something is wrong. When no signal comes back — no pushback, no questions, no visible confusion — they interpret that silence as confirmation. Silence equals agreement.

Silence equals alignment.
Silence equals, *"we're good."*
It does not.

What silence usually means in an operational environment is one of several things, almost none of which are agreement:

- **People did not understand** and **do not feel safe** saying so
- People **understood just enough to think they understand but are missing a critical piece**
- P**eople disagree** but have learned that **expressing disagreement in this environment is not worth the cost**
- People have decided to **handle it their own way** and see no need to announce that
- People simply **did not receive the information at all** and **do not know there is a gap**

Stage 2 is particularly insidious because the manager or supervisor experiencing it has a compelling, coherent story: *I told them, they had every opportunity to ask, nobody asked, therefore we are aligned.* That story feels airtight. It is built on evidence — the absence of objection. The problem is that absence of objection is not evidence of alignment. It is evidence that nobody is currently objecting out loud.

Organizations that have punished questions, dismissing them as timewasters or treating them as signs of incompetence, breed Stage 2 cultures. When people learn that *asking questions carries a social cost, they stop asking.* And the silence that results gets misread, over and over again, as consensus.

What This Looks Like in Your Monday Morning Meeting

1. **The manager wraps up and asks, "Any questions?" There is a three-second pause. Nobody speaks.** The manager says "Great, we're good then" and moves on.

2. **An operator has a specific concern about the new process but frames it as a general observation** — *"I mean, we'll see how it goes"* — and it gets absorbed as casual optimism rather than a warning.

3. **The team asks clarifying questions among themselves** in the parking lot, in the break room, and in the group chat — everywhere except the meeting room where it could actually be addressed.

4. **A supervisor notices that her team seems hesitant but tells herself they will figure it out once they get into it.** She does not probe because she does not want to slow down the morning.

5. **A critical question about handoff responsibility never gets raised** because everyone in the room assumed someone else would ask it or that it would get sorted out in practice.

6. The quietest, most deferential people on the team carry the most unasked questions, and **their silence is the most likely to be read as agreement.**

A Story From the Floor

A fulfillment facility was transitioning between two inventory tracking systems. The project lead, under deadline pressure, ran a single two-hour training session for all shift supervisors.

At the end of the session, she asked if there were questions. A few people asked about login credentials. One person asked about the reporting interface. Then silence.

She logged it as a successful training. Signed off on readiness. Sent up the green light to go live.

The go-live date arrived. Within seventy-two hours, inventory discrepancies started surfacing — items being counted twice, others not at all, location assignments going into the wrong fields. The error rate in the first week was four times the baseline.

When the project lead started talking to the people in the room, what she discovered was not carelessness. What she discovered was that most of the supervisors had left that training session with significant unresolved questions.

They had not asked them in the room for a mix of reasons: they did not want to look like they were behind everyone else; they assumed the confusion was their problem to sort out privately; they were not sure their questions were "training questions" versus "figure it out when you get there questions"; and one person had simply shut down after an hour and a half and was waiting for it to end.

None of them had walked out of that training in agreement. They had walked out in silence. And silence had been logged as green.

The project lead had run a training. She had not confirmed learning. The difference cost the facility a week of cleanup work and a significant amount of management credibility.

The Language of This Stage

1. *"Nobody said anything, so I figured we were fine."*
2. *"They had the whole meeting to bring it up."*
3. *"I gave them every opportunity to ask questions."*
4. *"No news is good news."*
5. *"If there was a problem, I would have heard about it."*
6. *"They seemed fine with it."*

7. *"I left it open for feedback and got nothing back."*

Pay attention to who these phrases center. Every one of them describes what the sender did or did not receive. None of them describe any effort to actively draw out the **receiver's actual understanding.**

What It Costs

1. **Compounding misalignment.** Every day of operation after a Stage 2 silence is a day of work building on an unstable foundation. The longer it runs undetected, the more has to be unwound.

2. **Failed implementations.** System go-lives, process changes, and policy rollouts that were signed off on the basis of silence frequently fail in execution — not because the ideas were bad but because understanding was assumed rather than confirmed.

3. **Underground question networks.** When people cannot ask questions in the official channel, they build unofficial ones. Information flows through whoever seems to know the most, whether or not that person actually knows the most. This creates misinformation pipelines disguised as institutional knowledge.

4. **Psychological safety erosion.** Once an organization establishes that silence is the safe response, the culture calcifies around it. You lose access to early warnings, dissenting views, and operational intelligence from the people closest to the work.

5. **The "we told you" trap.** When the failure eventually surfaces, management points to the meeting where nobody objected. Frontline workers point to the questions they did not feel safe asking. Both are right. Everyone loses.

STOP AND CHECK

Stop asking, *"Any questions?"* as your only check for understanding. That question puts the burden on the quietest person in the room to expose what they do not know in front of everyone else.

In a low-trust environment, most people will not do that. They will nod, stay silent, and try to figure it out later. Use questions that surface understanding instead:

"What is one thing you are taking from this that will change how you work tomorrow?" "What part of this still feels unclear?"

These questions shift the room from passive agreement to active processing and help you find the confusion while there is still time to fix it.

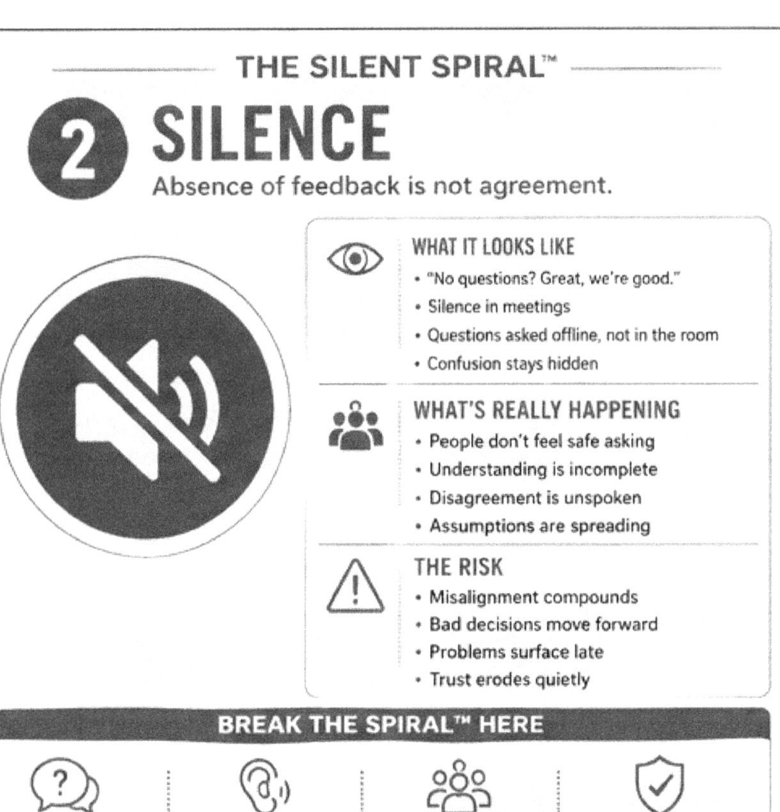

STAGE 3: FRUSTRATION

Consequences Attributed to People, Not Systems

What the Stage Is Really About

By Stage 3, something has gone wrong. The assumptions from Stage 1 failed to produce the results people expected. The silence from Stage 2 meant no one caught it in time. **Now the consequences are visible — missed targets, errors, delays, friction between teams — and everyone is looking for an explanation.**

The explanation that gets reached for first, in almost every organization, is people.

He doesn't listen. She never follows through. That team just doesn't care. He needs to be managed closer. They knew what was expected.

These explanations feel logical because they are *person-shaped*. You can point at them. You can put them in a performance conversation. They fit neatly into existing mental models about accountability and personal responsibility. *What they almost always miss is the system failure underneath.*

When **communication is broken** — when **expectations** were transmitted but **not confirmed,** when **feedback was absent** but **interpreted as agreement** — the **people in the system are set up to fail.**

They are working with incomplete or inaccurate information, operating under assumptions that were never validated, navigating processes that were never clearly defined. When the failure happens, it is a **communication design failure.** But because communication design is *invisible* and Marcus is *physically visible*, Marcus becomes the problem.

This is where Stage 3 **corrodes organizations from the inside.** The real cause goes unaddressed. The symptom — the person — gets managed, warned, reassigned, or replaced. New person steps into the same system. Same outcome. And everyone is baffled at why the "people problem" keeps coming back.

What This Looks Like in Your Monday Morning Meeting

1. **The manager opens by calling out, directly or indirectly, someone whose performance slipped** — without acknowledging that the expectations behind that performance were ever clearly communicated.
2. **The phrase "we've been over this" gets used to shut down a question that is actually a symptom of a communication gap** that was never closed.
3. **A process failure from last week gets attributed to a specific individual rather than to the hand-off point,** the unclear procedure, or the missing verification step where it actually broke.
4. **The team is told to "do better" or "pay more attention"** without any change to the process that produced the bad outcome.
5. Frustration is palpable on both sides of the table. **The manager is frustrated** that things keep going wrong. **The team is frustrated** that they keep getting blamed for outcomes they did not fully control.
6. **Someone who did catch the problem early,** and **tried to raise it** informally, **says nothing** in the meeting. They raised it before and **it did not go anywhere. They have learned.**

A Story From the Floor

A large-format print and production facility had been dealing with a recurring error in its finishing department — jobs were being trimmed to wrong dimensions, and the issue kept getting caught at the quality check gate, which meant rework, missed deadlines, and eventually client complaints.

Management's first response was to put the lead finisher on a performance improvement plan. The error rate was traced directly to her station, the logic went, so the problem was with her. She had been in the role for four years with a strong record. Nobody stopped to ask why the errors had started six weeks ago.

Six weeks prior, the production manager had verbally communicated a change in how finished-size specs were being noted on job tickets. The change was meant to simplify things. What it actually did was create an ambiguity — the new notation could be read two different ways depending on whether you assumed the spec was for the finished piece or the bleed-included cut.

Nobody had asked for clarification in the meeting where the change was announced. The lead finisher had left that meeting with one interpretation. Half the prep team had left with the other.

For six weeks, the error had been baked into the process. The lead finisher was doing her job correctly — by the interpretation she had been operating under. The performance plan added stress, damaged morale, and produced no improvement in accuracy because it was addressing the wrong problem.

It took a third-party process review to surface the real issue. By then, the damage to the lead finisher's standing in the organization was done, and she had quietly started looking for other work.

The Language of This Stage

1. *"He knew what was expected of him."*
2. *"I don't know why she keeps making this mistake — we've been over it."*
3. *"They just don't care enough to get it right."*
4. *"This is a performance issue, not a process issue."*
5. *"I can't hold everyone's hand."*
6. *"At some point it comes down to personal accountability."*
7. *"We need someone who can actually execute."*

Listen for these phrases carefully. They are not always wrong. Sometimes, there is a genuine individual performance issue.

But when they show up *consistently, across multiple people, in multiple roles, they are* ***almost always a signal that the system is the problem, and the people are the evidence.***

What It Costs

1. **Talent loss.** Competent people who are misidentified as performance problems leave. They take institutional knowledge, relationships, and hard-won skill with them. The gap they leave behind is expensive and rarely fully recovered.

2. **Morale damage.** The rest of the team watches what happens when something goes wrong. If the conclusion is always "someone did something wrong" rather than "the system had a gap," everyone quietly makes a calculation about how to protect themselves — which usually means less initiative, less transparency, and less communication upward.

3. **False fixes.** Replacing or disciplining people without fixing the underlying communication system produces no durable improvement. The next person inherits the same broken environment and produces the same results on a slightly different timeline.

4. **Management distraction.** Leaders consumed with personnel issues — performance improvement plans (PIPs), corrective actions (CAs), exit conversations — have less bandwidth to examine system design. The cycle accelerates.

5. **Permanent workaround culture.** Once people have been blamed for system failures enough times, they stop trying to fix the system and start building personal workarounds to protect themselves. That is where Stage 4 comes from.

STOP AND CHECK

The next time something goes wrong and your first instinct is to identify who is responsible, pause and ask a different question first:

What would need to be true about the system for a reasonable, experienced person to produce this outcome?

If you can construct that explanation — and you almost always can — you are looking at a system problem wearing a people costume. Fix the system first. Then, *and only then,* determine whether there is also an individual issue worth addressing separately.

THE SILENT SPIRAL™

3 FRUSTRATION

Confusion turns into frustration.

WHAT IT LOOKS LIKE

- People get short with each other
- Passive-aggressive comments
- "Why isn't this working?"
- Motivation and morale drop

WHAT'S REALLY HAPPENING

- Unanswered questions pile up
- Stress and doubt increase
- People blame the process or others
- Trust starts to break down

THE RISK

- Team tension rises
- Collaboration breaks down
- Focus shifts from solutions to complaints
- The real issue stays hidden

BREAK THE SPIRAL™ HERE

Acknowledge frustration early

Have the hard conversations

Find the real issue

Listen with empathy

STAGE 4: WORKAROUND

Shadow Processes Replace Formal Systems

What the Stage Is Really About

Stage 4 is adaptation. It is what humans do when the official system stops serving them — they build another system, creating a workaround. This one is informal, undocumented, and invisible to anyone who is not already part of it. *It works, at least for the people who built it.*

That is exactly the problem.

By the time an operation reaches Stage 4, **the people closest to the work have given up on the idea that the formal system will be fixed. They tried asking questions and learned that questions are not welcome. They tried flagging problems and found that the response was to be blamed for them.** They have watched enough people get burned by following official procedure in broken conditions that they have made a rational decision: figure out what actually works and do that instead.

So they do. A **team develops its own hand-off signals**. An operator keeps a personal spreadsheet that does what the inventory system is supposed to do but doesn't. A supervisor texts her counterpart on the next shift instead of using the communication log because the log is ignored and the text works. A group of shift leads has a standing "pre-meeting meeting" **where they actually figure out what is happening before the official meeting starts.**

None of this is in any manual. None of it is sanctioned. All of it is keeping the operation running.

And here is the dangerous part: because the workarounds work — at least locally, at least in the short term — the performance data looks acceptable. Management does not see the breakdown. They see outcomes that are close enough to target that nobody starts pulling threads. The organization believes it is operating on its official systems. It is not. It is operating on a parallel infrastructure built by the people who got tired of waiting for the real one to be fixed.

What This Looks Like in Your Monday Morning Meeting

1. **The official update given in the meeting does not reflect how work is actually being done on the floor.** Everyone in the room knows this. Nobody says it out loud.

2. **Institutional knowledge lives in specific people, not in documented processes.** When those people leave, the team scrambles for weeks because nobody outside the shadow system knows how things actually work.

3. **New hires are pulled aside by a veteran within their first few weeks and given the real orientation** — what the handbook says, and what you actually do.

4. **There are two versions of nearly every process: the official one that exists in documentation, and the real one that experienced operators follow.**

5. **Requests that go through formal channels take two weeks.** The same request routed through a personal relationship takes two hours. Everyone knows this. Nobody questions why.

6. **Meetings to "align on process" are treated with visible fatigue by the people in the room.** They have aligned on paper before. Nothing changed. They handle it themselves now.

7. **The people maintaining the shadow systems carry a disproportionate cognitive and relational load.** They are the ones everyone calls. They are also the ones at highest risk of burnout.

Story From the Floor

A regional grocery distribution center had been struggling with its inbound appointment scheduling system for the better part of two years. The official system required carriers to submit requests through an online portal, which then fed into a master schedule managed by the traffic desk. In theory, it was clean.

In practice, the portal submissions arrived without complete information about thirty percent of the time, the traffic desk was understaffed and chronically backlogged, and the master schedule had a forty-eight-hour minimum processing window that the actual dock could not accommodate.

Rather than surface the system failure repeatedly and be told to "work within the system," the dock supervisors built their own process. They maintained a running whiteboard schedule updated every four hours. Carriers who had been burned by the portal enough times started calling the dock directly, where they reached people who could actually make things happen. Appointments were confirmed via text with the supervisors' personal numbers. The portal submissions continued to be filed because compliance required them, but everyone knew they were ceremonial.

The informal system worked well enough that the facility's on-time receiving rate looked reasonable on monthly reports. There was no red flag compelling anyone to look deeper.

What the reports did not capture was the fragility of the arrangement. When one of the two supervisors who ran the shadow system left for another opportunity, her replacement walked into a dock where nobody could explain how the scheduling actually worked. The whiteboard was erased. The carrier contacts had been in her personal phone. The institutional memory walked out with her.

The facility spent six months relearning, at significant cost, how to do something it had technically already been doing — just not in any way that anyone had bothered to document.

The Language of This Stage

1. *"That's not how we actually do it."*
2. *"Go ask [person] — she knows how that really works."*
3. *"The system says X, but we stopped doing it that way a while back."*
4. *"Just text me directly. The ticket system is useless."*
5. *"That's the way it's supposed to work on paper."*
6. *"We figured out a better way — we just never got around to updating the SOP."*

7. *"Don't worry about the portal. Call the dock and they'll take care of you."*

When you hear these phrases regularly, you are not just looking at people who prefer shortcuts. You are looking at people who have formally concluded that the official system cannot be trusted — and have built a replacement.

What It Costs

1. **Single points of failure.** Shadow systems are person-dependent. When the person leaves — voluntarily, due to burnout, or otherwise — the system they maintained disappears with them. The operation loses capability it did not know it had until it is gone.
2. **Onboarding failure.** New team members who receive only the official training are immediately behind. They have to spend months figuring out the actual process, which they learn gradually through informal cues, mistakes, and the goodwill of veterans willing to bring them in. This is time, productivity, and goodwill that gets burned unnecessarily.
3. **Audit and compliance exposure.** When the documented process and the actual process diverge significantly, the organization is exposed. Audits, customer visits, regulatory reviews, and incident investigations all operate against what is documented. What is documented no longer reflects what happens.
4. **Scalability collapse.** Shadow systems cannot be scaled. They are built for the conditions that exist right now, by the people who are here right now. Any growth, restructuring, or geographic expansion exposes them immediately.
5. **Trust debt.** The existence of widespread shadow processes is evidence of a long-running failure of official systems to serve the people using them. That is not just a process problem — it is a trust problem between management and the floor that has been accumulating compound interest for years.

STOP AND CHECK

Before you attempt to eliminate a shadow process, **understand what need it was built to meet.** If you shut it down without addressing the underlying system gap, **you will create an operational vacuum** and **earn profound distrust from the people who built the workaround** in the first place.

Start by asking: *What problem does this informal system solve that the official system doesn't?* The answer to that question is your real remediation target.

The shadow process is just the symptom pointing you toward it.

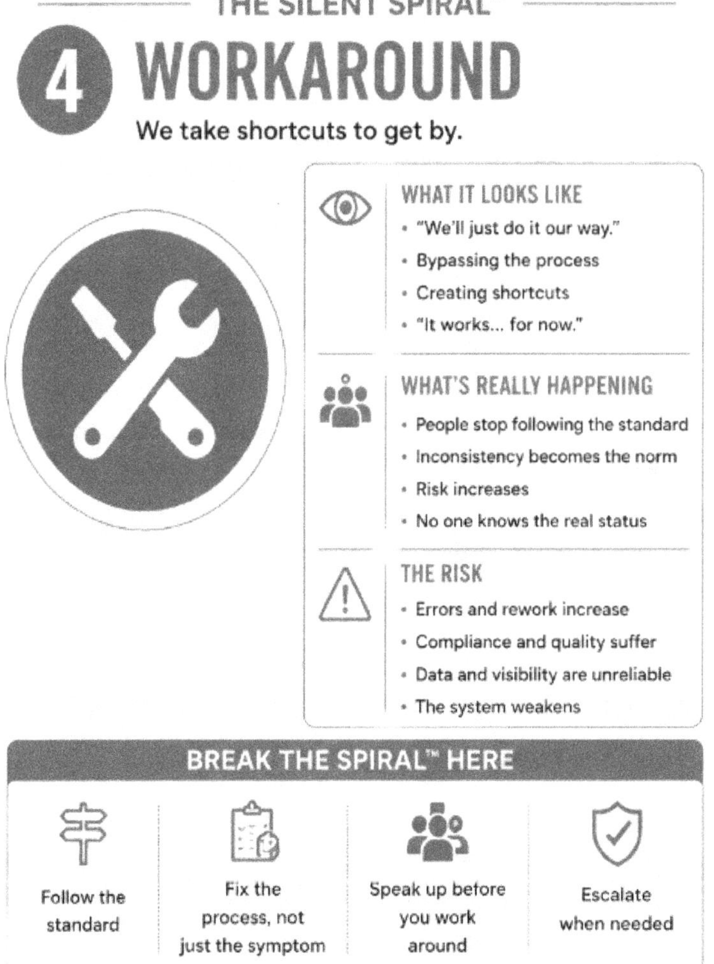

STAGE 5: FAILURE

Accumulated Damage Becomes Undeniable

What the Stage Is Really About

Stage 5 is not an event. It looks like one — there is usually a moment, a trigger, a thing that breaks publicly enough that it can no longer be absorbed or explained away. But that moment is not where the failure happened. The failure happened in Stages 1, 2, 3, and 4. Stage 5 is where the bill comes due.

This matters because organizations that experience Stage 5 almost always misread it. **They look at the specific crisis in front of them** — the client loss, the operations breakdown, the safety incident, the leadership departure — and treat it as the problem to be solved. They conduct incident reviews that focus on the precipitating event. They look for the specific decision or the specific person who was responsible for the thing that finally broke.

They find something. They call it the cause. They fix that thing. They go back to work.

And **because they did not address the communication system that produced all of it — the assumptions, the misread silences, the misdirected blame**, the shadow processes — the Silent Spiral™ **begins again.** Stage 1. Someone transmits without confirming. Someone else interprets silence as alignment. The whole structure rebuilds itself quietly, in the background, while the organization congratulates itself on having solved the problem.

Stage 5 is the proof that the spiral was running. **It is also the clearest opportunity to see it clearly enough to do something about it** — if you are willing to look past the crisis and into the system that produced it.

What This Looks Like in Your Monday Morning Meeting

1. **The Monday morning meeting is an emergency session, not a regular one.** Something happened over the weekend, or accumulated to a breaking point, and now there is a room full of people trying to figure out what to do about it.

2. **The post-mortem conversation focuses on the incident timeline and the immediate cause.** Nobody asks why the early warning signals were missed or why they were never surfaced in the first place.
3. **Key stakeholders are hearing about the full scope of the problem for the first time in that room.** Everyone else in the room knew pieces of it for weeks. Nobody connected the dots.
4. **The blame conversation happens quickly, quietly, and unofficially. By the end of the week, someone will be held responsible for the failure.** It will be the most visible person in the most recent part of the chain, not the person or process where the communication breakdown actually originated.
5. **People are careful with their words. Everyone in the room is doing some version of the same calculation:** what did I know, when did I know it, and how much of it do I say out loud right now.
6. **New communication initiatives are announced. New reporting requirements. New check-ins.** These measures address the form of communication without addressing the culture that broke it — and most of them will be quietly abandoned within ninety days.

A Story From the Floor

A mid-sized e-commerce fulfillment operation had been growing at a rate that strained its systems for the better part of three years. Headcount doubled. Volume tripled. The technology infrastructure scaled unevenly. Management was largely reactive, focused on hitting day-to-day throughput targets without significant investment in communication infrastructure or process documentation.

Over time, all five stages had played out in sequence. Information was announced without confirmation. Silence in team meetings was logged as alignment. When errors occurred, operators and supervisors were cycled through performance management while the system gaps underneath went unexamined. Veterans built informal networks and workaround processes to keep the place running. Management saw acceptable numbers and did not dig deeper.

The reckoning came during the peak season. A miscommunication about labor allocation — rooted in an assumption that a verbal confirmation in a hallway conversation constituted a firm commitment — left two critical shifts understaffed on the highest-volume days of the year. Orders did not ship. Customer service was overwhelmed. SLA violations triggered penalty clauses in three major retail contracts. The 72-hour crisis required emergency labor sourcing at premium rates, direct intervention from senior leadership, and a client communication process that revealed, for the first time, how widespread the service degradation had actually been.

The formal review that followed found the proximate cause: a miscommunication about staffing. What it did not fully investigate was why that kind of miscommunication had become possible — why two experienced managers could leave a conversation with different understandings of a commitment, why neither had followed up in writing, why nobody who knew there was a gap in coverage had raised it before it became a crisis, and why the workforce planning process had no verification step to catch it.

Those questions pointed to a communication system that had been failing quietly for years. The crisis was new. The failure was not.

The Language of This Stage

1. *"How did nobody catch this sooner?"*
2. *"This can't have just happened overnight — where was the breakdown?"*
3. *"We need to figure out who dropped the ball."*
4. *"Going forward, we need better communication."*
5. *"I feel like I was the last one to know."*
6. *"This should have been escalated."*
7. *"We can't let this happen again."*

Notice what the last phrase actually means in practice. "We can't let this happen again" spoken without a structural diagnosis of what produced

the outcome in the first place is not a resolution. It is a wish. And wishes do not change systems.

What It Costs

By Stage 5, costs are no longer abstract or future-oriented. They are present, documented, and attached to real numbers.

1. **Direct financial loss.** Contract penalties, expediting fees, emergency labor costs, rework, client credits, and refunds are all measurable. In many operations that reach Stage 5, the direct financial cost of the precipitating event runs to hundreds of thousands of dollars. The indirect costs — management distraction, employee disengagement, hiring to backfill departures — are typically two to three times that.
2. **Client and partner trust.** The relationships that are damaged at Stage 5 are often the ones that took years to build. Some of them will not be rebuilt. Not because the client is unreasonable, but because the Stage 5 failure demonstrated something about the organization's operational reliability that a strong recovery effort cannot fully erase.
3. **Workforce destabilization.** Stage 5 failures are demoralizing. People who were doing their best within a broken system watch the aftermath and make decisions about whether to stay. The exits that follow a public failure are rarely the ones organizations can afford — the competent, experienced people who have options leave first.
4. **Institutional scar tissue.** Organizations that survive Stage 5 often develop rigid, overbuilt communication requirements as a reaction — mandatory escalation paths, documentation requirements, approval chains — that add friction without addressing root cause. These structures protect against the specific failure that occurred, while the next spiral begins in the gaps they left open.
5. **The cost of the response to the cost.** The resources consumed by incident management, post-mortems, remediation plans,

client outreach, and internal repair are significant. Every hour spent on crisis response is an hour not spent on operation, development, or growth.

STOP AND CHECK

If your organization just came through something that looks like Stage 5, **resist the pressure to get to the solution before you fully understand the system.**

Map the spiral backward before you build anything forward. Where did the assumption enter? Where was silence misread as alignment? Where were people blamed for a system failure? Where did the workarounds form?

The answers to those questions are not comfortable. They will implicate decisions that were made with good intentions. They may implicate people who are well-regarded. They will almost certainly implicate structures and habits that the organization has operated under for a long time.

Do it anyway. A remediation plan that does not reach Stage 1 is a remediation plan that will bring you back to Stage 5.

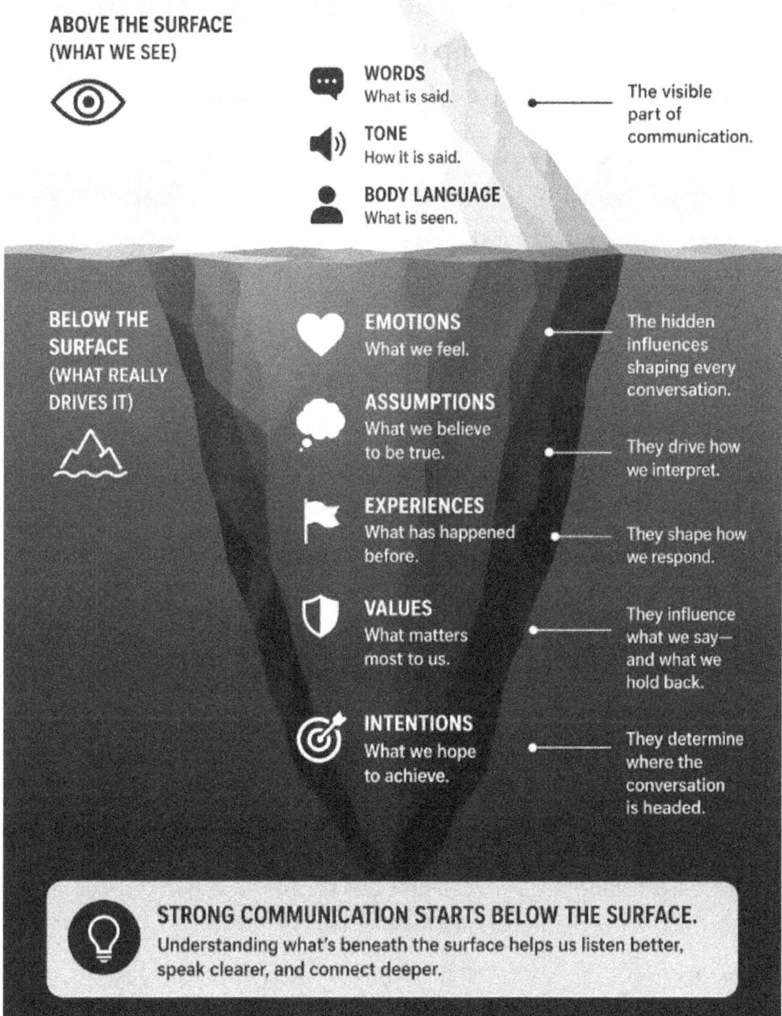

The Iceberg: What You See vs. What's Really There

The Silent Spiral™ works like an iceberg. **What's visible above the waterline** — the missed deadline, the blown budget, the resignation letter, the audit finding — **is only about 20 percent of the actual problem.** Below the surface sits the vast, hidden mass: the *unchecked assumptions, unanswered questions, conversations that never happened, workarounds that became permanent, and trust that eroded so slowly nobody noticed until it was gone.*

That is why post-mortems so often feel unsatisfying. They analyze the part of the iceberg that broke the surface. They document what was visible, measurable, and dramatic enough to show up in a report**. But the real story — the part that would actually prevent the next failure — is still underwater**.

Every visible failure event has a corresponding hidden history. The audit finding did not begin the day the auditor arrived. It started the day a handoff wasn't formalized, or the day a process changed without documentation, or the day someone noticed an inconsistency and stayed quiet because it did not feel like their place to speak up.

The resignation letter didn't start with a bad week. It began with a much smaller feeling, months earlier, that the person's *concerns were not landing, that their voice wasn't changing anything, that the effort of raising issues wasn't worth the outcome*. **By the time Stage 5 arrives, the iceberg has been forming for a long time.**

Above the Waterline (Visible)	Below the Waterline (Hidden)
Missed deadline	Scope change communicated verbally to one person
Budget overrun	Three versions of the requirements existed simultaneously
Client doesn't renew	Six months of unanswered concerns
Employee resignation	"I didn't feel heard" — said in the exit interview, felt for two years
Audit finding	A handoff that was never formalized
Project post-mortem	The same root cause identified three quarters ago
Team restructuring	Workarounds that masked the real problem for months
Escalation to leadership	Ten missed opportunities for a 5-minute conversation

This is what makes communication failure so persistent: **the events people treat as the problem are actually the end point of a much longer story.** And if you respond only to the visible event — fix the deadline, address the audit finding, replace the person who resigned — you are treating the tip of the iceberg while the mass beneath it remains intact, ready to surface somewhere else.

The intervention has to go below the waterline. That means asking different questions than most post-mortems ask.

- Not just *what went wrong* but *when did it first go wrong.*
- Not just *who was responsible* but *what information was missing from whom, and when.*
- Not just *how do we prevent this specific failure* but *how do we build a system where the below-the-waterline problems surface early enough to be cheap to fix.*

This book is built around the below-the-waterline work. The frameworks in Part II and the culture-building in Part III are designed to bring those hidden stages into the light — before they become the visible failure everyone is scrambling to explain.

Breaking the Spiral™ Stage 1 — Test the Assumption — is the direct intervention for the iceberg's base. When someone pauses and asks, "Are we sure we're all working from the same understanding," the entire structure below the waterline is exposed before it can grow. That one habit, practiced consistently, prevents more Stage 5 failures than any post-mortem framework ever will.

What You Walk Past, You Accept

In 2013, Australian Army Lieutenant General David Morrison delivered a statement that has since become one of the most quoted lines in leadership culture: ***"The standard you walk past is the standard you accept."*** He was addressing a specific institutional failure, but the principle travels. Brené Brown amplifies it in *Dare to Lead* as a cornerstone of accountable leadership — the idea that what we allow, we implicitly endorse. What we don't name, we normalize.

In the context of team communication, this principle lands with unusual weight. Most communication failures aren't caused by dramatic events. They don't begin with a single catastrophic decision, a spectacular misfire, or a moment anyone could point to and say: *there — that's where it started.* They begin with accumulation. The small things that good people walked past because it wasn't their job, wasn't the right time, or wasn't worth the risk.

The Silent Spiral™ doesn't need a dramatic trigger.

It just needs enough people to keep walking.

What You Walk Past in Each Stage of the Spiral:

What You Walk Past	What You Accept	Where It Leads
An assumption you suspect is wrong but don't question	A team operating on incomplete information	Stage 1 → Stage 2
Silence after a confusing update	The illusion that everyone understood	Stage 2 → Stage 3
A colleague's visible frustration that no one addresses	Resentment building underneath a functional surface	Stage 3 → Stage 4
A workaround that everyone uses but no one talks about	A broken system that will never be fixed	Stage 4 → Stage 5
A post-mortem that blames people instead of systems	The guarantee that the same failure will repeat	Stage 5 → Stage 1 (the spiral restarts)

Read that table slowly. Then think about the last month.

Notice that none of the "what you walk past" items require bad intentions. The assumption you didn't question — you may have let it go because you thought someone else would catch it, or because it seemed too small to escalate, or because you'd already raised something similar last week and didn't want to be the person who always raises things.

The silence after the confusing update — you didn't break it because you told yourself that maybe everyone else understood, and it would be embarrassing to be the one who didn't. The colleague's frustration — you noticed it, but it felt personal, and wading into someone else's emotional state didn't seem like your lane.

None of those calculations are malicious.
They're human. And together, they're catastrophic.

The Politeness Problem

Brené Brown writes in *Dare to Lead*:

"Clear is kind. Unclear is unkind."

This is one of those sentences that feels obvious until you sit with it. Most of us have been trained — explicitly or implicitly — to believe the opposite: that not saying difficult things is kind. That letting something slide is kind. That giving someone the benefit of the doubt rather than naming the gap is kind.

It isn't. This is avoidance dressed up as politeness.

When you walk past an assumption without questioning it, you're not protecting anyone. You're letting the team build on a foundation you suspect is unstable. When you let silence stand after a confusing update, you're not saving anyone from embarrassment. You're allowing everyone in the room to carry away a different version of the same message. When you don't address the frustration that's been leaking out of your colleague for three weeks, you're not preserving the relationship. You're letting it corrode slowly instead of quickly.

Clarity at the moment of the walk-past is kind. Silence is just silence — and silence is exactly what feeds the spiral.

This is not about perfection. You cannot catch every assumption, break every silence, or address every flicker of visible tension. Nobody can. The standard David Morrison and Brené Brown describe is not knowing everything; it is **intention**. It is **the difference between "I didn't know" and "I noticed and kept walking."**

Most communication breakdowns live in the **second category — not in the things we could not see, but in the things we saw and did not think were ours to address.**

There is a practical implication here worth naming directly: you do not have to be the manager to apply this standard. You do not have to be the team lead, the project owner, or the person with formal authority to intervene. **Walking past a broken standard is a choice available to everyone, and so is choosing not to walk past it.** The person who says, "I want to make sure I understood that correctly — can we take thirty seconds to confirm?" after a confusing update is not overstepping. They are doing what everyone else in the room wanted someone to do but was not sure was their job. **It is your job. It is everyone's job.**

The standard a team operates by is built from individual decisions made daily, in small moments that do not look like leadership decisions from the outside. Every time someone names the assumption, breaks the silence, or says, "I want to flag something before we move on," the standard lifts slightly for everyone.

And every time no one does, it settles slightly downward.

The Early Warning Signs

Most communication breakdowns do not begin with a dramatic event. They begin with **small signals that are easy to dismiss: a message that goes unanswered, a meeting that ends with no real clarity, or a concern that gets raised twice and then quietly dropped.**

That is what makes early warning signs so important. They are not minor irritants. They are evidence that information is not moving the way it should, that ownership may be unclear, or that people no longer trust the official path enough to use it. By the time a team reaches visible failure, the problem has usually been present much longer than anyone wants to admit.

The advantage of learning these signals is not that you will prevent every breakdown, but that you can intervene while the fix is still small, specific, and **far less expensive than recovery.**

Warning Sign	What It Signals	Your Move
Unanswered emails — pattern, not one-off	The communication system is overloaded, unclear, or no longer trusted to carry important information.	Audit urgency norms, expected response times, and whether the channel fits the message.
Meetings without agendas	No one clearly owns the outcome, so discussion replaces direction.	Require agendas and expected decisions; no agenda, no meeting.
Decisions made in hallways or sidebars	Real decisions are bypassing the team and never making it back into the official record.	Name it and create a visible decision log.
"Who owns this?" keeps recurring	Roles were never clearly defined, or they changed and no one reset accountability.	Run a role-clarity conversation or use a RACI-style ownership reset.
Nobody asks questions	People are disengaged, confused, or operating in a culture where questions feel risky.	Ask directly, invite dissent, and build response mechanisms into the conversation.
Attendance drops or replies get shorter	Someone has already started disengaging, even if they are still physically present.	Find out what is not being said before the silence hardens.
The same issue appears in three consecutive meetings	Information is not reaching the right people, or follow-through is failing.	Trace the information gap and ownership gap, not just the recurring symptom.
Shadow spreadsheets, side channels, or unofficial trackers appear	The official process is no longer trusted to get the work done.	Surface the workaround, understand why it exists, and repair the official path.
People say "I thought you knew" or "Nobody told me"	Assumptions are replacing confirmation, and shared understanding is breaking down.	Test the assumption; confirm receipt, understanding, and ownership explicitly.
Blame shows up before diagnosis and understanding	The team is reacting to visible failure without tracing the breakdown back to its origin.	Pause the blame cycle and map where information stopped flowing.

ARE WE IN THE SILENT SPIRAL?

A team diagnostic to uncover communication breakdowns before they become failures.

The Silent Spiral™ doesn't start with failure.
It starts with one assumption that goes untested.

Be honest. Check what's happening on your team today.

CHECK THE SIGNALS THAT SOUND FAMILIAR. CHECK ALL THAT ARE TRUE RIGHT NOW.

1. I sent a message in the last week and assumed it was received because no one responded. ☐
2. There is at least one issue on my team that everyone knows about, but no one has said out loud. ☐
3. In the last 90 days, a project or process stalled or failed because someone made an assumption. ☐
4. More than half of our team meetings end with no questions, no pushback, and no clarification. ☐
5. One or more people on my team have become noticeably quieter in the last 30 days. ☐
6. My team regularly uses at least one workaround to bypass an official process or communication channel. ☐
7. In the last month, a decision was made in a hallway conversation or sidebar and never brought back to the full team. ☐
8. Someone on my team has said, directly or indirectly, that they did not feel heard in the last six months. ☐
9. There are action items from past meetings that were never clearly followed up on. ☐
10. The same problem has surfaced in three or more consecutive meetings. ☐

HOW DEEP ARE WE IN THE SPIRAL?

Count your total checks. —

0–2 CHECKED

You may be catching issues early.

3–5 CHECKED

The Spiral is forming and beginning to affect team performance.

6+ CHECKED

You are in the Spiral.

NEXT STEPS

NEXT STEPS

Act this week, not next month.

Do not wait for more data.
Do not wait for confirmation.

Pick one communication breakdown and address it directly:

- clarify what was assumed
- surface what hasn't been said
- close one open loop

These tools are not about identifying failure.
They are about recognizing patterns early enough to change them.

The moment you can see the Spiral, you have the opportunity to break it.

Quick Check: Team Diagnostic — Early Warning Signs

Use these questions to pressure-test your team's communication patterns:

- How many of your last five team meetings had a written agenda?
- Are the same issues showing up across consecutive meeting notes?
- Who has become quieter in the last 30 days?
- When was the last time someone pushed back in a meeting, and how did the team respond?

Every Stage Has An Exit

Breaking the spiral doesn't require a different personality, a conflict resolution certification, or a perfect moment. **It requires one person** — a leader, a peer, sometimes the most junior person in the room — **choosing to say the harder, truer thing instead of the easier, familiar one.**

The spiral doesn't break itself. But it breaks faster than you think once someone decides to name what's actually happening.

FIELD NOTES: The Invisible Transition

A few years into my career, I was part of a team at a large logistics operation where a quality function was quietly shifted from one reporting line to another — no announcement, no transition meeting, no handoff documentation. On paper, the change made sense from a span-of-control standpoint.

In practice, the person in that quality role suddenly had a new chain of command, a new set of priorities, and an old team that still expected them to function as before — answering to two different sets of expectations, neither of which had been formally communicated to the other side.

It took months for anyone to name the dysfunction out loud. By then, several processes had drifted, relationships had been strained, and the person in the role had spent significant energy managing confusion that should never have been theirs to manage.

What failed wasn't the structural decision. What failed was the communication around it. The announcement that never came. The handoff meeting that was never scheduled. The conversation that assumed everyone would figure it out. They didn't. Nobody does.

The Shape of the Breakdown

The shape of a communication breakdown changes depending on where you're standing:

Vantage Point	What It Looks Like	The Real Problem
Top of organization	Execution failure — the team didn't deliver	Information never reached the people doing the work
Middle management	Resource problem — not enough time, clarity, authority	Caught between two sets of incomplete information
Ground level	Leadership is disconnected, changes direction without explanation	They weren't included in decisions that affected their work

All three perceptions can be simultaneously true. They're all symptoms of the same underlying breakdown. The failure travels through an organization the way a crack travels through a structure: it starts somewhere specific, and the stress radiates outward. The place where it finally breaks may be far from where it began.

Why This Matters More Than We Think

The organizations that get this right aren't doing so because they hired better communicators. They designed better communication. They built feedback loops. They created norms. They treated the flow of information as a process to be managed, not a hope to be held.

The breakdown doesn't start with bad people. It starts with missing structure, unexamined assumptions, and a culture that mistakes silence for consent.

KEY TAKEAWAYS: Chapter 1

- Communication breakdown is almost never a single dramatic event — **it's a slow accumulation of small failures that compound over time.**
- The five stages of The Silent Spiral™ follow a predictable pattern: **Assumption → Silence → Frustration → Workaround → Failure.** Each stage makes the next harder to prevent.

- **Early warning signs are opportunities for intervention,** not just annoyances.
- **Workarounds feel like solutions but are symptoms.** They make dysfunction survivable enough that no one fixes the root cause.
- PMI data places **poor communication as the primary driver of project failure** 56 percent of the time. This is a systems problem, not a people problem.
- **Breaking the Spiral™ offers the systematic antidote:** five stages of intervention that directly counter the five stages of failure. The framework is introduced fully in Part II.

REFLECTION QUESTIONS: Chapter 1

1. **Think about the last time a project, process, or working relationship broke down on your team. Which of the five stages was the actual point of origin — and when did you first notice the signs?**
2. **Where are the workarounds in your team or organization?** What do they tell you about where the official channels are failing?
3. **When you're in a meeting and nobody asks questions, what do you interpret that silence to mean?** Is your interpretation backed by evidence?

SEVEN COMMUNICATION FAILINGS THAT UNDERMINE TEAMS

1 ASSUMING THE MESSAGE WAS UNDERSTOOD

Insight: Delivery is not understanding.

Fix: Ask for feedback, confirm understanding, and assign ownership.

2 TALKING AT PEOPLE, NOT WITH THEM

Insight: Announcements may inform. Dialogue creates alignment.

Fix: Ask questions, invite response, and create real dialogue.

3 HOARDING INFORMATION

Insight: Held-back information weakens decisions and slows execution.

Fix: Share context early, document decisions, and increase visibility.

4 AVOIDING CONFLICT

Insight: Avoided tension becomes costly over time.

Fix: Address tension early with candor, respect, and facts.

5 BYPASSING THE CHAIN

Insight: Skipping levels may feel faster, but it creates confusion later.

Fix: Follow communication paths and escalate transparently when needed.

6 INCONSISTENT MESSAGING

Insight: Mixed messages erode trust and stall execution.

Fix: Align the message, the messenger, and the timing.

7 FAILING TO CLOSE THE LOOP

Insight: Unclosed communication creates repeated confusion.

Fix: Confirm actions, owners, deadlines, and follow-up.

Chapter 2: The Seven Failings

If you trace almost any team breakdown back far enough, you usually arrive at **the same few root causes**. Across healthcare, government, logistics operations, and cross-functional corporate environments, the **pattern is remarkably consistent:** the **visible failure may look unique**, but **the communication habits underneath it are not.**

I call these the **Seven Communication Failings that Undermine Teams**. They are not moral failings, personality flaws, or proof that the people involved do not care.

They are **recurring structural patterns — common**, **profoundly human**, and often **easy to justify in the moment** — that quietly wear away **clarity, trust, accountability,** and **execution.** That is what makes them so dangerous.

Most do not begin as dramatic acts of dysfunction. They begin as assumptions, omissions, avoided conversations, informal workarounds, and decisions made without full visibility. They look small, feel temporary, and are often defended as efficient, practical, or harmless. **Left unexamined, they become part of the team's operating logic.**

This chapter **names those seven failings**, **shows what they look like in practice**, and **explains what they cost**. More importantly, we reframe them as design problems rather than people problems. ***Once a team can see the pattern clearly, it has a chance to interrupt it.***

In the Room: The Seven Failings in One Meeting

You've probably sat in a version of this meeting.

Marcus sends the agenda at 8:57 a.m. for a 9:00 a.m. meeting. No pre-read. No context for the decision being made.

The meeting opens. Marcus: *"Okay, so we all know why we're here — the new reporting format goes live Monday."*

Silence. Priya hasn't heard about a new reporting format. Neither has Devon. But no one asks, because the way Marcus said *we all know* made it sound like asking would mean they missed something they were supposed to know.

Marcus: *"Great. Any issues?"*

Silence again. Devon has three issues. None of them feel worth saying out loud right now.

Marcus: *"Perfect. I'll send the format to the group."*

- He doesn't. That's a Friday.
- By Tuesday, Priya is using her own version.
- Devon built a workaround.
- Three other team members are waiting on the email that never came.

No one lied. No one was incompetent. Seven communication failings touched one meeting, and no one felt safe enough to say a word.

Failing	What it Looks Like	What it Costs
1. Assuming the message was received	A message is sent with no confirmation, follow-up, or check for understanding	Rework, errors, and repeated corrective conversations
2. Communicating at people	One-way broadcasts with no mechanism for response or clarification	Disengagement and poor decisions that persist too long
3. Hoarding information	Knowledge stays with one person or team and never reaches the people who need it	Duplicated work, knowledge loss, and weaker decisions
4. Avoiding conflict	People nod, stay quiet, or defer instead of pushing back	Artificial consensus that collapses under pressure
5. Ignoring the chain of responsibility	Work moves forward without clear ownership of decisions or outcomes	Role confusion, scope creep, and territorial disputes
6. Inconsistent messaging across levels	Strategy changes meaning as it moves from level to level	Workforce confusion and loss of trust in official channels

Failing	What it Looks Like	What it Costs
7. Failing to close the loop	Action items are discussed or assigned, but follow-up never happens	Stalled work, recurring problems, and eroded trust in meetings

Failing 1: Assuming the Message Was Received (and Understood)

This failing does not require bad intent. It happens in the absence of verification — no confirmation, no follow-up, and no check for understanding. **This is Spiral Stage 1 in its workplace form.**

A typical scenario:

- Email sent to 15 people about a process change
- 4 read it and understood it
- 3 read it and misunderstood it
- 2 skimmed it and *think* they understood it
- 4 haven't opened it yet
- 2 are on PTO
- Nobody responds
- Sender interprets silence as confirmation

The logic feels reasonable: we were clear, so anyone who was confused should have asked. But communication is not complete when a message is sent; it is complete when understanding is shared.

If the message was not understood, the communication was incomplete — regardless of how clear it felt to the sender.

This failing often grows out of familiarity. When the subject feels obvious to you, you stop hearing what is missing for everyone else. Important context disappears, steps go unnamed, and jargon slips in unnoticed.

- **The cost:** Rework, errors, and the same corrective conversation repeated multiple times.
- **The fix preview:** Test for understanding. Do not ask, “Do you have any questions?” Ask, “Can you tell me what you heard?”

Failing 2: Communicating At People Instead of With Them

There is a fundamental difference between distributing information and creating communication. One sends a message outward. The other creates a path for response, clarification, and adjustment.

Broadcasting	Conversation
"I have transmitted. My obligation is fulfilled."	"I need to know if this landed — and I need your response."
All-hands with pre-screened Q&A	Open dialogue with genuine response mechanism
Email blast announcing policy change	Discussion with the people affected before and after implementation
Status update that only travels up the chain	Information that flows in both directions

Communicating at people can feel efficient in the short term. Over time, it quietly disengages a team. When people are consistently expected to receive information but not shape it, they learn that their input is not necessary, and eventually they stop offering it.

This also weakens decision-making. The people with the closest view of how work actually happens often have the most useful information, but in a one-way system they have no reliable way to surface it. As a result, flawed decisions remain unchallenged until the cost of the decision becomes visible.

- **The cost:** Disengagement, weaker decisions, and a workforce that is present but no longer fully participating. People do not disengage only because they are uninformed. They disengage because they learn their knowledge is not part of how decisions get made.
- **The fix preview:** Build structured dialogue into significant communication. Create a response mechanism, make it safe to use, and show that what comes back affects what happens next.

Failing 3: Hoarding Information (The Knowledge Silo)

Information is power — and some people treat it that way. A knowledge silo forms when information **that should move stays trapped where it started**. Not always consciously, not always maliciously, but often just as damaging.

Knowledge silos tend to form in three ways:

- **Deliberate:** A manager or subject-matter expert believes that being the primary holder of information increases their value or control.
- **Incidental:** No clear system exists for sharing knowledge, so it accumulates where it originated and goes no further.
- **Structural:** Two teams depend on information that should inform each other's work, but no process or channel reliably connects them.

What the silo costs:

- **One person leaves →** years of **institutional knowledge disappears** overnight
- A **second team builds the same model,** makes the same calls, **produces redundant** or **contradictory work**
- **The next person in the role spends months rediscovering things** *that were already known*

Most silos do not form because people are intentionally secretive. They form because sharing knowledge requires effort, structure, and expectations that many organizations never deliberately build. **When documentation is inconsistent, handoffs are informal, and cross-functional visibility is weak, information stays local and decisions suffer.**

- **The cost:** Duplicated effort, knowledge lost to turnover, and teams making decisions without the information they need.
- **The fix preview:** Build information-sharing into the operating architecture. Use shared documentation, structured handoffs, and knowledge bases treated as operational infrastructure rather than optional admin work.

Failing 4: Avoiding Conflict to Preserve "Harmony"

In conflict-avoidant teams, "harmony" is often disagreement that has learned to stay quiet. The absence of open disagreement is not the same thing as genuine agreement.

Why conflict avoidance is seductive:

- It feels considerate; most people do not want to make a meeting more uncomfortable.
- Saying, "That plan has a flaw," is harder than nodding and moving on.
- The discomfort is immediate, but the cost shows up later.

What actually happens:

- Unspoken disagreement does not disappear; it goes underground.
- It turns into resentment, passive resistance, and quiet disengagement.
- Decisions move forward by default: nobody challenged the plan, so it survives — not because it is strong, but because nobody wanted to be the one to stop the room.

Patrick Lencioni makes this point well in *The Five Dysfunctions of a Team*: **when trust is weak, people avoid productive conflict, and the result is artificial consensus that starts to break the moment pressure hits it.**

I watched this play out in healthcare when the **data was telling a story nobody wanted to carry into the room.** The numbers were softened. The report was carefully framed. The meeting ended on a positive note. The problem did not go away; it kept growing while everyone acted as if the tone of the meeting mattered more than the truth in the data.

- **The cost:** Artificial consensus, decisions made without surfacing known risks, and resentment that lingers long after the original disagreement.

- **The fix preview:** Conflict avoidance is a habit, and habits can be replaced. The goal is to build structures where disagreement is expected, safe, and useful — not treated as a disruption, and not left to personality.

Failing 5: Ignoring the Chain of Responsibility

Every team has formal structures and informal ones. The **problem begins when the informal ones repeatedly override the formal ones** without being named, clarified, or corrected. **That is when responsibility starts to drift.**

How this failing shows up:

- A senior leader bypasses a direct manager and assigns work directly to that manager's team member, creating role confusion and undermining authority without ever addressing it openly.
- Tasks land on a team's plate because "it has to go somewhere," even when the work clearly belongs to another function and is assigned to whoever is willing to absorb it.
- People are quietly removed from decision-making without explanation; meetings disappear from their calendars, and decisions return later as directives.

One of the clearest signs of this failing is the gray zone experience: being assigned work that clearly belongs somewhere else, not because you are the right owner, but because responsibility was blurry enough for it to fall through the gap and land on you. That is not a compliment. **It is usually a sign that the organization has not done the work of defining who owns what.**

- **The cost:** Role confusion, scope creep, territorial tension, and the chronic experience of doing work that is not yours while your actual work waits.
- **The fix preview:** Ownership clarity is a design issue. RACI tools, role-definition conversations, and explicit communication about what belongs to whom are not administrative extras; they are structural safeguards.

Failing 6: Inconsistent Messaging Across Levels

What happens in practice: Nobody lied. But by the time the message worked its way down the chain, it barely resembled what started at the top.

This is also a leadership credibility problem:

- When your manager's direction directly contradicts what their manager said the week before, people start wondering which version is real and who to believe.
- Once trust in official communication starts to erode, people turn to the rumor mill, the text thread, or the colleague who "always knows what's really going on."
- None of those channels is consistent, accountable, or reliable.

In organizations where **supervisors in the same department apply the same policy differently — one enforcing it tightly, another barely acknowledging it** — the team's experience of the organization changes depending on who they report to. That is not a management style difference. **It is a communication failure at the leadership level.**

- **The cost:** Workforce confusion, uneven enforcement of standards, loss of credibility in official communication, and the growth of informal channels people trust more than the formal ones.
- **The fix preview:** Message consistency **requires discipline, documentation, and a deliberate cascade plan**. Leaders at each level need to understand the message, deliver it the same way, and have a way to clarify it before it spreads.

Failing 7: Failing to Close the Loop

The meeting happened. The decision was made. Action items assigned. Then: nothing. No follow-up, no accountability check, and no confirmation that anything actually moved. **This is Spiral Stage 4 forming in plain sight — the moment when the official channel quietly gets replaced by whatever workaround the team builds to compensate for it.**

Two weeks later, someone asks about it. A month later, the same issue shows up again in a slightly different form.

Why closing the loop matters:

- Without follow-up, commitment becomes optional.
- People are busy; the work that gets done is usually the work that gets tracked.
- Every unclosed loop teaches the team that commitments made in this room do not carry much weight.

The deeper damage is cultural. *When follow-up repeatedly does not happen, people stop treating meetings as places where real commitments are made.* They become more cautious with their own promises, less confident in other people's promises, and more likely to assume that today's agreement will be tomorrow's forgotten conversation.

- **The cost:** Stalled work, recurring problems, and the slow erosion of trust in the team's meeting and decision-making structure.
- **The fix preview:** Closing the loop is both a habit and a process. It requires visible ownership, clear deadlines, and a reliable method for checking what was done, what was not, and what happens next.

FIELD NOTES: Who Owns This? Nobody, Apparently.

The setup: cross-functional defect tracking in a high-volume distribution environment. One shared document. One "Responsible" field — supposed to be the spine of the whole system, the answer to the question every corrective action starts with: who owns this?

What I found: the field was blank. Routinely, chronically, institutionally blank.

Not because someone forgot to fill it in. Because no one had ever resolved the underlying question:

- Was the receiving team responsible for defects caught at intake?
- Was the floor supervisor responsible for defects caught at the line?
- Was quality responsible for documenting the issue, assigning corrective action, following up, or all three?

Nobody had ever sat in a room and answered those questions explicitly. So the field stayed empty, meeting after meeting. What I watched play out was not one isolated problem, but several communication failings running at the same time:

- The assumption that someone else would fill in the field.
- Silence when no one did.
- Frustration when defects recurred without resolution because the resolution had no owner.
- Workarounds, as supervisors quietly kept informal notebooks to track what the official report was not capturing.
- Failure at review time, when asked why quality metrics had not improved and the honest answer was this: for four months, we had been tracking problems without assigning anyone to fix them.

The fix was not sophisticated. We added one standing agenda item to the weekly cross-functional meeting: before any new defect data was reviewed, every open item with a blank "Responsible" field had to be resolved. Someone had to take ownership on the record — not by default, not because they happened to be in the room, but because the team agreed the work belonged to them.

We built the conversation into the structure, because leaving it to chance had already shown us the outcome.

What I learned: ambiguity in accountability is not neutral. It is not a placeholder. It is a decision not to decide, and it produces consequences as real as any wrong decision would.

A blank "Responsible" field does not mean nobody owns the issue.

It means everyone can assume somebody else does.

That assumption is where the failure begins.

FIELD NOTE TAKEAWAY: **Unclear ownership is not a neutral condition; it is an open invitation for the failure to continue.** If your tracking system includes a field that routinely goes blank, that blank is not a formatting issue. It is the problem. **Name the conversation, assign the owner, and build the decision into the structure. The blank will not fill itself.**

Breaking the Spiral™: The Same Meeting, *Done Differently*

Same cast. Different choices.

Marcus sends a two-sentence pre-read Thursday afternoon: *"We'll be deciding on a new reporting format Monday. I'm attaching the draft — please flag anything that won't work for your process before the meeting."*

Devon flags two issues. Marcus reads them.

Monday, 9:00. Marcus: *"Before we finalize this, I want to make sure I've heard from everyone. Devon flagged a concern about the data pull — Devon, can you walk us through it?"*

Devon does. Priya realizes she has the same problem and says so.

Marcus: *"Good. I want to get this right before Monday. Let's hold the launch until we've resolved those two items. Who owns the data pull piece — and can we get that resolved by Thursday?"*

Ten minutes. Two real problems surfaced. One decision made clearly, with a name and a date attached. That's closing the loop. That's what *actually* ending a meeting looks like.

How Many of These Are Happening on Your Team Right Now?

That's not a rhetorical question. It's a diagnostic one.

- **Are people assuming messages were received** without confirmation?
- **Is communication flowing in one direction,** with no structured way for people to respond or clarify?
- **Is there a person, or a team, *holding information* others need** without a reliable way of sharing it?
- **Are important conversations not happening because the conflict feels too uncomfortable?**
- **Are tasks landing wherever they land because nobody clearly defined ownership?**
- **Do people at different levels hold noticeably different understandings of the same priorities?**
- **Are commitments made in meetings actually being followed through on?**

If you answered yes to two or more, you're not in crisis — ***you're normal.*** These failings are common in organizations, but common does not mean harmless. The goal is not to feel bad about them. It is to see them clearly, name them honestly, and start making deliberate choices to change them.

KEY TAKEAWAYS: Chapter 2

- **The Seven Communication Failings that Undermine Teams are patterns, not character flaws** — recurring breakdowns that produce predictable consequences.
- **Assuming messages are received and understood is a foundational failing, and one of the most correctable,** because simple habits like testing for understanding can reduce it quickly.

- **Conflict avoidance creates artificial harmony that often collapses under pressure**; productive disagreement in the room prevents unproductive fallout outside it.
- **Inconsistent messaging across levels is a leadership design problem**, not a supervision or personality problem.
- **Failing to close the loop systematically destroys accountability by making commitments optional.**

REFLECTION QUESTIONS: Chapter 2

1. **Which of the seven communication failings is most prevalent in your current team or organization?** What is one concrete change in process, structure, or habit that could begin to address it?
2. **Think of a time when conflict avoidance led to a worse outcome than honest disagreement would have.** What would the more productive version of that conversation have looked like?
3. **What is the last significant commitment made in a meeting in your organization that was actually followed through on?**

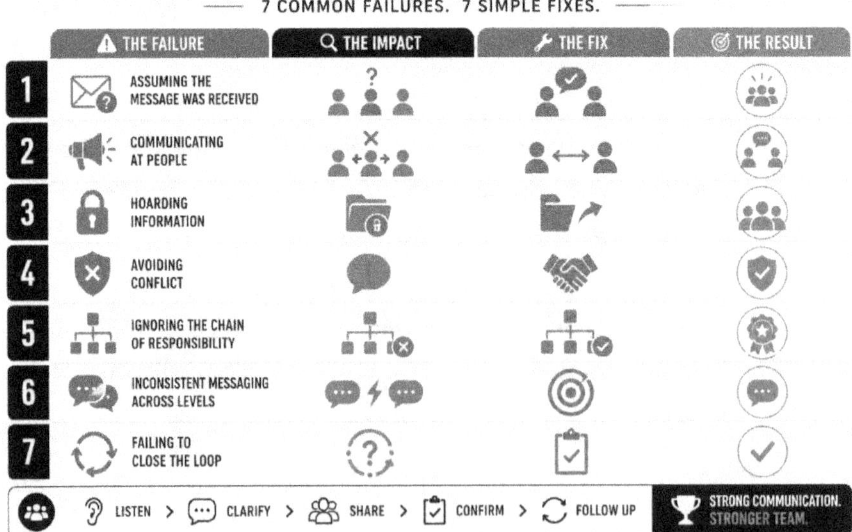

Chapter 3: The Human Element — Why Smart People Communicate Poorly

Here is the **uncomfortable truth** this chapter is built around: **communication failure is not a problem of intelligence.** Some of the worst breakdowns I've witnessed happened in rooms full of intelligent, well-credentialed, experienced people — people who knew better, in every sense of the phrase.

This matters because it means the solution isn't to hire smarter people or train everyone **to communicate well**. The barriers are largely psychological — rooted in how the brain works, what fear does to behavior, and what happens when a culture systematically rewards certain communication patterns while punishing others.

Understanding the human element is not a detour from practical work. It is a prerequisite, a MUST.

Before communication breaks down in process,
it usually breaks down in perception.

Ego, Fear, and the Illusion of Transparency

Two forces sabotage communication more reliably than almost anything else: **ego** and **fear**. They work in tandem, reinforcing each other in ways that make both harder to recognize.

Ego, in this context, does not mean arrogance. It means the deeply human need to appear capable, competent, and in control. It is the **instinct to protect the image of ourselves as people who understand, who can handle things, who do not need help, and who are not the weak link in the room.**

That kind of ego shows up in familiar ways. It **keeps people from asking questions** because asking would reveal a gap in understanding. It **shapes status updates that emphasize what is going well and minimize what is not.** It encourages people to answer **with confidence about things they are not entirely sure of, because confidence is often mistaken for competence.** It sends people out of meetings with unresolved questions and into *decisions made inside that fog.*

Fear operates at a different register, but it drives people toward the same result. There is fear of judgment. Fear of consequences for delivering bad news. Fear of what happens when you push back on a leader's idea. Fear of being the person who raises the problem that was supposed to have already been fixed.

Together, ego and fear create one of the most dangerous distortions in communication: **the illusion of transparency**. **We think we are being clear when we are actually being partial. We think we are being direct when we are sounding cautious, hedged, or ambiguous.** We think we are asking a precise question when the other person hears three possible meanings and has to guess which one we intended. We think we have communicated that input is welcome, while never actually saying so. We think we have signaled that a project matters, while our behavior quietly communicates the opposite.

In practice, the gap often looks like this:

What You Think You're Doing	What The Other Person Actually Receives
Being honest and direct	Hedged, cautious, or ambiguous messaging
Asking a clear question	A request that could be interpreted several different ways
Communicating that you value input	No explicit invitation to speak honestly
Signaling that the project is a priority	Mixed signals suggest other priorities matter more

Leaders are often the last to realize how wide this gap can become. They judge their communication by what they intended to convey. Their teams judge it by what was actually said, modeled, reinforced, and made safe to respond to **honestly**.

And the power differential matters. A manager who gives a vague directive and a team member who accepts it without asking for clarification have both participated in the breakdown, but responsibility is not distributed equally. The person with more power, more context, and more control bears more responsibility for creating the conditions in which clarity is possible.

In the Room: The Curse of Knowledge in Action

This exchange is so common it almost has a script.

Keisha is a senior project manager. She's running a handoff meeting for someone new to the team.

Keisha: *"So the client wants the deliverable in the standard format — you know, the one we use for all the regional accounts."*

James nods. He does not know the standard format. He's been here four weeks. He doesn't know what a regional account is, exactly, versus other accounts. He doesn't want to ask, because Keisha said *you know* and the room moved on.

Keisha: *"Just make sure it goes through the normal approval chain."*

James nods again.

Three days later, James submits the deliverable in the wrong format, to the wrong approver, two days after the actual deadline — because he hadn't known there was a deadline.

Keisha's reaction: *"I told him everything he needed."*

She did. She just didn't know she hadn't.

The Cognitive Biases Behind the Breakdown

Ego and fear explain a great deal, but they do not explain everything. Communication also breaks down because human beings are not neutral processors of information. We hear selectively. We assume too much. *We fill in missing context with our own beliefs. We mistake silence for agreement and familiarity for clarity.*

These failures are not random. They are **driven by predictable cognitive biases: recurring mental shortcuts and distortions that shape how people interpret information, judge intent, and make decisions.**

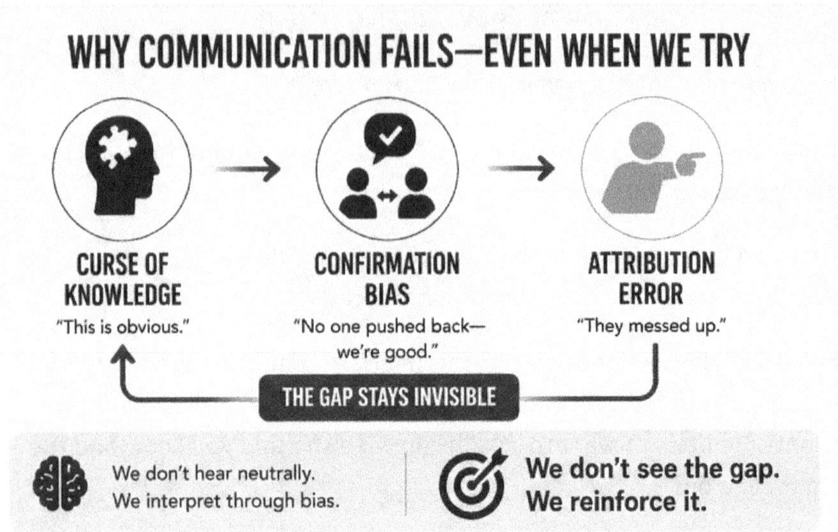

These biases affect *everyone*: leaders, frontline employees, experts, newcomers, confident people, anxious people, and well-intentioned people alike. *No one enters a conversation as a neutral observer.* That does not make clear communication impossible, but it does make it far more dependent on environment, power, and process than most organizations are willing to admit.

Three biases are especially destructive:

- **The Curse of Knowledge makes it difficult to remember what it was like not to know something.** Once you understand a process, a system, or a decision, it becomes surprisingly hard to see what a newcomer cannot see. *You skip context. You use jargon.* You refer to assumptions so foundational that you forget they were ever assumptions at all. **The person who built the process is often the worst person to explain it to someone new, because they can no longer see what they are leaving out.**
- **Confirmation Bias makes us interpret new information through the lens of what we already believe.** A leader who believes their communication is working may treat the absence of complaints as proof that everything is fine. **What they may be**

missing is that complaints were tried, ignored, and eventually stopped. The silence is not confirmation. It is surrender.

- **Fundamental Attribution Error leads us to explain other people's failures as character flaws while explaining our own as products of circumstance.** When a process breaks down, we **look for the person to blame instead of the structural weakness that made the failure likely.** When someone communicates poorly, we label them a poor communicator instead of asking what kind of environment makes good communication difficult. This is one reason so many communication workshops underdeliver: *they are designed to fix the person when the deeper problem is the system.*

Seen Side-By-Side, the Pattern Becomes Difficult to Ignore

Bias	What It Is	How It Damages Communication
Curse of Knowledge	Expertise makes it hard to remember what it was like not to know something	You skip context, use jargon, rely on unstated assumptions, and cannot see what you are leaving out
Confirmation Bias	We interpret new information through the lens of what we already believe	We hear what we expect to hear, and silence gets mistaken for confirmation when it may actually be surrender
Fundamental Attribution Error	We attribute others' failures to character and our own to circumstance	Systemic failures get diagnosed as people problems, so the system itself never gets fixed

Ego and fear supply the emotional fuel. Cognitive bias supplies the mental mechanism. Together, they widen the gap between what was intended, what was said, and what was actually received.

Psychological Safety and Why It Changes Everything

This is where **psychological safety** becomes decisive. **Psychological safety is what determines whether people will speak honestly** when clarity is missing, whether they will raise concerns before problems spread, and whether information can move upward before it becomes too costly to ignore.

Amy Edmondson's research on psychological safety offers one of the most powerful frameworks for understanding why teams communicate well or badly.

What happens without it:

- **Problems stay hidden**
- **Errors don't get reported**
- **Bad news doesn't travel upward**
- **Innovation gets killed at birth**
- **Decision quality degrades because decision-makers don't have the full picture**

Edmondson's counterintuitive finding: Teams with high psychological safety actually report more errors — not fewer.

What changes isn't the error rate. It's the reporting rate. In safe teams, errors surface early when they can still be addressed. In unsafe teams, errors are hidden until they become catastrophic.

That distinction changes everything. The most communicative team may not be the one with the fewest problems. It may be the one willing to reveal them. A quiet team is not automatically a healthy team. It may simply be a team that has learned what not to say.

And that is the central misunderstanding at the heart of so many organizational failures: **leaders often assume communication is broken because people are not skilled enough, disciplined enough, or brave enough.** But many communication failures are not failures of individual character. They are failures of environment. People do not communicate clearly in conditions that punish clarity. They do not tell the truth freely in systems that make truth dangerous. They do not raise risks early when experience has taught them that speaking up changes nothing — or makes them the problem.

Communication is more than sending a message. It is whether the conditions exist for reality to move between people without being distorted by ego, fear, power, and self-protection.

That is why psychological safety does not sit beside communication as a secondary topic. It sits underneath it. It is the condition that determines whether communication is real at all.

What creates psychological safety:

Factor	What It Looks Like In Practice
Leader models fallibility	"I got that wrong. Here's what I should have done differently." — said in a normal, matter-of-fact tone
Questions over performed expertise	Asking genuine questions rather than signaling certainty you may not have
Acknowledging uncertainty with a plan	"I don't have all the information yet, and here's how I'm going to get it."
Response to failure = learning, not punishment	Mistakes are debriefed, not prosecuted

These behaviors seem small. Their impact is not. When the leader says, "I made a mistake," every person on the team receives permission to say the same thing. That permission is the foundation of honest communication.

Breaking the Spiral™: Stage 1 → Test the Assumption

The same moment. One small change.

Keisha: *"So the deliverable goes out in the standard regional format — let me pull that up and walk you through what that looks like, because it's not obvious the first time."*

She shares her screen. Two minutes.

Keisha: *"The approval chain has three steps — I'll send you the name of the person at each step and flag who tends to be the bottleneck.*

Deadline is Thursday. Does that track with what you've got on your calendar?"

James: *"I have Friday — let me double-check."*

Keisha: *"Let's confirm right now."*

It takes four minutes total. James delivers on Thursday. In the right format. To the right person.

The curse of knowledge doesn't go away. But **it breaks the moment you stop assuming your expertise is visible to everyone in the room.**

When the Culture Rewards Silence

Psychological safety can be built over time and destroyed in a single conversation.

The unspoken rules that kill communication:

- The micro-calculation in every group setting: *Is it safe to say what I actually think?*
- The shift in meeting dynamics when certain people enter the room
- Who gets invited to which conversations
- Who finds out about decisions after the fact

The experience of being gradually, quietly removed from decision-making:

- Meetings you used to be included in stop appearing on your calendar
- Decisions that touch your work arrive as directives
- You find out about things in emails rather than in conversations
- Because nothing was ever explicitly communicated, you can't even name what changed

This experience is particularly common for people who aren't part of the informal networks that run the real business. A colleague once put it plainly, with no particular bitterness:

"The real meetings happen before the meeting."

They weren't being dramatic. They were naming the *structural reality* of a team where the informal power network operated through channels that were never announced and never documented — and that functionally excluded anyone who hadn't been part of it from the beginning.

Any honest discussion of why people communicate poorly has to acknowledge: **the system doesn't always fail the same way for everyone.** Some people's silence is chosen. Some people's silence is enforced.

Cultures of Fear: When Silence Becomes Survival

Psychological safety operates on a spectrum. At one end, teams speak freely, flag problems early, and treat honest disagreement *as part of doing good work.* At the other end, silence isn't common — *it's the rational survival strategy.* **This is the far end of the spectrum: a culture of fear.**

Fear-based cultures don't usually announce themselves. They're built through *accumulated signals*, each one small enough to be deniable, together *forming a pattern that everyone can read*. The signals teach a lesson: here, speaking up is dangerous. **And once that lesson is learned, it's remarkably hard to unlearn.**

How Fear-Based Cultures Become Self-Reinforcing

The first time someone raises a concern and gets punished for it — visibly sidelined, publicly dismissed, quietly reassigned — everyone in the room learns something. Not just the person who spoke. Everyone. The room files that lesson away. And the next time there's something uncomfortable to say, the calculation happens: *what happened to the person who said the last uncomfortable thing?*

This is how the silence compounds. One incident teaches caution. Two incidents teach calculation. Three teach silence. By the time a fear culture is fully formed, most of the people in it will tell you, privately, that they knew the problems were there. They didn't see a path to raising them that didn't end badly.

The Link Between Fear And The Silent Spiral™

Fear doesn't produce silence in isolation — it accelerates every stage of the Silent Spiral™. **When fear is the operating system:**

- **Stage 1 (Assumption)** becomes more dangerous, because no one asks the clarifying question that would catch the wrong assumption before it compounds
- **Stage 2 (Silence)** becomes structural, not situational — people don't stay quiet because they forgot to speak up; they stay quiet because they've learned what happens when they do
- **Stage 3 (Frustration)** goes underground. People are frustrated, but frustration expressed is a risk, so it travels sideways: venting to peers, eroding morale from the inside out
- **Stage 4 (Workaround)** becomes invisible. Shadow systems, unofficial channels, and quiet workarounds multiply — and because no one will flag them, they never get fixed
- **Stage 5 (Failure)** arrives without warning, because every early signal was suppressed along the way

Fear isn't one variable among many. It's the fuel. The same breakdown that a psychologically safe team catches in Stage 1 or 2 will run all the way to Stage 5 in a fear-based environment, because every mechanism that would have stopped it earlier depends on someone being willing to say something.

When People Don't Just Stay Silent — They Actively Hide

In a moderately unhealthy culture, people stay quiet about problems. ***In a fear culture, they do something worse:*** they actively manage the picture.

- Status reports get smoothed.
- Bad news gets delayed.
- *Numbers get reframed.*

Not because people are dishonest — most aren't — but because **they've learned that the messenger gets shot**, and they're calculating the risk of delivering a message that lands badly.

This is what the green dashboard / red room dynamic looks like from the inside. It's not that the team doesn't know the project is in trouble. Each person has independently decided that today is not the day to be the one who says so.

How Leaders Create Fear Without Intending To

Most leaders who run fear cultures did not intend to. Fear is rarely built on purpose — it is built by default.

It is built through four everyday patterns:

- **Reactions to bad news.** A visibly frustrated, sharp, or dismissive response to a problem report teaches the team exactly what happens when someone brings bad news. One reaction, watched by everyone in the room, is remembered for months.
- **Punishing the messenger.** It does not have to be formal. A person who flags a problem and then finds themselves sidelined, excluded from key conversations, or passed over for the next opportunity teaches everyone else exactly what flagging problems costs.
- **Rewarding only good news.** When praise flows freely toward people who report wins and recognition is absent for people who flag risks or catch problems early, the incentive structure is clear: surface the positive, bury the negative.
- **Public dismissal of ideas.** When questions and suggestions are met with dismissal, eye rolls, or *"we already tried that"* — in front of peers — the cost of contributing visibly goes up for everyone in the room.

None of these require malice. They require only a leader who has not examined what their reactions are teaching. Fear cultures are not what leaders say. They are what leaders do in the moment when it would be easier not to.

The Difference Between Healthy Caution And Toxic Fear

Not all caution is fear, and not all risk-calculation is dysfunction. Healthy caution is proportionate and recoverable: someone weighs the risk of speaking up, decides it's manageable, and speaks. **Toxic fear** is anticipatory and permanent: someone has learned that *the risk is never manageable*, so they stop calculating and start defaulting to silence.

The test is what happens when someone does speak up. In a healthy culture, the outcome — even when the feedback isn't what they hoped for — is survivable. The person isn't penalized for trying. In a fear culture, the outcome teaches **The Art of "Everything Is OK" — The Most Dangerous Sentence in Any Organization.**

I've sat in hundreds of meetings. Maybe thousands. And I've watched it happen so many times I can feel it coming before the words leave someone's mouth.

The project manager takes a breath. The room gets that specific kind of quiet — not comfortable quiet, the other kind. And then, right on cue: "Yeah, we're good. No issues."

Everyone nods. **The meeting moves on. And somewhere underneath that nodding, three people know the deadline is a fiction, one person knows the client is furious, and another has been duct-taping a critical process together for six weeks because they didn't want to be the one who said it out loud.** This is a cultural habit so deeply wired into how most organizations operate that people don't even notice they're doing it. And it is one of the most organizationally destructive behaviors I have ever observed. Not dramatic destructive. Quiet destructive. **The kind that doesn't show up until you're already in the rubble.** It is also the beating heart of Silent Spiral™ Stage 2: Silence.

Why We Say "Fine" When We Mean "Help"

When someone tells you "everything is OK" and it isn't, they're not being lazy or cowardly. They have usually learned, through direct experience, that telling the truth about problems in this organization does not go well for the person who tells it.

They've been the bearer of bad news and watched the room treat them like they caused it. They've raised a concern, and had it minimized or turned back on them — "Well, what's your plan to fix it?" — as though ***noticing a problem and solving it are the same person's job.*** Maybe, nothing dramatic happened at all. They noticed that people who keep their heads own get fewer hard conversations than people who flag things. That's

A CULTURE OF FEAR

When people stay quiet to stay safe, the organization stops learning.

- People avoid speaking up.
- Bad news travels slowly.
- Questions are treated as challenges.
- Mistakes are hidden, not examined.
- Silence is mistaken for alignment.

2 COMMON SIGNALS

Meetings are quiet, but hallway conversations are not.

Concerns are raised privately, not publicly.

People wait for permission to say obvious things.

Workarounds grow because formal channels feel unsafe.

Employees become careful, guarded, and less candid.

3 WHAT IT CAUSES

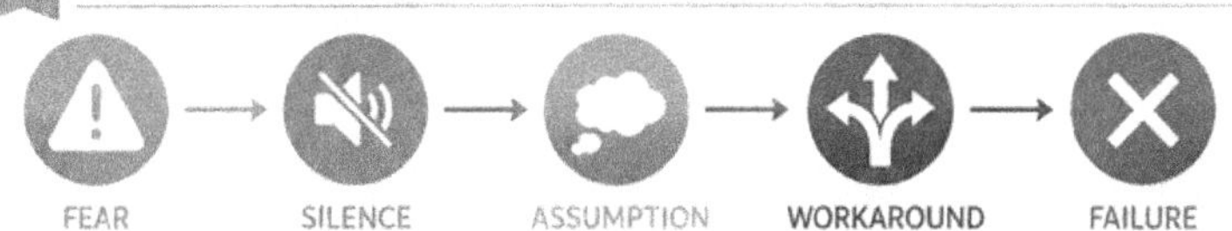

A culture of fear does not create discipline. It creates distortion.

4 WHAT TO BUILD INSTEAD

Make it safe to raise concerns early.

Reward candor, not just compliance.

Respond to bad news constructively.

Close loops so people know they were heard.

Model calm, direct leadership communication.

PSYCHOLOGICAL SAFETY IS NOT SOFTNESS. IT IS OPERATIONAL STRENGTH.

enough.

There Are Other Flavors, And They All Have Their Own Logic

- **The Self-Rescuer.** "If I just work harder this week, I can fix this before anyone notices." **They're building the plane while flying it** — patching systems, absorbing gaps, and carrying risk that leadership doesn't even know exists. Sometimes they pull it off. More often they burn out trying, the problem catches up anyway, and now it's bigger and they're exhausted.
- **The Hierarchy Reader.** "It's not really my place." They can see the problem clearly, but the **implicit message they've absorbed is that ground-level employees don't weigh in on executive-level decisions.** So they don't. And the executive makes a decision that the person three floors down could have corrected in thirty seconds.
- **The Room Reader.** The meeting is running long, everyone is visibly done, and raising a real concern right now means being *that person* — the one who kept everyone late. **So, they save it for later. Except later never comes,** because by then the decision has already been made.
- **The Professional.** They've internalized the cultural premium on optimism, and they've noticed that people who raise problems are sometimes **quietly filed under "not a team player."** So, they keep the concern internal and carry the full weight of knowing things aren't fine.

Every one of these people is trying to survive in the environment they've been given. **The fault is not theirs.** *The fault is the environment — and the leaders who built it, usually without meaning to.*

The Walk-By

There's an unspoken rule in most workplaces: when someone asks, "How are things going?" — the only acceptable answer is "fine."

FINE. It might be the most dangerous word in organizational communication. *Not because it's a lie — but because it's a signal.*

It means *I don't want to talk about it,* or *I don't trust this conversation enough to be honest,* or *I've learned that the truth isn't welcome here.*

Here's where it usually happens. A director passes a supervisor in the hallway. "How are things going?" he asks — already walking, already half-turned toward his next meeting. The supervisor says, "Good." Because what else is she supposed to say? He didn't stop. He didn't sit down. He didn't ask a question that had room for a real answer.

And then, almost as an afterthought: *"Let me know if you need anything."*

Anything. **The most generous-sounding, least useful word in leadership.** What does anything mean? Budget? Headcount? Air cover on a decision? Permission to push back on a policy that's failing? The person being asked has no idea what's actually on the table — so they nod, say "will do," and go back to solving it alone. Not because they don't need help. **Because they don't know what help is available, and the offer wasn't specific enough to test.**

This is the other side of "fine." Leaders ask questions they haven't built the space to hear honest answers to. They offer help they haven't defined. **And then they interpret the silence as confirmation that everything is working.**

It isn't working. *They just made it too expensive to say so.*

The supervisor who says "fine" isn't dishonest. She's doing math. She's calculating the risk of honesty against the likelihood that it changes anything. And most days, the math says: *just handle it yourself.*

The question isn't why people say "fine." The question is *what have we built that makes "fine" the safest answer?*

Breaking the Walk-By: If You're the Supervisor

The instinct is to match the energy of the question. Vague question, vague answer. But "fine" keeps you invisible — and invisible people don't get resources, air cover, or support.

You don't have to unload everything in a hallway. **But you can replace "fine" with one specific, low-risk sentence:**

- **Instead of "Good" → "We're managing, but I could use five minutes on the staffing gap this week."**
- **Instead of "All good" → "Mostly solid — I do have one thing I'd like your input on when you have a minute."**
- **Instead of "Fine" → "I'm working through something. Can I grab 10 minutes on your calendar this week?"**

Each of these does the same thing: it converts a throwaway exchange into an opening without requiring trust you haven't built yet. You're not being vulnerable. You're being specific. That's different.

And when a leader says, "let me know if you need anything" — ask them to define it. **Not confrontationally. Just practically:**

"I appreciate that. Can you help me understand — if I came to you with a staffing issue versus a process issue versus a decision I need air cover on — what's realistically on the table?"

Most leaders have never been asked that question. It resets the entire relationship.

Breaking the Walk-By: If You're the Leader

Stop asking questions while you're walking away. If you don't have time for the answer, don't ask the question. A check-in that happens in passing tells your team exactly how much their answer matters to you: not enough to stop moving.

Replace the walk-by with these:

Instead Of...	Try...
"How's it going?" (while walking)	Sit down. Even 3 minutes. "What's the hardest thing on your plate this week?"
"Everything okay?"	"What's one thing that's working and one thing that's frustrating you right now?"
"Let me know if you need anything"	"I can help with [X, Y, or Z]. Which of those would make the biggest difference?"
"Any issues?"	"If something was slipping that I couldn't see from where I sit, what would it be?"

The shift is small but structural: you're asking questions that have room for an honest answer, and you're defining what help actually looks like.

"Let me know if you need anything" puts the burden on the person with less power to figure out what you're willing to do.

That's backwards.

The leader should be the one who names the menu. You're not handing someone a blank check — you're showing them the options.

The Test

Here's how you know if you've built an environment where people can stop saying "fine":

- **Someone tells you something you didn't want to hear — and nothing bad happens to them.**
- ***That's it.*** That's the whole test. Not once. Repeatedly. Until the pattern is undeniable, and the team believes it.

What Performative OK Actually Costs

Leaders lose ground truth. This is the most operationally critical cost. If the people with direct knowledge of what's happening are consistently telling you everything is fine, you will make decisions based on a reality that does not exist. You will set timelines that can't be met and walk into client conversations with confidence that isn't backed by facts. You will be the last to know.

Problems compound. I've watched this happen too many times to count. A concern that could have been addressed in a single Monday conversation becomes a crisis by Friday. Not because the problem was hidden — but because by the time it was visible enough that no one could pretend otherwise, it had been growing, untouched, for weeks. A $500 fix becomes a $50,000 fix. A recoverable client relationship becomes a lost contract.

The people saying "ok" burn out. When someone presents calm publicly while privately absorbing dysfunction, they are doing two jobs simultaneously: their actual work, and the work of managing the gap between the official story and the real one. They are building the plane while flying it — and no one in the cockpit knows the wings aren't finished.

That gap has weight. Carrying it, alone, over time, is exhausting in a way that's hard to explain to someone who hasn't done it. These are often your most conscientious people — the ones who care enough to notice but have learned that surfacing it isn't safe. **You are quietly burning out your best employees.**

Trust erodes. Not quickly, and not loudly. Trust doesn't leave organizations all at once. It leaves in small increments, every time someone realizes the gap between the official story and the lived reality is wider than they thought. Eventually, people stop believing the official story about anything. The credibility debt accumulates, and by the time leadership notices, it's staggering.

How to Recognize It

- **Everyone agrees too quickly.** Real teams have friction. When a proposal sails through with zero pushback and unanimous enthusiasm, that is not a sign of a healthy, aligned team. It is often a sign that people have learned their questions aren't welcome.

- **Status updates are suspiciously clean.** No risks. No flags. Green lights, on time, on budget, every single week — right up until suddenly it isn't. Real projects have noise. Perfect status reports aren't a sign of excellent execution. They're a sign that someone is editing reality before it reaches you.

- **The same problems keep recurring.** If an issue gets "resolved" and surfaces again three months later, it was not resolved. Something was patched while the underlying cause was never discussed — usually because that conversation never fully happened.

- **People who used to speak up have gone quiet.** When someone who used to flag things, ask hard questions, push back — stops doing that — they didn't suddenly become more agreeable. They made a calculation. Something taught them it wasn't worth it.

- **The meeting ends in five minutes when the topic warranted thirty.** Quick meetings feel efficient. But when a genuinely complex issue gets a clean five-minute resolution with no dissent, what you're often watching is a room full of people who have already decided this isn't the place to say what they actually think.

DANGER ZONE: The Open Door That Never Heard Bad News

There is a particular kind of leader — well-intentioned, often genuinely warm — who says, sincerely, "My door is always open." **And means it. And has never once, through that open door, received a piece of bad news.**

If this is you: the problem is not that your team has no concerns. The problem is that your behavior — however unintentionally — has communicated that you don't actually want to hear them.

Maybe you responded to a concern with visible frustration once. Maybe you asked for solutions before you acknowledged the problem. Maybe **you just always seem so busy that people feel guilty interrupting.**

It doesn't take much. "My door is always open" is a passive invitation in an environment that may require active permission. If the people closest to your work have never told you anything was wrong, the honest question isn't whether they have concerns. It's what you've taught them happens when they share them.

Before and After: What It Sounds Like

BEFORE — The "Everything Is Fine" Meeting

- **Manager:** Quick check-in — how's the client deliverable looking for Thursday?
- **Team member:** Yeah, should be good.
- **Manager:** Any blockers?
- **Team member:** No, we're on track.
- **Manager:** Great. Anyone else? No? Perfect.

What you don't see: the team member has known for four days that a key dependency is running late. They've been building the plane while flying it — reworking timelines, pulling favors, quietly absorbing a problem that isn't theirs to carry alone. They didn't say anything because the last time they flagged a cross-team issue, they spent two weeks in uncomfortable meetings and nothing got resolved.

Thursday is going to be a problem.

AFTER — Breaking the Pattern

- **Manager:** Quick check-in — what's the one thing that's *not* working on this deliverable right now?
- **Team member:** *(pause)* I need to flag something. We have a dependency on the data team that's running late. I'm not confident we'll have what we need by Thursday.
- **Manager:** I'm glad you said that. How far off are we, and what do you need from me?
- **Team member:** Maybe two days. If you could talk to their lead, that would help — I didn't want to go over anyone's head.
- **Manager:** That's exactly where you should go over someone's head. Let's figure this out now.

The same problem existed in both versions. In the first, it surfaces as a crisis Thursday. In the second, it becomes a solvable problem Monday. The difference was one question and one response that didn't punish the honesty.

WHAT TO SAY: Replace "Is Everything OK?" With These

1. "What's the one thing that's not working right now?"
2. "If you had to pick one concern about this project, what would it be?"
3. "What would you want me to know that you haven't told me yet?"
4. "What's keeping you up at night about this?"
5. "What are we pretending isn't a problem?"

Each of these questions assumes that something is wrong. That assumption is the work. You are giving people permission, in the structure of the question itself, to tell you the truth. "Is everything OK?" does the opposite — it invites, and almost requires, a yes.

How to Break It

Asking better questions is necessary but not sufficient. You cannot ask your way out of *a culture of performative OK* if the conditions that created it haven't changed.

- **Normalize "I need to flag something."** When someone says it, stop what you're doing. Don't rush to solutions. Don't make them defend the concern before you've heard it. The goal is to make flagging a problem feel like a professional act, not a personal risk.
- **Model it yourself.** Say it out loud, in meetings: "I want to be honest — I'm concerned about X, and I'd rather say it now than pretend it's fine." When leadership demonstrates that uncertainty is speakable, the entire organization gets permission to do the same. This cannot be delegated or put in a values deck. It has to be modeled, repeatedly, by the people at the top.
- **Create structure where "no concerns" is not a valid answer.** Build into recurring check-ins a moment where every person names one risk or concern — not as a performance of negativity, but as a professional practice. Every project has friction. The only question is whether you know about it.
- **Follow through visibly.** When someone flags something and the response works — the problem gets addressed, and nothing bad happens to the person who raised it — make sure that outcome is visible to the rest of the team.

Trust in the safety of honesty is built by precedent.

People are watching what happens to the first person who says it. If the outcome is invisible, the team learns nothing. If the outcome is visible, the team learns that flagging problems is safe — and the next person is a little more willing to speak.

The Connection to The Silent Spiral™

This is where Stage 2 lives. Not in the dramatic breakdown, not in the resignation letter or the crisis meeting. Right here, in the **small, daily, almost invisible decision to say "we're fine" when you know you're not.**

The Spiral accelerates every time someone makes that choice. They are usually making the rational choice given the environment they're in. Silence is the symptom, not the problem. The problem is the environment that made silence feel safer than honesty.

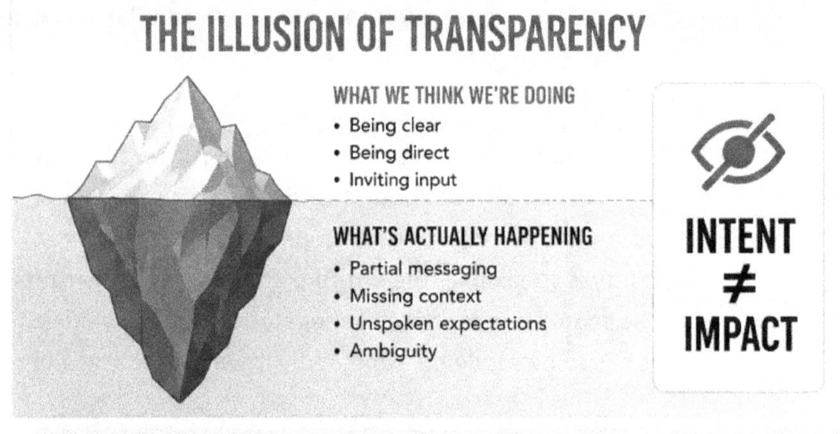

Breaking the Spiral™ at Stage 2 — Break the Silence — requires making honesty structurally safer than the alternative. Not just tolerated. Not just invited. Actively, visibly, repeatedly rewarded. Ask different questions. Model vulnerability from the top. Build structures that require rather than merely permit candor. And treat the person who flags the problem as an asset, not an inconvenience.

"Everything is OK" will keep getting said until the people saying it **genuinely believe that something else is possible. Give them a reason to believe it.**

Signs You're Working in a Fear Culture	Signs You're Working in a Safe Culture
Bad news arrives late, after it's too late to act	Problems surface early, while there's still time to fix them

Signs You're Working in a Fear Culture	Signs You're Working in a Safe Culture
Status reports are consistently optimistic until they suddenly aren't	Status reports include risk flags and early warnings
People vent privately but go quiet in meetings	People raise concerns in the room where they can be addressed
"I told you so" travels fast; "I was wrong" is rare	Leaders model fallibility openly and without drama
Questions from leadership feel like interrogations	Questions from leadership are curiosity, not accountability theater
Messengers get managed; problems get ignored	Problems get investigated; messengers get protected
Workarounds multiply and go unacknowledged	Workarounds get surfaced and traced back to root causes
High performers leave without warning	High performers stay and engage

The Words That Push People Out

Not all communication failures involve missing information or broken systems. Some are built from language — specific phrases, delivered often without awareness, that tell people their contributions aren't wanted.

No single phrase does catastrophic damage. A person can absorb "we already tried that" once and move on. They can hear "you'll understand once you've been here longer" and chalk it up to someone having a bad day. **What they can't absorb indefinitely is a pattern — the accumulation of small dismissals that, over weeks and months, builds into a clear signal: *your input doesn't change anything here.***

This is how organizations lose the voices they most need. Not through dramatic exclusion. Through the slow, consistent deflation of every attempt to contribute.

What They Say. What You Hear. What It Produces.

What They Say	What You Hear	The Effect
"That's just how we do things here."	Your ideas don't matter.	Person stops proposing improvements.

What They Say	What You Hear	The Effect
"You're overthinking it."	Your concerns are invalid.	Person stops flagging risks.
"You'll understand once you've been here longer."	You don't belong yet.	Person waits instead of contributing.
"We already tried that."	Don't bother.	Person stops innovating.
"That's above your pay grade."	Know your place.	Person stops escalating important issues.
"Let's not boil the ocean."	You're asking too much.	Person scales back ideas before sharing them.
"We don't have time for this right now."	Your priorities aren't priorities.	Person stops raising non-urgent issues — including the ones that become urgent.
"That's really a question for someone else."	You're in the wrong room.	Person stops asking questions in the room they're in.
"We've been doing this a long time."	Your perspective is irrelevant.	Person defers rather than contributing.
"You'll just have to trust the process."	Don't ask questions.	Person disengages from understanding the work they're doing.
"That's not what I asked for." (in front of peers)	Public incompetence.	Person defaults to minimum interpretation of every request.

The point is not that these phrases are always toxic or always intentional. Sometimes "we already tried that" is genuinely useful context. Sometimes "that's above your pay grade" is a reasonable boundary. What matters is frequency and pattern.

A person who hears one of these phrases occasionally and sees evidence to the contrary — sees their idea considered, sees a concern genuinely taken seriously — files it away and moves on. A person who hears these phrases consistently, and never sees evidence to the contrary, learns the real policy: *contribution is not what this organization is asking for.*

Once that lesson is learned, the cost of unlearning it is high. Trust, once eroded this way, requires patient, consistent evidence to rebuild. You cannot undo a year of dismissal with one energetic offsite.

The Ripple Effect: How One Communication Failure Becomes Ten

Drop a coin in still water. The coin is small. The ripple isn't.

This is the principle that makes communication failures so much more expensive than they appear at the moment they happen. The failure itself — an unchecked assumption, a missed handoff, a message that landed differently than it was sent — is rarely the full cost.

The full cost is what the failure produces in the hours, days, and weeks that follow, as each downstream consequence creates the conditions for the next one.

Communication failures are not isolated events. **They compound.**

Tracing A Single Failure Through Its Ripple Effects

Example: A scope change is communicated verbally — in passing, to one person, with the assumption that they'll pass it along. It's a small thing. It doesn't merit a formal update.

Except:

- **That person tells two colleagues their interpretation of what they heard**
- **Two interpretations become three versions of the plan,** each slightly different, each held with confidence by the person who heard it
- **Work diverges along those three lines, quietly, for days, each** *person executing on their understanding*
- The divergence surfaces at a team check-in — or worse, at a delivery point — **when the gap between versions is too large to close without rework**
- The **deadline slips**

- Someone asks **who dropped the ball,** and the honest answer is a verbal conversation that was never confirmed, a week ago, by **someone who assumed** it would travel correctly
- **Trust takes a hit.** "How does that keep happening?" becomes the question that doesn't have a satisfying answer.
- **People start creating workarounds:** more individual verification, more back-channel confirmation, more time spent making sure they have the right version rather than doing the work itself
- **The spiral accelerates**

The Ripple Timeline:

Timeline	What's Happening
Day 1	Scope change communicated verbally to one person. Confirmation not requested.
Day 3-4	Two team members have different versions of the plan. Each is executing on theirs.
Day 7	Work begins diverging visibly. Nobody flags it because each person believes they have the right version.
Day 14	Integration point reveals the gap. Rework required. Deadline under pressure.
Day 30	Delivery delayed. Root cause attributed to "miscommunication." No structural change made.
Day 90	Team is operating with more redundant verification, more informal check-ins, lower trust in formal channels. The workarounds are now standard practice.

Note what the ripple timeline doesn't include: a dramatic failure, a visible conflict, or a bad actor. The original failure was a single verbal communication that never got confirmed. Everything else followed from that.

The point isn't that every unchecked assumption will produce a ninety-day crisis. Most won't. The point is that the failure never ends at the moment it happens. It continues downstream — in the rework, in the eroded trust, in the workarounds that multiply, in the future conversations where people are slightly less willing to assume that things landed correctly.

Every unchecked assumption is a coin dropped in still water. You may not see the ripple reach the far edge. But the water moves.

Example: "The Email That Wasn't Read"

A policy change affects how twelve people on a cross-functional team handle a compliance-sensitive process. The policy is real, the change is important, and someone did the right thing — they put it in writing and sent it to the full distribution list.

Three of twelve people read it. Nine continue following the old process.

Nobody knows that nine people are working off outdated guidance. There's no meeting to confirm receipt. No acknowledgment is requested. No follow-up is sent. The email sits in twelve inboxes with twelve different statuses: read, skimmed, missed, buried, and in two cases, filtered into a folder that hasn't been opened since Q1. Then a customer complaint surfaces. An investigation follows.

Except:

- The investigation doesn't find a bad actor — **it finds nine people who were never told the rules changed**
- The nine people **are blamed anyway,** because the email exists. "It was sent." Sent, in this context, is being treated as the same thing as received, understood, and implemented
- The **people who received the complaint blame the people who should have changed their process.** The people who should have changed their process say nobody told them. The people who sent the email say they did tell them.
- *All three groups are, in their own way, correct*
- **Trust takes a hit in every direction:** the team loses faith in email as a reliable channel, leadership loses faith in the team's "follow-through," and the nine people who got blamed for following the old process now carry quiet resentment about a failure that wasn't theirs

- **Communication about that process becomes guarded.** People start CC-ing more people on more emails, not because it improves information flow, but because documentation has become self-protection

- ***The spiral tightens***

The Email That Wasn't Read — Ripple Timeline:

Timeline	What's Happening
Day 1	Policy change emailed to 12 people. Read receipts not requested. No confirmation required.
Day 7	3 of 12 have read it and adjusted. 9 are still following the old process, unaware anything changed.
Day 14	Customer complaint surfaces. Investigation begins.
Day 30	Blame distributed. Relationships strained. Trust in official email communication erodes.

FIELD NOTES: The Information You Were Never Supposed to Have

The setup: A team member — competent, high-performing, brought in specifically because the organization needed what they knew — gradually realized they were operating one step behind everyone else. Not on technical matters. On decisions. On context. On the conversations that shaped the work before it ever appeared on the agenda.

They had come in from a different department. Before that, from outside the organization entirely. Every formal process said they were fully integrated. The organizational chart said they reported to the right people. Their deliverables were visible. Their contributions were acknowledged in the appropriate settings.

But the information flow told a different story.

What the exclusion actually looked like — nothing overt:

- No announced policy. No one said the quiet part out loud.

- Decisions moved through informal channels — a lunch conversation, a quick message between people who'd worked together for years, a standing check-in that nobody was sure was still happening
- Those conversations arrived as directives. The decisions were already made. The discussion was already over.
- And because none of it was written down, because none of it was a meeting, there was nothing formal to point to — and nothing formal to challenge

The inner circle wasn't malicious. It had simply never actually opened up to include someone new. The relationships were old, the habits were set, and the information continued to travel the routes it always had.

What formal performance discussions missed: Every formal checkpoint confirmed that this person was meeting expectations. The deliverables were on time. The relationships were professional. The contributions were noted.

What the formal process could not capture: they were executing on decisions without the context that shaped them. Doing the job well — without access to the information that would have let them do it better.

What the research misses: The cognitive biases covered in this chapter — the curse of knowledge, confirmation bias, fundamental attribution error — all assume the primary communication barriers are internal. And they often are. But internal barriers sit inside a context.

When that context is a team where the informal information network was built before you arrived and never extended to include you, the most sophisticated communication skill in the world will not put you in the conversation where the real decisions happen.

What I carry from it: When I am in a position to influence who is in the room — or more precisely, who is in the message thread, who gets the early draft, who gets asked before the meeting rather than told after it — I think carefully about who isn't and why.

The most important question at the start of any decision-making process is not *who is available* — it is *who has standing we haven't recognized?* **That answer shapes everything that follows.**

FIELD NOTE TAKEAWAY: Exclusion from decision-making often operates through information flow, not formal policy. The question isn't who was formally barred from the room — it's who learned about the outcome after it was already made, who got the context after the plan was already set, who was never quite on the thread where the real conversation happened. If someone competent and capable keeps showing up one step behind, audit the information flow before assuming the problem is theirs.

When You're Communicating and the System Doesn't Respond

There's one more scenario that deserves direct attention: what happens when someone is doing everything right — communicating clearly, following up, escalating appropriately, documenting everything — and the system still doesn't respond?

Examples of systemic non-response:

Situation	What It Signals To The Employee
PTO request submitted 30+ days ahead, no acknowledgment	Your planning doesn't merit consideration
Performance review says "fine" but provides no clarity on what progress looks like	The conversation happening about you ≠ the conversation happening with you
Question emailed, Teams-messaged, then walked over — answered with a non-answer	Communicating through proper channels produces nothing

The conventional advice — communicate better, communicate more clearly, use different channels — doesn't address this. The problem isn't the communication. The problem is the receiving end.

When this lesson takes hold, the organization has created exactly the conditions it claims to want to prevent. It has taught a competent person that their voice doesn't count. What follows isn't insubordination. It's adaptation.

The loss is on both sides. The organization loses an engaged voice. The person loses investment in a system that doesn't invest in them.

KEY TAKEAWAYS: Chapter 3

- **Communication failure is not a function of intelligence — it's a function of psychology, bias, and culture.**
- **The illusion of transparency leads both leaders and team members to overestimate how clearly they're communicating and how well they're being understood.**
- Three cognitive biases that reliably undermine communication: **the curse of knowledge** (expertise creates blindness), **confirmation bias** (we hear what we expect to hear), and **fundamental attribution error** (we blame people for systemic failures).
- **Psychological safety is not comfort — it's the belief that speaking up is safe.** Its presence predicts better decisions, faster error correction, and more honest communication.
- When the culture consistently rewards silence over speech, the people with the most important things to say are the first to stop saying them.

REFLECTION QUESTIONS: Chapter 3

1. **Think of the last time you didn't say something you needed to say in a professional setting.** What was the risk you were calculating — and was that calculation based on reality, or on an assumption about how speaking up would be received?
2. **Where in your organization might the fundamental attribution error be at work — situations where you're diagnosing a "people problem" that might actually be a systems problem?**
3. **How would you honestly rate the psychological safety of your current team?** What's one behavior — yours or a leader's — that either builds or erodes it?

Chapter 4: The Organizational Element — When the System is the Problem

There's a version of the communication breakdown conversation that stops at individual behavior: **fix how people talk to each other, train them, coach them, hold them accountable.** Individual behavior matters, and much of this book addresses it directly.

But there's a harder, more important conversation that doesn't happen often enough:

What happens when the *system itself* is producing the breakdown?

When structure, reporting lines, role definitions, tools, and processes actively work against clear communication — not because anyone designed them to, but because nobody designed them with communication in mind at all.

This chapter is about that conversation.

Reporting Structures That Create Confusion

Most organizational charts are drawn with authority in mind, not information flow. They show who reports to whom. They rarely show who needs to know what, when, from whom, and through what channel.

The core problem:

What Org Charts Manage	What Org Charts Don't Address
Who can approve what	Who needs to be in the loop
Who has budget discretion	Who needs to be consulted
Who can hire and fire	Who needs to be informed and when

The most common version of this problem: a role with functional responsibilities across multiple teams, reporting to only one of them. The reporting line clarifies authority but obscures information access. The role has accountability for outcomes that depend on information from multiple directions, but only has a formal channel to one direction. Everything else is relationship-dependent — which means it works when relationships are strong and collapses when they're not.

What Happens When Structures Change

Reorganizations are common. **What's rare is the reorganization with an explicit transition plan for how information will flow in the new structure.**

- The person in the restructured role now receives direction from a new chain of command with different priorities, different vocabulary, different expectations
- Their old team still needs things from them that the new structure doesn't account for
- Nobody runs a transition meeting or creates a communication plan
- The assumption is that the org chart update is sufficient — it is not

The org chart update tells people who to report to. It says nothing about who to loop in, who to consult, where the boundaries sit, or how to handle situations that don't map cleanly onto the new structure. The person in the middle figures it out alone — managing competing demands without the authority or context to do it well.

In the Room: The Reorganization Nobody Explained

Two weeks after a restructuring. Two people who used to work together, now unclear whether they still do.

Terrell: *"Hey — I sent that over to you Tuesday for review. Did you get a chance to—"*

Sandra: *"Oh. I wasn't sure if that was still mine to review. I thought after the reorg, that function moved to Marcus's team."*

Terrell: *"I thought it moved to you."*

Sandra: *"Nobody told me either way."*

Terrell: *"So… who's been reviewing it?"*

Sandra: *"I assumed you were handling it until I heard otherwise."*

Terrell: *"I assumed you were."*

Three seconds of silence. The deliverable has been sitting unreviewed for nine days **because two competent people each assumed the other was accountable.** The org chart changed. No one ran the communication transition. By the time anyone notices, the client deadline is four days away and the review still hasn't started.

Role Ambiguity and Scope Creep

"Who owns this?"

If this question has ever genuinely arisen in your team — as in, nobody actually knew — you've experienced role ambiguity. If you've ever heard it answered with "well, I guess we do" w**hile everyone in the room knows that "we" means "you" — you've experienced scope creep.**

How role ambiguity develops:

- Job defined clearly at hire; the work evolves while the shared understanding doesn't
- New priorities emerge, teams grow or shrink, structures shift
- Job description from 18 months ago bears little resemblance to actual work being done today

How scope creep operates:

Pattern	What It Looks Like	The Real Problem
Work expands to fill available capacity	"Can you just handle this?"	The accommodating person absorbs work that has no formal home
Quality functions absorb neighboring tasks	Safety reports, incident logs, vendor communications "land" on quality	Organizations exploit the instinct to not let things fall through the cracks
Informal assignment calcifies	One time becomes "always"	Nobody ever has to address the structural gap

The real cost of scope creep:

- **Every absorbed responsibility creates a gap in your formal work that nobody sees,** because informal work is invisible in metrics
- You **operate at the edge of your lane** — managing processes you didn't design, communicating with stakeholders you weren't introduced to
- The **organization is never required to confront the fact that the work has no legitimate home**

The ambiguity of accountability is a specific version I have encountered repeatedly in quality and continuous improvement roles: when a defect occurs, who is responsible? In well-designed systems, the answer is unambiguous. In most real organizations, the answer is: it depends on who you ask — and the "Responsible" field on the tracking document is blank.

One useful test is simple: think about the last three tasks that "landed" on your team without ever being formally assigned. Who did they actually belong to? And if there is a "Responsible" field in your tracking systems that routinely goes blank, what conversation has been avoided to keep it that way?

Blank "Responsible" fields are not an administrative oversight. They are a symptom. The organization has not done the work of deciding who owns the outcomes that matter.

FIELD NOTES: The Work That Just Appears

The experience: Anyone who has worked in a quality or compliance function will recognize this. You're focused on what your role actually requires — and a task arrives. Not assigned. Not requested. Not discussed. Just *arrived* — in your inbox, on your desk, in a meeting invite — with the implicit understanding that it is now yours.

What this looked like in practice:

- A safety report that Operations didn't want to write
- An incident log that nobody in Procurement had time to maintain

- A vendor communication that fell between Supply Chain and Quality — and therefore landed on Quality, because quality people are detail-oriented and surely they'll handle it

The task has no formal home. But it is now yours, because taking it is easier than the conversation about whether you should.

The concrete cost:

- Every hour spent on a report that belonged to a different department = an hour not spent on my actual mandate
- Informal work is invisible in metrics — nobody sees the gap it creates in your formal responsibilities
- Because I was handling it, the organization was never required to confront the fact that the work had no legitimate home
- The structural problem never got addressed, and the informal assignment calcified into expectation

The conversation that needed to happen: *Who actually owns this?*

- If the answer is "nobody," the organization has a structural gap that needs to be filled through proper channels — not absorbed quietly by whoever is closest and most willing

What happened when I did push back (documented, framed as a capacity and accountability concern, not a complaint):

Outcome	What It Told Me
Work got dropped entirely	It wasn't as essential as the default assignment implied
Work got properly assigned	It had a legitimate home — it just hadn't been sent there
Real conversation about formally expanding my role	This work should be mine, but with appropriate resources

All three outcomes were better than silent accumulation.

What made them possible: Refusing to let the ambiguity stay comfortable. When scope creep goes unnamed, it stays. When it gets named — calmly, professionally, with evidence — the organization has to respond to something it had successfully ignored.

FIELD NOTE TAKEAWAY: Scope creep only stops when someone names it. Quietly absorbing work that doesn't belong to you doesn't protect your relationship — it protects the organization from having to resolve a structural gap. Frame the conversation around accountability and capacity, not complaint. That framing is what makes it actionable.

The Handoff Problem

Transitions are the most dangerous moment in any process or project. They require active, intentional knowledge transfer — and they almost never get it.

What needs to travel in a handoff:

- Relevant knowledge and context
- Relationship history
- Authority and decision-making scope
- The history of failed approaches (so the new person doesn't repeat them)

What actually transfers:

- The title change
- The org chart update
- Maybe a 30-minute coffee with the outgoing person

The result: Person B inherits a situation they don't fully understand. The gaps surface as problems over the following weeks and months.

Teams spend months rediscovering things their predecessors already figured out — not because predecessors were withholding, but because nobody thought to encode the knowledge before the person left the building.

Where handoff failures happen most:

- Personnel transitions (someone leaves, retires, transfers)
- Project phase changes (Phase 1 completes; work moves to a different team)

- Process ownership changes (new person assigned to manage a process they've never worked in)
- Organizational restructuring (a function is moved; institutional knowledge doesn't travel with it)

In every case, the same failure: the assumption that the org chart transfer is sufficient to transfer the actual work. Authority transfers. Understanding does not — unless you deliberately design it to.

Breaking the Spiral™: Stage 1 → Test the Assumption

What the conversation looks like when someone stops to check.

Sandra: *"Before we get into this — I want to make sure I understand who owns what after the reorg. In the new structure, does the deliverable review sit with me or with Marcus's team?"*

Terrell: *"Honestly? I'm not sure. I was going to ask you."*

Sandra: *"Then let's figure it out now instead of after something falls through. Give me ten minutes — I'll send a message to both our managers and copy you. We'll get a clear answer before end of day."*

Terrell: *"That works. And if we can't get an answer, can you keep it for now just so it doesn't sit?"*

Sandra: *"Yeah. But I want the written confirmation so we're not making this call again in three weeks."*

Accountability starts before someone drops the ball. That question — *who actually owns this?* — is worth asking the moment you're not sure. The answer is always faster to get than the rework costs later.

When Tools and Processes Replace Actual Conversation

There is a particular organizational fantasy that technology enables: the idea that if we build the right system, use the right software, implement the right process — communication will take care of itself.

This fantasy is responsible for an enormous amount of organizational dysfunction.

The reality:

The Assumption	What Actually Happens
"The tool will create a single source of truth"	The tool captures what's easy to capture, not what matters
"Everyone will know what they need to know"	People who need to act on information aren't reading it
"If the tracker is maintained, we're aligned"	The tracker is maintained; the teams using it are siloed
"The process documentation = process adherence"	Documentation is excellent; actual adherence is nominal

I've worked in environments with excellent tools and terrible communication — where the project tracker was meticulously maintained and the team using it was completely siloed from the team whose work it tracked.

I've also worked in environments with almost no formal tooling where the communication culture was so strong that information traveled efficiently and reliably through conversation, brief emails, and structured stand-ups.

The tools are not the problem. Substituting tool deployment for communication design is the problem. Tools do not create alignment; they reveal whether alignment already exists.

The question is not what tool you are using. The question is:

- **Do the people who need information have access to it? Do they understand it?**
- **Do they act on it? When something goes wrong in the information flow, can you identify where and why?**

No tool answers those questions on its own.

Cross-Functional Teams Without Cross-Functional Communication Plans

The rise of the cross-functional team is one of the most significant organizational developments of the past few decades. The logic is sound: complex problems require people with different kinds of expertise. The reality is frequently messier.

What bringing different experts into the same room actually produces:

What Organizations Hope For	What They Often Get
Integrated problem-solving	Proximity without communication
Shared ownership	Unclear accountability across departments
Aligned execution	Different vocabularies, metrics, timelines, loyalties

A cross-functional team without a cross-functional communication plan is a collection of people from different departments who are now in meetings together.

What has to be designed explicitly:

- How decisions get made
- Who communicates what to which stakeholders
- How conflicts between departmental priorities get resolved
- Who is ultimately accountable for the team's outcomes

None of that gets answered by the org chart or the team roster.

A real example: I've seen cross-functional teams where quality data generated by one function was used by another, with no formal agreement on how data would be collected, what it would measure, who would review it, or what would happen when the numbers told a story that one team's leadership didn't want to hear.

The result: data attribution conflicts, parallel and contradictory tracking, a shared reporting process nobody trusted because nobody had agreed on its terms.

The fix required something disproportionately simple: a joint session where each function walked through the process step by step and agreed — in writing, with all parties present — on which function owned each step.

Three hours. A shared glossary of exactly four terms.
The data stabilized the following month.

The Cost of Organizational Communication Failure

Missed Deadlines:

- The project on schedule until the handoff revealed a six-week gap
- The deliverable that arrived wrong because requirements changed and only one team knew
- The approval that stalled because nobody was sure whose sign-off was required

Duplicated Work:

- Two teams building the same tracking tool, unaware the other existed
- Two sets of training materials developed in parallel for the same process
- Two departments purchasing the same vendor service — no centralized visibility into what had already been contracted

Turnover:

The most consistent finding in honest exit interview data: people don't leave companies because of money. They leave because of management, culture, not feeling heard, included, or valued. All of these are communication failures. Turnover is expensive: recruiting, training, knowledge loss, team disruption.

Erosion of trust:

Perhaps most importantly, organizational communication failure erodes trust — in leadership, in systems, in the organization itself. And trust, once lost, is extraordinarily expensive to rebuild.

Organizational communication failure is rarely a matter of poor wording or missed intention. More often, it is built into the way work is structured, handed off, tracked, divided, and led. Until those conditions are examined, teams will keep blaming people for failures the system made likely.

KEY TAKEAWAYS: Chapter 4

- **Organizational reporting structures are designed around authority, not information flow** — this creates information barriers.
- **Role ambiguity and scope creep are communication design failures:** when nobody defines who owns what, workflows to whoever will take it, and the structural gap never gets addressed.
- **The handoff problem is universal: what transfers in a transition is authority;** what doesn't transfer, unless created to, is understanding.
- **Tools and processes are channels through which communication may occur.** Substituting **tool deployment for communication design solves nothing.**
- **Cross-functional teams require more communication infrastructure,** not less — the informal channels that work within teams don't work across them.

REFLECTION QUESTIONS: Chapter 4

1. **In your current role or organization, where are the seams in the information flow — the places where information routinely fails to travel because of structural gaps rather than individual failures?** Who is living in those seams right now?
2. **Think about the last major transition — personnel, project, or structural — in your team or organization. What knowledge was lost in that transition, and what would a real handoff plan have looked like?**
3. **What tools or processes in your organization were implemented to solve a communication problem? Are they solving it?** If not, what's the conversation that the tool was meant to replace — and is that conversation happening?

—End of Part I—

PART II

THE FRAMEWORK

Breaking the Spiral™

How People Actually Communicate – Styles, Clashes, and Bridges

This is where communication begins to work:
In the styles *people* ***default to under pressure,*** *the* ***rules teams live by,*** *and the* ***language that turns intention*** *into* ***shared understanding.***

Chapter 5: Breaking the Spiral™

You have seen the Silent Spiral™. You have seen the seven failures, the psychology that makes silence feel safer than speaking, and the structures that turn individual habits into systemic ones. Naming the problem is where the work starts. It is not where it ends. What follows is the work itself.

The five stages below are not a cure. They are a practice. Teams that do this work do not stop having miscommunications — they stop letting miscommunications compound into something nobody can fix. That is the difference.

Most leaders look for the breakdown. They watch for the missed deadline, the project that derails, the team member who quits without warning. By then, the spiral has already turned five or six times. The signals were there for months. The work in this chapter is not about catching the breakdown. It is about catching the turn.

A turn is small. An assumption left unspoken in a meeting. A question someone almost asked and didn't. A workaround that becomes the new default because nobody pushed back the first time. These are the moments where the spiral picks up speed — and the moments where it can still be stopped without anyone losing face.

You will not catch every turn. Nobody does. But the difference between a team that recovers and a team that erodes is not whether the spiral starts. It is how many turns happen before someone names what is happening and asks the room to stop. That is what the five stages teach you to do.

Each stage has a signal you can hear, a question you can ask, and a move you can make. None of them require permission. None of them require a meeting. Most of them take less than a minute. What they require is that you stop waiting for someone else to go first.

The Silent Spiral™ in Language: Before and After

The dialogues in the next pages capture the exact phrases that signal each stage of the Silent Spiral™ is taking hold — and the phrases that interrupt it.

These are not hypothetical. They are pulled from real teams, real meetings, and real moments where a single sentence either kept the conversation alive or shut it down. Recognizing the language is the first step to intervening. You cannot catch what you cannot name.

Stage 1: Assumption → Test the Assumption

The Silent Spiral™ in Action	Breaking the Spiral™ in Action
"I emailed them — they know."	"I sent the email, but I want to confirm — can you tell me what you understood the next step to be?"
"We covered that in the meeting. Everyone was there."	"We covered it in the meeting, but I noticed a couple of people were quiet. I'm going to follow up individually."
"It's in the shared drive. They have access."	"It's in the shared drive, but I'm going to walk through the key changes in person. Access isn't the same as understanding."
"They'll figure it out — they're smart people."	"Before we move forward, I want to hear each person say back what they think they own."
"I assumed we were aligned. We had the same conversation."	"I think we're aligned, but let me check — what's your read on what we agreed to?"

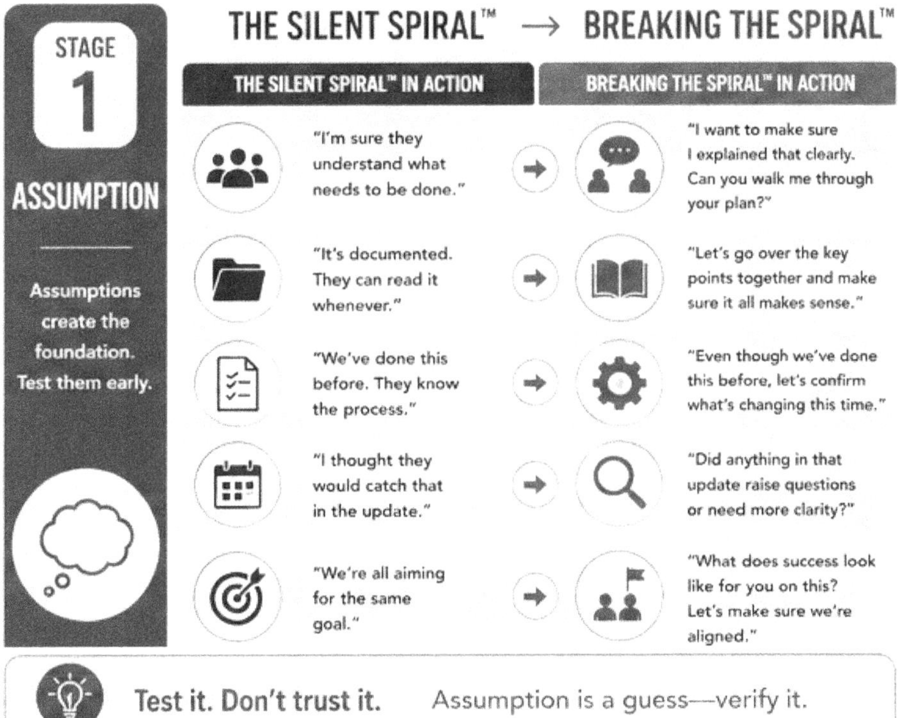

Stage 2: Silence → Break the Silence

The Silent Spiral™ in Action	Breaking the Spiral™ in Action
"No questions? Great, we're all set."	"No questions usually means people are still processing. I'm going to check in with each of you individually this afternoon."
"Nobody pushed back, so I think we're good."	"Nobody pushed back, and that actually concerns me. What are we not saying?"
"I didn't want to be the one to say something."	"I have a concern I've been sitting on, and I think it's better to raise it now than let it grow."
"I figured if it was a real problem, someone would speak up."	"I'm going to ask directly — does anyone see a problem with this that they haven't said out loud yet?"
"It's not my place to raise that."	"If this were going to fail, what would be the reason? I'd rather hear it now."

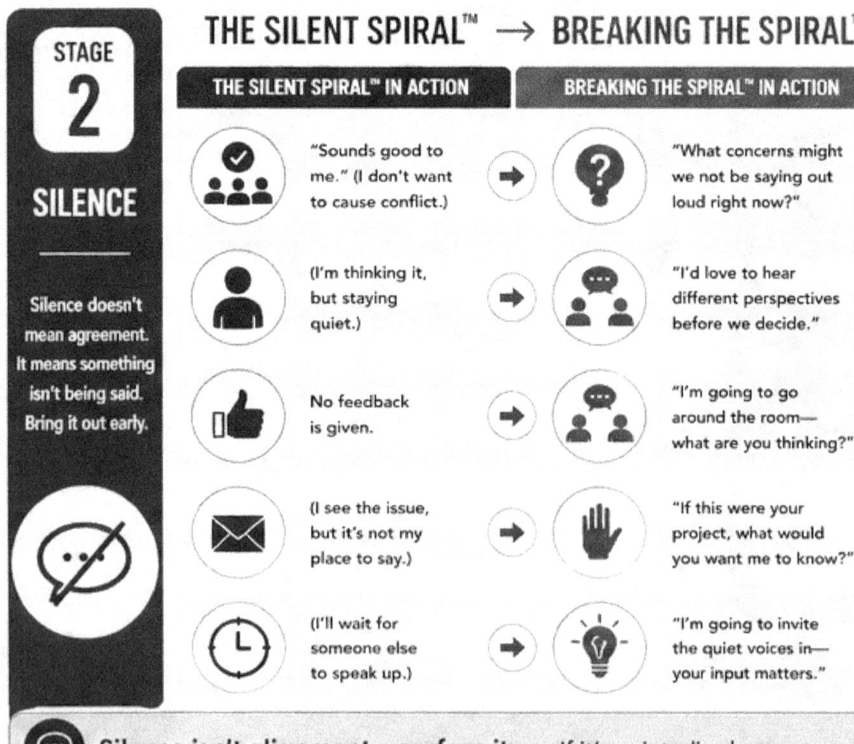

Stage 3: Frustration → Make It Safe

The Silent Spiral™ in Action	Breaking the Spiral™ in Action
"Why doesn't anyone tell me anything?"	"I can see you're frustrated. Tell me what's happening from your side — I want to understand."
"I've brought this up three times and nothing changes."	"You've raised this before and I hear you. This time, let's document it together and put a name and a deadline on the fix."
"They don't listen. They never listen."	"I know it feels like nothing changes. What would make you feel like your input actually landed this time?"
"I'm done trying to fix this. It's not my problem."	"What would need to be true for you to feel safe raising this in the team meeting instead of just to me?"
"Every time I raise a concern, I get told it's being handled. It's never being handled."	"I'm going to be honest — I think we've made it hard for people to bring problems forward. What would make it easier?"

Stage 4: Workaround → Close the Loop

The Silent Spiral™ in Action	Breaking the Spiral™ in Action
"I just handle it myself now. It's faster."	"I noticed you've been handling this yourself. That tells me the process is broken — can we talk about what's not working?"
"I built my own spreadsheet because the official system doesn't work."	"If you needed to build your own system, that's a signal I need to hear. Walk me through what the official process is missing."
"I stopped going through the process. I go straight to the person who can actually help."	"I'd rather fix the process than have you work around it. What would make the real system actually usable?"
"Everyone knows the real way to get things done around here."	"Who owns this process? Because if everyone's routing around it, we need to either fix it or replace it — not just accept the workaround."
"The official process is a joke. Nobody follows it."	"Let's close this loop. What was the original intent of this process, what's actually happening, and what do we need to change?"

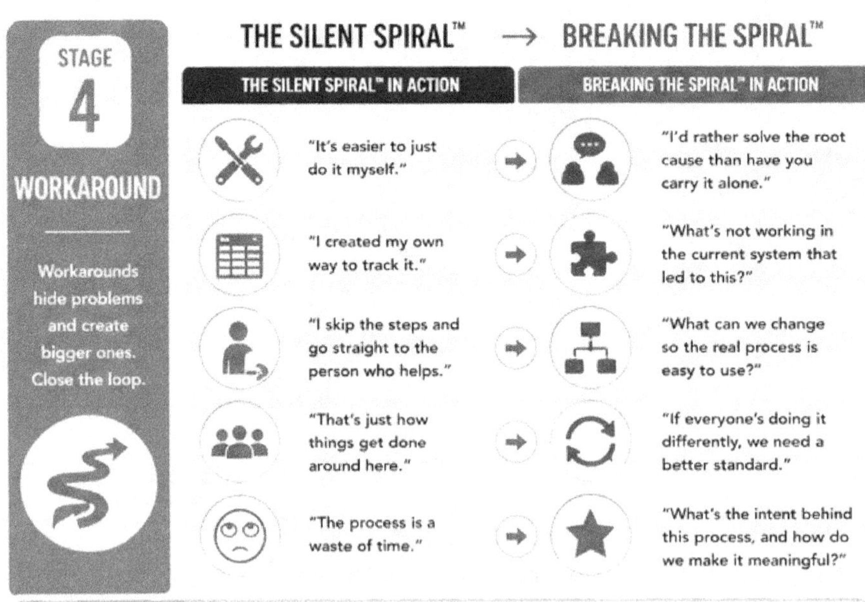

Stage 5: Failure → Name It

The Silent Spiral™ in Action	Breaking the Spiral™ in Action
"How did this happen? Who dropped the ball?"	"This failed. Before we assign blame, let's map exactly where the information stopped flowing — and why."
"Nobody told me. I had no idea this was coming."	"The question isn't who dropped the ball. The question is where in our system did the handoff break down."
"We need to figure out who's responsible for this."	"We have a communication failure. I'm naming it so we can fix it — not so we can punish someone."
"This is what happens when people don't communicate."	"This is a system problem, not a people problem. Let's trace it back to the first assumption that went unchecked."
"I don't even know where to start fixing this."	"Here's what I know, here's what I don't know, and here's what I need from each of you to start the recovery."

Recognizing the language is the work of pages. Practicing the antidotes is the work of years. **The five stages that follow give you the practice.**

Stage 1: Test the Assumption

The Antidote to: Assuming Transmission Equals Reception

The first stage of the Silent Spiral™ is deceptively simple: someone sends a message and assumes it landed. A supervisor explains a new process once, in a noisy environment, to a group of people who are half-watching because their shift is about to end. The supervisor walks away thinking *they got it*. The team walks away having heard something — just not necessarily what was said. Nobody checks. Nobody confirms. Everyone proceeds on their own version of what was communicated.

The result is not a dramatic failure. It is a slow drift. Decisions get made on different assumptions. Work gets done the wrong way — not because people don't care, but because no one verified the map matched the territory.

Testing the Assumption is the practice of actively confirming understanding instead of trusting that transmission equals reception. It treats comprehension as something you verify, not something you presume.

What This Looks Like When a Team Gets It Right

1. **A team lead doesn't just explain a change to the pick-path procedure — she asks one person to walk her through the new sequence before the shift starts.**

2. **A project manager sends out meeting notes and follows up:** "Before we move forward, can you flag anything here that doesn't match your understanding of what we decided?"

3. A dispatcher who hands off mid-shift doesn't say "you're all caught up" — **he asks the incoming driver, "What's your read on the afternoon? What are you walking into?"**

4. Training doesn't end with a signature on a checklist. **It ends when someone can demonstrate the task without prompting.**

5. When a new policy comes down from corporate, the floor supervisor reads it, **then asks two frontline workers to explain it back in their own words** — and uses the gaps in their answers to figure out where the original communication was unclear.

None of this is about doubting people. It is about *respecting how easily communication degrades*. A message passed from person to person is like a photocopy of a photocopy: still recognizable, but less precise each time it moves. Context fades. Urgency softens. Ownership blurs. Meaning shifts. That is why we check. Not because we assume people failed, but because the cost of confirming understanding is almost always lower than the cost of repairing the damage later.

A Story: The Inventory Count That Almost Wasn't

Marcus had been a warehouse receiving lead for eleven years. He prided himself on running a tight ship — clear instructions, no drama. When the company switched to a new cycle count methodology, he got the briefing, understood it, and passed it along to his team in a fifteen-minute meeting before a Monday shift.

The cycle count happened. The numbers were off. Not catastrophically, but enough to require a recount — which meant overtime, which meant complaints, which meant Marcus sitting in his manager's office explaining what went wrong.

When they dug into it, the issue wasn't attitude. It wasn't effort. Two of his best counters had genuinely understood the new method differently than Marcus intended — one had been counting bundles as individual units because the briefing was ambiguous, and another had been applying the old exception process because nobody had explicitly told her it changed.

Marcus had explained it. He'd never checked what they'd heard.

The second time a methodology change came through, Marcus did something different. After the briefing, he pulled Darnell and Priya aside — the two who'd had the gaps last time — and said, "Walk me through how you'd start the count tomorrow morning. From the first bay." They walked him through it. He caught two misunderstandings before the count started.

The recount didn't happen. The overtime didn't happen. And Marcus stopped believing that explaining something was the same as communicating it.

The Language of This Stage

People who are practicing Stage 1 — Testing the Assumption — say things like:

1. *"Before I let you go — can you walk me through how you'd handle this?"*
2. *"I want to make sure I explained that clearly. What's your understanding of the next step?"*
3. *"Help me close the loop — what are you taking away from this conversation?"*
4. *"I may have been unclear. Let's check before you get started."*
5. *"Can you give me a quick summary so I know we're on the same page?"*
6. *"What questions do you have? And if you don't have any right now, come find me when you do."*
7. *"I'm going to check back in after the first hour. Not because I don't trust you — because this is new and I want to catch anything early."*

Notice what's absent: *"Does everyone understand?"* — the question that produces the most nodding and the least actual comprehension. That question puts the burden on the person who least wants to admit they're lost. The phrases above shift the burden to the communicator, where it belongs.

What It Unlocks

When teams normalize assumption-testing, the downstream effects compound quickly.

Training becomes more efficient because gaps get caught at the point of instruction, not after a costly mistake. Rework drops, because people are working from a shared understanding of what "correct" actually looks like. New hires ramp faster because their questions get surfaced earlier instead of suppressed by social pressure.

More importantly, it changes the culture around "not knowing." When checking for comprehension is what you do — when it's built into handoffs, meetings, and training moments — it stops being a signal that someone is confused or behind. It becomes the standard. And when it's the standard, people stop faking understanding. That change alone prevents more problems than most organizations realize.

QUICK WIN Replace "Does everyone understand?" with "Tell me what you're going to do first." You don't need a new program, a new policy, or a new hire. One different question at the end of every set of instructions. Do it consistently for two weeks and watch what surfaces.

Stage 1 is where the Silent Spiral™ begins, and where it is easiest to break. An assumption costs nothing to surface and almost everything to leave alone. The teams that catch it here rarely need the rest of this chapter.

Most teams do not catch it here.

Stage 2: Break the Silence

The Antidote to: Staying Quiet Because It's Safer

The second stage of the Silent Spiral™ is the one most leaders underestimate. People know something is wrong — a process is broken, a safety step is being skipped, a number doesn't add up — and they say nothing. Not because they don't care. Because they've done the math, consciously or not, and speaking up doesn't pencil out.

Maybe someone got shut down last time. Maybe they watched a coworker get labeled "difficult" for raising an issue. Maybe they're three weeks into a new job and they're not sure they've earned the right to have an opinion. Whatever the specific trigger, the logic is the same: the risk of speaking up outweighs the benefit. So silence becomes the rational choice.

This is not a character flaw. It is a response to environment. **Breaking the Silence** means changing the environment — making it more dangerous to stay quiet than to speak up. That requires active work from leadership, not passive hope.

What This Looks Like When a Team Gets It Right

1. **A shift supervisor opens every pre-shift with the same two questions: "What's working that we should keep?" and "What's getting in your way that I should know about?" He** writes the answers on a whiteboard. He follows up the next day on anything that was raised.

2. A director who receives a concern from someone two levels below her doesn't escalate it back down through channels — **she responds directly, thanks the person by name, and reports back on what happened.**

3. When a cross-functional team meeting surfaces a problem, the facilitator **doesn't skip past it to stay on schedule. She says, "This sounds important. Let's give it five minutes now and schedule time to go deeper."**

4. **New employees are explicitly told in their first week: "If you see something that doesn't make sense, we want to know. You don't need tenure to have a valid observation."**

5. **Anonymous feedback channels exist — and are visibly acted on. *Not just acknowledged. Acted on.***

The key word in all of these is *active*. Silence doesn't break on its own. It breaks when leadership consistently signals, through behavior not just speech, that the information is wanted and will be handled with care.

A Story: The Intake Log Nobody Wanted to Fix

At a regional distribution hub, there was a known problem with the incoming shipment log. Items that arrived damaged were being logged in a way that made them look like shortages — which meant the damage was invisible to the vendor claims process, and credits that should have been recovered were being left on the table. Everyone on the receiving dock knew it.

Nobody said anything for nearly eight months.

When the new operations manager, Delphine, came in, she spent her first two weeks walking the floor, specifically asking: "If you could fix one thing about how information flows through this building, what would it be?"

She asked it one-on-one, not in group settings. She wrote the answers in a notebook. She didn't defend anything or explain why things were the way they were.

On her third week, she scheduled a thirty-minute working session with four dock workers. She brought the notebook. She said, "I want to talk about the intake log. I've heard there's a problem. I need you to show me."

Two people in that room had been wanting to surface that issue for over a year. Within forty-five minutes, they'd mapped the gap. Within three weeks, the log format had been corrected. Within a quarter, vendor credit recovery had improved enough to be flagged at the regional level.

The fix took three weeks. The silence had cost eight months of lost credits. Delphine didn't break the silence by being exceptional. She broke it by being consistent and by making it safe to be the first one to say something.

The Language of This Stage

People who are practicing Stage 2 — Breaking the Silence — say things like:

1. *"I've been noticing something and I wanted to bring it up before it becomes a bigger problem."*
2. *"I don't know if this is my place to say, but I think it matters, so I'm saying it."*
3. *"I'm asking because I genuinely want to know — what's getting in your way?"*
4. *"If something's not working, I'd rather hear it from you than find out from a metric three months from now."*
5. *"You don't have to have a solution to bring me a problem. Just bring it."*
6. *"What would you change about this if you could?"*

What It Unlocks

When silence breaks, two things happen that money can't buy directly.

First, problems surface earlier. The operational cost of a problem almost always compounds over time. Something caught in week one is a conversation. The same thing caught in month six is a project. Breaking silence compresses that timeline.

Second, people invest differently when they believe they're heard. Discretionary effort — the work people do beyond the minimum — is heavily correlated with whether someone feels like their input matters. It doesn't take a survey to know this. Ask any long-tenured employee about a time they stopped going above and beyond, and most of them can name the moment they decided their observations weren't welcome.

That moment doesn't have to happen. And when it doesn't, you keep something you can't hire: people who still care.

WHAT TO SAY When someone brings you a problem, before you respond with context, explanation, or a fix, say this: *"I'm glad you told me."* Three words. It sounds small. It isn't. It signals that the decision to speak up was correct, and it makes the next conversation easier to start.

By Stage 2, the assumption has hardened into a pattern. The silence is no longer accidental — it is learned. People have decided, individually and without saying so, that speaking up is not worth what it costs.

This is the stage where intervention shifts from naming an assumption to naming a pattern. That is harder. It is also the last point where the work is still cheap.

Stage 3: Make It Safe

The Antidote to: Letting Frustration Become Blame

By the time the Silent Spiral™ reaches stage three, the dynamic has shifted. People aren't staying quiet anymore — they're expressing what they feel, but sideways. Frustration that should go into a conversation gets vented in the break room. Blame circulates through informal channels while official channels stay clean. Meetings end with agreement and hallways fill with the real verdict.

This is not cynicism or immaturity. It is what happens when feedback is systematically punished — even subtly, even unconsciously. If the last few times someone raised a concern it came back to haunt them, if candor in meetings is met with defensiveness, if the person who names a problem gets treated as the problem — then the feedback doesn't stop existing. It stops going where it could do some good. It goes sideways instead.

Making It Safe is the stage where psychological safety gets built — not as a feel-good concept, but as a functional one. The question is not "do people feel comfortable?" The question is "does frustration in this environment get expressed as feedback, or as blame?" One is actionable. One compounds.

What This Looks Like When a Team Gets It Right

1. A manager who receives criticism in a team retrospective **doesn't go quiet, get defensive, or pivot** to "what we did right." **She writes it on the board under her own name and says, "That's fair. Here's what I'm going to do differently."**
2. When a cross-functional project goes sideways, the debrief **focuses on process, not people.** "Where did the handoff break?" rather than "who dropped the ball?"
3. A team lead notices two workers have been sniping at each other for a week. **Instead of waiting for an HR incident, she pulls them in separately and asks each one what they need the other person to know.**
4. **Feedback flows in all directions** — and when a frontline worker tells a supervisor something isn't working, the supervisor **doesn't treat it as insubordination. She treats it as data.**
5. After a hard quarter, the VP of Operations doesn't send a performance email. **He gets on a call and says, "I know that was rough. I want to hear what you saw on the ground that I couldn't see from here."**

Psychological safety is not the absence of hard conversations. It's the presence of enough trust that hard conversations are possible.

A Story: When the Shift Lead Stopped Being Defensive

The cross-functional planning team at a mid-sized logistics company had a morale problem that nobody was naming. The weekly cadence calls had become performance theater — everyone reported green, nothing was ever actually green, and the real conversations happened in side channels after the call ended.

At the center of it was a specific dynamic: whenever the ops team flagged a problem that touched the planning function, the planning lead, Connor, had a habit of immediately explaining why it wasn't his team's fault. Not aggressively — but consistently. The explanation always came before the acknowledgment. After a while, the ops team stopped flagging things on the call and started routing their concerns through the VP's office, which made everything slower and more political.

A peer coach who worked with Connor didn't frame it as a behavior problem. She asked him: "When something goes wrong that involves your team, what's your first instinct?" He said, "Honestly? To make sure people know it wasn't us." She said, "How's that working?" Long pause. "It's not."

The next week, when the ops team flagged a sequencing error that had knocked out two days of planning work, Connor did something different. He said, "That's a mess. I can see why that's frustrating. Let me understand what you need from us to recover." Not an admission of fault — an opening. The call ran fifteen minutes long that day because people had things to say that they'd been sitting on for months.

Three months later, the side-channel conversations had mostly migrated back into the room. Not because trust was perfect — because it was good enough to make directness the easier option.

The Language of This Stage

People who are practicing Stage 3 — Making It Safe — say things like:

1. *"That's fair feedback. I'm writing it down."*
2. *"I can see why that was frustrating. What would have made it better?"*
3. *"I don't need you to be polished about this. I need to know what's happening."*

4. *"I'm not interested in assigning blame. I'm interested in understanding where it broke down."*
5. *"You can bring me the ugly version. I'd rather hear the ugly version than not hear it at all."*
6. *"If I ever respond in a way that makes you feel like you shouldn't have said something, tell me. I mean that."*
7. *"Let's separate what happened from who caused it, at least for the first part of this conversation."*

What It Unlocks

When psychological safety is real — not just stated in a values document, but demonstrated in how leadership responds to bad news — the quality of information available to decision-makers changes fundamentally.

Accurate data surfaces. **Problems get named at the source instead of laundered through layers of escalation.** Retrospectives produce insight instead of performance. And people who have been absorbing friction quietly — the informal glue of the organization, the ones who compensate for broken processes without complaining — finally have a place to put what they've been carrying.

This is not soft. **Decisions made on accurate information are better decisions. When people feel safe enough to tell the truth, organizations stop flying blind.**

QUICK WIN In your next team debrief, or project retrospective, before the group does anything else, say: *"I'll go first."* Share one thing you personally would do differently. Make it real — not performative humility, something you'd actually change. It sets a tone that can't be set any other way, and it gives everyone else permission to be honest too.

By Stage 3, the team has stopped noticing what it has stopped saying. Silence becomes the default. Workarounds become the system. The original problem is no longer the problem — the avoidance is. You cannot reach Stage 3 by accident. You reach it by repetition. Which means the move out of it is also repetition — the deliberate, uncomfortable kind.

Stage 4: Close the Loop

The Antidote to: Working Around Broken Processes Instead of Fixing Them

By stage four of the Silent Spiral™, the damage is structural. People have stopped expecting that problems will get resolved. When something breaks, they don't submit a ticket or escalate through proper channels — they develop a workaround, share it informally, and keep moving. The workaround becomes the process. The broken thing underneath continues to break.

This is what organizational scar tissue looks like. Every workaround represents a decision someone made, consciously or not, that going through official channels isn't worth the effort. They may have been right — in that moment, for that problem. But workarounds accumulate. They hide the true failure rate of underlying systems. They create shadow processes that new employees learn from experienced employees instead of from documentation. And they make the actual problem progressively harder to diagnose, because its symptoms have been managed into invisibility.

Closing the Loop is the practice of replacing workarounds with accountable follow-through and genuine process fixes. It means doing what you said you would do, by when you said you would do it — and when you can't, saying so. It means treating unresolved issues as open items, not closed books.

What This Looks Like When a Team Gets It Right

1. **When a concern is raised in a team meeting, it goes on a visible tracking list with an owner and a date.** Not a parking lot — a commitment register. Items don't disappear; they get resolved or explicitly reprioritized.

2. **A supervisor who says "I'll look into that" sends a follow-up by end of week, even if the answer is "still working on it" or "here's why this one isn't going to change."**

3. **Process improvement ideas from the floor don't go into a suggestion box and disappear.** They get a response — yes, no, or "here's what we can do instead" — within a defined window.

4. **When a workaround is discovered, the immediate question is: "What does this workaround tell us about the process it's working around?"**

5. **Cross-functional issues get a named owner.** Not "we'll figure it out" — one person accountable for bringing back a resolution.

The **distinction between closing the loop and responding is accountability.** Acknowledging a problem is not the same as resolving it. Teams that close loops make that distinction explicit and track against it.

A Story: The Ticket That Finally Got Closed

At a regional fulfillment center, the inbound quality check process had a recurring issue: items flagged for re-inspection were getting lost between the quality station and the re-inspection queue. It happened often enough that the quality team had developed an informal system — they kept a personal list on a shared spreadsheet that wasn't connected to any official system. Everyone knew about it.

Nobody had fixed the underlying issue because it had been raised to IT twice and both times the ticket had gone into a queue and not come back out.

When a new operations director, Yolanda, came through the facility on her listening tour, a quality tech named Rosalee mentioned the spreadsheet. Yolanda asked her to explain it. Rosalee did. Yolanda asked, "Has this been raised before?" Rosalee showed her the two tickets — both marked "resolved," neither actually resolved.

Yolanda did something simple and unusual: she sent an email to the IT director with both ticket numbers and one question — "Can you help me understand the current status of these?" Then she told Rosalee, "I'm going to follow up on this. Give me two weeks, and if you haven't heard anything, come find me."

Two weeks later, Rosalee hadn't heard anything, so she found Yolanda. Yolanda had already had two conversations with IT and gotten a scope estimate. She walked Rosalee through where it stood and gave her a revised timeline. The fix took six weeks. The spreadsheet finally retired.

The resolution mattered. What Rosalee remembered — and told people — was that someone had said they'd follow up and actually had. That one kept loop changed the credibility of the entire escalation process on that floor.

The Language of This Stage

People who are practicing Stage 4 — Closing the Loop — say things like:

1. *"I said I'd get back to you on this. Here's where things stand."*
2. *"This is still open. I haven't forgotten it, and here's the next step."*
3. *"That workaround tells me there's a process underneath it that needs attention."*
4. *"I'm going to put this on the tracking board with a date. If that date passes and you haven't heard from me, please flag it."*
5. *"I can't fix this one, but I want to tell you why — and what we can do instead."*
6. *"Who owns getting this resolved? Let's put a name on it."*

What It Unlocks

Closing loops rebuilds organizational credibility — the kind that makes people willing to raise problems in the first place.

When people see that concerns lead to action, they keep raising concerns. When they see that concerns disappear into a void, they stop. It is that simple. Every closed loop is a deposit into an account that funds future transparency. Every open loop that stays open is a withdrawal.

There is also a direct operational benefit: workarounds are expensive to maintain. They require tribal knowledge, informal coordination, and ongoing human effort to substitute for broken systems. Every time a workaround gets replaced by a fixed process, that effort gets freed up. Multiply that across a facility, a department, or a company, and the productivity recovery is meaningful.

WHAT TO SAY When you can't fix something someone raised, don't go quiet. Say: *"I looked into this. Here's what I found out, here's what I can and can't do, and here's why."* That response — transparent, direct, honest about limits — does more for trust than a fix that takes three months and arrives without explanation.

Stage 4 is where the cost becomes visible. Missed deadlines. Failed launches. People leaving without telling anyone why. By the time the breakdown surfaces, the spiral has been turning for months — sometimes years.

Leaders often discover the team is in Stage 4 the same week they discover they are also in Stage 5. The two are rarely far apart.

Stage 5: Name It

The Antidote to: Treating Communication Failures as Random Events

The fifth stage of the Silent Spiral™ is the most insidious because it doesn't look like failure. The immediate problem has been handled. The miscommunication got sorted out, the deadline got met, the situation got managed. But nothing about how it happened was examined. No one asked why the wires crossed. No one traced the pattern back to its source. The incident becomes a data point that disappears instead of a signal that gets read.

And so the same failure happens again. Differently shaped, different people, different project — same root cause. Because the system was never fixed. Only the symptom was addressed.

Naming It is the practice of calling a communication failure by its actual name so the system — not the incident — can be understood and improved. It means having the vocabulary to identify what kind of breakdown occurred, the willingness to say it out loud, and the organizational muscle to use that identification to make structural changes.

This is the stage where everything before it consolidates. You have been testing assumptions, breaking silence, creating safety, and closing loops. Stage 5 is what makes all of that learning transferable. It is how a team stops repeating the spiral.

What This Looks Like When a Team Gets It Right

1. After a **project debrief** where a miscommunication is identified, the **team doesn't note "we should communicate better." They name the specific failure:** "We assumed the handoff protocol was shared knowledge. It wasn't. We need a documented handoff checklist."

2. **A manager who keeps seeing the same conflict between two teams says it plainly to the leadership team**, "This is a recurring communication breakdown at the boundary between planning and ops. We keep treating it as a personality issue. I think it's a structural one."

3. When a **crisis is post-mortemed, the language is specific:** "We didn't close the loop on the supplier change notification. That's a loop-closing failure, and here's how we're building the check into the process."

4. **Teams develop shared language for communication patterns** — not to shame anyone**, but to make the invisible visible.** "That feels like a Stage 2 issue — are we creating conditions for people to actually speak up here?"

5. **Leaders model the naming:** "I made a Stage 1 error in that briefing. I assumed everyone understood the priority. I'm going to check that assumption directly."

Naming is not blame. It is diagnosis. And you cannot fix what you cannot name.

A Story: The Pattern Nobody Had a Word For

For eighteen months, a cross-functional product launch team at a consumer goods company had a recurring problem that everyone experienced and nobody could articulate. Every launch had a version of the same breakdown: somewhere between the product team finalizing specs and the operations team beginning production planning, something important got lost. The result was always recoverable, but always expensive — late changes, expedited production runs, strained relationships between two teams that needed to work together constantly.

The launches kept happening. The breakdowns kept happening. The post-mortems kept concluding "communication needs to improve between product and ops."

The turning point came when a process consultant the company brought in for a different engagement sat in on one of the debrief sessions. She listened for an hour and then said: "I want to name what I'm hearing. This isn't a general communication problem. This is a loop-closing failure at a single handoff point — the moment specs are finalized. Product closes their loop internally and considers it done. Ops doesn't know the loop is closed because nobody told them specs were final. The fix isn't 'communicate more.' It's a defined trigger: when specs are final, a specific person sends a specific message to a specific distribution list, and ops doesn't begin planning until they receive it."

The room was quiet for a moment. Then the ops director said, "We've been having this problem for a year and a half and that's the first time I've heard it described in a way I could do something with."

The fix took two weeks to implement. It held. Not because the people changed — because the system did, once someone had named what was wrong.

The Language of This Stage

People who are practicing Stage 5 — Naming It — say things like:

1. *"I want to name what happened here so we can fix it."*
2. *"This isn't a one-time thing. This is a pattern, and it has a name."*
3. *"We keep treating this as a people problem. I think it's a process problem. Let me explain why."*
4. *"What kind of communication failure was this? Let's be specific."*
5. *"If we only fix the symptom, we'll be back here in six months. What's the root cause?"*
6. *"I've seen this before. It's a handoff problem — and here's the specific break in the chain."*

7. *"Let's not leave this debrief without naming the pattern, not just the incident."*

What It Unlocks

When organizations develop the habit and vocabulary to name communication failures accurately, something fundamental changes: institutional learning becomes possible.

Without naming, organizations repeat. The same misalignments, the same spiral, the same expensive recoveries — all handled individually, never addressed systemically. Naming breaks that cycle. *It turns isolated incidents into pattern recognition.* It gives leaders something concrete to act on instead of vague mandates to "do better."

There is also a cultural shift that comes with naming. When the language exists and it is used without blame, communication failures stop being personal failures. They become system signals. And that reframe — from "who messed up" to "what is the system telling us" — is what makes sustained improvement possible instead of a one-quarter initiative that fades when pressure returns.

Breaking the Spiral™ does not mean communication becomes frictionless. It means friction becomes useful. Every breakdown becomes information. Every pattern becomes fixable. That is not perfection — but it is, genuinely, better. And better is achievable.

QUICK WIN After your next project postmortem or incident review, add one question to the debrief agenda: *"What kind of communication failure was this?"* Not "what went wrong" in general — specifically, where in the communication chain did it break, and what would we call that? You don't need a formal framework to start. You need the habit of asking the question and staying in the room long enough to get a real answer.

Stage 5 is what most leaders mean when they say communication has broken down. It is also the stage where most leaders first decide to act. That is too late to prevent the damage. It is not too late to stop the next one.

The five stages are not a ladder you climb once. They are a pattern that recurs — in new projects, new teams, new pressures. The practice is not getting to the end. The practice is catching the spiral earlier each time.

The next chapter starts where this one ends – with the styles people default to when the pressure rises, and the silence sets in.

Key Takeaways

- **Communication breakdowns are rarely random; they follow patterns, and those patterns can be named.**
- **The Silent Spiral™ begins when assumptions go untested, silence feels safer than truth, and small omissions start to compound.**
- **Most team communication failures are not caused by bad intent;** they are caused by **unclear ownership, weak feedback loops, and unspoken risk.**
- **Silence is not neutral.** When teams stop speaking up, the cost shows up later as rework, frustration, workarounds, and missed opportunities to correct course early.
- **The goal is not perfect communication. The goal is deliberate communication:** clearer expectations, better follow-through, and more room for honest input.

Reflection Questions

1. **Where on your team do you see assumptions being treated as understanding?** What is one concrete way you could test for understanding more reliably?
2. **Where has silence been mistaken for agreement in your work?** What was left unsaid, and what did it cost?
3. **What is one recurring breakdown on your team that could be traced back to unclear ownership, weak follow-up, or inconsistent messaging?**
4. **Which pattern in the Silent Spiral™ feels most familiar in your current environment** — and what is one small action you could take this week to interrupt it?

Chapter 6: How People Actually Communicate — Styles, Clashes, and Bridges

At a Glance

What This Chapter Does	Why It Matters
Names the four most common communication styles on real teams	You cannot adjust for what you cannot see
Shows how style mismatch accelerates the Silent Spiral™	Most "people problems" are style problems with no shared language
Gives you a clash matrix and three real examples	The fix is almost never a new meeting structure
Ends with a two-minute self-check	Style starts with you

Before frameworks, tools, or scripts, there is a prerequisite most communication books skip: **not everyone communicates the same way.** Style mismatch is one of the most common, and most invisible, causes of breakdown on real teams.

This is not about personality tests. You do not need an assessment tool or a four-letter type to use what follows. You need to **watch how people process, express, and respond to information** — and then *adjust your approach.*

That adjustment is the skill.

What This Is Not

This is not a personality test. It is not a typology you sort people into and stop thinking. It is not a label you put on a colleague to explain why they are difficult.

Personality assessments have their place, but they are the wrong tool for what this chapter is trying to do. Assessments freeze a person in a moment. Communication style, the way I use it here, is the opposite — it is a moving read on how someone is processing this conversation, in this room, under this pressure.

The same person can be Direct in a budget meeting and a Processor in a performance conversation. The skill is not pinning the label. The skill is reading the behavior in front of you and adjusting.

The Four Communication Styles

These are not neat categories people fit into once and for all. They are tendencies — patterns you will recognize in yourself and in the people you work with. Most people have a dominant style and can flex into others. The best communicators are not the ones with the "right" style; they are the ones who can meet other people where they are.

Style	How They Process	What They Need	What Frustrates Them	How to Communicate With Them
The Direct Communicator	Thinks fast, speaks fast, wants the bottom line	Brevity, clarity, action items	Long explanations, indecisiveness, "just thinking out loud"	Lead with the ask. Add context only as needed.
The Processor	Needs time to think before responding	Space, written summaries, time to reflect	Being put on the spot, rapid-fire questions, "What do you think right now?"	Send the agenda ahead of time. Follow up in writing. Give them time to think.
The Verbal Thinker	Processes by talking; needs to say it out loud to figure out what they think	A sounding board, patience, room to circle back	Being told to "get to the point," having their thinking aloud mistaken for a final position	Listen through the full thought. Ask, "Is that where you landed, or are you still working through it?"
The Conflict Avoider	Prioritizes harmony and may agree in the room while disagreeing later	Safety, private channels, explicit permission to dissent	Public confrontation, "Why didn't you say something in the meeting?", being called out	Create private channels for honest input. Ask, "What concerns do you have that you have not shared yet?"

If you have managed teams for any length of time, you have seen all four of these styles collide. You have seen the Direct Communicator read the Processor's silence as disengagement. You have seen the Verbal Thinker work through ideas out loud while someone else mistakes the process for a decision. You have seen the Conflict Avoider nod in the meeting and raise the real concern later, in the hallway.

None of those failures required bad intent. They required a style mismatch and no shared awareness of it.

How The Silent Spiral™ Accelerates When Styles Clash

The Silent Spiral™ accelerates when styles clash without awareness. Once you start looking at the stages through that lens, the pattern gets easier to see.

- A **Direct Communicator** becomes the manager of a Processor. The Direct Communicator gives direction quickly, in a meeting, and expects immediate acknowledgment.
- **The Processor** needs time to think and a written summary, so they say nothing. The Direct Communicator reads that silence as agreement and moves on. Stage 1 — assumption — has already started.
- A **Verbal Thinker** manages a team that includes Direct Communicators. Planning meetings turn into extended brainstorms. The Verbal Thinker is processing in real time, out loud, with no guarantee that every idea is final. The Direct Communicators hear the last thing said and start acting on it. Two weeks later, the Verbal Thinker has moved to a different position, and the team realizes they executed on a thought, not a decision. That is Stage 3 — frustration — triggered by a style mismatch.
- A **Conflict Avoider** sits in every meeting and nods. They have real concerns, but the room does not feel safe enough for pushback, and nobody has created another channel. The manager leaves thinking the team is aligned. The Conflict Avoider leaves carrying unspoken concern. Over time, that silence hardens into the kind of problem that does real damage. That is Stage 2 — silence — being sustained by a style the room never made room for.

Style Clash: What Goes Wrong and How to Fix It

Your Style	Their Style	What Goes Wrong	The Fix
Direct	Processor	You think they are slow; they think you are dismissive	Send context in advance and give them response time
Processor	Verbal Thinker	You feel overwhelmed by their volume; they think you are disengaged	Ask them to summarize their top two takeaways
Verbal Thinker	Direct	They cut you off; you feel unheard	Lead with your conclusion, then explain the reasoning
Conflict Avoider	Direct	You agree to avoid conflict; they think you are aligned	Name it privately: "I want to share something I held back."
Direct	Conflict Avoider	You think they agree; they are surviving the conversation	Follow up one-on-one and ask what they are really thinking

The table above is worth sitting with. Not because every interaction maps perfectly onto these pairings — it does not — but because it trains the habit of asking a better question: what is this person's style, and what does that mean for how I read their response?

The silence after your question might not mean agreement. The pushback in the hallway might not mean someone is difficult. The long monologue might not mean the person is self-absorbed. It might mean you are looking at a Processor, a Conflict Avoider, or a Verbal Thinker and reading them through the wrong lens.

Read the behavior. Adjust the approach.

Style Under Pressure

Style is not fixed. Most people have a dominant tendency in calm conditions and a different one when the room gets hot. Workload, conflict, an unhappy customer, a stretched deadline — these are the moments your team's communication style actually matters, and they are also the moments people stop communicating in their default mode.

A **Direct Communicator** under pressure can compress further — fewer words, sharper edges, less context. To the rest of the room, that reads as anger or dismissiveness even when it is neither.

A **Processor** under pressure goes quieter. The same person who would normally ask for a day to think now says nothing at all. Silence in a calm meeting and silence in a stressed meeting look identical, and they mean different things.

A **Verbal Thinker** under pressure talks more, not less, and the gap between "I am processing" and "I have decided" gets wider — exactly when the team most needs to know which one they are hearing.

A **Conflict Avoider** under pressure becomes invisible. They will agree faster, leave earlier, and reroute every concern into a private channel that may or may not reach you in time.

Watch for the shift. The most useful question a leader can ask in a tense meeting is not, "Does anyone disagree?" It is, "What am I not hearing right now that I would be hearing if the stakes were lower?"

Your Style Sets the Room's Default

Whatever style a leader brings into a meeting becomes the meeting's default style. A Direct manager runs short, action-focused meetings — and Processors quietly stop contributing. A Verbal Thinker manager runs long, exploratory meetings — and Direct Communicators quietly start tuning out. A Conflict Avoider manager runs polite meetings — and the real concerns leave with people in the parking lot.

This is not a flaw. It is physics. People match the energy of the person running the room.

The work, then, is not to change your style. It is to notice what your style filters out, and build a deliberate counterweight. If you are Direct, the counterweight is a written agenda sent ahead of time and a follow-up channel after. If you are a Verbal Thinker, the counterweight is a clear "I am still processing" signal. If you are a Conflict Avoider, the counterweight is a structured place — even a one-question form — for the dissent your meetings will not produce on their own.

You cannot run a meeting that accommodates every style at once. You can run a meeting that knows what it is leaving out, and catches it somewhere else.

Three Real Examples from Real Teams

Example 1: The operations meeting that was breaking down. A logistics manager I worked with could not figure out why his planning meetings kept producing rework. He was Direct — he covered the issues quickly and moved on. Two of his team leads were Processors. By the time they had a real response, the meeting had moved on. They stopped raising concerns in the room and started flagging them afterward, which created the exact sidebar dynamic the manager did not want.

The fix was not a new meeting structure. It was a fifteen-minute heads-up email before each meeting with the questions he planned to ask. The Processors had time to think, and the meeting sharpened immediately.

Example 2: The Verbal Thinker and the misunderstood commitment. A project lead I know — sharp, creative, genuinely collaborative — had a pattern of frustrating the people who reported to her. She would brainstorm direction with the team, they would execute, and then she would return two weeks later with a different direction. From her side, she had been thinking out loud and had not landed yet. From their side, she had given direction, and they had spent ten days delivering it.

Neither version was dishonest. They had no shared language for the difference between "I am processing" and "I have decided." Once they named it, and she began ending brainstorms with, "I am still working through this — I will come back tomorrow with where I have landed," the rework pattern stopped.

Example 3: The Conflict Avoider and the invisible red flag. In a large government operation I was brought in to work with, a project had been stuck in Stage 4 — Workaround — for over a year before anyone named it out loud. The project manager asked, "Any concerns?" in every status meeting and got nothing but nods.

The concerns existed. Three different team members had identified the same critical risk independently, and none of them had said a word because the room did not feel like a safe place for pushback, and nobody had created another channel.

When a simple anonymous input form was introduced before each status meeting — a text field, two questions — the same three team members flagged the same risk within a week. It had been there the whole time. The meeting format had not been designed for the people in it.

Style Inventory: A Quick Self-Check

Before you move on, take two minutes with these questions:

1. **What is your default style?** When you are under pressure or moving fast, do you go Direct? Do you withdraw and process? Do you talk it through? Do you smooth things over?
2. **Who on your team has a style most different from yours?** Not who you find difficult — who is simply different? What does their style tell you about what they need from you?
3. **Where have style clashes produced the most friction on your team in the last 90 days?** Not "who is difficult" — where did different styles collide without a bridge?

You do not need to share the answers. They are diagnostic. Once you start seeing the style dimension in your team's communication, you will not be able to unsee it — and that is the point. Most team silence is not random; it is what happens when different communication styles collide without a bridge.

Style is the first layer. The next layer — what people *say* once you have made room for them to say it — is the subject of the chapter that follows.

Key Takeaways

- **Style differences matter.** People do not all process information the same way, and ignoring those differences creates avoidable friction.
- **There are four common styles** — Direct, Processor, Verbal Thinker, Conflict Avoider — and most people have a dominant tendency that shifts under pressure.
- **Style mismatch is invisible until it is named.** Silence read as agreement, brainstorming read as direction, harmony read as alignment — these are the costs of running a team without a shared style vocabulary.
- **The fix is rarely a new meeting structure.** The fix is a small adjustment in how information is delivered, when, and through what channel — sized to the people in the room.

Reflection Questions

1. **Which communication style on your team tends to be misunderstood or overlooked?** What would it look like to adjust your approach for that person or group?
2. **Where on your team has a single style — yours, or someone else's — set the default for everyone?** What gets lost because of it?
3. **What is one specific change you could make in your next team meeting** to give a different style room to land?
4. **When was the last time you noticed your own style shift under pressure?** What changed in how you communicated, and what did the people around you most likely read into it?
5. **If a new person joined your team tomorrow with the style most different from yours, what is the first adjustment you would owe them — and would you actually make it?**

Chapter 7: Build the Foundation — Trust and Psychological Safety

There is a team I think about often. Smart, credentialed, motivated professionals were handed a significant project — and watched it fall apart over eighteen months. Nobody missed a deadline on purpose. Nobody was incompetent. Nobody wanted to fail.

It failed anyway, because no one ever said, out loud: *"I don't know what I'm doing,"* or *"I'm worried this isn't going to work,"* or *"Can someone help me?"*

I have done this kind of diagnostic work many times — in operations rooms, conference calls, and one-on-ones that ran far longer than planned. The answer is usually the same: the problem was not skill, strategy, or resources. The problem was that nobody felt safe enough to tell the truth.

That is the foundation problem. Before communication plans, RACI matrices, standups, and dashboards, there has to be something underneath all of it: trust. In team settings, the operational expression of trust is psychological safety — the shared belief that the team is safe for interpersonal risk-taking.

If you think back to The Silent Spiral™ from Part I, trust is what determines whether Stage 2 — Silence — takes root. When people feel safe, silence does not get a foothold. Building trust is not a soft prerequisite. It is the intervention that stops the Spiral before the damage compounds.

At a Glance

Section	What You'll Learn
Lencioni's Model	Why trust is the base of every team dysfunction
Building on Psychological Safety	How psychological safety connects to the trust you build day to day
Vulnerability as a Tool	Why leaders who admit uncertainty get better information
What Kills Trust	Five behaviors that undo months of trust-building in a single conversation

Section	What You'll Learn
Building Trust	Four structured exercises teams can use right now
Rebuilding Trust	A four-step playbook when trust is already broken
Trust-Repair Scripts	Word-for-word language for hard conversations
Hostile Environments	How to create micro-safety when the culture resists it

Lencioni's Model

Patrick Lencioni's *The Five Dysfunctions of a Team* became a cliché because the core insight is correct. Teams fail because dysfunction stacks, and you cannot solve the higher levels until the lower ones are addressed.

1. **Absence of trust:** team members are unwilling to be vulnerable with one another.
2. **Fear of conflict:** teams avoid productive ideological debate.
3. **Lack of commitment:** without honest debate, decisions do not get genuine buy-in.
4. **Avoidance of accountability:** without commitment, people do not hold each other to standards.
5. **Inattention to results:** without accountability, individual ego wins over team outcomes.

Communication breakdowns show up at every level of that pyramid:

Dysfunction	Communication Impact
Absence of trust	People do not share information
Fear of conflict	Critical concerns go unspoken
Lack of commitment	Progress communication becomes performative
Avoidance of accountability	Nobody follows up
Inattention to results	Nothing worth communicating about remains

The foundation is trust — specifically vulnerability-based trust. Not liking each other. Not good chemistry. Not a retreat where everybody falls backward into somebody else's arms.

Trust is being able to say in front of your peers and leadership:
"I was wrong."
"I do not know."
"I need help."
"I made a mistake, **and here is what I am doing about it."**

That *sounds* simple. **In practice, it is one of the hardest things to create in a professional environment.**

I have worked in places where admitting you did not know something felt like handing someone a weapon. I have watched people present data they had not verified, give assurances they could not keep, and nod along in meetings rather than ask the question that would expose a gap. Every time, the communication that should have happened at moment one got pushed to moment ten — usually too late.

The antidote is **intentional trust-building.** Not *hoped-for trust*. Not assumed trust because everyone seems friendly. Intentional, structured, practiced trust.

Building on Psychological Safety

The Human Element chapter covered psychological safety in depth — Amy Edmondson's research, the four conditions that produce it, and the way teams in high-pressure work end up reporting more errors when they feel safe, not fewer. That is the underlying mechanism.

This chapter is the operating manual. The work that follows — vulnerability as a tool, the four trust exercises, the rebuild playbook, the scripts — is how psychological safety stops being a concept and becomes a daily practice.

In the Room: The Moment Trust Gets Killed

It rarely happens with a dramatic blowup. Usually, it is quieter than that.

The weekly ops review. Dominic has been tracking a production issue for ten days. He thinks he has finally found the root cause — a scheduling gap that keeps recurring.

Dominic: *"I want to flag something before we close. I've been watching this pattern in the line output for the last two weeks, and I think there's a scheduling gap that's—"*

His manager, Paul, looks at the clock. *"Send me the data. We're out of time."*

Dominic sends the data. Hears nothing.

Next week, Dominic prepares a one-page summary. Paul does not open it before the meeting.

The week after that, Dominic says nothing. The scheduling gap is not in the root cause analysis three months later — because by then, Dominic had decided it was not worth the effort. Nobody asked. Nobody remembered he had mentioned it twice.

The failure was not dramatic. It was two meetings where it was not the right time. That is all it took.

What Kills Trust

You can spend months building trust and lose it in a single conversation.

Trust Killer	What It Looks Like	Why It Damages Trust	Instead, Do This
Public blame	Calling out a mistake in a group setting	Tells everyone that failure means humiliation	Address mistakes in private
Inconsistency	Saying one thing in a 1:1 and another in a meeting	Makes your words unreliable	Align your message across channels

Trust Killer	What It Looks Like	Why It Damages Trust	Instead, Do This
Taking credit	Presenting team work as your own	Signals that support flows upward, not outward	Name your team's contributions publicly
Breaking confidences	Sharing what someone told you privately	Tells people private information is not safe	Ask permission before sharing
Saying nothing when something is wrong	Letting problems slide to keep the peace	Teaches that standards are optional	Address it directly, privately, and promptly

Vulnerability as a Leadership Tool

In many workplaces — especially industrial, government, and traditionally hierarchical settings — there is an unspoken rule that leaders project confidence at all times. Questions look weak. Uncertainty looks unstable.

The problem is that when leaders perform certainty they do not actually have, people stop telling them things that would disrupt that certainty. The leader ends up operating blind, making decisions on filtered information while believing they have the full picture. Used strategically and authentically, vulnerability breaks that cycle.

What strategic vulnerability looks like in practice:

- **In a project kickoff:** "I want to be honest — I do not have all the answers on how this comes together. What I need from this team is your eyes and your brains, not just your hands."
- **When someone brings a concern:** "Thank you for bringing this. I do not know the answer right now, but let's figure it out together."
- **After a failure or near-miss:** "Here is what I think I missed on my end. Here is what I am going to do differently."

These are not confessions of incompetence. They are demonstrations of integrity. They tell your team that the standard is not perfection. The standard is honesty, effort, and course correction.

I once managed a quality process that produced a significant error that reached a customer. My instinct was to identify who made the mistake. My better instinct was to ask: what did the process allow? And what did I miss in my oversight?

When I had that conversation openly, the defensive posture dropped. People started offering information they had been sitting on: “I had a feeling that step was going to be a problem, but I did not know if I should say something.” That information was gold. It only surfaced because I made it safe to surface.

Trust Translations

Instead Of...	Try...
“Let’s stay focused — we’ll address concerns offline.” “That’s not what we’re here to discuss.”	“What concerns should we address before moving on?” “That’s worth capturing for follow-up.”
“I’ve already thought through all the risks.” “We need to project confidence to the client.”	“Here’s what I’ve considered — what am I missing?” “Honesty is worth more than false certainty.”
“Figure it out. That’s what I’m paying you for.”	“What support would help most right now?” “Honesty is more credible than false certainty.”

THE TRUST AUDIT

Before you can build or repair trust, you need to know where you actually stand.
Answer honestly – not as you wish things were, but as they are.

SCORE EACH STATEMENT: 1 = Rarely | 2 = Sometimes | 3 = Usually | 4 = Consistently

#	STATEMENT	SCORE
1	Team members admit mistakes to each other without fear of blame	______
2	People ask for help when they are stuck rather than struggling silently	______
3	Concerns and risks get raised before they become crises	______
4	Disagreement is expressed directly, not through back-channels	______
5	I follow through on what I say I will do	______
6	When I give feedback, it is specific and timely, not vague and delayed	______
7	My team gets consistent information from me across channels	______
8	Bad news reaches me quickly; people do not bury it	______
9	Team members credit each other's contributions openly	______
10	I respond to problems with curiosity, not judgment	______

SCORING

34–40	**STRONG TRUST FOUNDATION.** Protect it and keep building.
25–33	**FUNCTIONAL BUT FRAGILE.** Identify the lowest scores and act on them specifically.
15–24	**TRUST IS A REAL RISK.** Pick one item and start there this week.
BELOW 15	**THE TRUST GAP IS ACTIVELY COSTING YOU.** Treat this as urgent.

Building Trust

Trust is built in moments — the accumulated weight of small interactions. There are also structured exercises teams can use deliberately.

Behavior	What it looks like	Impact on trust
Do what you said you would do	Follow through on commitments, visibly and consistently	Builds predictability and reliability
Tell uncomfortable truths	Name problems early, even when it is awkward	Signals that honesty is safe
Make space for other perspectives	Ask before asserting; listen before responding	Creates equity of voice
Acknowledge mistakes openly	"Here is what I missed on my end."	Models the behavior you want to see
Separate the person from the problem	Address behavior and process, not character	Makes it safe to surface issues
Show up for people	Respond when someone brings a concern	Teaches that problems are welcome here

Personal Histories Exercise

In a team meeting, ask every member to briefly share:

- Where they grew up
- What their career path looked like, including any unexpected turns
- One professional challenge they have faced

This is not therapy. It is a **bounded exercise that humanizes team members to one another.** I have run it in rooms full of engineers, government workers, and logistics supervisors — people who would roll their eyes at anything that *smelled like a feelings exercise*. Every time, something in the room shifted. People **stopped being job titles** and **started being people.**

Team Agreements

Build a collaboratively written document that answers: how are we going to work together?

At minimum, cover:

- How will we make decisions? Who has final say?
- How will we handle disagreement in meetings?
- What are our expectations for response times?
- How will we handle it when someone drops the ball?
- What does good feedback look like on this team?

Keyword: collaboratively. A team agreement the leader wrote is a policy. One the team built together is a commitment.

The Appreciation Practice

At the end of team meetings, take three minutes for one person to name something they appreciated about a colleague's contribution that week. Not performance feedback — specific, genuine appreciation:

- "I noticed you stayed late to get that report out, and it made a difference."
- "When I was stuck on that problem, you asked me exactly the right question."

This sounds small. It compounds quickly. Within weeks, teams start noticing and naming contributions as a default.

The Pre-Mortem

Before a project launches: "Imagine we are twelve months from now and this project has failed. What happened?"

Let people identify the things they are worried about but have not said yet. What comes out is almost always useful — and often includes the exact failure that later happens.

When Trust is Broken

By the time a team or leader starts paying attention to the trust problem, they are usually already in it. The project is in trouble, the relationships are frayed, and everyone is in self-protection mode. This is recoverable — but not easily.

The Four-Step Trust Rebuild Playbook

Step	What to do	What not to do
1. Name it	"I think we have lost some trust on this team, and I want to talk about how we got here and what we are going to do about it."	Pretend it is not there
2. Acknowledge your role	Name your piece of the breakdown before asking others to name theirs	Assign blame before taking ownership
3. Define what good looks like	Get specific about what behavior is changing and what systems are being put in place	Apologize and move on without specifics
4. Follow through visibly	Do the stated change consistently, where people can see it	Say it and then slide back into old patterns

Trust is rebuilt in small actions over time. Not in a single meeting, a heartfelt apology, or a team offsite.

The common thread in every success story I have seen is this: ***someone had the courage to name the problem and start the work.***

Trust-Repair Scripts

When trust has been damaged, the hardest part is starting the conversation. The goal is not to over-explain or defend yourself. The goal is to name the issue clearly, take responsibility where appropriate, and show what changes going forward.

When You Broke a Commitment

"I said I would do this, and I did not follow through. I understand that affects trust. Here is what happened, what I should have done differently, and what I am doing to prevent it from happening again."

When You Said Something Damaging In Public

"I want to go back to something I said earlier. The way I said it was too sharp, and it was not helpful. That is on me. What I meant to say was..."

When Trust Has Been Broken Between Two Team Members

"I can see there is a trust issue here, and it is affecting the work. I do not want to force a quick fix, but I do want us to name what happened and what needs to change so we can work effectively again."

When You Are Addressing a Pattern, Not Just a Single Incident

"This is not about one moment. It is a pattern, and it is affecting how people are working together. I want us to look at what is driving it and what we are going to do differently."

When You Need To Rebuild Trust With Leadership

"I know I have not always been consistent in how I have communicated, and that has affected confidence. I want to reset that. Going forward, here is what you can expect from me."

When Someone Brings You a Hard Truth

"Thank you for telling me that. I know it was not easy to say. I would rather hear it now than find out later after it has grown into something bigger."

When You Need To Own a Miss Without Spiraling Into Self-Protection

"I missed this, and I want to own it directly. I am not going to spend time defending it. What matters now is correcting it and making sure we do not repeat it."

A Few Guidance Notes

- Keep your tone steady. Do not over-apologize.

- Do not explain so much that the ownership gets buried.
- Do not turn the moment into a speech.
- Say the thing, own the thing, and move to the change.

Being Vulnerable in Environments That Do Not Reward It

Not every workplace is open to change. Some leadership cultures actively punish people who speak up, admit uncertainty, or refuse to perform false confidence. Some teams are so cynical from past dysfunction that anything resembling a team-building exercise lands as a joke. **You cannot single-handedly transform a culture that does not want to be transformed.** *But you can create micro-environments of safety within the larger dysfunction.*

When This Happens / Do This

When This Happens	Do This
Leadership punishes honest status updates	Frame updates in terms of risk management: "I am flagging this so we can address it before it affects the outcome."
A team member is mocked for asking a question	Follow up privately: "That was a good question. I am glad you asked it." Do this consistently until the norm shifts.
Your vulnerability is used against you	Note it. Adjust what you share with that person specifically, not with the whole team. Do not let one bad actor change your standard.
The cynicism in the room is too thick	Do not try to convert the room. Find the one or two people who seem open and build from there. Change happens in relationships, not announcements.
Your manager does not model the behavior you want to see	Be explicit about the standard with your team: "I want us to operate differently from what some of us have seen elsewhere. Here is what that looks like."

What that looks like:

- Be the manager whose team knows they will not be punished for bringing a problem.
- Be the colleague who responds to a mistake with, "Thank you for telling me. Let's figure this out," instead of, "How did this happen?"
- Be the person who models the behavior you want to see, even when the environment around you is not there yet.

This is not passive acceptance of a broken culture. It is strategic resistance. Build trust where you have influence. Document the impact. Make the case — with data and results — that this way of operating is not soft. It is effective.

Sometimes — not always, but sometimes — the micro-environment you create becomes visible enough that it starts to change the macro-environment around it. That is communication as leadership. That is the foundation the rest of this book is built on.

Key Takeaways

- **Trust** — specifically vulnerability-based trust — is the non-negotiable foundation of every communication framework. Without it, the rest becomes performance rather than function.
- **Psychological safety is not about being nice.** It is about creating conditions where honest, complete information flows, including bad news, mistakes, and uncertainty.
- **Vulnerability is a leadership tool.** Leaders who model intellectual honesty and respond curiously to problems build teams that communicate honestly.
- **Trust can be built deliberately through structured exercises:** personal histories, team agreements, appreciation practices, and pre-mortems.
- **Trust, once broken, can be rebuilt** — but only through consistent action over time and through specific trust-repair conversations, not general apologies.

Reflection Questions

1. **Think of a time when you withheld important information from your team or leadership.** What made it feel too risky to share, and what was the cost of that silence?
2. **As a leader or team member, what is one behavior you currently model that might be teaching your team that honesty is not safe?** What would it look like to change that?
3. **Where on your current team do you see the absence of vulnerability-based trust?** What is one concrete step you could take this week to begin building it?

FIELD NOTES: The Review That Said Everything Was Fine

I have received performance reviews that told me I was doing well and left me less certain of my footing than when I walked in.

That sounds like a paradox. It is not. It is the predictable result of a performance conversation built around what people are comfortable saying rather than what a professional needs to hear.

What the formal review said versus what was actually true:

- **The review said:** Positive, or at worst neutral
  The reality was: Concerns existed
- **The review said:** No warnings, no flags, no documented concerns
  The reality was: Conversations about my work and prospects had already been happening without me
- **The review said:** “On track”
  The reality was: Nobody had defined what “on track” actually meant
- **The review said:** Fine
  The reality was: Corrective direction had already been forming in someone’s mind for some time

What I did not know until later — sometimes months later — was that the corrective direction I eventually received had already been established as fact before it ever reached me. No prior warning. No prior conversation. No opportunity to address the concern while it was still small enough to address.

What broke trust was not the corrective feedback itself. Corrective feedback, given clearly and early, is one of the most respectful things a leader can offer. What broke trust was the gap: fine to corrective action, with no bridge between them. That sequence does not feel like feedback. It feels like a setup.

The pattern is not rare. I have talked to enough professionals across industries to know the shape of it: the review that leaves the receiver with less clarity than they arrived with, the corrective action that lands as the first explicit signal of a problem leadership has been tracking for months, the moment when you realize the conversation happening about you is not the conversation happening with you.

What I know now, having been on both sides, is this: the review that says everything is fine when everything **is not fine is not kindness.**

It is a debt being deferred. And when it comes due — as it always does — **the interest rate is trust.**

Field Note Takeaway: A performance conversation that produces no clarity is not a kindness; it is a missed opportunity that will cost twice as much later. If you are in the position of giving feedback, say the real thing early.

If you are receiving a review that leaves you with less clarity than you arrived with, ask direct follow-up questions: "What would progress look like in the next 90 days?" Do not leave the conversation carrying ambiguity that was never yours to carry.

Chapter 8: Define the Rules of Engagement

I have seen impressive communication plans in my career. Beautifully formatted. Color-coded. Complete with stakeholder matrices, escalation trees, and distribution lists so thorough they might as well have included building maintenance.

I have watched those plans get presented, approved, filed, and never looked at again. The team checks a box, believes they have structure, then operates on instinct while the plan collects digital dust. Two months in, when something breaks, no one opens the document — they call the person they think might know. That is the cost of a plan that was never built to be used.

Most communication plans fail not because of content, but construction:

- *Built once by one person, without input from those who execute them*
- *Built at project start when everything is theoretical, never updated when reality arrives*
- *So comprehensive they are unusable*

This chapter interrupts the Silent Spiral™ at Stage 1 — Assumption. The tools that follow replace guesswork with structure before silence takes root.

At a Glance

Section	What You'll Get
Communication Plans	Three principles that make plans usable, plus a practical template
RACI Matrix	A role-clarity tool, common mistakes, and a sample
Communication Cadence	Daily, weekly, monthly, and quarterly rhythms
Channel Decision Tree	A framework for choosing the right communication channel
Meeting Agenda Template	A simple structure for meetings that produce decisions

Section	What You'll Get
SOS/EOS Reporting	A handoff discipline that preserves critical context
Escalation Path	When, how, and to whom issues should be escalated

Communication Plans That Actually Get Used

A functional communication plan is not a ceremonial document. It is an operating tool.

Three principles determine whether it gets used.

1. Solve real problems, not theoretical ones

Do not begin by asking what a "good communication plan" usually includes. Begin by asking the team where communication breaks down.

- Where do handoffs fail? What information arrives late?
- What gets trapped in one function and never reaches another?
- What does leadership find out too late? What do frontline teams wish they had known sooner?

Those answers should shape the plan.

2. Simplicity beats comprehensiveness

A one-page plan the team references is more valuable than a twelve-page masterpiece no one opens after kickoff. The goal is not maximum coverage. The goal is operational usefulness.

Start with the five or six communication flows that matter most. Weekly status. Escalations. Decision records. Shift handoffs. Stakeholder updates. Risk communication. Build the plan around the communications that, if neglected, would create confusion, delay, rework, or distrust.

3. Assign specific ownership

Every communication line item needs a clear owner.

- Not a department.
- Not "the team."
- Not "as needed."
- **A person.**

"Sarah sends the weekly status update by noon every Friday" is a **communication plan**. "Status updates will be distributed regularly" **is a wish.**

Communication	Audience	Frequency	Format	Owner	Channel
Weekly status update	Core team + sponsor	Every Friday	Email summary	Project Lead	Email
Stand-up check-in	Core team	Daily, 9:00 AM	15-minute meeting	Rotating facilitator	In person / Video
Escalation report	Leadership	As needed	Structured memo	PM + Supervisor	Email + verbal
Stakeholder update	Extended stakeholders	Bi-weekly	Slide deck	Project Lead	Email
Issue / risk log	Core team	Updated weekly	Shared tracker	PM	Shared drive
Decision log	All participants	Per meeting	Meeting notes	Note-taker	Shared drive

Build the plan with the people who will use it. Review it quarterly. When a communication failure happens, update the plan. Treat it as a living operating document, not a project deliverable.

In the Room: When Nobody Defined the Rules

The project is four weeks in. Things are starting to slip.

Alicia: *"I sent that to Marcus for approval three days ago. No response."*

Ben: *"I thought I was reviewing it first?"*

Alicia: *"I thought Marcus was."*

Ben: *"Does Marcus know he's the approver?"*

Alicia: *"...I assumed the project lead would have told him."*

Ben: *"Who's the project lead?"*

The deliverable is four days from deadline. Three people think someone else is accountable. The communication plan listed *"Quality team"* as the approver — no name, no timeline, no definition of what approval means. Everyone filled in the blank differently.

***"Quality team"* is not an owner.**
It is a placeholder for a conversation nobody had.

The RACI Matrix: Who Does What and Why It Matters

If the communication plan defines how information moves, the RACI matrix defines who is expected to make things happen. One governs flow. The other governs ownership. You need both.

RACI works because it makes implicit assumptions explicit. In many teams, accountability is felt but not assigned. That gap is where some of the most damaging breakdowns begin.

Letter	Role	Meaning
R	Responsible	Does the work; owns execution
A	Accountable	The single person answerable for the outcome
C	Consulted	Must provide input before a decision is made
I	Informed	Needs to know the outcome after the decision is made

The most important rule in the matrix is this: there can only be **one A per task.** When accountability is shared, it is diluted.

Mistake	Why It Fails	Fix
Multiple people listed as Accountable	When everyone is accountable, no one is	Assign one A per task
Confusing Responsible and Accountable	The doer and the decision-owner are not always the same	Separate execution from final ownership

Mistake	Why It Fails	Fix
Too many Consulted roles	Excess consultation turns process into committee	Consult only where input is necessary
Building it once and never revisiting it	Teams and scopes change	Review it when people, scope, or risk changes

Most common mistakes:

- Multiple A's per task (when everyone is accountable, no one is)
- Confusing R and A (doer ≠ decision-owner)
- Too many C's (15 consultees = committee)
- Never updating it

Instead of...	Try...
"Everyone is responsible for this."	"Marcus is accountable. Sarah and Devon are responsible for execution."
"Just make sure the right people know."	"Inform the site director and customer contact only."
"We need more input."	"We need input from Quality and Procurement before deciding."
"Who owns this?"	"Let's assign an owner before we move on."

Sample RACI (quality reporting):

Task	QA Sup	OM	Director	Customer	Corporate
Document VNC	R	C	I	I	I
Initiate Containment	R	R	I	I	C
Communicate to customer	C	C	A	I	C
Conduct root cause analysis	R	C	I	I	C
Submit corrective action report	R	I	A	I	C
Approve and close	C	C	A	I	R

Build your RACI with the people named in it. Pay attention to disagreements. Those disagreements are not annoyances. They are early warnings. They reveal the ambiguity that would have become a breakdown later.

Establishing Cadence: The Rhythm of Information Flow

One of the most underestimated elements of communication is rhythm. **Teams with a reliable cadence spend less time chasing status, sending reminder emails, or discovering important information three days late.** Cadence reduces drag because it removes uncertainty about when information will surface. Cadence is not bureaucracy. It is the operating rhythm that keeps people from having to guess when critical information will move.

Cadence	Purpose	Format	Key Question
Daily stand-up	Surface blockers and create awareness	15 minutes max	What changed since yesterday?
Weekly review	Assess trajectory and make decisions	30-60 minutes	Are we on track?
Informal check-in	Capture what formal reports miss	Brief 1:1 or walk-through	What is not being said in meetings?
Monthly review	Evaluate health over time	Structured review	What patterns are emerging?
Quarterly review	Reassess strategic alignment	Leadership + team review	Are we still solving the right problem?

The Daily Stand-Up: Keep It Ruthlessly Simple

1. What did I complete since the last stand-up?
2. What am I working on next?
3. What is blocking me?

Stand-ups work when they are brief, consistent, and followed by action. They fail when they turn into mini status presentations, get skipped because "nothing changed," or surface blockers that no one resolves.

The Weekly Review

A good weekly review answers four questions:

1. What commitments were completed?
2. What was not completed, and why?
3. What risks or issues changed this week?

4. What decisions need to be made in the next seven days?

Choosing the Right Channel

The channel is part of the message. An accurate communication can still fail if it is delivered through the wrong medium. **The wrong channel creates friction, misunderstanding, defensiveness, delay, or unnecessary escalation.** ***Is action needed in the next two hours?***

If yes:

- If the issue is simple, use a call, a Teams chat, or a radio.
- If the issue is complex, sensitive, or emotionally charged, call or walk over first. Document afterward.

If no:

- If the topic requires discussion, schedule a meeting.
- If it needs a durable record, use email.
- If it is lightweight and informational, use a brief message.

Do not start with email for a performance issue, a rapidly developing problem, or a sensitive concern where tone can easily be misread. I learned that lesson the hard way. I once sent a carefully worded email about a process concern. It was read as an accusation. The email chain stretched for three days and solved almost nothing. The face-to-face conversation that followed took fifteen minutes and solved the problem completely. The issue was not the wording. It was the channel.

Channel	Use When	Avoid When
Email	Formal records, summaries, non-urgent updates, complex info people may need to reread	Urgent issues, tone-sensitive topics, emotionally charged concerns
Phone / Teams	Quick questions, urgent coordination, fast clarification	Decisions that need documentation, complex multi-party alignment
Meeting	Complex problems, hard conversations, significant decisions	Information that could be read
Walk over	Urgent, nuanced, or sensitive issues with someone nearby	Anything that must begin with a formal record

A meeting without an agenda is a conversation with overhead.

MEETING NAME:

DATE / TIME:

LOCATION / LINK:

FACILITATOR:

NOTE-TAKER:

PURPOSE: ☐ Decision ☐ Discussion ☐ Update ☐ Problem-solving

PRE-READ MATERIALS:

[List or link anything participants need beforehand]

DECISION(S) TO BE MADE TODAY:

[List them clearly]

MEETING FLOW (AGENDA ITEMS)

#	TOPIC / AGENDA ITEM	TYPE	OWNER	TIME
1		☐ D ☐ Disc ☐ U ☐ PS		
2		☐ D ☐ Disc ☐ U ☐ PS		
3		☐ D ☐ Disc ☐ U ☐ PS		
4		☐ D ☐ Disc ☐ U ☐ PS		
5		☐ D ☐ Disc ☐ U ☐ PS		

D = Decision **Disc** = Discussion U = Update **PS** = Problem-solving

POST-MEETING:

- **Notes distributed by:** ______________________ [date/time]
- **Action log updated by:** ______________________ [date/time]

TIP:

If a meeting requires a decision, name the decision in advance.
If no decision is needed, be honest that it is an update.
A surprising number of bad meetings happen because
no one knows what kind of meeting they are in.

Context Transfer: The Discipline Every Team Needs

Every handoff is a risk.

One person leaves with key information in their head. Another arrives without it. The setting changes, but the communication failure stays the same. End of shift. Vacation coverage. Sprint rollover. Phase transition. Leadership change. Contractor handoff. In every case, critical context disappears unless it is deliberately transferred. That is why handoffs deserve their own discipline.

What Context Transfer Captures

- What happened
- What is still open
- What must carry forward
- What the next person or team needs to know immediately

A Simple Three-Part Template

CONTEXT TRANSFER
From: [Name]
To: [Name]
Date: [Date]

What Happened
[Three bullets max: key outcomes, decisions, issues]

Open Items

Issue	Owner	Next Step	By When
[Item]	[Name]	[Action]	[Date/Time]
Must-Know — for urgent risks, critical context, non-obvious constraints, pending decisions			

This structure works because it forces explicit transfer. It reduces the number of times someone says, "I assumed you knew."

It applies to:

- end-of-shift transitions
- vacation coverage
- project phase handoffs
- contractor-to-employee transitions
- team lead changeovers
- sprint-to-sprint continuity

Context transfer is not administrative overhead. It is continuity made visible.

The Power of SOS/EOS: Shift Reporting as a Communication Discipline

Start-of-shift and end-of-shift reporting may sound operational, but the discipline behind them applies far beyond shift work. The core problem they solve is universal: every handoff creates the possibility that something important will be lost.

In high-risk environments such as logistics, manufacturing, healthcare, field operations, and customer response teams, handoff failures have direct consequences. In office settings, poor transitions create rework, delay, confusion, and duplicated effort.

Escalation Path: Build It Before You Need It

Escalation without a predefined path is guesswork under pressure. When teams do not know what qualifies as an escalation, who owns it, how fast it should move, or how it should be communicated, they do one of two things: they escalate too late, or they escalate chaotically.

Both are expensive.

Issue Type	Level 1	Level 2	Level 3	Timeline
Missed task / deliverable	Responsible party + direct supervisor	Project Manager	Department Head	24-48 hours
Resource conflict	Team leads	Operations Manager	Site Director	Same day
Customer-impacting quality issue	Quality Supervisor	Quality Manager + Operations Manager	Site Director + Corporate QA	Immediate
Budget overrun >10%	Project Manager	Finance + Sponsor	Executive Sponsor	Within 48 hours
Safety incident	Direct supervisor	Safety Officer	Site Director	Immediate
Scope change request	Project Manager + Sponsor	Steering Committee	Executive Sponsor	Within one week

The Escalation Message Structure: Situation — Impact — Ask (SIA)

Every escalation should answer three questions:

1. **Situation** — What is happening?
2. **Impact** — What happens if this is not resolved?
3. **Ask** — What do you need from the person you are escalating to?

A simple escalation message sounds like this:

"I need to escalate an issue on the project. Here is the situation: [facts only]. The impact if unresolved is [schedule, cost, quality, safety, customer, or operational consequence]. What I need is [specific decision, support, or action] by [timeframe]."

That structure matters because vague escalation wastes time. Good escalation communicates risk without drama and urgency without confusion.

Escalate When:

- The issue has sat unresolved at your level for too long
- You have tried to solve it and lack authority or resources
- Leadership would be blindsided hearing it from someone else first
- You are unsure if it rises to escalation and need a judgment call

A useful phrase in that last case is:

"I want to give you an early heads-up on something. I'm not escalating for action yet, but I do want to know whether you want visibility now." That sentence creates transparency without panic.

A Full Communication Plan: Seven Sections

A complete communication plan does not need to be massive. In most cases, three pages is enough.

Section	Contents
1. Project / Team Overview	Purpose, scope, time period covered
2. Stakeholder Matrix	Who needs what information, preferred channel, primary contact
3. Communication Schedule	Type, audience, frequency, format, owner, channel
4. Escalation Path	Thresholds, issue categories, chain, response timing
5. Meeting Structure	Recurring meetings, purpose, participants, outputs
6. Document Management	Where information lives, naming rules, access control
7. Plan Maintenance	Who updates the plan, how often, and what triggers revision

That is enough structure to create clarity without creating a document no one will use.

Rules of engagement are not bureaucracy. They are the agreements that keep work from unraveling under pressure. They define what matters, who owns what, when to speak up, and how information moves before it becomes a problem. Without them, teams fall back on instinct, personality, hierarchy, and hope. That may work for a while, but it does not work reliably. **The healthiest teams are not the ones with the best intentions. They are the ones that make communication explicit before stress tests it.** If the Silent Spiral™ begins with assumption, then rules of engagement are one of the first ways to stop it.

Breaking the Spiral™ Stage 1 says: Test the Assumption. This chapter gave you the tools to replace assumption with structure — before the silence starts.

Key Takeaways

- A communication plan that gets used is built collaboratively, kept simple, assigned to real owners, **and maintained as a living document.**
- RACI prevents one of the most common causes of breakdown: **ambiguity about ownership.**
- Communication cadence **creates rhythm, which reduces status chasing and late surprises.**
- **Channel choice shapes meaning. The right message in the wrong channel can still fail.**
- **Handoffs need structure. Context does not transfer itself.**
- SOS/EOS reporting **is not for shift work alone. It is a universal continuity discipline.**
- **Escalation paths should be designed before pressure arrives, not improvised in the moment.**

Reflection Questions

1. **Think about the most recent communication failure you experienced or observed. What assumption was sitting underneath it?**
2. **Where are the handoff points in your current work?** What information is most likely to get lost there?
3. **What is one communication habit your team normalizes today that creates unnecessary friction?**
4. **Which issues in your environment are being discussed repeatedly because ownership has never been made explicit?**

Chapter 9: Say What You Mean — And Make Sure It Lands

The message you sent is not the message that was received.

Not as a metaphor. As a literal description of how communication works. The words leave your mouth or keyboard carrying your intention, your context, your assumptions, your history with the issue, and whatever urgency you believe is obvious.

By the time they arrive, they have been filtered through someone else's experience, assumptions, workload, distractions, priorities, history with you, and current emotional state.

What you meant and what they understood are almost never identical. The gap between those two things is where an astonishing number of professional failures live.

We treat communication as a sending problem. Choose better words. Tighten the email. Make the slide cleaner. Speak more directly. Use a better subject line. All of that matters. It is half the equation.

Communication is not complete when something has been said. It is complete when meaning has been received, understood, and, when necessary, able to travel back.

That is the part organizations underestimate. Most workplaces invest heavily in transmission. They teach people how to present, how to brief, how to report, how to write, how to speak with confidence, how to cascade messages downward. Far fewer invest in the receiving side: how to confirm understanding, how to listen for signal, how to catch what is not being said, how to structure meetings so real input surfaces, how to create conditions where concerns rise early instead of dying quietly where they were first noticed.

This chapter is about clarity — making the message land in the first place. The other half — listening as an operating capability — has its own chapter and gets the depth it deserves there.

If the previous chapter was about the rules of engagement, this chapter is about what happens after the words leave you. The Silent Spiral™ does not begin with catastrophe. It begins much earlier, in the ordinary gap between what was said and what was actually received.

At a Glance

Section	What You'll Get
Test for Understanding	Practical ways to confirm comprehension, not just acknowledgment
Feedback That Lands	Direct, useful feedback — five methods that work
SIA Framework	A simple structure for hard communication
Clarity Checklist	A final review for messages that need to land
Communication Translations	Twelve translations from vague to specific

The Test for Understanding

Most people think they have communicated once they have explained something clearly. That assumption causes more trouble than poor wording ever could.

Understanding is not proven by silence. It is not proven by a nod. It is not proven by “Got it,” “Makes sense,” or “I’m good.”

If you want to know whether something landed, you have to test for understanding.

That does not mean quizzing people. It means checking whether meaning was constructed on the other side.

Here are four methods that work:

- **Ask for playback:** “Can you tell me back what you heard, so I can make sure I explained it clearly?”
- **Ask an application question:** “If this comes up while I’m out, what would you do first?”

- **Watch behavior:** compare what was communicated with what happened.
- **Use structured written response:** "After reviewing this, what part do you think will be hardest to implement?"

The reason these methods work is simple: they move communication out of the world of assumed understanding and into the world of observable evidence.

I started using this more deliberately when I realized how often people were being labeled careless, inattentive, or resistant when the real problem was simpler. The message had not landed.

A better question than *What do I need to explain?* is *How will I know they understood it correctly?*

That one shift changes everything.

It forces you to build communication backward from what someone will need to do, decide, or carry forward, rather than forward from what feels clear in your own head. What feels obvious to you may not survive contact with another person's context. If you are not checking for understanding, you are guessing.

When This Happens, Do This

When This Happens	Do This
You have given a complex set of instructions	Ask them to walk you through the first few steps before they begin.
Someone seems confused but won't say so	Ask: "What part feels least clear right now?" — gives them permission to name it
A task comes back wrong	Don't re-explain the same way. Ask what they understood the ask to be. Then fill the gap.
You're about to send a critical email	Read it out loud. If you'd have to add "what I mean is..." in conversation, the email isn't clear enough.

When This Happens	Do This
Nobody responds to your email	The message felt like information, not an action request. Re-send with a specific ask and a deadline.

Feedback That Lands

Most people think of feedback as a speaking skill. It is at least as much a listening skill.

You cannot give useful feedback if you have not understood what happened. You cannot coach well if you are responding only to the version of the situation you constructed in your own head. You cannot correct behavior effectively if you are not listening carefully enough to distinguish between refusal, confusion, overload, lack of clarity, competing priorities, missing skill, and poor judgment.

Poor feedback often begins with poor listening. That is why useful feedback is not about directness. It is about attention.

Feedback that lands has two traits at the same time: it is clear enough to act on and grounded enough to be credible.

Why vague feedback fails:

- “You need to communicate better.”
- “You’re not paying attention to details.”
- “You need to be more proactive.”

Statements like these do almost nothing. They are not tied to observed reality. They leave the other person guessing what you mean, which behavior matters, and what success would look like instead.

Useful feedback sounds different:

- “In yesterday’s briefing, the vendor delay was left out, and that was the update leadership needed most.”
- “You’ve been quiet in the last few team meetings. That is not like you. Is something going on that I should know about?”

- "The issue log was not updated before handoff, and the incoming lead spent the first forty-five minutes rebuilding the picture. Help me understand what happened there."

All three examples begin from attention, not assumption. They also create space for information to come back. That matters because many feedback conversations fail for the same reason other communication fails: the speaker treats the act of saying it as the whole job. The job is to make the message clear enough to act on and safe enough to respond to honestly.

Kim Scott's *Radical Candor* framework: great feedback requires both care and directness, simultaneously.

The Four Quadrants:

	High Directness	**Low Directness**
High Care	Radical Candor — tell the truth because you want them to succeed	Ruinous Empathy — soften the message until it is useless
Low Care	Obnoxious Aggression — direct but lands as an attack	Manipulative Insincerity — vague, hedge-everything, avoids discomfort

In many industrial and government settings, feedback culture leans toward either silence (pointing things out feels dangerous) or bluntness that strips out the care. Neither works. Silence compounds problems. Bluntness without care creates defensiveness — and the behavior you wanted to change often gets worse.

Why the Feedback Sandwich Does Not Work — And What Does

There is a nearly universal piece of management advice that sounds reasonable in theory and fails almost every time in practice: the feedback sandwich. Say something positive. Insert the real message — the correction, the concern, the performance issue. Close with something positive again. Positive-negative-positive. Easy to remember. Easy to teach. Easy to detect. And that is the problem.

The feedback sandwich fails because everyone knows it is a sandwich. The person on the receiving end hears the first positive and immediately braces for what is coming.

The praise does not land because it is perceived — correctly — as a setup. The middle message, the actual feedback, gets diluted because it is cushioned on both sides. And the closing positive is processed as a consolation, not a genuine observation.

The entire structure teaches people to distrust your compliments. I stopped using it years ago. Here is what I use instead.

The Direct-and-Specific Method

The most effective feedback I have ever delivered — and the most effective feedback I have ever received — followed a pattern that has nothing to do with sandwiches. **It has three qualities:**

1. **It is specific.** Not “your communication needs work.” Instead: “In yesterday’s briefing, the status on the vendor delay wasn’t included, and that’s the one piece leadership was waiting for.”
2. **It is tied to impact.** Not “you need to be more careful.” Instead: “When the cycle count came back with three discrepancies that could have been caught on a second pass, it triggered a full recount that took four people two hours.”
3. **It is delivered privately, quickly, and without ambush.** The best feedback happens within 24 hours of the behavior, in a private setting, with a tone that communicates “I’m telling you this because I want you to succeed” — not “I’m telling you this because I need to document that I told you.”

That is it. No sandwich. No preamble. No performance. A clear statement of what happened, what it affected, and what needs to change — delivered by someone who the recipient believes genuinely cares about their success.

Five Feedback Methods That Actually Work

Here are the approaches I have seen produce real behavioral change — in warehouses, in offices, in government agencies, and in cross-functional teams where the stakes were high and the relationships were complicated.

Method 1: SIA — Situation, Impact, Ask

Before this becomes a feedback tool, it is a structure for any high-stakes communication. The Rules of Engagement chapter introduced SIA as the format for *escalation*; here, it does double duty as the most versatile feedback tool I know. **It forces you to lead with facts, not judgment.**

Example:

- **Situation:** "In the last two shift handoffs, the open issue log was not updated before the incoming team arrived."
- **Impact:** "The incoming supervisor spent the first forty-five minutes figuring out what was still open — and one issue that needed immediate attention got missed until midshift."
- **Ask:** "I need the log updated before you clock out. Can we set a 15-minute window at the end of every shift for that?"

No sandwich. No "you're great, but..." Here is what happened, here is what it cost, here is what I need.

Method 2: The Observation + Question

Sometimes the most powerful feedback is not a statement — it is a genuine question that invites the other person to reflect.

Example:

- "I noticed the client asked for the timeline twice during the call, and both times we moved to a different topic. What was going on there?"
- "The report went out without the variance analysis. Walk me through your process — I want to understand what happened so we can prevent it."

- "You've been quiet in the last few team meetings. That's not like you. Is something going on that I should know about?"

This works because it treats the other person as a competent adult who may have context you do not. It opens a conversation instead of delivering a verdict. And it often surfaces the real root cause — which is frequently not what you assumed.

Method 3: The Forward-Focused Redirect

Not all feedback needs to dwell on what went wrong. Sometimes the most effective approach is to name the gap and immediately move to what "right" looks like going forward.

Example:

- "The process we followed on that last project did not work — here is what I want to do differently this time, and here is what I need from you specifically."
- "That presentation did not land the way we needed it to. For the next one, let's build it around three key decisions we need from leadership, not a status walkthrough. I'll work through the first draft with you."

This method works especially well with high performers who already know they missed. They do not need you to explain what went wrong — they need to know what "better" looks like and that you are invested in getting there with them.

Method 4: The Pre-Commitment Conversation

The best feedback often happens *before* the behavior, not after. When you know someone is about to face a high-stakes situation, set the standard in advance.

Example:

- "Tomorrow's meeting with the client is high-stakes. Here is what I need from you: own the quality section, have the data ready, and if a question comes up that you can't answer, say 'let me get back to you on that' — don't guess. Can you commit to that?"

If the behavior does not match, the feedback conversation is simple: "We agreed on X. What happened?" That is not a sandwich. That is accountability based on a mutual commitment.

Method 5: Delivering Genuinely Bad News

Sometimes the message is not "here's how to improve." Sometimes it is "this isn't working," or "this position is being eliminated," or "you didn't get the role." These are the hardest communications, and no framework makes them painless. There is a structure that makes them honest, humane, and clear.

The structure:

1. **State the decision.** Don't bury it. Don't build up to it. Say it in the first two sentences. "I need to let you know that we've made the decision to restructure the team, and your current role is being eliminated." The person needs to hear the headline before they can process anything else.
2. **Give the reason — briefly and honestly.** Not corporate euphemisms. Not "strategic realignment." The actual reason, stated plainly. "The volume shift means we need fewer quality roles and more operations capacity. This isn't about your performance."
3. **Acknowledge the impact.** "I know this is not what you wanted to hear, and I understand what this means for you." One sentence. Genuine. Not performative.
4. **Provide what comes next.** Logistics, timeline, support available. Don't make them ask. "Here's what happens from here: [specific next steps, dates, resources]."
5. **Create space for their response.** After you have delivered the message, stop talking. Let them react. Don't fill the silence with more words. They need a moment to process, and trying to make them feel better in that moment is about your discomfort, not theirs.

Delivering Bad News	Do This	Don't Do This
Timing	As soon as the decision is final — delays erode trust and fuel rumors	Wait until Friday afternoon "so they have the weekend to process" — that's for your convenience, not theirs
Setting	Private, in person (or video if remote), with enough time for a real conversation	In a group, via email, or in a 15-minute slot between other meetings
Opening	State the decision clearly in the first 30 seconds	Build up slowly, hedge, use phrases like "I wanted to chat about something"
Honesty	Give the real reason. People can handle hard truths better than they can handle feeling lied to	Use corporate language that obscures the actual reason — they will decode it anyway and resent the packaging
Empathy	Acknowledge the impact on them specifically. One genuine sentence beats five minutes of platitudes	Say "I know how you feel" (you probably don't) or "this is harder for me than it is for you" (it isn't)
Space	After delivering the message, pause. Let them respond. Silence is appropriate here	Fill the silence with explanations, justifications, or attempts to fix their emotions
Follow-through	Provide specific next steps, dates, and who they can contact	Leave them with vague promises of "we'll figure it out"

What All Five Methods Have in Common

None of them require you to manufacture a compliment you do not mean. None of them ask you to disguise the message. None of them treat the other person as someone who cannot handle direct communication.

What they do require:

- **Specificity.** Vague feedback is useless feedback. “You need to communicate better” teaches nothing. “In yesterday’s briefing, the project risk section was missing, and that’s what the steering committee needed to make their decision” teaches everything.
- **Timeliness.** Feedback delivered three weeks after the behavior is a performance review, not a development conversation. The closer to the event, the more useful it is.
- **Privacy.** Never deliver corrective feedback in front of others. This is non-negotiable. Public correction does not build accountability — it builds resentment, fear, and a team that learns to hide mistakes.
- **Genuine investment in the person.** If you do not actually care whether this person succeeds, they will know. You cannot fake care, and you cannot deliver effective feedback without it. If you find yourself not caring, that is a signal about the relationship that needs to be addressed — not papered over with a framework.

The goal of feedback is not to make people feel bad. It is not to document that you said something. It is to change behavior in a way that makes the person, the team, and the work better. Every method above serves that goal. The sandwich does not.

The Clarity Checklist: Before You Send It

This is your pre-send review for any communication that matters – email, report, message, or presentation slide.

10-POINT CLARITY CHECKLIST

1. **THE ASK IS EXPLICIT.** ☐
   What do I need from the recipient?
   (Decision / Action / Information / Awareness)
2. **THE DEADLINE IS STATED.** ☐
   If action is needed, by when?
3. **THE OWNER IS NAMED.** ☐
   Is it clear who needs to act – not just who's on the distribution?
4. **THE CONTEXT IS SUFFICIENT.** ☐
   Does the recipient have enough background to act on this without asking me for more?
5. **THE "SO WHAT" IS CLEAR.** ☐
   Have I explained why this matters – the impact if it doesn't happen?
6. **THE TONE IS APPROPRIATE FOR THE CHANNEL.** ☐
   Is this an email that should be a phone call? A chat message that needs to be a meeting?
7. **I'VE CUT THE HEDGE WORDS.** ☐
   "Kind of," "sort of," "might want to," "it seems like" – remove them. Say it directly.
8. **THE SUBJECT LINE OR OPENING TELLS THE READER WHAT THEY'RE READING.** ☐
   No burying the lead.
9. **IT'S AS SHORT AS IT CAN BE.** ☐
   Every sentence that doesn't earn its place makes the message harder to act on.
10. **I'VE READ IT FROM THE RECIPIENT'S PERSPECTIVE.** ☐
    Does someone unfamiliar with my context understand what I need from them?

ONE LAST CHECK:
If you're not 100% clear on all 10 points, **your recipient won't be either.**

Clarity is respect.
Make it easy for people to act.

Escalation — when to do it, how to structure the message, and to whom — is covered throughout the book. The *Rules of Engagement* chapter sets up the structural piece — who gets escalated to and when. *Lead Through Communication* is where the act of escalating, including escalating upward when it is professionally costly, gets handled.

Instead of This, Try: 12 Communication Translations

Instead of...	Try...
"Does anyone have questions?"	"What questions do you have?"
"Your communication has been a problem."	"In the last two project updates, the vendor delivery status was missing — and that's what leadership needs to make their decision."
"You're not a detail-oriented person."	"This report had three errors caught by the client before us. I need you to build a check step before submitting."
"You were late to the meeting and that was disrespectful."	"You were fifteen minutes late — I want to understand what happened, because these meetings matter for the team."
"Great job, everyone."	"The way you handled that client pushback on the timeline last week was exactly what the situation needed — Marcus, specifically, the way you reframed the ask was sharp."
"Let me know if you need anything."	"I'm going to check in with you on Thursday. If you hit a wall before then, come find me."
"We need to do better."	"The defect rate this week was 4.2% against our 2% target. Here's what I think is driving it, and here's what I need from each of you this week."
"Can you handle this?"	"I need you to own this deliverable. The due date is Friday at noon. What do you need from me to make that happen?"
"I thought you understood what I needed."	"Let me be clearer about what I was expecting — here's what the finished product should look like."

Instead of...	Try...
"That's not what we discussed."	"I want to make sure we're aligned — here's what I captured as the agreement. Where does your understanding differ?"
"I'll try to get to that."	"I'll have it to you by [specific date and time] or I'll let you know by [earlier date] if something's come up."
"We should probably loop in [person]."	"I'm adding [person] to this conversation because they own [specific piece] and their input is needed before we decide."

Key Takeaways

- **Communication is complete only when understanding is confirmed**, not when the message has been sent. Test for understanding actively and build feedback loops into all critical communications.
- **Clarity is a courtesy.** Vague messages create rework. The time you invest in making your communication precise is time you save for everyone on the receiving end.
- **Effective feedback** is specific to behavior (not character), delivered soon, and combines directness with genuine care for the person's success. It lands better when it begins with attention, not assumption.
- **The SIA framework** — Situation, Impact, Ask — is the most versatile tool for structuring any critical professional communication. Lead with facts, name the impact, make the ask specific.
- The quality of communication is measured not just by what was said, but by what was truly received and **what was able to come back**.

Reflection Questions

1. **Think about the last time you believed you had communicated clearly, and the result proved otherwise. Where did the message break: expression, understanding, or follow-through?**

2. **Where in your team do messages get sent without a built-in check for understanding?** What is one place you could add that check this week?

3. **What is one piece of feedback you have been holding because you did not know how to deliver it cleanly?** Which of the five methods would fit it best?

Closing

The strongest communicators are not the people who speak the most, write the longest, or sound the smartest. They are the people who **understand that communication is not finished when it leaves them. It is finished when it lands. That requires more than clean wording.**

It requires attention, confirmation, structure, and the humility to accept that meaning is never guaranteed because your intention felt clear in your own head. The next chapter takes up the other half of that discipline — listening — and treats it as the operating capability it is.

Chapter 10: The Other Half — Listening

Most research on workplace communication focuses almost entirely on how people **send messages.** We have frameworks for writing emails, techniques for delivering feedback, scripts for difficult conversations, and entire seminars dedicated to public speaking. What we barely talk about — in training rooms, in leadership development programs, in books like this one — is the other half of the equation.

Listening.

Not hearing. Listening. There is a difference, and it matters more than most organizations are willing to admit.

Hearing is passive. Listening is active. *Hearing is physiological. Listening is cognitive.* Hearing means sound reached you. Listening means **meaning did.**

That distinction becomes expensive the moment teams start mistaking presence for comprehension.

The manager who nods and moves on without a single follow-up question may look engaged from across the room. The supervisor who says, "I hear you," and then makes the same decision they walked in with may believe they have listened. The team lead already rehearsing their response while the other person is still talking may not realize they are no longer receiving anything.

From the outside, hearing and listening can look similar. The difference reveals itself later, in the quality of the response, the quality of the decision, and the quality of what happens next.

At a Glance

Section	What You'll Get
Hearing vs. Listening	Why the difference matters more than most teams admit
Listening Failure at Scale	How organizations become good at talking and bad at receiving

Section	What You'll Get
Four Levels of Listening	A framework for recognizing shallow versus real listening
Five Tests for True Listening	Practical diagnostics that catch listening breakdowns in the room
Listening in Groups	Why meetings suppress signal and how to surface it
Cultural Silence	How not listening becomes part of the environment
Listening as a Leadership Practice	Why this is leadership, not a soft skill

Hearing Is Not the Same as Listening

Your ears are always on. As you read this, your auditory system is passively registering ambient sound — the hum of an HVAC unit, a forklift backing up somewhere on the floor, a conversation two desks over, the notification chime from someone's phone in the break room. You are hearing all of it. You are processing almost none of it.

Hearing is physiological. It is the mechanical process of sound waves entering the ear canal, vibrating the eardrum, and triggering nerve signals to the brain. It requires no effort, no intention, and no engagement. You cannot turn it off without physical intervention. A brick wall hears the safety announcement on the PA system in the same way an inattentive supervisor does — the sound waves reach it, and nothing meaningful happens on the other end.

Listening is something else entirely. Listening is a *cognitive and intentional act*. It requires you to process, interpret, and assign meaning to what you are hearing. It requires you to track not the words alone but the context, the tone, the hesitation, the emphasis — and to hold all of that information long enough to formulate a meaningful response. Listening is active work. Like most active work, it can be done well or badly, and it can be avoided altogether in favor of something that looks similar from the outside.

That is the problem. **In most workplaces, the majority of people in most meetings are *hearing*, not *listening* — and nobody can tell the difference until something goes wrong.**

- The person with their phone angled slightly below the table edge? **Hearing.**
- The manager who nods at everything but asks no follow-up questions? **Hearing.**
- The team lead who talks over the quiet team member for the third time this week? **Hearing.**
- The executive who says, "I hear you" and then makes the same decision they walked in with? **Definitely hearing.**

Compare that with what listening looks like in practice:

Hearing	Listening
Passive; requires no conscious effort	Active; requires deliberate focus and engagement
Registers words and sounds	Processes meaning, tone, and context
Allows for parallel thinking ("What's for lunch?")	Requires cognitive presence — single-threaded attention
Reacts to what was said	Responds to what was meant
Waits for a turn to speak	Waits to understand before speaking
Misses subtext, hesitation, and emotional cues	Picks up on what is not being said
Produces generic acknowledgment ("Got it," "Sounds good")	Produces specific, relevant follow-up or paraphrase
Ends when the speaker stops talking	Continues — reflecting, connecting, following up
Can be faked without detection	Reveals itself through the quality of response
Focused on self (what do I need to say next?)	Focused on the speaker (what do they need to communicate?)

When someone brings a process problem to a supervisor who is only hearing, that problem goes into a conversational void. The supervisor nods, says something non-committal, and moves on to the next thing. The person with the problem walks away unsure whether they were understood. They file it under "not worth bringing up again." And the problem sits untouched — waiting for the day it becomes a defect, a safety incident, or a failed audit.

That is the Silent Spiral™ at work, Stage 2 (Silence) in action — not because the person chose to stay quiet, but because the *organization's listening infrastructure* gave them nowhere to go.

In the Room: Level 1 Listening in a Status Meeting

The update has been raised twice before. Watch what happens the third time.

Maria: *"The vendor lead time is still running two weeks longer than expected. If we don't adjust the schedule, we'll miss the installation window."*

Her manager, Rob, is typing. He nods. *"Mm-hmm. Okay. Anyone else have updates?"*

Dave: *"Procurement is good."*

Rob: *"Great. Same time next week."*

After the meeting, Maria stops by Rob's desk.

Maria: *"Did you catch what I said about the lead time?"*

Rob: *"Yeah, the vendor thing. I'll loop in with you."*

He doesn't. The installation window is missed. In the post-mortem, three people say they raised the risk. None of them are wrong.

The problem was not that Maria did not communicate. The problem is that Rob was hearing, not listening — and the meeting was not designed to tell the difference.

Why Organizations Are Designed for Talking, Not Listening

Take a look at almost any formal organizational structure and you will see the same thing: a beautifully engineered machine for transmitting information downward, and almost nothing built to receive it upward.

Consider the standard communication mechanisms in most operations environments:

- **Briefings where one person talks and everyone else is expected to absorb.** One supervisor talks, incoming shift listens (or hears).
- **Performance reviews led almost entirely by the manager.** Manager talks, employee responds to prompts.
- **All-hands presentations designed for distribution, *not exchange*.** Workforce informed, leadership has spoken.
- **Dashboards that travel upward as numbers and downward as talking points.**
- **Meetings where questions are** *technically allowed* but **structurally crowded out.**

At each level, the dominant communication mode is *transmission*. There is a sender with information. There is a receiver who is expected to absorb it. The feedback mechanism — if it exists at all — is usually a survey administered once a year, a suggestion box that has not been emptied since the last administration change, or an open-door policy that everyone knows carries invisible risks if you actually use it.

This is not a conspiracy. It is the natural byproduct of how organizations evolved.

- **Efficiency favors top-down communication because it is fast, consistent, and scalable.**
- **Listening is slow.** It is asymmetrical — one person's three-minute concern might take ten minutes to properly unpack and respond to.

Listening is also uncomfortable because it sometimes surfaces things that organizations would rather not know:

- That the new procedure creates a bottleneck nobody anticipated
- That the rescheduled shift is quietly destroying morale

- That the person running the receiving dock has been manually correcting a recurring system error for six months because nobody fixed it the first time they reported it

The result is an organization structurally optimized for broadcasting and structurally blind to the signals.

Here is where this connects to the Silent Spiral™. The model identifies Stage 2 as Silence — the point where someone stops communicating a concern because their prior attempts were not received. Most people assume that silence is a *choice* — that the employee decided to stop sharing. In the majority of cases I have encountered across industries, silence is not a choice. It is a *rational response* to a structural reality. It can be misread as *disengagement, apathy, or lack of courage*.

Sometimes it is those things. More often, it is a rational response to repeated evidence that the signal has nowhere to go. When people do not believe their input will be caught, processed, or acted on, they stop spending effort to generate it. That is not a personality problem. That is a system problem. It matters because the people closest to the work usually know first where the failures are. They know which steps are being skipped, which vendor keeps creating issues, which workaround has become routine, which equipment is about to fail, which deadline is already unrealistic, and which assumption leadership is making that does not survive contact with the floor.

The question is never whether the signal exists. The question is whether anyone has built a reliable way to receive it.

The Four Levels of Listening

Not all listening is equal. Over the course of my career — in warehouses, distribution centers, clinical environments, and government facilities — I have watched people communicate at radically different levels of engagement, and the outcomes varied accordingly. Here is a framework that captures those distinctions.

Level 1: Cosmetic Listening

This is the performance of listening without any actual listening happening. The cosmetic listener maintains eye contact (intermittently), nods at appropriate intervals, and occasionally produces affirmative sounds — "Mm-hmm," "Right," "Okay" — to signal engagement. Their phone is under the table, or they are composing their response in their head, or they are watching the clock, or they are thinking about a completely different problem. *If you asked them to repeat what was said, they could get through maybe the last sentence.* They will not remember this conversation in two hours.

Cosmetic listening is not just an individual failure. **When it becomes the norm in a team or organization, it creates a culture where people learn to give short answers and expect nothing back.** Why develop a complete thought if nobody is going to catch it?

Level 2: Selective Listening

The selective listener is genuinely engaged — but only with the parts of the message that align with what they already think. They are listening through a filter. If you say something that confirms their existing view, it registers and strengthens. If you say something that contradicts their existing view, it tends to get processed as noise, misheard, or reframed as "that's not what you meant."

Selective listening is especially dangerous in decision-making contexts because it feels like listening. The selective listener believes they are being attentive. They are — they are attentive to the parts of reality that match their mental model and inattentive to the parts that don't.

This is how bad decisions survive every warning sign: someone was listening, just not to the right signals.

Level 3: Active Listening

This is what most communication training programs mean when they say "listen better." *Active listening is deliberate, engaged, and structured. The active listener asks clarifying questions. They paraphrase back. They take notes. They withhold judgment until they have a complete picture. When the conversation ends, they have genuinely processed the content.*

Active listening is significantly better than Levels 1 and 2**, and most organizations would be dramatically better off if their managers consistently operated here. *It is not the ceiling.***

Level 4: Empathic Listening

Empathic listening is active listening plus context. The empathic listener is not only tracking what is being said — they are tracking what is *not* being said. They notice the pause before the answer. They see the body language that does not match the words. They pick up on the associate who has not spoken in 30 minutes despite clearly having an opinion.

Empathic listening requires the listener to hold multiple channels simultaneously: the content, the tone, the context of the relationship, the broader team dynamics, and the organizational pressures shaping what the speaker is or is not willing to say aloud. It is the hardest form of listening and the most valuable — particularly in high-stakes environments where people have learned to self-censor.

How to Test for True Listening

Most people think they are listening. Most teams believe they have open communication. They have sat through the training. They nodded at the slides. They can define "active listening" if you ask them nicely. Then they walk back to their desks and nothing changes.

Here is what nobody says out loud: there is a gap between *hearing words* and *actually processing, retaining, and acting on information.* That gap is where misunderstandings are born. It is where projects quietly go sideways. It is where workarounds get built in silence because someone did not want to admit they had no idea what you said.

"Active listening" has become a workplace buzzword — something people perform during one-on-ones and then abandon the moment the meeting ends. The head nod. The "totally." The "got it." None of that tells you whether a message landed.

What you need are tests. Not theory. Not more training. Concrete, practical diagnostics you can use in real time to find out whether genuine listening is happening — and to catch the breakdown before it turns into a crisis.

The "Tell Me Back" Test

This is the most powerful listening verification tool available to you, and it costs nothing. **After sharing important information, don't ask *"Do you understand?"* That question is useless.** Everyone says yes. Nobody wants to look confused, uninformed, or slow — so they say yes even when they have no idea what happened.

Instead, ask: **"Tell me back what you just heard."** Not "what I said." What *you heard.* That distinction matters. You are not quizzing them on your words — you are asking them to reflect back their understanding. What comes back tells you everything.

- If it matches what you sent, great. Communication happened.
- If it does not, you have just found the breakdown before it becomes a workaround.

Example: The Perfect Tell-Back

Manager: "The client moved the final review to the 14th, not the 21st. That means our internal draft deadline is now the 10th. Can you tell me back what you heard?"

Team member: "Client review is the 14th instead of the 21st, so our draft is due the 10th — a week earlier than we planned."

That is a clean receive. The key detail (internal deadline) came back intact. Move on.

Example: The Tell-Back That Reveals a Misunderstanding

Manager: "The client moved the final review to the 14th, not the 21st. That means our internal draft deadline is now the 10th. Tell me back what you heard."

Team member: "Okay, so the client review is on the 14th. I'll adjust my calendar for the 21st."

The person heard the date but missed the implication. They are still planning to deliver on the 21st. The communication failed — but you caught it now, not on the 11th when the draft is missing.

Example: The Tell-Back That Reveals Someone Was Not Listening at All

Manager: "The client moved the final review to the 14th, not the 21st. That means our internal draft deadline is now the 10th. Tell me back what you heard."

Team member: "...Wait, sorry — can you repeat the second part?"

That is the best-case scenario when someone was not tracking: they admit it immediately rather than faking comprehension. The tell-back created a safe, expected mechanism for saying *I missed that.* No shame, no performance — a chance to re-send the signal cleanly.

STOP AND CHECK: Make "Tell Me Back" a Team Norm, Not a One-Time Trick

The first time you ask someone to tell you back what they heard, it can feel like an interrogation. That is a training issue, not a technique issue. The fix is consistency.

When "tell me back" becomes standard practice — something you use in both directions, something you invite your own manager to use on *you* — it stops feeling like a test and starts feeling like a team habit. Say it out loud: *"We use tell-backs around here because we'd rather catch misunderstandings in the room than chase them down later."* Then model it by asking your peers to use it with you. Once it is mutual, it is culture.

The 48-Hour Test

Real listening produces action. Not immediately — people have other things on their plate — but within a reasonable window, something should shift.

The rule of thumb: if someone genuinely heard you, something changes within 48 hours. A follow-up email. A question. A task started. A behavior that looks slightly different than it did yesterday.

If nothing changes in 48 hours — no acknowledgment, no action, no follow-up — the message did not register. They were in the room. They may have been looking at you. But they were not listening.

This is a diagnostic, not an accusation. You are not trying to catch someone slacking. You are identifying a signal failure. The question is not *why didn't they act?* — it is *did the message actually land?*

Run this test after any communication where action is expected. When the 48-hour window closes and nothing has moved, that is your signal to re-send — and to reconsider your delivery. Did you make the action clear? Did you give them a timeframe? Did you state what success looks like?

The 48-hour test holds both parties accountable: the listener for processing and responding, and the sender for being clear enough that a response was obviously warranted.

The Question Test

People who are truly listening generate questions. Not performative ones — not *"Great presentation, really insightful!"* — but substantive questions that could only come from someone who was actively processing.

- *"You mentioned the timeline shifted — does that affect the vendor deliverable?"*
- *"When you said we're moving away from the old process, does that apply to the projects already in flight?"*
- *"That's a significant change. Who else needs to know about this?"*

Those questions show that the person was not hearing — they were connecting the new information to things they already know, testing it against context, looking for gaps. That is listening.

If nobody asks questions after a briefing, you have two possible explanations: either you were so perfectly clear that nothing was ambiguous (unlikely, but it happens), or **nobody was processing deeply enough to generate genuine questions.**

Silence after a presentation is not respect. It is disengagement, or fear of looking uninformed, or a team that has learned their questions do not lead anywhere productive. If you are consistently getting no questions, that is the thing worth investigating — not because your team is disrespectful, but because something in the environment is suppressing the most natural indicator of real attention.

The Silence Test

1. After delivering important information, stop talking.
2. Count to five in your head.
3. The silence will be uncomfortable. That discomfort is productive. It creates space for people to process, react, formulate a response, or admit confusion. You are not waiting for a standing ovation — you are creating the conditions where a real response can emerge.

Most communicators fill their own silence. They deliver a message and then immediately start explaining it, qualifying it, cushioning it, checking in nervously. **Every word you add after the message is delivered tells the room that their response is not required.** You are signaling that you will handle it yourself.

Practice this: make the statement, then stop. Fully stop. Eyes up, mouth closed, comfortable with the pause. Let someone else fill it. What fills the silence — a question, a pushback, a clarification, a long beat of nothing — tells you exactly where you stand.

If five seconds of silence causes visible distress in your meetings, that is worth noting. Teams that cannot tolerate a pause are often teams that have been trained to react quickly rather than think carefully. Slow the room down. Make space. It pays off.

The Contradiction Test

This one requires care — it is one of the most revealing.

Deliberately introduce a small inconsistency or change from what was previously communicated. Not to trick anyone. Not to embarrass anyone. *To find out if anyone is reading and listening closely enough to catch it.*

- Say the deadline was the 15th. Mention the 22nd in passing during a meeting. **See if anyone flags it.**
- Say the process requires three approvals. In a document update, reference two. **See if a reviewer notices.**
- **If people catch the inconsistency, you have an engaged audience.**
- **If nobody catches it, the earlier communication was not received carefully enough to serve as a baseline** — and that tells you something important about how your team is processing information day to day.

The contradiction test is a team attention diagnostic. It is not a gotcha, and it should never be used to punish or embarrass.

If someone catches it, acknowledge it immediately:

- *"You're right — good catch, that was a test of whether we're all working from the same information. We are."*

If nobody catches it, treat the finding with curiosity, not judgment:

- *"What does this tell us about how we receive information, and what do we need to change?"*

The Tests at a Glance

Test	How to Use It	What It Reveals	Red Flag Signal
Tell Me Back	After sharing key information, ask "Tell me back what you just heard."	Whether the content was received accurately and completely	Silence, deflection, or a return summary that's missing the point
48-Hour Test	After communicating an expected action, observe what changes in the next two days	Whether the message translated into behavior	No follow-up, no questions, no visible change in approach
Question Test	After a briefing, notice what questions (if any) people ask	Whether the audience was processing deeply enough to engage	Zero questions — especially from people who typically have them
Silence Test	After making a key statement, stop talking and count five seconds	Whether the room is waiting for you to lead or able to respond	You fill your own silence every time; others show visible discomfort at any pause
Contradiction Test	Introduce a small, deliberate inconsistency and observe whether it gets flagged	Whether your team is reading and listening with enough attention to hold you accountable	Nobody notices; the error propagates without comment

STOP AND CHECK: Testing for Listening vs. Testing for Compliance

These tests are not loyalty checks. They are not performance reviews in disguise. The goal is shared understanding — not obedience.

There is a meaningful difference between *did they absorb and internalize the information?* and *will they do what I said?* These tests measure the first question, not the second. Someone who tells back your message perfectly, asks a sharp follow-up question, and then disagrees with your decision is a better listener than someone who nods, says nothing, and complies silently while building a workaround at their desk.

If you start using these tests as accountability traps — keeping score, catching people out, leveraging the results in performance conversations — you will train your team to game them. They will tell back exactly what you want to hear, ask a performative question, and stay quiet for the rest of the meeting. You will have the appearance of listening without the substance.

Use these diagnostics the way you would use a thermometer: to take a reading, find the problem, and address it — not to assign blame.

The Connection to the Silent Spiral™

These five tests share a common purpose: **they break the assumption that communication happened just because words were exchanged.**

That assumption is Stage 1 of the Silent Spiral™. Someone sends a message. The receiver nods. Both parties walk away believing they are aligned. Neither confirms. Neither asks. Neither follows up.

And then the gap quietly widens.

The Silent Spiral™ starts not with conflict, **but with the absence of verification.** Someone assumed understanding had occurred. Someone else assumed they understood when they did not. The words were transmitted. The meaning was not. And because nobody built in a mechanism to check — no tell-back, no follow-up, no question, no silence — the assumption calcified into a shared fiction: *we're on the same page.*

These tests are early detection systems. They interrupt Stage 1 before it becomes Stage 2, Stage 3, or a full-blown communication breakdown that takes weeks to unravel.

You do not need all five tests in every conversation. You need the habit of checking. The discipline of not assuming. The willingness to say — regularly, without defensiveness — *"Tell me back what you just heard."*

That single question is the fastest path to finding out whether your communication is actually working.

When This Happens...	Do This
Someone raises the same concern for the second or third time	Treat it as a signal of urgency, not repetition. Ask: "This keeps coming up — what would it take to actually close this out?"
A team meeting produces no pushback or alternative ideas	You are not seeing healthy alignment. You are seeing cosmetic listening. Add structure: round-robin, written input, or a cold-call on the quietest person in the room.
Someone says "I already mentioned this"	Stop. Acknowledge it specifically. Find out where it went and why it did not land. Then fix the process, not the person.
A decision gets reversed because the front line knew something leadership did not	Run a listening post-mortem. Don't just fix the decision — figure out where the information was and why it did not travel.
You notice someone has stopped contributing in meetings	They did not become less engaged by accident. Something killed the signal. Find out what, and fix the underlying cause.
A concern gets logged but never followed up	The person who raised it is watching. Lack of follow-up teaches the whole team that raising concerns produces nothing. Close the loop — even if the answer is "we looked into it and here's why we're not changing it."
You're in a high-stakes conversation and you realize you missed something earlier	Say so. "I want to back up — I don't think I fully caught what you were describing. Can you walk me through that again?" This takes two minutes. Pretending you caught it costs far more.

Small Group Communication Dynamics

It is easy to assume small groups make better decisions than individuals. More people, more perspectives, more information. **Research on group decision-making tells a messier story. Small groups have access to more information than any single person in the room — they are notoriously bad at using it.** Group conversation has a shape, and that shape quietly suppresses some voices while amplifying others.

Three Dynamics Cause Most of the Damage

The Dominant Voice Problem. In most small groups, **one or two people take up more airtime than everyone else.** Not always because they have the best ideas. Often, they are the most comfortable speaking in a group, and they fill the silence others leave behind. The more an idea gets discussed, the more weight it takes on — not because it is better, but because it had more room to develop.

The Quiet Expert Problem. Every operation has at least one person who knows the work better than almost anyone else and rarely speaks in meetings. They know where handoffs fail, which workaround is holding the shift together, and which recurring issue nobody upstream has named yet. They have learned to wait. They have been talked over. They have watched the meeting move on before they finished a sentence. They have seen the first idea become the plan before their insight could enter the room. Unless someone asks them directly, they walk out carrying information the team needed.

The "First Idea Wins" Bias. Small groups tend to anchor on the first workable idea raised. Once that idea is on the table, discussion shifts from *"What are our options?"* to *"Can we make this one work?"* That shift quietly shapes the outcome. **The first speaker sets the boundaries of the conversation, and everyone else ends up refining within those boundaries instead of generating alternatives.**

The Fix Is Structure

All three dynamics share the same solution: structure. The goal is not to silence confident voices. It is to make sure **confidence is not mistaken for correctness, speed is not mistaken for clarity, and silence is not mistaken for agreement.** Better group listening does not happen because everyone has good intentions. It happens because the meeting is designed to make it possible.

Structures That Improve Group Listening

- **Round-Robin Check-Ins.** Open every substantive discussion with a brief round-robin. **Each person gets sixty to ninety seconds to share**

their initial take — no interruptions, no rebuttals, no cross-talk. A full lap around the table. This single practice surfaces quiet-expert input better than almost anything else because it makes participation structural, not optional. Everyone's perspective is expected.

- **The Two-Minute Think-Before-We-Talk Rule.** Before opening the floor on any significant question, give the group two minutes of silent reflection. **It feels awkward the first time. Do it anyway.** The pause breaks the habit of reacting to whoever speaks first and gives quieter thinkers time to organize their ideas. What surfaces after two minutes of quiet is almost always stronger than what gets tossed out in the first ten seconds.

- **Written Input Before Verbal Discussion.** For decisions that matter, **ask each participant to write down their initial position before anyone speaks.** A sticky note, a shared document, or a one-line chat response will do. Written input reduces anchoring because each person commits to a view before the first voice shapes the room — and it creates a record of where people started, which is useful when you need to understand how a decision got made.

- **The Facilitator as Listening Architect.** The facilitator's most important job is not keeping the meeting on time. **It is listening on behalf of the group.** Facilitators track who has and has not spoken, notices when someone is trying to enter the conversation but not getting the floor, **catches the comment that deserved more development**, and **creates room for the quietest voices to contribute.** That is not passive work. **It is active, intentional, and structural.** The facilitator's real job is to make sure the meeting surfaces the best thinking available — and that requires active listening as a leadership function.

THE LISTENING AUDIT

Before you can fix your team's listening culture, you need an honest read on where it actually stands. This self-assessment is designed to be done twice: once as an individual reflection on your own listening habits, and once as a team exercise where everyone rates the team's collective listening culture and you compare the results.

HOW TO SCORE

Score each statement 1–5 based on how often it is true.

1	2	3	4	5
ALMOST NEVER	RARELY	SOMETIMES	OFTEN	ALMOST ALWAYS
Rarely or not at all true	Happens occasionally	About half the time	Most of the time	Consistently or nearly every time

PART 1: INDIVIDUAL LISTENING HABITS

#	Statement	1 (Almost Never)	2	3	4	5 (Almost Always)
1	When someone is explaining a problem to me, I wait until they are completely finished before I begin formulating my response.	○	○	○	○	○
2	When I disagree with what someone is saying, I can accurately summarize their position before I offer my counterargument.	○	○	○	○	○
3	When I am in a meeting, my phone is put away and I am not working on other tasks.	○	○	○	○	○
4	After a significant conversation, I can recall the key points the other person made without referencing notes.	○	○	○	○	○
5	I ask follow-up questions that address the specific content of what was just said, rather than redirecting to my own perspective.	○	○	○	○	○

PART 2: TEAM LISTENING CULTURE

#	Statement	1 (Almost Never)	2	3	4	5 (Almost Always)
1	Team members in our meetings regularly paraphrase or check their understanding of what others have said.	○	○	○	○	○
2	Quieter or more junior team members have genuine opportunities to contribute in group discussions, not just token invitations.	○	○	○	○	○
3	When a concern is raised by someone on our team, there is a clear follow-up – either action taken or an explanation of why action wasn't taken.	○	○	○	○	○
4	Our meeting structures give people time to think before responding, rather than rewarding whoever speaks first.	○	○	○	○	○
5	People on our team feel confident that raising a concern will result in it being heard – not dismissed, redirected, or used against them.	○	○	○	○	○

THE LISTENING AUDIT

HERE'S WHAT YOUR SCORE MEANS

SCORE RANGE	INTERPRETATION	WHAT THIS MEANS FOR YOU
41–50 STRONG LISTENING CULTURE	**Strong listening culture.** The gaps you have are likely situational. Focus on sustaining what works and identifying edge cases.	Keep reinforcing the behaviors and systems that work. Look for edge cases: specific people, topics, or situations where listening still breaks down. Share what's working so others can learn from it.
31–40 FUNCTIONAL BUT INCONSISTENT	Functional but inconsistent. Listening happens when it's convenient; the structure isn't there to ensure it when it's uncomfortable.	Build structure and habits that make listening the default, not the exception. Focus on consistency across meetings, teams, and leadership levels. Make listening part of how work gets done — not an extra step.
21–30 SIGNIFICANT GAPS	Significant gaps. People may feel unheard more often than you realize. Begin with structural fixes before addressing individual behavior.	Strengthen meeting structures and accountability loops. Actively create space for dissenting voices and quieter team members. Rebuild trust by showing people their input leads to real outcomes.
10–20 LISTENING HAS LIKELY BROKEN DOWN AS A CULTURAL NORM	Listening has likely broken down as a cultural norm. The Silent Spiral™ is almost certainly active. This needs leadership attention now.	This is a culture issue — it won't fix itself. Start with leadership: model the behavior and change the systems. Prioritize listening as a business critical capability.

REMEMBER:
This audit isn't about perfection — it's about awareness. Awareness drives change. Change builds a culture where people feel heard, ideas surface, and teams perform.

Revisit this audit regularly to track progress and keep listening a priority.

When Not Listening Becomes the Culture

Listening failure does not arrive dramatically. It accumulates.

Someone raises a concern and gets a nod with no follow-up. Then it happens again. Someone else watches that pattern and learns from it.

Over time, people recalibrate what is worth saying, when it is worth saying, and whether speaking up is worth the effort at all.

Here is how the pattern unfolds:

- **Stage 1: Individual silence.** Someone raises a concern and gets a non-response — not a "no," a nod and a pivot. They bring it up again a week later in a different way. Same result. They try one more time, and this time the conversation gets cut short because the manager has another meeting. They stop bringing it up.
- **Stage 2: Peer modeling.** Others watch this happen. They note the outcome and adjust their own behavior accordingly. Why spend energy raising concerns that do not go anywhere? The tacit knowledge of "what's worth saying" gets calibrated downward across the team.
- **Stage 3: Leadership loses ground truth.** Management is now operating on the information that *makes it through the filter* — which is, increasingly, the information that reflects well, confirms existing beliefs, or travels up through people who have learned to package feedback in ways that do not create friction. The difficult signal does not make it.
- **Stage 4: Decisions degrade.** Leaders make decisions without access to the full picture. They allocate resources based on what they are being told rather than what is happening. They approve changes that the people on the floor could have told them were going to create problems, if anyone had asked — and if asking had ever produced results.
- **Stage 5: Outcomes fail, blame goes to execution.** The results come back wrong. A process breaks. A shipment fails. A metric

collapses. The natural organizational response is to ask why "execution" fell short — why the front line did not perform to the plan. The answer, buried under layers of culture and structure, is that the front line *was* performing to the plan. They knew the plan was wrong for six months and had no effective way to say so.

This is the iceberg that sinks the ship. What is visible above the waterline — the missed KPI, the failed audit, the customer complaint — is always smaller than what is sitting underneath. Below the surface: the concern that went unheard, the workaround that went unreported, the employee who checked out six months ago because nobody seemed interested in what they knew.

The Silent Spiral™ is not just an individual communication pattern. *At scale, it becomes an organizational culture — one where silence is the rational, learned response to a system that stopped listening somewhere along the way.* **Breaking the Spiral™** at the cultural level requires more than better individual listening skills. **Breaking that pattern requires more than telling people to "listen better."**

It requires structural intervention:

- Mechanisms that *force* the organization to receive information it would otherwise filter out.
  - Skip-level conversations.
  - Anonymous input systems with genuine follow-up accountability.
  - Regular after-action reviews that specifically ask "what did we not know that we should have?"
  - Leader rounding that goes to where the work happens, not just to where things look good.

A visible pattern of leaders saying "we heard this, and here's what we did" — because without that pattern, people assume nothing happens even when it does.

Listening becomes cultural only when it becomes visible.

Field Note: The Update That Never Made It Upstairs

I spent time in an environment where speed was valued, meetings were tight, and the unwritten rule was simple: keep it brief or lose the room.

There was a coordinator there who knew the inbound process better than most of the people managing it. She was methodical, quiet, and not the kind of person who filled the room with her voice.

For most of a quarter, she had been tracking a pattern in vendor shipments. The manifests were consistently off just enough to create downstream discrepancies that kept resurfacing in counts and reconciliation. She documented it. She mentioned it twice in routine briefings and got some version of "we'll look into it" both times. She raised it to her supervisor in passing. He told her to send it in writing. She did. **Nothing came back.**

At quarter close, the site had a variance that took days and multiple people to unwind. Eventually, the cause was traced back to the same shipment issues she had already flagged.

During the debrief, someone asked how long the problem had been happening. *A supervisor estimated it probably started around the middle of the previous quarter. She was in the room. She said nothing.*

Later, I asked why. Her answer was simple: "I said something twice. I sent the email. Nobody asked me anything. So, I figured it must not be that important."

That is what organizational listening failure looks like in practice. Not dramatic. Not loud. Signal that had nowhere reliable to go.

Listening as a Leadership Practice

Listening does not make the agenda. It does not show up in most job descriptions, performance reviews, or leadership competency frameworks. It is treated as a background skill — something people either have or don't, something that develops naturally with experience, something that does not require deliberate cultivation.

That belief is wrong, and it is expensive.

The most operationally costly moments I have witnessed across twenty years in operations, healthcare, government, and logistics were almost never caused by a failure of process design, resource allocation, or technical skill. They were caused by information that existed — somewhere in the organization, in someone's experience, in someone's careful tracking of a pattern — and that never made it to the place where it could do something.

Listening is how information travels. When organizations treat it as an afterthought, they lose access to the real-time intelligence that their most experienced people carry. They operate on filtered signal. They make decisions in the dark and wonder why execution keeps failing.

The Silent Spiral™ ends at Stage 2 — silence — every single time someone chooses not to listen. It breaks — actually breaks, permanently — when the people at every level of the organization learn that raising concerns produces a response, that speaking up is worth the effort, that there is someone on the other end of the conversation who is receiving what they say.

That is not a communications training program. That is a culture. It starts with one person deciding, in one meeting, to put the phone down and listen to what is being said.

Key Takeaways

- **Listening is not passive. It is an active, cognitive, operational skill.**
- **Most organizations are better at broadcasting than receiving.**
- **Silence is often the outcome of repeated listening failure,** not personal reluctance.
- The Four Levels of Listening — **Cosmetic, Selective, Active, Empathic** — name the difference between performance and reception.
- **Five tests** — Tell Me Back, 48-Hour, Question, Silence, Contradiction — turn listening into something you can diagnose in real time.

- Group meetings suppress signal unless they are structured to surface it. Round-robins, silent reflection, and written input are the fix.
- Listening becomes cultural only when it becomes visible. People believe what they see leaders do, not what they hear leaders say.

Reflection Questions

1. **In your current environment, what mechanisms truly exist for information to travel upward, and which ones are mostly symbolic?**
2. **Where in your team do people hear one another without really listening?** What concern, if raised today, would people on your team quietly assume is not worth the effort?
3. **Who are the quiet experts in your environment, and what would need to change for their signal to reliably reach decision-makers?**
4. **Which of the five listening tests would tell you the most about your team's current listening culture?** Try it this week. Note what you learn.

Closing

The strongest listeners are not the people who say the most about listening. They are the people whose responses prove they received what was said.

When listening breaks down, the consequences rarely announce themselves all at once. First the signal gets missed. Then it gets repeated. Then it gets shortened. Then it stops.

That is how the Silent Spiral™ begins. Not with dramatic failure, but with the quiet moment when someone realizes the organization can hear them perfectly well and is not really listening.

And that is why listening is not passive. It is an act of leadership.

Chapter 11: Close the Loop — Accountability Without Blame

I want to tell you about the action log that saved a relationship.

Late in a project that had already been through two restarts and a scope change. The team was tired. The client relationship was strained. Trust between two departments had eroded to the point where both sides had stopped sharing information proactively and started treating every interaction as potential evidence in a case they might someday need to make against each other.

In a meeting meant to be a status review, someone raised a concern that had supposedly been addressed three months earlier. Both sides were certain they were right about what had been agreed. The conversation was heading in exactly the direction those conversations always go when they're driven by memory and reputation rather than record.

What broke the impasse wasn't a tense exchange or a formal escalation. It was an action log. Someone pulled up a shared document — consistently maintained, meeting by meeting, action by action — with dates, owners, and status notes. The item was there. The commitment had been made. The follow-through had not happened. The documentation was clear, and it was not personal.

The conversation that followed was not easy. But it was productive. **Because the record wasn't about who was telling the truth — it was about what needed to happen next.**

That is the difference documentation makes. Not as a weapon. Not as a CYA file. As a shared reality that everyone can navigate by.

At a Glance

Section	What You'll Get
Why Follow-Through Fails	The systems gap — not the character gap
Building Feedback Loops	Four practices that return information to the people who generated it
Accountability vs. Punishment	The distinction that changes everything

Section	What You'll Get
Tracking Commitments Visibly	What a real action log looks like, plus a tool comparison
When Someone Drops the Ball	A 5-step process for the conversation that has to happen
Follow-Up Email Template	Word-for-word template for post-meeting accountability
Documentation	Why it's not CYA — it's the team's collective memory

Why Follow-Through Is the Hardest Part

Here's something I've observed across industries, organizations, and team sizes: **people are far better at starting things than finishing them.**

Conversations that produce clear agreements still result in actions that never get taken. Decisions made in meetings evaporate between the conference room and Monday morning. Commitments get made with sincerity and then quietly abandoned when other priorities arrive. **This is not primarily a character issue. It is a systems issue.**

When organizations rely on memory, goodwill, and professional norms to ensure follow-through — without structural reinforcement — they are **engineering failure into their communication process:**

- **Memory is unreliable and selective.**
- **Goodwill is finite** and consumed by competing demands.
- **Professional norms are invisible and inconsistently enforced.**

What closes the loop is not trying harder to remember or care more. What closes the loop is **building follow-through into the process itself** — so action items have owners, deadlines, and visibility, and the state of those items is reviewed on a predictable schedule.

The organizations I've seen do this well don't have more disciplined people. They have better systems.

FIELD NOTES: Thirty Days, No Response

The situation. A PTO request, submitted more than a month in advance — more notice than required. Coverage arranged. Transitions planned. Every box checked on my end.

What happened:

- Day 1. Request submitted through the appropriate channel.
- Days 30–35. Request still unacknowledged, sitting in the approval queue.
- Follow-up #1. Response redirected me to a different platform I hadn't known existed.
- After re-submitting. Another week passed.
- Follow-up #2. Acknowledgment of receipt. No indication of review, approval, or decision.
- Ongoing. Trip arrangements couldn't be finalized. A professional commitment existed in uncertainty.

The Message Underneath

What I want to draw out here isn't the inconvenience. It's the message the silence sends. When a reasonable, properly submitted, appropriately timed request goes unacknowledged for more than a month, the professional on the receiving end learns four things:

- Their request does not require a response.
- Their planning does not merit consideration.
- The loop they opened will stay open indefinitely.
- They should not expect it to close.

The Slow Erosion

This kind of failure doesn't feel dramatic. There is no incident. No conflict. No wrong words spoken. It's a silence that accumulates — until the person on the receiving end quietly recalibrates their expectations. About the organization's responsiveness. About whether following proper channels is worth the outcome.

Every unacknowledged request teaches the same lesson:

Communicating through official means in this system produces nothing. String enough of those lessons together and you have trained a capable professional to route around the official channels — because the official channels have demonstrated they do not reliably respond.

- **The Math on Acknowledgment.** Consider the cost of a ten-second reply against the cost of saying nothing. A short acknowledgment — *"Received, will review by Friday"* — takes about ten seconds. It prevents the loop from staying open, and it keeps trust intact.
- **Silence for thirty-plus days takes zero effort in the moment.** But it produces disengagement, workarounds, and recalibrated expectations that are far harder to rebuild than they were to lose.

Accountability is not only about whether commitments are kept. It is about whether acknowledgment happens at all.

FIELD NOTE TAKEAWAY: An unacknowledged request is not a neutral event. It is a lesson — and the lesson is that using official channels doesn't get results. String enough of those lessons together and you've trained a capable person to route around the process. Acknowledgment is the minimum viable commitment. If your systems can't produce a "received" response within forty-eight hours, that is the problem to fix first.

Building Feedback Loops Into Every Process

A feedback loop returns information about outcomes back to the person or system that generated them. Most organizations have feedback loops for their technical processes — quality checks, financial closes, test results. Most do *not* have equivalent feedback loops for their communication processes.

Did the message land? Did the action item get completed? Was the handoff successful? These questions go unasked — which means teams are operating a communication system with no quality control.

Four Practices for Communication Feedback Loops

Practice	What It Looks Like	What It Catches
End every meeting with an action review	Read back action items, confirm owners and deadlines — two minutes	Items that weren't captured clearly
"Completed since last meeting" at the top of recurring agendas	Before talking about now, account for what was supposed to happen	Commitments that quietly dropped
Structured review cycles	Weekly or monthly review of all open action items, risks, and commitments — not to blame, to maintain shared awareness	Items stuck "in progress" that need different treatment
Solicit feedback on communications themselves	After major announcements or policy changes: brief follow-up, check-in, or one-question survey	Confusion, resistance, and gaps in understanding

Instead of / Try: Accountability Language

Instead of...	Try...
"Let me know if you have any issues."	"I'll check in with you on Wednesday. What's the most likely blocker?"
"You said you'd have this done."	"The deliverable for Wednesday didn't come through — can you walk me through what happened?"
"Does everyone know what they're doing?"	"Let's do a quick playback — can each person name their action item and due date?"
"We'll follow up on that."	"[Name] will follow up on [specific thing] by [specific date] — I'm putting that in the notes right now."
"I assumed you were handling it."	"We never explicitly named who was owning this — let's do that now."

The Difference Between Accountability and Punishment

This distinction matters enormously and is more poorly understood than it should be.

- **Accountability** is the condition of being answerable for your commitments. You said you would do something; there is a clear expectation that you will either do it or proactively communicate that you cannot, and explain why. It is a professional contract, not a moral judgment.
- **Punishment** is what happens when accountability is conflated with shame, blame, and consequence for its own sake.

	Accountability	Punishment
Purpose	Maintain shared expectations; learn what's in the way	Assign blame; signal consequences
What it teaches	Your commitments matter; when something fails, we figure it out together	Hide failures, manage perception, point at systemic factors to deflect
Information it produces	Why the commitment failed; what needs to change	A defensive story, not accurate information
Effect on relationships	Preserves the working relationship	Damages it — often permanently
Effect on future behavior	People communicate proactively about problems	People hide problems until they can't

The Practice Difference in Conversation

- *Punishment framing:* "You said you'd have this done by Wednesday. It's Friday. Why wasn't it done?"
- *Accountability framing:* "The deliverable for Wednesday didn't come through — can you walk me through what happened? I want to understand whether there was a resource problem, a clarity issue with the ask, or something else, so we can figure out how to support you in meeting the next deadline."

The second framing is not soft. It does not lower the standard. It investigates rather than accuses — which produces more accurate information and better outcomes. **And it preserves the relationship you need to function effectively after this conversation is over.**

In the Room: The Same Conversation, Two Ways

One version closes the relationship. The other closes the loop.

Version 1 — Punishment:

Manager: *"You said you'd have this done by Wednesday. It's Friday. This is the second time."*

Team member: *"I had three other things on fire —"*

Manager: *"I don't need an explanation. I need it done."*

What gets produced: a completed deliverable and a team member who will now delay telling you the next time something is at risk. Because they learned that telling you costs more than hiding it.

Version 2 — Accountability:

Manager: *"The report didn't come in Wednesday — can you walk me through what happened? I want to understand what got in the way."*

Team member: *"The data from Operations came in late, and I wasn't sure if I should wait or submit with what I had."*

Manager: *"Good to know. Going forward, if a dependency is going to push your timeline, flag it before the deadline — not after. What do you need from me to get this closed today?"*

Same standard. Completely different outcome. Breaking the Spiral™ at Stage 4 means closing the loop on missed commitments — not punishing the person, but surfacing what broke down so the system can be fixed.

Tracking Commitments Visibly

Nothing in this chapter works without a system for making commitments **visible** — not just tracked somewhere, but accessible, current, and shared with the people who made the commitments and those affected by them.

What Visible Commitment Tracking Looks Like

Element	What It Looks Like	What Fails Without It
Shared action log	One shared, living document — every action item, one owner, target date, current status	Items living in personal to-do lists or email chains nobody else can see
Current status	Updated by owners on a predictable schedule, reviewed by the team on a predictable schedule	A log last updated three weeks ago is a museum, not a tool
Escalation when items go red	Items past their deadline get flagged visibly and trigger an immediate conversation — not wait for the next review	Red items hiding in plain sight until it's too late
Decision log (parallel)	What was decided, by whom, on what date, on what basis	Memory-dependent accountability conversations

Tracking System Comparison: Choose What Fits Your Team

Tool	Best For	Strengths	Limitations
Shared spreadsheet	Small teams, simple projects, any environment	No software cost; everyone knows how to use it; highly customizable	Manual updates; no notifications; can fall out of date
Project management software	Larger teams, complex multi-track projects	Automated reminders; built-in status tracking; visual dashboards	Setup overhead; license costs; team adoption required

Tool	Best For	Strengths	Limitations
Shared document	Small teams, meeting-heavy environments	Easy to embed in meeting notes; low friction	Hard to sort or filter; not built for status tracking
Whiteboard or physical board	Floor-level teams, same-location daily stand-ups	Visible to everyone in the space; no login required	Not accessible remotely; hard to archive
Email thread	One-off items only	No new tool required	Loses visibility quickly; no aggregate view; no status tracking

The right choice is the one your team will use. A complex tool with 10 percent adoption is worse than a simple spreadsheet with 100 percent adoption. I have built these tracking systems in multiple contexts using nothing more sophisticated than a shared Excel file and a standing agenda item. The sophistication of the tool is irrelevant.

The practice of maintaining it and reviewing it is everything.

What to Do When Someone Drops the Ball

It happens. Commitments get missed. Deadlines pass. *How you handle this moment determines whether your team is becoming more accountable or less.*

Two Wrong Responses:

- **Say nothing** — let the miss slide in the interest of harmony; quietly pick up the work yourself; adjust the timeline and move on. Teaches the team that commitments are optional.
- **Make an example** — public callouts, sharp questioning in front of peers, CC-ing the supervisor without a prior direct conversation. Punishes rather than corrects; damages psychological safety.

The 5-Step Missed Commitment Conversation

Step 1: State the observable fact without judgment.

- *"The report due Wednesday didn't come in. I wanted to connect with you about it."*

Step 2: Create space for the explanation.

- *"Can you walk me through what happened?"* — and listen. Was the ask unclear? Did something shift in their workload? Was there a dependency that wasn't met? The answer shapes everything that comes next.

Step 3: Problem-solve together.

- Based on what you learned: revised deadline? Additional support? Clearer deliverable definition? A conversation with someone whose cooperation they needed and didn't get?

Step 4: Restate the commitment explicitly.

- *"So what I'm hearing is that you'll have the revised version to me by Friday at noon. Is that right?"* Confirm the new commitment. Write it down.

Step 5: Follow through on your own side.

- If you said you'd provide support, a resource, a clarification — do it. Your follow-through teaches the person whether accountability is a one-way or two-way street.

Most of this takes five minutes.

The discipline is not in the length of the conversation — it's in having it at all, rather than letting the miss go unaddressed.

THE FOLLOW-UP EMAIL TEMPLATE

This is the email you send after the accountability conversation – or after any meeting where commitments were made.
It doesn't need to be long. It needs to be clear.

SUBJECT

Subject: Follow-up – [Meeting Name or Topic], [Date]

GREETING

[Name],

Thanks for the conversation today. I want to capture what we discussed and make sure we're aligned on next steps.

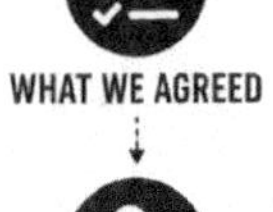

WHAT WE AGREED

What we agreed:

- [Action item] – Owner: [Name] – Due: [Date]
- [Action item] – Owner: [Name] – Due: [Date]
- [Action item] – Owner: [Name] – Due: [Date]

MY COMMITMENT

What I'm doing on my end: [Your specific commitment]

NEXT CHECK-IN

Next check-in: [Date and format – brief call, email update, or next meeting]

CLOSE

Please let me know if I've missed or misrepresented anything.

[Your name]

THIS EMAIL DOES THREE THINGS:

It confirms what was agreed (preventing later confusion).

It makes commitments visible.

It models the follow-through you're asking for.

THE ROLE OF DOCUMENTATION IN ACCOUNTABILITY

In many organizations, "document everything" sounds like "protect yourself in case this goes wrong." So, documentation gets treated as a defensive act – something you do when you're worried, not a professional standard. That's a misread. **Documentation is the collective memory of the team.**

THREE PURPOSES DOCUMENTATION SERVES IN ACCOUNTABILITY

PURPOSE	WHAT IT DOES
 CLARITY	**Written commitments eliminate interpretation.** "Draft ready by Thursday" can mean five things in memory. It means one thing in a shared action log with a deadline.
 FAIRNESS	**The record is shared, so accountability isn't about who has a better memory or a louder voice.** It's about what the document says – protecting both the person who kept their commitment and the person who missed it.
 LEARNING	**When you document not just what happened but why – the reason an item was delayed, the thinking behind a decision – you build organizational knowledge.** The next team can learn from this one.

Documentation done right is a communication act of respect for your team and your future colleagues.

It says: *what we did here mattered, and we want to remember it clearly.*

Accountability Conversation Script — When a Pattern Has Developed

When This Happens / Do This: Documentation

When This Happens	Do This
A decision is made verbally in a meeting	Send a summary email within 24 hours: "We decided [X] on [date]. Owner: [name]."
An agreement is reached in a one-on-one	Follow up with a brief written note confirming the commitment
Someone claims they never agreed to something	Pull the record — meeting notes, email, or action log. Address the discrepancy factually.
You're about to do something that wasn't explicitly authorized	Document your understanding and send it for confirmation before you act
An action item goes past its due date	Update the status in the log immediately — don't leave it showing "in progress"

Key Takeaways

- **Follow-through is a systems problem, not a character problem.** Build action tracking, feedback loops, and regular review cycles into your processes so accountability doesn't depend on memory or individual motivation.
- **Accountability and punishment are fundamentally different.** Accountability is being answerable for your commitments. Punishment is consequence for its own sake. The first improves performance; the second drives failure underground.
- **Visible commitment tracking** — shared action logs, decision logs, regular reviews — creates the shared reality that allows fair, clear accountability conversations.
- **When someone drops the ball**, the productive path is a private, direct, fact-based conversation that surfaces the reason, problem-solves together, and restates the commitment.

- **Documentation is not defensive.** It is the team's collective memory — the foundation of clarity, fairness, and organizational learning.
- **The follow-up email is not optional.** It is the step that turns a conversation into a commitment. Without it, the conversation was just a conversation.

Reflection Questions

1. **In your current team or organization, what happens when an action item is missed?** Is there a consistent, structured response — or does it depend on who's involved and what mood the room is in? What would a more consistent approach look like?
2. **Think about a commitment you made recently that you didn't fully follow through on. What got in the way?** Was the obstacle something the system could have caught earlier — a resource gap, an unclear ask, a conflicting priority that wasn't surfaced?
3. **Where in your current work is documentation treated as optional or as a defensive measure rather than a professional standard?** What would it look like to build documentation into the process itself, rather than bolting it on after the fact?

Chapter 12: Bridge the Silos — Cross-Functional Communication

Nobody builds a silo on purpose. I've never walked into an organization where leadership stood up and said: *"From this point forward, each department will operate as its own insular unit, information will be hoarded, and we will refer to other departments primarily as obstacles."* **Nobody says that. Nobody wants that.**

And yet, across organizations I've worked in or worked with — the silos exist. They form organically, inevitably, and they are remarkably resistant to destruction. Understanding *why* silos form — despite everyone's stated preference for collaboration — is the first step to preventing them.

At a Glance

Section	What You'll Learn
Why Silos Form	The structural forces stronger than anyone's good intentions
McChrystal's Team of Teams	Shared consciousness plus empowered execution
Shared Language	How to find and fix the definitions colliding between functions
The Connector Role	The person who translates between worlds — and why you need them
Stakeholder Mapping Table	Who needs what — and how to manage each relationship
Joint Problem-Solving Tools	Gemba, A3 thinking, cross-functional reviews
Cross-Functional Meeting Template	A fill-in structure for meetings that span departments
Information Handoff Checklist	What must transfer at every cross-functional boundary
Partnership Communication	What makes inter-organizational coordination work

Why Silos Form Even When Nobody Wants Them

Silos form because of how organizations are **designed**, not because of how people feel about collaboration. Structural forces create silos; social forces can't overcome them. That's why team-building exercises and "break down the barriers" slogans don't work.

The 5 Mechanisms That Create Silos

Mechanism	How It Works	Why Good Intentions Don't Fix It
Competing reporting structures	Quality reports to one leader measured on defect rates; Operations reports to another measured on throughput. Goals conflict.	People optimize for the metric they're evaluated on. That's rational, not selfish.
Physical or geographic separation	Co-located teams develop informal habits; separated teams don't. Without ambient communication, formal channels are all that's left — and they're insufficient.	You can't relationship-build across a time zone at the volume needed.
Specialized vocabulary	Every function builds its own glossary. Quality's "inspection" ≠ Operations' "inspection." Neither party realizes they're speaking different languages.	Both parties believe they're using common language — the collision is invisible.
Past conflict	After a blowup or blame assignment, the natural response is to reduce interaction surface. Less sharing. More formalized, defensive communication.	The protection is understandable. The cost is that the collaboration the organization needs doesn't happen.
Busyness	Heavy workloads deprioritize proactive coordination. People reach out when they need something — by which	Good intentions plus no structure equals reactive, not preventive, communication.

Mechanism	How It Works	Why Good Intentions Don't Fix It
	point the gap has already formed.	

FIELD NOTES: The A3 That Saved the Project

The setup: Two departments. A recurring quality issue that had been generating friction for the better part of a quarter. The kind of problem that had its own name in both teams — a shorthand that everyone recognized and nobody had resolved.

The meetings had not been unproductive in the conventional sense. Attendance was good. The conversation was substantive. People showed up prepared. But every session ended roughly where it began: both teams having made their case, neither team having changed their position, and the quality issue still present in the next production cycle.

The dynamic: Each department had a perfectly coherent explanation for what was causing the problem. The explanations were not compatible with each other. In four months of meetings, no one had yet noticed that.

What changed: Someone suggested pulling out a blank sheet of paper and filling out an A3 together. Not separately and then sharing. Together, in real time, starting with the problem statement.

The problem statement took forty-five minutes. Not because people were being difficult. Because when you ask two departments to agree on one sentence describing what the problem is — specific, measurable, factual, no solutions embedded — the differences in how each team was experiencing the issue come to the surface fast. *And what surfaced in that room, over those forty-five minutes, was the following:*

- **Department A's version:** Quality failures at the output stage, caused by process gaps in Department B's workflow.
- **Department B's version:** Rework requirements arriving from Department A that didn't match the spec as originally communicated.

Same meetings. Same calendar invite. Two different problems being solved in the same room for four months — because no one ever forced the problem into a single shared sentence both sides had to agree on.

What the A3 did in that session:

Once they had a shared problem statement, not a compromise, but an actual agreed-upon description of the gap between current condition and target, the next sections moved faster than anyone expected. The current condition surfaced the point in the process where the two teams' workflows intersected and where the specification had never been formally reconciled between them.

That was the root cause.

- ***Not a person.***
- ***Not a department.***
- **A process gap that had existed since the original workflow design and had never been closed.**

The resolution: Two weeks after that single A3 session, the issue was resolved. Not because anyone worked harder or communicated better in some general sense.

Because for the first time, both teams were looking at the same picture of what was broken — and the picture made the fix obvious.

What I carry from it: The A3 did not give anyone information they didn't already have. Every fact on that page was known to someone in the room. What the A3 did was force all of those facts into a shared, structured format that neither team could interpret in isolation. The problem was visible. The gap was visible. The fix was visible.

All of it had been invisible before — not because anyone was hiding anything, but because the information had never been organized into a form that both teams could see simultaneously.

Making thinking visible on one page can accomplish what months of meetings cannot. *Not because the page is magic. Because the act of filling it out together is.*

FIELD NOTE TAKEAWAY: When two groups have been talking about the same problem for months without resolution, stop trying to solve it and start trying to define it — together, out loud, in a format everyone has to agree on.

The moment you write the problem statement and ask both parties to sign off on a single sentence, you'll find out how aligned you are. In most cases, the answer is: less aligned than anyone realized.

That discovery, as uncomfortable as it is, is worth more than any proposed solution that came before it.

CREATING SHARED LANGUAGE ACROSS DEPARTMENTS

Early in a cross-functional quality role, I attended a meeting where a word was used fourteen times in forty-five minutes and meant something different to at least four people in the room.

THE WORD WAS "INSPECTION."

QUALITY TEAM: formal, documented process with specific pass/fail criteria and required documentation

OPERATIONS: a visual check a supervisor might perform in thirty seconds

CUSTOMER: a quarterly audit they conducted

RECEIVING TEAM: opening the box and confirming the count

Not one person knew the others were working from different definitions. The decision the meeting was supposed to produce – about whether "inspection" at a particular step was required – was incoherent, because everyone was answering a different question.

This is so common it should be treated as the rule, not the exception.

HOW TO BUILD SHARED LANGUAGE

STEP		
	FIND THE HIGH-FRICTION TERMS	In any cross-functional work, five to ten terms consistently cause miscommunication. Ask each function to define their most important terms, then compare. The differences will surprise you.
 	CREATE A JOINT GLOSSARY	For major cross-functional projects, build a shared glossary of the terms where definitions diverge and that divergence causes operational problems. Not every term – just the high-friction ones.
 	NAME THE CONFUSION IN THE ROOM	When you suspect a word means different things: "I want to check – when you say 'review,' what does that process look like on your side?" Brief, non-threatening, prevents significant downstream confusion.
	 BUILD TRANSLATION INTO PROCESSES	Identify someone who understands both functions well enough to catch language mismatches in real time.

Shared language isn't about being picky with words. It's about making sure we're solving the same problem.

McCHRYSTAL'S SOLUTION: TEAM OF TEAMS

SHARED CONSCIOUSNESS / EMPOWERED EXECUTION

General Stanley McChrystal's Team of Teams documents what he learned leading the Joint Special Operations Command in Iraq: a highly capable, traditionally organized force struggling against a network that was decentralized, fast-moving, and deeply coordinated.

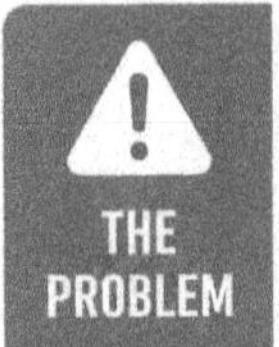

THE PROBLEM

The problem wasn't competence. It was that the traditional command structure – hierarchical, information-controlled, decisions concentrated at the top – was too slow for its environment.

- **Intelligence from the field reached decision-makers too late.**
- **Decisions reached the field too late.**

By the time the organization could respond, the situation had already changed.

MCCHRYSTAL'S SOLUTION

SHARED CONSCIOUSNESS

Every part of the organization has access to a common picture of what's happening across the whole system.

EMPOWERED EXECUTION

Authority to act on that information delegated to the people closest to the situation.

WHAT SHARED CONSCIOUSNESS REQUIRED

RADICAL INFORMATION SHARING

previously closely-held information made available across units.

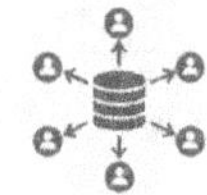

REGULAR CROSS-UNIT COMMUNICATION FORUMS

that became operational necessities, not administrative overhead.

THE ORGANIZATIONAL LESSON:

You cannot coordinate across functions without shared information.
And shared information requires **deliberate structures** – because the default is information hoarding, whether anyone wants it or not.

WHAT THIS LOOKS LIKE IN PRACTICE

MECHANISM	MANUFACTURING/LOGISTICS EXAMPLE	GOVERNMENT/AGENCY EXAMPLE
CROSS-FUNCTIONAL VISIBILITY DASHBOARDS	Production and quality share one daily visual board.	Program and compliance teams review the same project dashboard.
ALL-HANDS BRIEFINGS	Multiple functions in one room, each sharing current state openly.	Cross-team stand-up instead of separate siloed reviews.
SHARED METRICS	Metrics reflecting whole-system performance, not just one function's output.	Joint KPIs that span delivery and risk status.
ROTATION AND EMBEDDING	Quality reps spending time on the operations floor.	Program staff spending time with compliance teams.

THE POINT IS THE SAME IN EVERY CONTEXT:
THE INFORMATION NEEDS TO BE COMMON BEFORE THE COORDINATION CAN BE EFFECTIVE.

Breaking the Spiral™: Stage 1 → Test the Assumption

The same conversation. Someone asks the question.

Quality Supervisor: *"Before we decide whether we're covered at Step 7 — can we take two minutes to make sure we mean the same thing? When you say 'inspection,' what does that look like specifically on the Operations side?"*

Operations Manager: *"Supervisor visual check, logs the shift report."*

Quality Supervisor: *"Okay. When I say 'inspection' for compliance purposes, I mean a documented check against the spec sheet with a pass/fail logged in the quality system. Those are different things."*

Operations Manager: *"So we don't have what you need at Step 7."*

Quality Supervisor: *"Right. But now we both know that. Can we figure out what adding that step would take — and whether there's a version that works for Operations?"*

Five minutes. One assumption named. One definition compared. Months of compliance risk avoided.

This is what shared language looks like being built in real time — not in a glossary document, but in the moment, *someone decides to ask.*

In the Room: The Word That Meant Four Different Things

Imagine you'd been in this meeting.

Quality Supervisor: *"We need to make sure there's an inspection at Step 7 before the product ships."*

Operations Manager (OM): *"We do inspection at Step 7."*

Quality Supervisor: *"Is it documented?"*

OM: *"Sure — the supervisor signs off."*

Quality Supervisor: *"That's not what I mean by inspection. We need a formal check against the spec sheet with a logged result."*

OM: *"That's an audit. We don't do audits at Step 7."*

Quality Supervisor: *"Then we're not compliant."*

OM: *"We've been doing Step 7 this way for three years."*

No one is wrong. They have been using the same word to mean different things for three years — and they are discovering this for the first time in a meeting where a client is waiting on an answer. **The silence that follows is the sound of two people realizing they've been aligned on a word and misaligned on everything underneath it.**

Instead of...	Try...
Assuming everyone uses the same definition	"When you say [term], what does that look like specifically on your end?"
"We all know what [term] means."	"Let's make sure we're aligned on definitions before we go further — especially for [term] and [term]."
Using your department's internal jargon in a cross-functional setting	Plain language, every time — or define the term the first time you use it
Presenting findings in your function's native format	Ask what format the other function reads and uses

The Role of the Connector: People Who Translate Between Worlds

In every organization I've worked in, there have been **individuals with an unusual ability to move between departments** — who understood the Quality and the Operations perspective, knew the right person in Finance and in Procurement, and **could walk into a room of people who barely spoke to each other and get a productive conversation going.**

Connectors are typically people who have worked in multiple functions, or who have natural curiosity about how other parts of the organization work. **They invest in relationships across boundaries, not just within their own team.**

In operational environments, I've played this role informally — sitting between a client organization and a service provider, **translating the concerns of one into language the other could hear. It's not glamorous. It requires patience, active listening, and comfort with ambiguity. The operational value it generates is enormous.**

WHAT CONNECTORS DO:

	FUNCTION	WHAT IT LOOKS LIKE
	TRANSLATE	Convert the concerns of one function into language the other can hear.
	CARRY RELATIONSHIPS	Know the people on each side personally – which makes formal communication easier.
	CATCH MISMATCHES	Spot when two functions are using the same word to mean different things.
	BRIDGE THE GAP	Facilitate conversations that wouldn't happen otherwise.

WHAT TO DO WITH CONNECTORS:

IDENTIFY
the connectors on your team – the people who move fluidly between functions.

RECOGNIZE
their cross-functional capacity explicitly; protect their time for this work.

RESIST
pulling them into purely functional roles where their boundary-spanning is unused.

WHEN BUILDING A CROSS-FUNCTIONAL TEAM:
explicitly assign the connector function – don't assume it will emerge organically.

Connectors turn silos into conversations and information into action.

Templates and Working Tools Table

Before you can communicate across functions, you need to know who you're dealing with — what they care about, what they know, and what they need from you.

Use this map to identify key stakeholders across functions, understand what matters to them, and build stronger, more effective working relationships.

STAKEHOLDER / FUNCTION	WHAT THEY CARE ABOUT	WHAT THEY NEED FROM YOU	WHAT YOU NEED FROM THEM	BEST CHANNEL	RELATIONSHIP WARMTH
FUNCTION A	[Their primary metric / concern]	[Updates, decisions, access]	[Data, input, approval]	[Email / Meeting / Walk-over]	[Cold / Warm / Strong]
FUNCTION B	[Their primary metric / concern]	[Updates, decisions, access]	[Data, input, approval]	[Email / Meeting / Walk-over]	[Cold / Warm / Strong]
FUNCTION C	[Their primary metric / concern]	[Updates, decisions, access]	[Data, input, approval]	[Email / Meeting / Walk-over]	[Cold / Warm / Strong]
EXECUTIVE SPONSOR	[Their primary metric / concern]	[Updates, decisions, access]	[Data, input, approval]	[Email / Meeting / Walk-over]	[Cold / Warm / Strong]
CUSTOMER / EXTERNAL PARTNER	[Their primary metric / concern]	[Updates, decisions, access]	[Data, input, approval]	[Email / Meeting / Walk-over]	[Cold / Warm / Strong]

HOW TO USE THIS MAP

1. IDENTIFY
List the key stakeholders across your project or initiative.

2. UNDERSTAND
Capture what matters to them and how you can support them.

3. ALIGN
Clarify what you need from them – and how you'll exchange value.

4. STRENGTHEN
Choose the best channel and invest in building a stronger relationship.

STRONG STAKEHOLDER RELATIONSHIPS DRIVE BETTER DECISIONS AND BETTER OUTCOMES.

Joint Problem-Solving Tools

The tools that make cross-functional collaboration real are the ones that physically bring different perspectives into contact with the same problem.

Silo-Breaking Strategies: When to Use What

Strategy	When to Use	Primary Owner	What It Produces
Gemba Walks	The reported work does not match the actual work. Functions describe the same process in different terms.	Leader or problem-solver; ideally cross-functional team	First-hand observation; information that never appears in formal reports
A3 Thinking	Two or more functions disagree about a recurring problem. Root cause analysis is needed.	Cross-functional team; A3 owner	One-page shared problem picture; aligned root causes; actions with owners and dates
Cross-Functional Review	For ongoing coordination; whenever multiple functions share accountability for the same outcome	Facilitated; rotating or permanent	Shared data, shared decisions, cross-functional action items
Shared visual board	Daily coordination between two adjacent functions (e.g., production + quality)	Joint team	Common operating picture replacing two separate, often conflicting pictures
Joint glossary build	A cross-functional project is starting. Communication failures keep recurring.	Cross-functional team; documented owner	Explicit shared language that prevents invisible misalignments

Gemba Walks: Go See the Work Together

A Gemba walk is one of the simplest and most powerful joint problem-solving tools because it moves the conversation out of the conference room and into the place where the work happens. The purpose is not to inspect, audit, blame, or correct people in the moment. **The purpose is to understand the real condition of the work.**

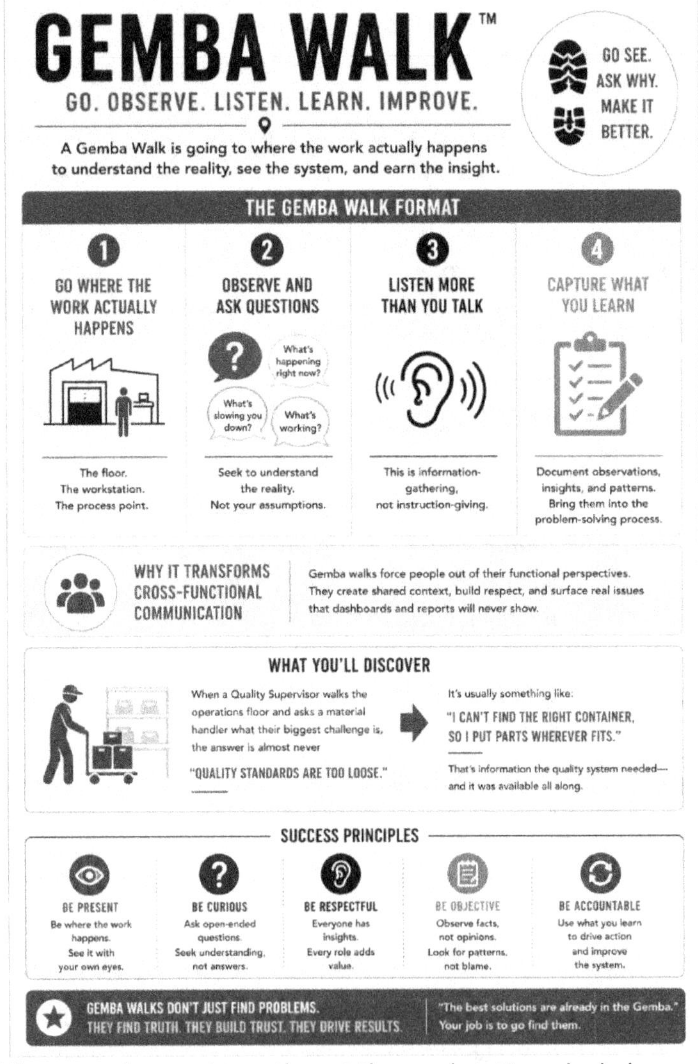

When people stand together at the workstation, dock door, staging lane, pack table, system screen, or handoff point, the conversation changes. The problem, the workarounds, the missing information — all become visible.

A3 Thinking

THE A3 THINKING MODEL™
SEE THE PROBLEM. UNDERSTAND THE SYSTEM. FIX WHAT MATTERS.
1
PROBLEM STATEMENT
What's happening? Be specific.
• What is the issue?
• Where is it showing up?
• Why does it matter?
CLARITY CHECK:
If we can't define it clearly, we can't solve it correctly.
2
CURRENT CONDITION
What is actually happening today?
• What do we see? (facts, not opinions)
• What data do we have?
• What patterns are repeating?
WATCH FOR:
Missed handoffs, unclear ownership, rework loops.
3
ROOT CAUSE ANALYSIS
Why is this happening?
• Use: Fishbone (6M)
• 5 Whys
• Pattern recognition
SILENT SPIRAL™ CONNECTION:
Assumptions → Silence → Frustration → Workarounds → Failure
4
TARGET CONDITION
What should "good" look like?
• Clear expectations
• Defined ownership
• Visible communication flow
DEFINE SUCCESS CLEARLY BEFORE FIXING ANYTHING.
5
COUNTERMEASURES
What will we change?
• What action will address the root cause?
• Who owns it?
• When will it be done?
FOCUS ON:
Fixing the system, not the person. Eliminating workarounds.
6
FOLLOW-UP / PDCA
Did it work? What did we learn?
• Measure results
• Adjust if needed
• Standardize if successful
NO FOLLOW-UP = NO IMPROVEMENT.
"WE DON'T CHASE SYMPTOMS. WE SOLVE ROOT CAUSES.
WHERE A3s FAIL
Problem is vague
Root cause is assumed
Actions fix symptoms
No ownership
No follow-up
WHY THIS WORKS
Focuses on the real problem
Aligns the team on true causes
Drives lasting improvement
THE COMMUNICATION PROCIESS THAT DRIVES RESULTS
CLARITY → ALIGNMENT → ACTION → FOLLOW-THROUGH → RESULTS
REFLECTION
What is the real problem we are trying to solve?
What assumption needs to be tested first?

Templates and Working Tools:

CROSS-FUNCTIONAL MEETING TEMPLATE

> Most cross-functional meetings fail because they're structured like internal team meetings - without the extra scaffolding needed when people don't share context, terminology, or priorities.

CROSS-FUNCTIONAL MEETING AGENDA

Meeting Name: ______

Date / Time / Location: ______

Purpose: (One sentence - decision, coordination, or problem-solving) ______

Functions Represented:

Function	Attendee	Role in This Discussion
[Function A]	[Name]	[Decision-maker / Subject matter expert / Informed party]
[Function B]	[Name]	
...		

CONTEXT-SETTING (5 MINUTES):

Before discussion begins – one sentence per function: ______

"From [Function]'s perspective, here's what matters most about today's topic:" ______

AGENDA ITEMS:

#	Topic	Decision/Discussion/Update	Owner	Time
1	Context alignment (shared current state)	Update	Facilitator	5 min
2	[Issue or topic]	Decision/Discussion	[Owner]	[X min]
3	Cross-functional dependencies	Discussion	All	10 min
4	Action items + owners	Decision	Facilitator	5 min

KEY QUESTIONS TO RESOLVE TODAY:

1. ______
2. ______

DECISIONS TO BE MADE:

1. ______
2. ______

CROSS-FUNCTIONAL ACTION ITEMS (FROM THIS MEETING):

Action	Owner (Function + Name)	Due Date	Follow-up Method

NEXT TOUCHPOINT: [Date, format, purpose] ______

At one facility, the most effective communication change I ever made was also the simplest. We were running two separate stand-ups every morning — one for each function — and by mid-morning, the two teams were colliding over something that could have been solved in five minutes if they had started the day in the same room. So we stopped running them separately. One cross-functional brief. One shared picture of the day. It did not add time to anyone's schedule. It gave time back, because the rework, the late catches, and the daily firefighting finally had somewhere to go before they became problems.

Information Handoff Checklist

Every time work, decisions, or accountability crosses a departmental boundary, information needs to transfer with it. Most of the time, it doesn't — or it transfers incompletely. Use this checklist at every cross-functional handoff from a warehouse setting (example).

Before the Handoff:

- Is the receiving function or person identified by name?
- Do they know this handoff is coming?
- Is the deadline and format agreed in advance?
- Have I confirmed they have the access and tools needed to receive this?

In the Handoff:

- **Current status** — what's done, what's not done, what's in progress
- **Open items** — what's still unresolved and who owns each
- **Context** — what decisions were made and why (don't just send the output; explain the thinking)
- **Dependencies** — what does the receiving team need from other parties to proceed?
- **Red flags** — what's the thing most likely to go wrong, and what should they watch for?

- **Escalation contact** — if they hit a wall, who do they call?

After the Handoff:

- Did the receiving team confirm receipt and understanding?
- Have I updated the shared action log to reflect the transfer?
- Is there a follow-up checkpoint scheduled to verify the handoff was complete?

When This Happens / Do This: Cross-Functional Coordination

When This Happens	Do This
Two departments are repeatedly blaming each other for the same problem	Run an A3 together. Make the problem definition joint property before assigning any solutions.
A cross-functional project is stalling	Map the stakeholders and identify who's blocking — formally or informally. Then have the conversation directly.
You're not getting cooperation from another function	Ask to sit in on one of their team meetings. Understanding their pressures changes how you ask.
Nobody agrees on what "done" looks like	Stop. Define success criteria together before proceeding. Write it down.
A key connector leaves the organization	Immediately identify their replacement and invest in building those relationships before the gap widens.

Building Communication Into Partnerships

The most challenging communication scenario: the inter-organizational partnership — two separate organizations that are operationally entangled, reporting to different leadership, measured by different metrics, expected to function as a unit.

I've lived in this space, operating between a service provider and a client organization. The communication complexity is at least double what you encounter within a single organization, because you have all the internal challenges plus the boundary between the organizations themselves.

What makes inter-organizational partnerships work:

Element	What It Requires
Defined interfaces	Who talks to whom, about what, through which channels, at what frequency — agreed by both organizations and documented
Joint metrics	If each organization is measured only on its own performance, each will optimize at the boundary, shifting costs and delays to the other side. Shared metrics tied to the whole partnership's outcome create aligned incentives.
Regular joint reviews	Both organizations in the room, reviewing the same data, owning their respective pieces together. Not separate reports exchanged and compared — a joint session with shared accountability.
Clear escalation paths across the boundary	Who calls whom when something needs senior-level attention? Agreed in advance. Tested before the crisis.
Relationship investment	The formal structures above are necessary but not sufficient. The working relationships between individuals — the quality manager who knows the operations supervisor by name — keep information flowing between the formal touchpoints. These relationships don't develop by accident.

Key Takeaways

- **Silos form because of structural and incentive design**, not attitudes toward collaboration. Structural solutions — shared metrics, cross-functional visibility, regular joint forums — are more effective than exhortations to "be more collaborative."
- **McChrystal's shared consciousness** framework applies directly to organizational silos: you cannot coordinate effectively without a common information picture, and that picture requires deliberate structures to create and maintain.

- **Language differences between functions** are a major source of cross-functional miscommunication that goes unrecognized. Building a shared glossary of high-friction terms is a practical, high-value investment.
- **Connectors** — people who translate between functions — are operational assets. Identify them, protect their cross-functional capacity, and cultivate more of them.
- **Joint problem-solving tools** — Gemba walks, A3 thinking, cross-functional reviews — work because they physically bring different perspectives into contact with the same problem. That contact is where cross-functional understanding is built.
- **Every cross-functional handoff is a communication risk.** Use the handoff checklist to ensure context, status, and ownership transfer completely — not just the deliverable.

Reflection Questions

1. **In your current organization, where do the most significant silos exist?** Are they between departments, between shifts, between organizational levels, or between internal and external partners? **What structural factors created them?**
2. **Think about a recent project or problem that touched multiple functions. Was there a single, shared picture of the current state that everyone was working from?** If not, what information did each function have that the others didn't, and what was the cost of this gap?
3. **Who are the connectors on your team or in your organization — the people who move fluidly between functions and translate between perspectives?** What would happen to cross-functional communication if those people left? How could you reduce that dependency?

Chapter 13: Lead Through Communication

There's a version of leadership that treats communication as a task — something on the to-do list between the real work. Send the update. Attend the meeting. Respond to the email. Check the box.

Communication *is* the work of leadership. It is not a supporting function. It is not a soft skill layered on top of technical expertise. It is the core way leaders organize people, align effort, create accountability, prevent failures, and build the conditions for results. When leadership fails — real failure, the kind where projects collapse and teams fracture and organizations lose months of momentum — the root cause is **almost always a communication failure**.

Not strategy. Not competence. A failure in how information moved, how decisions were shared, how problems were surfaced, how expectations were set, how trust was built or destroyed. If you lead anything — a team, a project, a process, an organization — your first job is to communicate. Everything else depends on it.

At a Glance

Section	What You'll Get
Communication IS the Job	Four things that are leadership communication — whether you treat them that way
What Good Leaders vs. Bad Leaders Say	Side-by-side comparison across 10 real situations
Daily Communication Checklist	An AM-to-PM structure for communication discipline
Leading Up	What to do when the communication problem is the people above you
Leading Down	The most common failures in downward communication — and the fixes
Leading Sideways	How peer communication works at the working level
Difficult Conversation Prep	A pre-conversation planning tool
When You're the Only One	How to sustain when no one else reciprocates

Section	What You'll Get
The Courage to Escalate	Why documentation is a professional act, not a defensive one
Modeling the Standard	The most powerful communication act you have

Communication IS the Job

When I say "communication is the job," I don't mean "talk more" or "hold more meetings." I mean this specifically:

4 Leadership Communication Acts

Act	What It Looks Like	What Happens When You Don't Do It
Information architecture	Actively ensuring the right information reaches the right people, in the right form, at the right time	Your team works without context; your leadership makes decisions without reality
Setting clear expectations	Defining what success looks like, who has decision authority, and what the actual deadline is — explicitly	Every ambiguity in your team's understanding originated in something never said clearly
Creating conditions for honest information flow	Responding to problems with curiosity, not blame; welcoming bad news	The team sends only good news; you operate on a systematically distorted picture of reality — while believing you have full visibility
Modeling the standard	Behaving the way you want your team to behave — your behavior is the loudest communication you produce	Your actions contradict your stated expectations; the team adopts what you do, not what you say

That last one carries more weight than most leaders realize:

- Send emails at 11 PM → tells others that the workday doesn't end.

- Take credit for team accomplishments in leadership meetings → communicates that credit flows up, not down.
- Cut people off in meetings → communicates that some voices matter more than others.

None of this requires saying a word.
Your behavior is the loudest communication you produce.

What Good Leaders Say vs. What Bad Leaders Say

Situation	What a Bad Leader Says	What a Good Leader Says
Someone brings a problem	"Why didn't you catch this earlier?"	"Thank you for telling me. Walk me through what you're seeing."
A deadline is missed	"This is unacceptable. Who's responsible?"	"The deadline passed — can you walk me through what happened? I want to understand what got in the way."
The team asks for direction	"Figure it out — that's what I pay you for."	"Here's what I need the outcome to look like. Let's talk through the approach and make sure you have what you need."
A decision is being made	Decides privately, announces the result	"Here's the decision I'm leaning toward and why — what am I missing?"
Something goes wrong publicly	Deflects or stays silent	Addresses it directly: "Here's what happened, here's what we're doing about it, and here's what I should have done differently."
Someone performs well	"Good work."	"The way you handled the client pushback on Tuesday — specifically how you reframed the ask — that was exactly right."
Feedback needs to be given	Six-week delayed review, vague and general	Private, specific, timely: "Here's what I observed, here's the impact, here's what I'm asking you to do differently."

Situation	What a Bad Leader Says	What a Good Leader Says
Uncertainty exists	Projects false confidence	"I don't have all the answers yet — here's what I know and here's how we'll figure out the rest."
The team gave input that wasn't used	Makes the decision and moves on	"I heard [specific feedback]. I wasn't able to act on it because [reason]. Here's what I could change: [specific item]."
A team member is struggling	Waits for the performance review	"I've noticed you seem stretched right now — what's getting in the way and what can I do to help?"

Leader's Daily Communication Checklist

This is not a comprehensive to-do list. It is a set of habits that can change the information environment your team operates in.

Morning (before 10 a.m.):

- Am I accessible today — does my team know how to reach me and whether I'm available?
- Is there anything my team needs to know to start their day that they don't have yet?
- Are there any open commitments from yesterday that need a status update?
- Is there anyone I should proactively check in with today?

During the Day:

- Am I listening more than I'm talking in my conversations?
- When someone brings me a problem, am I responding with curiosity before judgment?
- Are my messages clear enough that the recipient knows exactly what I need and when?
- If I made a commitment today, did I write it down?

End of Day:

- Did I close every loop I opened today — or did I communicate a delay with a new timeline?
- Did I give at least one piece of specific, timely positive feedback?
- Are there open items my team is waiting on from me that I can advance or respond to before tomorrow?
- Did I learn anything today that leadership needs to know?

Weekly:

- Did I hold all my 1:1s? If not, did I reschedule them promptly?
- Is my team's action log current?
- Have I given feedback this week — not just praise, but specific, developmental feedback to at least one person?
- Did I communicate proactively, or was I reactive all week?

Leading Up: When Your Leadership Isn't Listening

This is the situation that doesn't get enough attention in leadership books: **what do you do when the communication problem is the people above you? You will, at some point, work for a leader who does not listen. Who makes decisions without relevant information because they haven't asked for it and the culture doesn't invite it.**

Who responds to concerns with minimization. Who treats updates as confirmation of what they already believe rather than information that could change their thinking. **This is not unusual. It is extremely common.**

Leading Up Effectively — 3 Principles

1. Lead with what they care about, not what you care about.

The executive focused on cost will not be moved by a concern framed in quality terms. The operations leader measured on throughput will not engage with a problem framed as a process compliance issue. Frame your information in the terms that matter to the person you're communicating with — while being completely honest about the content. This is not dishonesty. It is effective communication.

2. Make the decision easy.

When you bring a problem without a recommendation, you're asking them to do work you could have done. When you bring a problem with a proposed solution and a clear Ask (SIA — Situation, Impact, Ask), you're respecting their time and demonstrating you've thought it through. Leaders who feel like they're being given work by the people below them eventually stop being receptive. Leaders who feel supported by capable people who bring complete packages become more engaged, not less.

3. Know when to escalate despite the resistance.

There are situations where you've tried to communicate a concern to your immediate leadership, it has not been received, and the risk is significant enough that you cannot accept the non-response. In those situations, the responsible professional choice is to escalate further, through appropriate channels, with documentation of what you communicated and when.

This requires courage. Escalating over or around a leader who hasn't been receptive is professionally risky — anyone who tells you otherwise hasn't worked in a real organization. The question is not whether it's risky. The question is what the cost of staying silent is, and whether you can live with that.

I have made this calculation more than once. Looking back, the times I did not escalate — the times I let the communication failure stand because escalating felt too risky — those are the ones I regret.

Instead of / Try: Leading Upward

Instead of...	Try...
"I have a concern about [topic]."	"I want to flag a risk that I believe needs a decision at your level — it's affecting [specific impact]."
"I've been trying to tell you this for weeks."	"I want to make sure I'm communicating this in a way that's useful to you — here's the one-page summary."

Instead of...	Try...
Burying the ask at the end of a long update	Leading with the ask: "I need a decision on [specific thing] by [date]. Here's the context."
Waiting for the issue to resolve itself	Proactive flag: "I don't have a crisis, but I have an emerging situation you should know about before it becomes one."

Leading Down: Giving Your Team the Clarity They Need

The most common failure mode in downward communication is not cruelty or dishonesty. It is **insufficient clarity, delivered with the assumption that the team will fill in the gaps.**

Leaders who understand the full context of a decision communicate only the decision itself — without the reasoning that would help the team execute it well, adapt when circumstances change, or understand what success looks like. The fix is not complicated: **tell people why.** Not a dissertation — a sentence or two.

Common Downward Communication Failures:

Failure	What It Sounds Like	What It Costs
Withholding the reasoning	"Prioritize this metric this quarter."	Team executes blindly; can't adapt when circumstances change
Inconsistency across channels	Different messages in 1:1 vs. team meeting vs. email	Team loses trust in both channels simultaneously
Praise without specificity	"Great job, everyone."	Noise. Team doesn't learn what you value.
Not closing the loop on input	Ask for input → make decision → move on without acknowledging what you heard	Team learns their input is irrelevant; stops giving it

The fix for not closing the loop on input, even when the decision is not what people advocated for: *"I heard the team's concerns about the timeline. Here's what I was able to change, and here's what I wasn't able to change and why."* **That's it. That's all it takes to keep input flowing.**

Difficult Conversation Prep Sheet

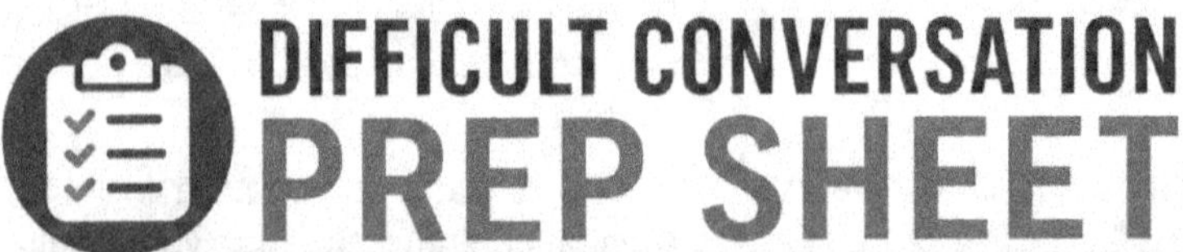

Use this before any conversation you've been avoiding – feedback, performance, escalation, or conflict resolution.

WHAT IS THIS CONVERSATION ABOUT?
One sentence.
Observable situation,
no judgment.

WHAT IS THE SPECIFIC BEHAVIOR OR SITUATION I NEED TO DESCRIBE?
Facts only. No adjectives like "unprofessional" or "irresponsible."
What did I actually see or hear?

WHAT IS THE IMPACT OF THIS BEHAVIOR OR SITUATION?
On the work, the team, the project, the relationship.
Be specific.

WHAT IS MY ASK?
What specific, observable change do I need?
What is the timeline?

WHAT IS THEIR LIKELY PERSPECTIVE?
Before you sit down, genuinely try to see it from their side.
What are they trying to accomplish?
What pressures are they under?

WHAT DO I NEED TO LEARN FROM THEM?
What question do I need to ask – and actually listen to – before I arrive at my ask?

WHAT AM I WILLING TO DO ON MY SIDE?
Accountability is two-way. What will you change, provide, or do differently?

WHAT IS THE FOLLOW-UP?
When will you check in?
What will "better" look like, specifically?

MY OPENING SENTENCE:
Write it out word for word.
Starting strong sets the tone for the whole conversation.

EXAMPLE OPENING SENTENCES:

"I want to talk with you about something that I think is getting in the way of [the project / our working relationship / your growth], and I want to approach it in a way that's useful for both of us."

"I've noticed something over the past few weeks that I'd like to address directly – not to put you on the spot, but because I think it matters."

"I want to give you some feedback. I want to do it now, while it's still recent, because I think it's important and I care about how you're developing."

PREPARE WELL. SPEAK CLEARLY. LISTEN FULLY. FOLLOW THROUGH.
THAT'S HOW DIFFICULT CONVERSATIONS BECOME STRONGER RELATIONSHIPS.

Leading Sideways: Communication Across Peer Functions

Sideways communication — between peers, across functions, among people with equivalent authority and no reporting relationship — is where organizational coordination happens at the working level. It also gets the least structured attention.

Leading sideways effectively:

Principle	What It Looks Like
Build relationships before you need them	Regular check-ins, mutual support on low-stakes items, genuine interest in what they're working on — six months before you have an urgent request that requires their cooperation
Make mutual dependencies explicit	"I can't produce an accurate forecast without your input by Tuesday." Not a complaint — a dependency made visible, which opens a conversation about how to manage it
Take the zero-sum dynamic off the table	Relentlessly focus on the shared outcome. Start from shared purpose rather than competing metrics. Information stops flowing when peer communication is zero-sum competition for budget, credit, or executive attention.

When This Happens / Do This: Peer-Level Communication

When This Happens	Do This
A peer isn't sharing information you need	Make the dependency explicit and the impact specific: "Without [X], I can't complete [Y] by [date]."
A peer is getting credit for joint work	Address it directly with them first — not with leadership. "I want to make sure we're presenting this as a joint effort."
A peer's function is creating problems for yours	Don't escalate first. Ask for a direct conversation: "Can we find twenty minutes to walk through the friction points?"
You need cooperation that requires their leadership's involvement	Give the peer a chance to solve it first. If they can't, escalate with their knowledge: "I told [peer] I was going to loop in [their boss] — they're aware."

When You're the Only One Communicating

At some point in every professional career, there is a period where you find yourself being the only one actively working the communication problem. You're sending updates nobody acknowledges. You're asking questions that go unanswered. You're building the action log, running the stand-ups, chasing the decisions — while the rest of the team operates as though these mechanisms don't exist.

This is one of the most demoralizing experiences in professional life. It is also more common than anyone admits.

How to navigate it:

Approach	What to Do	Why It Matters
Document your communication	The email you sent on March 14 with the status update and risk flag. The meeting notes you circulated. The action log you maintained.	Not paranoid. Professional records that make the situation visible and protect you if questions arise about what was known when.
Name the pattern, not the individual incidents	"I want to raise a concern about our communication process on this project — information isn't traveling consistently, and I think it's creating risk."	Addresses the systemic issue; avoids the appearance of complaint
Decide what you can sustain	Assess honestly: fixable problem you're compensating for, or unfixable dysfunction you're propping up?	You cannot carry the entire communication burden indefinitely. Know the difference.

FIELD NOTES: The Meeting You Stopped Being Invited To

The operational signature: No announcement. No conversation. No updated organizational chart. What happens instead is quieter and more disorienting.

What it looks like:

- Meeting invitations stop arriving — not all of them, just the specific ones.
- The cross-functional review where strategy gets set.
- The session where leadership aligns before the broader team is briefed.
- The working group shaping the thing your team will be asked to execute.
- Because they were never formally part of your role, nothing written says you should have been included — so the absence is deniable.

I have been in this situation. Not once, but across different contexts, at different points in my career. Each time felt different. Each time had the same operational signature: **I was learning about decisions that affected my work from their downstream effects rather than their upstream conversations.**

Why this was particularly costly in a quality function:

Quality doesn't operate in isolation. It is downstream of decisions made by operations, by leadership, by cross-functional working groups. When those decisions arrived without context:

- I was ensuring standards I had not been consulted on.
- Executing processes I had not helped design.
- Responding to problems I had not been given information to anticipate.

My work became necessarily reactive — not because of my capability, but because of information timing.

The communication skill that mattered most: Not getting back into the rooms I'd been removed from. I didn't always manage that.

What mattered was the discipline to keep communicating clearly in the rooms I was still in:

- Document what you know.

- Flag what you need.
- Name information gaps without making them interpersonal.
- Create a record of the impact of those gaps on the work you're accountable for.

The harder form of leadership: Leading through communication in a system that has partially excluded you means refusing to let the exclusion become an excuse for the failure of your own clarity.

You cannot control whether the decision table includes you. You can control whether your voice is documented, whether your concerns are on record, and whether the people with decision authority know what you know — even when they did not think to ask.

That is a harder form of leadership than operating within a well-functioning system. But it is the one that most directly tests whether your commitment to clarity is conditional on being recognized for it.

FIELD NOTE TAKEAWAY: Being excluded from the room doesn't end your obligation to communicate clearly. It changes the terrain. Document what you know. Flag what you need. Name information gaps without making them interpersonal. The goal isn't to force your way back in — it's to ensure that the people with decision authority know what you know, whether or not they thought to ask.

The Courage to Escalate and Document

There is a particular kind of professional courage that communication requires — not about confrontation or bravado, but about telling the truth when it's uncomfortable and creating a record when doing so feels politically risky.

I have worked in environments where escalating a concern felt like career risk. Where documenting a decision meant someone above me might someday be held accountable for it — and they knew it, and they preferred ambiguity. Where the unspoken norm was: resolve problems quietly, without evidence, without the accountability that comes from a paper trail. I understand the pressure to go along with that norm. I have, at times, yielded to it.

What I know now: the professional who consistently escalates concerns appropriately, documents decisions accurately, and maintains a record of what was communicated is not a troublemaker. They are a professional asset. They are the person organizations can rely on when the picture needs to be clear. They are the person who, when something eventually goes wrong, can show exactly what they said and when.

The culture that punishes this behavior is optimizing for appearance over reality. It will eventually pay the price of that optimization. The professional who maintained their integrity and their record will be in a far better position than the one who disappeared into the norm.

Modeling the Standard You Expect

Habit	What It Looks Like	What It Signals to Your Team
Communicate proactively	Update before they ask; flag risks before they become crises	Information is welcome; you won't be blindsided
Follow through on your commitments, visibly	Do what you said. When you can't, say so in advance.	Accountability goes both directions
Respond to problems with curiosity	"Tell me more about what you're seeing." (Not: "How did this happen?")	Problems are safe to bring; you won't shoot the messenger
Be consistent across channels	What you say in a 1:1, in a meeting, and in email should align	No hidden agenda; trust in both directions
Close the loop	"I said I'd get back to you — here's where we landed."	Your word means something
Name your own misses	"I should have updated you last week — I didn't, and I'm sorry. Here's where we are now."	Models the behavior you want when they drop a ball

Habit	What It Looks Like	What It Signals to Your Team
Make praise specific	Name the behavior, not just the outcome	Teaches what you value
Protect time for direct conversations	Don't email what should be a conversation	You're willing to do the harder thing when it matters

You cannot expect from your team what you don't demonstrate yourself. If you want proactive communication, communicate proactively. If you want transparency, respond to transparency with curiosity, not defensiveness. If you want accountability, maintain a visible tracking system for your own commitments.

The standard is set by what you model, not what you mandate.

This is not a counsel of perfection. Nobody communicates perfectly. What matters is the pattern — and the response when you fall short. **When you notice you've dropped a communication ball, name it:**

"I should have updated you last week on where this stood — I didn't, and I'm sorry. Here's where we are now."

That response does two things at once: it closes the loop that was left open, and it models the behavior you want your team to demonstrate when they drop a ball.

Being the Bridge Between Dysfunction and Function

Not everyone who leads communication change does it from formal authority. Sometimes you're the individual contributor who sees the problem and takes it upon themselves to build the action log, draft the communication plan, and facilitate the cross-functional meeting that nobody else was going to organize. Sometimes you're the middle manager whose own leadership doesn't model good communication and whose team is looking to you for stability.

These positions are harder than having organizational mandate. They are also more important — because the people who choose communication discipline in the absence of organizational support are the ones who change culture from within.

What you don't need a title to do:

- Send a clear, well-structured email.
- Suggest that the meeting needs an agenda and a note-taker.
- Say, at the end of a conversation: "I want to make sure we're aligned — can I read back what I heard?"
- Build a shared tracker for your team's action items.
- Establish a standing communication with your counterpart in another department.
- Start every handoff with a structured summary of what's open and who owns it.

When you do these things — consistently, professionally, with the discipline of someone who understands that communication is the infrastructure of everything else — you become the bridge. Between where your team is and where it can be. Between the dysfunction of poor communication and the function that good communication makes possible.

You are the bridge between what your organization intends and what it delivers.

Every clear message. Every honest escalation. Every followed-up action item. Every team agreement built and honored. Every moment you made space for someone to tell the truth.

Those are the bricks. You're building the bridge one conversation at a time. **That is leadership. That is the job.**

Chapter 14: Communicating Through Change

There is a particular kind of exhaustion that comes from leading a team through change — not the honest tiredness of hard work, but *the grinding fatigue of being caught between what leadership announced and what the floor is experiencing.*

I have been in that gap more times than I care to count. I have stood in the middle of a shift change and tried to explain, with a straight face, why the new process looked nothing like the one we trained on. I have watched good workers shut down, disengage, and walk out — not because they couldn't handle the change, but because no one ever told them what was happening.

Change is not the enemy. Poor communication about change is.

Every major operational shift I have been part of — new systems, restructured workflows, facility transitions, process overhauls — has had one thing in common regardless of whether it succeeded or failed: the outcome was determined less by the quality of the plan and more by the quality of the communication surrounding it. A good plan communicated badly will fail. A decent plan communicated exceptionally well has a fighting chance.

This section is not a primer on change management theory. If you have studied Prosci, you already know the framework. If you haven't, I'll introduce the pieces that matter most for communicators on the ground. What this section is about is the practical, unsexy, often-overlooked work of making sure the people who have to live inside a change understand it — before, during, and after it happens.

Why Change Fails — And It's Almost Always Communication

Study after study has confirmed what most operations leaders already know from hard experience: the majority of organizational change initiatives fail to achieve their intended outcomes. Estimates place the failure rate at approximately 70 percent, a number that has remained stubbornly consistent for decades despite advances in project management methodology, change management certification, and organizational development theory.

Why? Researchers and practitioners have pointed to dozens of root causes — poor sponsorship, insufficient resources, misaligned culture, unrealistic timelines. But cut through the post-mortem reports and you will find one consistent thread underneath almost all of them: somewhere, at some critical moment, the right information did not reach the right people in the right way at the right time.

That is a communication problem.

The Prosci ADKAR model gives us a useful lens here. ADKAR stands for Awareness, Desire, Knowledge, Ability, and Reinforcement — and it maps the psychological journey an individual takes through any change. What most people miss about ADKAR is this: every single stage is, at its core, a communication problem.

- **Awareness** — Does the person know the change is coming and understand why? If not, that's a communication failure.
- **Desire** — Does the person want to support the change? Desire is built (or destroyed) by what they hear, see, and observe from leadership. Communication again.
- **Knowledge** — Does the person know how to make the change work? Training is communication. Documentation is communication. Job aids are communication.
- **Ability** — Can the person perform the new way? When ability gaps persist, it traces back to inadequate feedback loops — no one was listening well enough to know where the gaps were.
- **Reinforcement** — Does the change stick? Or does the organization slide back to old habits because success was never recognized, progress was never communicated, and accountability was never established?

You cannot shortcut any of these stages. People who skip from Awareness straight to Ability and **wonder why no one is embracing the change have bypassed Desire and Knowledge — and they are usually baffled when their perfectly designed process falls apart on implementation day.**

ADKAR Stages Mapped to Communication Actions

ADKAR Stage	What People Need	Comm. Actions	Who Should Deliver	When
Awareness	To know the change is happening and why	Town halls, leadership memos, team briefings, posted announcements	Senior leadership (credibility requires rank)	As early as possible — before rumors fill the gap
Desire	To understand what's in it for them (or what's at risk)	One-on-ones, team discussions, honest Q&A sessions, connecting change to values people already hold	Direct supervisors (trust required)	During the "why" phase — before details are finalized
Knowledge	To know how the new process, system, structure works	Training sessions, job aids, SOPs, shadowing, FAQs	Subject matter experts and trainers	Before go-live — with time to absorb and practice
Ability	To perform the change correctly under real conditions	Coaching, observed practice, feedback loops, help desks	Frontline supervisors and peers	During and immediately after go-live
Reinforcement	To feel their efforts are recognized and the change is permanent	Recognition programs, updated metrics, accountability conversations, visible leadership behavior	All levels — but especially direct supervisors	Ongoing — for 60-90 days minimum post-launch

Here is the uncomfortable truth embedded in that table: most change communication plans focus almost entirely on Awareness. **Leadership**

sends the announcement, checks the box, and wonders why people "aren't on board."

They built a runway.
They didn't build the plane.

The Scope Discovery Problem

Before you can communicate a change, you have to understand what you are changing. This sounds obvious. It is not.

The most expensive communication failure in any change initiative is not saying the wrong thing — it is not knowing what needs to be said because nobody fully mapped the landscape before the launch. It is discovering mid-stream that entire categories of work exist that were never accounted for. It is finding out in week three that the new system cannot handle a transaction type that accounts for 30 percent of daily volume because no one asked the right questions before go-live.

I have lived this. The cost — in rework, in trust, in people's willingness to show up for the next initiative — is staggering.

Why Scope Gaps Happen

Scope gaps are not usually the result of negligence. They are the result of a predictable set of assumptions that feel reasonable in a conference room and fall apart on the floor.

- **The first assumption is *we know what we're getting into.*** Organizations **with experienced teams have the most dangerous blind spots** because their *expertise creates confidence* — sometimes justified, sometimes not. The familiarity that allows them to move fast also causes them to stop asking basic questions. "We've done this before" is one of the most dangerous phrases in change management.
- **The second assumption is *we don't have time to fully scope this.*** Timeline pressure is real. But compressing scope discovery does not save time — it borrows time at a very high interest

rate. Every hour not spent mapping the landscape pre-launch becomes ten hours of firefighting post-launch.

- **The third assumption is *we already know who the stakeholders are.*** Stakeholder identification is almost always incomplete on the first pass. The people who will be most affected by a change are frequently the ones least visible in planning conversations — the floor workers, the third-shift supervisor, the carrier rep who handles the exception freight no one documented.

The Cost of Discovering Scope Mid-Implementation

Consider two scenarios. In Scenario A, a team spends two weeks before a launch doing thorough scope discovery — mapping every workflow, interviewing every stakeholder group, stress-testing their assumptions. They find three significant gaps they hadn't planned for. They address them. The launch is delayed by one week.

In Scenario B, the same team skips the deep dive, launches on schedule, and discovers the same three gaps in weeks two, three, and five of live operations. Each discovery triggers emergency problem-solving, rework, expedited resources, and a fresh wave of team frustration.

Scenario A costs one week of delay. Scenario B costs months of chaos, rework, and credibility. I have never once, in twenty years, seen an organization regret Scenario A. I have seen many organizations live in Scenario B for far longer than they ever should have.

The Role of Trained Process Experts

This is where the combination matters. Lean Six Sigma helps identify where the process is breaking. Change management helps explain why people may resist, misunderstand, or work around the fix. **When both disciplines are at the table, organizations are far more likely to solve the real problem — and make the solution stick.**

LSSBB-credentialed professionals are trained specifically in the kind of process mapping, waste identification, and end-to-end flow analysis that exposes scope gaps before they become operational crises. They bring structured methodology — SIPOC (Supplier, Inputs, Process, Outputs,

Customer) diagrams, process maps, voice of the customer analysis — to a conversation that otherwise tends to run on assumptions and instincts.

Category	Question to Answer	Why It Matters
Process Scope	What are ALL of the workflows, tasks, and transaction types that will be affected — including low-volume and exception processes?	Low-volume processes are the ones most likely to be missed and most likely to create chaos when discovered mid-launch
People Scope	Who performs work that touches this change, including indirect roles, support functions, and third parties (carriers, vendors, temps)?	Stakeholders you didn't identify cannot be prepared
Technology Scope	What systems, integrations, and data flows are involved? What happens to current workarounds when the new system goes live?	Technical gaps surface at the worst possible moment if not discovered pre-launch
Volume Scope	What is the full range of transaction volumes, including peak periods and seasonal spikes?	A process that works fine at average volume may collapse at peak, and nobody planned for it
Dependency Scope	What upstream and downstream operations depend on the processes being changed? What will break if this change is delayed or partially implemented?	Cascading dependencies are the most common source of "we didn't know that would happen" surprises
Exception Scope	What are the known exceptions, special handling requirements, and edge cases in the current process?	Exceptions are where scope gaps hide. "We handle about 200 of those a week" is a sentence that surfaces too late more often than it should

Category	Question to Answer	Why It Matters
Knowledge Scope	Where does critical process knowledge live? Is it documented? Is it in one person's head? What happens if they're out?	Tribal knowledge is invisible scope — and it disappears at exactly the wrong moment during transitions
Communication Scope	Who needs to know what, and from whom do they need to hear it? Is there a communication infrastructure in place to reach all affected stakeholders?	The change communication plan is part of the scope — not a separate add-on

If your organization is about to launch a significant operational change and there is no trained process expert involved in the scope discovery phase, that is a risk that should be surfaced to leadership immediately. It is not a nice-to-have. The absence of that expertise is a gap with a price tag.

Scope Communication Checklist
Answer these questions first. If you cannot answer them, find out why.

This is the point in our framework where the Silent Spiral™ most often begins at the **organizational level.** Remember the **Stages: Assumption → Silence → Frustration → Workaround → Failure.**

Major change initiatives that skip thorough scope discovery are making an organizational-level Assumption at Stage 1. The silence that follows — the unasked questions, the unidentified stakeholders, the undocumented processes — is already building toward the Frustration and Workaround stages before the launch even happens.

Progress over perfection — *always.*

But "we'll figure it out as we go" is not progress.

It is a **deferred cost with compound interest.**

The Three Phases of Change Communication

Change communication is not an announcement. It is an ongoing process — managed before, during, and after the change itself. Most organizations invest heavily in the announcement and then wonder why the change didn't stick.

The announcement is not where change communication begins. By the time the all-hands meeting happens, the people in the room have already decided whether to trust what they're about to hear. They formed that opinion in the weeks before — from what they overheard, what they did not hear, and what they pieced together from the silence around them. The announcement either confirms what they already suspected or contradicts it. Neither outcome is what leadership thinks it's delivering. Here is a framework built from floor-level experience — communication architecture that works in operational environments.

Phase 1: Before the Change — Preparing the Ground

The pre-change phase is where you build the foundation. Your goals are to create Awareness and begin cultivating Desire — the first two stages of ADKAR. Understanding starts long before go-live.

Awareness is not the same as having been told. People are aware of a change when they can describe it in their own words — what is changing, why, and what it means for the work they do tomorrow morning. If they cannot answer those three questions, they have been informed, not made aware.

Desire is harder. It cannot be installed by repetition or pressured into existence. It builds when people see that the change is being managed by adults who have thought it through, that the costs are being acknowledged, and that the rollout will not leave them looking foolish in front of their teams. Desire is the byproduct of credibility. You earn it before you ask for it.

This phase should begin early — before the plan is finalized, before the vendor is selected, before the org chart has been redrawn. People who feel like decisions happened to them are harder to bring along than people who had visibility into the process. **You do not have to share everything. You do have to communicate something.**

PHASE 1: BEFORE THE CHANGE

PREPARING THE GROUND

Great change starts before the change begins.

The pre-change phase is where you build the foundation. Your goals in this phase are to create Awareness and begin cultivating Desire— the first two stages of ADKAR.

WHY THIS PHASE MATTERS

- People cannot support a change they don't understand, and understanding starts long before go-live.
- As early as possible, communicate the plan, the "why," and what people can expect.
- As much as possible, create clarity and visibility before the details are finalized.

OUR OBJECTIVES IN THIS PHASE

AWARENESS
Let people know the change is happening and why.

UNDERSTANDING
Share what is known, what is still being figured out, and how people will be kept informed.

TRUST
Build credibility by being transparent and consistent, even when the full picture is not complete.

KEY MESSAGES TO COMMUNICATE EARLY

Here's why the change is needed.

Here's what we're trying to achieve.

Here's what we know (and when decisions will be made).

Here's who is involved and how you can stay informed.

Here's how you can ask questions and give input.

BEFORE THE CHANGE: STAKEHOLDER-SPECIFIC COMMUNICATION PLAN

COMMUNICATION NEED	AUDIENCE	CHANNEL	FREQUENCY	OWNER
Status updates – where we are in preparation	All employees	Posted updates / email / shift briefing	Weekly	Operations manager
Two-way Q&A – surface concerns early	Small group sessions (10–15 people max)	Facilitated sessions	2–3 weeks before go-live	Direct supervisors
Detailed briefing – impact by role	Frontline supervisors	In-person briefing	Once per supervisor any employee communications	Operations leadership
FAQs – awareness & what's why	All employees	Intranet / posted FAQs	Once per week	Communications lead
Stakeholder-specific announcements	Supporting departments, vendors, carriers	Direct outreach / email	As scope is confirmed	Change lead
Internal alignment – leadership team updates	All supervisors	Direct conversation + written clarification	As needed / rapid response	All supervisors
Training lead time	Affected workers	Written + verbal	2–3 weeks before training begins	Training lead

SUCCESS IN THIS PHASE LOOKS LIKE:
- People know a change is coming.
- They understand the why.
- They trust that communication will continue.

REMEMBER
Silence → frustration → workaround → failure.
Visibility and honesty now prevent resistance later.

START EARLY. COMMUNICATE OFTEN. BUILD TRUST.
If people don't understand it before go-live, they won't support it after.

Phase 2: During the Change — Sustaining Through the Messy Middle

This is where most communication plans collapse. The "messy middle" is the space between go-live and stability — and it is almost always messier than anyone planned. Unexpected problems surface. Training doesn't cover everything. Systems behave in ways nobody anticipated. Key people are unavailable, and backups are learning in real time.

This is not a failure of the plan. It is the reality of change. In this phase, **your people are asking three questions — whether they say them out loud or not:**

- *Are you paying attention?*
- *Do you care what this is like on the ground?*
- *Are you doing something about it?*

If they believe all three, they will keep showing up and working through the friction. If they doubt even one, resistance accelerates. During this phase, feedback loops become non-negotiable. "Let me know if something's wrong" is not a system. **This is the phase where the Silent Spiral™ either accelerates — or gets interrupted.**

You need structure:

- Daily huddles that surface issues in real time
- A visible way to track and prioritize problems
- A clear owner for answering questions and closing gaps

Problems that are not surfaced cannot be solved. Problems that are **not solved** become the permanent **new normal.**

PHASE 2: DURING THE CHANGE

MAKING IT HAPPEN

Communication keeps people aligned, capable, and moving forward.

This phase is where people put the change into action. Your goals are to build Knowledge and develop Ability—the middle two stages of ADKAR.

WHY THIS PHASE MATTERS

- People are learning, adjusting, and applying the change in real time.
- Questions, frustration, and slips will surface—communication prevents small issues from becoming big setbacks.
- Consistent, two-way communication builds confidence and keeps momentum strong.

OUR OBJECTIVES IN THIS PHASE

KNOWLEDGE

Ensure everyone has the information, tools, and training they need to do the new way of working.

ABILITY

Support people as they practice, adapt, and perform the change correctly under real conditions.

CONFIDENCE

Reinforce progress, address concerns quickly, and keep people engaged and moving forward.

KEY MESSAGES TO COMMUNICATE OFTEN

Here's what's going well.

Here are the common challenges—and how we're solving them.

Here's how to get help and where to find resources.

Here's what's next.

Thank you—your efforts are making a difference.

DURING THE CHANGE: STAKEHOLDER-SPECIFIC COMMUNICATION PLAN

COMMUNICATION NEED	AUDIENCE	CHANNEL	FREQUENCY	OWNER
Real-time updates – what's happening and what's changed	All employees	Email / shift huddles / team briefings	Weekly (or as needed)	Operations leadership
Q&A and issue resolution – address questions quickly	All employees	Help desk / dedicated channel / huddles	Daily (or as needed)	Change team / Help desk lead
Coaching and feedback – support learning and improve performance	Frontline employees	One-on-ones / side-by-sides / coaching sessions	Ongoing (daily / weekly)	Frontline supervisors
Training refreshers – reinforce key skills and knowledge	Frontline employees	Training sessions / job aids / videos	As needed / based on gaps	Training lead / SMEs
Performance check-ins – track adoption and outcomes	Managers / supervisors	Weekly reports / dashboards / team meetings	Weekly	Operations manager
Cross-functional alignment – stay coordinated	Supervisors / key stakeholders	Stand-up calls / team syncs	Weekly	Change lead
Celebrate wins – recognize progress and effort	All employees	Recognition boards / emails / huddles	Weekly	All supervisors / HR / Comms

SUCCESS IN THIS PHASE LOOKS LIKE:

- People know how to do the new way of working.
- Questions are answered quickly.
- Issues are addressed before they grow.
- Early wins are recognized and shared.

REMEMBER

Learning happens in the flow of work.
Communicate, coach, and listen every day.
Small conversations now prevent big resistance later.

STAY CLOSE. LISTEN OFTEN. REMOVE ROADBLOCKS.

Support today creates the results you need tomorrow.

Phase 3: After the Change — Reinforcing and Closing the Loop

This is the most neglected phase — and the one that determines whether the **change actually sticks.** ADKAR calls this **Reinforcement**, and it's where many organizations quietly fall apart. The change has launched. Things are "mostly working." Leadership shifts focus to the next initiative. And then, slowly and predictably, the organization drifts back to the old way of working.

Not because people are resistant:

- Because the new way was never fully locked in. No one kept reinforcing the standard.
- No one consistently recognized the effort.
- No one closed the communication loops that were opened during the transition.

In this phase, people are watching for three signals:

- *Is this permanent?*
- *Did this work?*
- *Did what I did matter?*

If they don't hear those answers clearly, they wait. And waiting turns into reverting. *Reinforcement is not a one-time message — it is a pattern.*

It shows up in what leaders say, what gets measured, what gets recognized, and what gets corrected. When those signals are consistent, the change becomes the new normal. When they are not, the old system quietly reasserts itself. This phase also requires a structured after-action review.

Not a blame session — an honest discussion:

- What did we plan?
- What happened?
- What did we learn?
- What will we do differently next time?

When that reflection is documented and shared, it becomes more than a debrief — it becomes institutional knowledge. **And that is one of the highest-value communication investments an organization can make.**

PHASE 3: AFTER THE CHANGE

MAKING IT STICK

Reinforcement turns change into the new way forward.

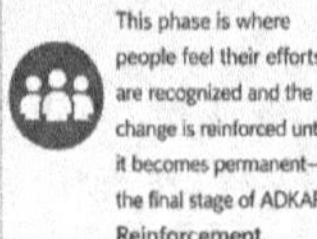

This phase is where people feel their efforts are recognized and the change is reinforced until it becomes permanent—the final stage of ADKAR: Reinforcement.

WHY THIS PHASE MATTERS

- Without reinforcement, old habits return and the change fades.
- Recognition, accountability, and consistent leadership behavior lock in the change.
- Sustained communication ensures the change is valued, measured, and here to stay.

OUR OBJECTIVES IN THIS PHASE

REINFORCEMENT

Recognize effort, celebrate wins, and reinforce the behaviors that align with the change.

SUSTAINABILITY

Build systems, processes, and accountability to make the change last.

CONTINUOUS IMPROVEMENT

Gather feedback, learn, and keep improving based on what's working and what's not.

KEY MESSAGES TO COMMUNICATE OFTEN

Here's what's working—and the impact we're seeing.

Thank you—your efforts are making this stick.

Here's what we expect to continue doing.

Here's what we're learning and how we'll keep improving.

This is our new normal—let's keep moving forward.

AFTER THE CHANGE: STAKEHOLDER-SPECIFIC COMMUNICATION PLAN

COMMUNICATION NEED	AUDIENCE	CHANNEL	FREQUENCY	OWNER
Recognize and celebrate – highlight wins and impact	All employees	Recognition programs / shout-outs / newsletters / town halls	Weekly / Monthly	All supervisors / Communications
Share results and impact – show progress and value	All employees, leadership	Dashboards / reports / town halls	Monthly	Operations manager
Reinforce expectations – remind and hold the line	Frontline employees	Team huddles / one-on-ones / posters / reminders	Weekly	Frontline supervisors
Gather feedback – keep listening and adapting	All employees	Surveys / feedback forms / team discussions	Monthly / Quarterly	Change team / HR / Operations
Accountability conversations – review performance and adherence	Managers / supervisors	One-on-ones / performance reviews / coaching conversations	Bi-weekly / Monthly	All supervisors / Managers
Update systems and tools – embed into policies, processes, and metrics	Managers, key stakeholders	Policy updates / SOPs / team meetings	As changes occur / Quarterly review	Change lead / Operations manager
Share stories – success stories and lessons learned	All employees	Newsletters / videos / town halls	Monthly	Communications lead

SUCCESS IN THIS PHASE LOOKS LIKE:

- People consistently use the new way of working.
- Positive results are visible and measured.
- Old habits don't return.
- The change is part of how we work—every day.

REMEMBER

Reinforcement is not a one-time event—it's a pattern. 60–90 days of consistent reinforcement is the minimum to make the change permanent.

REINFORCE. RECOGNIZE. LOCK IT IN.

Sustained communication and visible leadership make the change permanent and set the stage for the next improvement.

The Communication Void

When leaders go quiet during change, something always fills the silence.

It is never good. The **Communication Void** is the space that opens when the people responsible for communicating a change — leaders, managers, project sponsors — stop transmitting information.

It rarely happens for bad reasons. Leaders don't have full answers yet. They don't want to make commitments they can't keep. They're overwhelmed by the operational reality of the transition. **The intention is not malicious.** *The effect is.*

What Fills the Silence

In the absence of official information, people do not wait patiently for clarity. They generate their own explanations. And those explanations follow a pattern. They are *almost always worse than the truth.*

- Silence about a reorganization becomes *"there are layoffs coming."*
- Silence about a system change becomes *"the system is failing and no one knows how to fix it."*
- Silence about a contract becomes *"we lost the work."*

This is not irrational behavior. People have learned — often through experience — that silence precedes bad news. So when communication stops, they prepare for the worst.

The Leadership Mistake

The instinct to wait until you have the full picture before saying anything feels responsible. It is not. It is a decision to cede the narrative to the rumor mill.

THE 3 THINGS RULE

When you don't have all the answers, cover these three things—every time.

It keeps you communicating. It builds trust. It prevents the Communication Void.

You don't need all the answers. You need a standard for how you communicate until you do.

In any communication about an ongoing change—any briefing, any update, any floor conversation—cover three things:

WHAT WE KNOW

State it clearly.

Even if it's only one thing, say it.

Example:
"We know the system go-live date is still May 15."

2 WHAT WE DON'T KNOW YET

Name the uncertainties explicitly.

Saying "I don't know" is not weakness—it is credibility.

Example:
"We don't know yet how reporting will be impacted."

3 WHEN WE'LL KNOW MORE

Commit to a timeline for the next update.

Even if that timeline is "by end of week," honor it.

Example:
"We'll have more information by Friday."

WHY IT WORKS

BUILDS TRUST

Honesty about what you know—and don't know—earns credibility.

MANAGES EXPECTATIONS

People know what's settled and what's still being worked.

PREVENTS THE VOID

There is always something being transmitted, so rumors don't fill the gap.

KEEPS THE MOMENTUM

Consistent updates keep people engaged and moving forward.

COMMUNICATE SOMETHING. COMMUNICATE CONSISTENTLY.

THE 3 THINGS RULE KEEPS YOU LEADING THE MESSAGE—
SO THE RUMOR MILL NEVER DOES.

The Silent Spiral™ Connection

The Communication Void is **Stage 2 of the Silent Spiral™ operating at scale**. When organizational silence sets in, **Frustration is already building below the surface**. By the time leadership realizes how far the rumors have spread, the team has already moved into Workaround:

- Making decisions based on assumptions
- Creating their own versions of the process
- Solving problems that may not exist

At that point, you are no longer leading the change. You are reacting to it. Silence doesn't create neutrality. It creates distortion. If you don't fill the space with clarity, someone else will fill it with assumptions.

Resistance Is Feedback, Not Defiance

The natural instinct when a team pushes back on a change is to interpret the resistance as a performance problem — people who aren't willing to adapt, workers who are too set in their ways, supervisors who are protecting their turf. ***Resist that instinct.***

Resistance is almost never defiance for its own sake. *It is information.* **When people resist a change, they are telling you something about the gap between what they understand and what you are asking them to do.** That gap is a communication problem — and it is yours to solve, not theirs to overcome on their own.

Think about what resistance actually looks like in an operational environment: the worker who keeps reverting to the old way, the supervisor who "hasn't gotten around to" implementing the new process, the team that keeps raising the same objection in every meeting. From the outside, these look like compliance failures. From the inside, they are almost always something else entirely.

Resistance Reframe — What It Looks Like, What It's Saying, and the Communication Fix

What Resistance Looks Like	What It's Saying	The Communication Fix
"We tried something like this before and it didn't work."	I don't trust that this time will be different. Nobody has told me what's changed.	Acknowledge the history directly. Explain specifically what is different this time — don't dismiss the past.
Reverting to the old process when supervisors aren't watching	I wasn't trained well enough to feel confident in the new way.	Return to Knowledge and Ability in the ADKAR model. More training, coaching, and practice time — not more accountability conversations.
"Nobody asked us before they decided this."	I feel excluded, and my expertise was not respected.	Build in retrospective input mechanisms. Acknowledge the gap. Ask for input going forward — and use it.
Silent compliance — doing it, but with zero engagement	I have given up trying to raise concerns. Nobody listens anyway.	This is the most dangerous resistance. Proactively seek out the quiet ones. Create safe channels for concerns to surface.
Escalating the same issue repeatedly	My concern has not been addressed, and I don't feel heard.	Close the loop. Either address the concern or explain clearly why you cannot — and what you are doing instead.
"This is going to create more work, not less."	I don't see the benefit. Nobody has made the case in terms I understand.	Connect the change to outcomes that matter to this specific person or team. "Here is what this means for your shift specifically."
Increased absenteeism or turnover among key players	The stress of this change is unsustainable, and I am voting with my feet.	This is a Stage 4/5 failure in the Silent Spiral™. Emergency intervention — not an email, but direct conversation with the people you cannot afford to lose.

The most dangerous form of resistance is the last one in that table — and it is also the most invisible. When your best people start quietly disengaging, the problem has been building for a long time. By the time you see it in turnover data, you have already missed most of the signals.

Resistance that is treated as feedback is a gift. Resistance that is treated as defiance becomes a battle — and in my experience, operations leaders who go to battle with their own teams over change consistently lose.

The Ripple Effect of Poorly Scoped Change

When a change initiative launches without a thorough understanding of the end-to-end operation, the consequences do not arrive all at once. They come in waves — each one triggered by the wave before it, each one hitting a different part of the organization that had no warning it was coming.

This is the Ripple Effect of poorly scoped change. It is not a single failure. It is a cascade.

The initial failure — the scope gap — is usually discovered by the people closest to the work. A process that was assumed to be straightforward turns out to include categories of volume, transaction types, or specialized requirements that were never accounted for. The people who designed the change did not know about them. The people who knew about them were never asked.

What happens next is predictable: **emergency problem-solving, resources, workarounds.** The immediate team absorbs the impact and does what operational teams always do — they hold it together with duct tape and extra shifts while the formal process scrambles to catch up. But the work doesn't stay contained. It ripples.

The team that built the workaround now has a different process than the training documents describe. The downstream team is now getting something different than what they planned for. The carrier or vendor is being asked to accommodate changes to requirements they were never briefed on. The supervisors trying to hold performance metrics are now managing to a standard that the team cannot physically meet with the resources allocated.

And underneath all of it, **something quieter but more lasting is happening: trust is eroding.**

Stage	What Happens	Who Is Affected	The Comm. Failure
Gap Discovery (Week 1-2)	A category of work surfaces that was not planned for — specialized handling, exception processing, assembly requirements	Launch team, frontline workers	The scope discovery phase didn't involve the people who knew about this work
Immediate Workaround (Week 2-3)	The launch team improvises a solution — manual process, extra headcount, temporary bypass	Launch team, supervisors	Workers are following a process that doesn't match their training — and the discrepancy isn't officially communicated
Downstream Impact (Week 3-5)	The downstream team begins receiving output that doesn't match specifications — wrong format, incomplete data, missing documentation	Downstream operations, support functions	Downstream team was not briefed that the process changed mid-launch
Resource Strain (Week 4-6)	Unplanned volume and extra process steps are consuming resources budgeted for a different scope	Operations management, finance	Budget owners don't know why actual costs are diverging from plan
Trust Erosion (Week 4-ongoing)	Workers and supervisors who raised the scope gap early and were told to "keep moving" stop volunteering information	All levels	The feedback loop is broken — people have learned that raising problems has no payoff

Stage	What Happens	Who Is Affected	The Comm. Failure
Credibility Impact (Ongoing)	Leadership's ability to sponsor future changes is diminished. "Remember last time" becomes part of the cultural vocabulary	All employees	No formal acknowledgment of what went wrong, no lessons-learned communication, no closure
Retention Risk (3-6 months out)	Key people who carried the heaviest load during the cascade begin looking at their options	Your most capable workers — the ones who always find a way	Nobody followed up to acknowledge their contribution or address their exhaustion

Ripple Effect of a Failing Scope Gap

That last row is the one that keeps me up at night. Organizations routinely underestimate the retention cost of poorly managed change initiatives. The people who stayed, adapted, and held things together during a chaotic launch are the same people who have the most options when they decide they've had enough. When they leave, they take institutional knowledge, hard-won process expertise, and the capacity to stabilize the next change with them.

The scope gap that seemed like a manageable operational problem in Week 2 is now, six months later, a talent problem, a culture problem, and a performance problem — and its origins are traceable back to a conversation that didn't happen in the planning phase.

FIELD NOTES: The Launch That Didn't Know What It Was Launching

> The transition looked simple on paper. A regional distribution operation — mid-sized, established carriers, experienced team, known SKU counts — being absorbed into a larger network. Everyone involved had done transitions before. The plan covered what you would expect: standard receiving, standard put-away, standard pick and pack. Staffing model built. Technology integration scheduled. Communication cadence set.

They weren't wrong about what they planned for.
They were wrong about what they didn't know existed.

What no one had uncovered — because no one had asked the people doing the work — was that a significant portion of daily throughput didn't behave like standard freight.

There were products with environmental requirements that demanded specific staging sequences. Assembly and kitting operations with their own workflows, labor demands, quality checkpoints, and downstream dependencies.

This wasn't edge-case volume.
It was core to the operation.

And it didn't exist in a single scope document.

- The first week after go-live was rough, but manageable. By the second week, the first unplanned workflow surfaced. An emergency bridge was built.
- By the third week, a second surfaced. Another bridge.
- By the fourth week, the downstream team filed a formal complaint: what they were receiving didn't match what they had been told to expect. A third bridge.
- By week six, the operation was running on three improvised processes layered on top of the original plan.
- The staffing model was wrong.
- The technology configuration was wrong.
- The SLAs committed to carriers and customers were based on a scope that didn't reflect reality.

And the team — working extended hours to hold it together — had stopped raising problems through official channels.

Not because the channels didn't exist. Because using them hadn't produced solutions. It had produced pressure to keep moving.

The impact didn't show up all at once. It compounded.

- Unbudgeted rework.

- Unplanned retraining.

Strained relationships with partners who had spent weeks receiving output no one warned them about. A supervisor who had tried to flag the gap before launch — and had been told the timeline was fixed — quietly started looking. She left four months after go-live. Three members of her team followed within the quarter.

What would have changed this?

Two weeks. Two weeks of structured scope discovery with the people who do the work — not just the managers who describe it.

- A process mapping exercise on the floor, not in a conference room.
- A trained practitioner challenging assumptions and documenting what was found.

And one honest pre-launch communication to every downstream team:

- Here is what this operation does.
- Here is what you should expect.
- Here is who to call when something doesn't match.

The scope gap was expensive. The communication failure made it catastrophic. And the most lasting cost wasn't measured in overtime or rework. **It was measured in the team that stopped trusting:**

- The next announcement
- The next initiative

The next time someone stood in front of them and said,
"We've got a solid plan."

Putting It Together: Change Communication as a Leadership Discipline

Change is not a project phase. It is a continuous condition in operational environments. The organizations and leaders who thrive are not the ones who manage change best in isolation — they are the ones who build the communication muscle over time, so that when the next transition arrives, the infrastructure is already in place and the team already knows how to move through it.

That means **investing in scope discovery before it feels urgent.** It means maintaining communication even when you have nothing to announce. It means treating resistance as data and silence as a warning sign. **It means closing the loop after every transition — not just moving on when things stabilize, but formally acknowledging what was hard, what was learned, and what you will do differently.**

The ADKAR framework gives us the map. The three phases give us the timeline. The Scope Communication Checklist gives us the pre-work discipline. And the Ripple Effect table reminds us of what is at stake if we skip any of it.

But underneath all of the frameworks and tables and checklists is a simpler truth that I keep returning to after twenty years on the operations floor: people can handle almost any change if they feel respected, informed, and heard. They will struggle through ambiguity if they trust that someone is paying attention and will tell them what they know as soon as they know it.

Your job as a leader communicating through change is not to have all the answers. It is to maintain the connection — to be the person your team can count on to show up, be honest, and keep the information moving even when the ground is shifting underneath everyone's feet.

Progress over perfection. But know your scope first.

Key Takeaways

- **Communication is not a task on the side of leadership during change. It is the mechanism by which leadership functions during change.** Setting expectations, modeling the behavior, and keeping honest information flowing are not soft work — they are the work.
- **ADKAR is a communication framework.** Awareness, Desire, Knowledge, Ability, and Reinforcement each fail or succeed based on what was communicated, by whom, and when.

- **Scope discovery is a communication act.** The most expensive failure in change is not knowing what needs to be said because nobody mapped the landscape before launch.
- **Silence is not neutrality.** The Communication Void during change always gets filled — and what fills it is almost always worse than the truth.
- **Resistance is feedback, not defiance.** Treat pushback as information about the gap between what people understand and what you are asking them to do.
- **The Ripple Effect** of poorly scoped change cascades from gap discovery through workaround, downstream impact, resource strain, trust erosion, credibility loss, and retention risk. Every stage compounds the last.
- **Reinforcement is a pattern, not a memo.** What gets said, measured, recognized, and corrected after launch determines whether the change sticks or quietly reverts.

Reflection Questions

1. **Name the change your organization is currently working through — declared or undeclared.** What phase are you actually in: scope discovery, the messy middle, or reinforcement? Where would the people on the floor say you are?
2. **Think about a change that succeeded under your leadership.** Strip away the project plan and the tooling. What did people *hear* from you, and how often, that made the difference?
3. **Think about a change that stalled or failed.** Where did the communication actually break — in what was said, in what was not said, or in what was said too late? Be specific. The diagnosis is the first repair.
4. **Who in your operation is most likely to fill a Communication Void with the wrong story when information goes quiet?** What would change if you got to them first — every time, on purpose?

Chapter 15: The Screen Between Us — Remote and Hybrid

Here's what most books about remote work won't tell you, because it complicates the narrative they're trying to sell. **Remote work did not create new communication problems. It inherited all the ones you already had and *gave them more room to run.***

Every organization that went remote in 2020 — most of them overnight, under significant stress — took its existing communication culture and put it on a larger stage. Teams with clear norms, documented decisions, and disciplined follow-through adapted reasonably well. Teams that ran on ambient awareness, hallway consensus, and informal relationships felt the floor drop out. The underlying difference wasn't technology or tools or whether people were in the same building. It was whether the communication infrastructure existed independently of physical proximity. **Most of it didn't.**

What followed — and what persists in hybrid teams today — is the Silent Spiral™ running at double speed:

Assumption (I was clear) → **Silence** (nobody said anything, so it must be fine) → **Frustration** (why didn't anyone tell me?) → **Workaround** (I'll just handle it myself) → **Failure** (how did this happen?)

In co-located environments, the spiral is slowed by friction — the natural checkpoints that exist when people share physical space. You see your colleague's face when you say something and notice the confusion. Someone overhears a conversation and flags a conflict. The project manager catches you at the coffee machine and asks the follow-up question that closes the loop.

These **micro-interactions** don't show up in any meeting agenda. But they do real work, constantly, and we built our organizational communication habits on the assumption that they would always be there. In remote and hybrid environments, they aren't. The spiral has no friction.

Breaking the Spiral™ adapted for distributed teams is exactly what this chapter is about. Every tool here — the default-to-writing principle, the documentation discipline, the structured check-ins, the source-of-truth architecture — is an application of the five-stage Breaking the Spiral™ framework to an environment where the organic friction that used to slow the Spiral has been removed.

This chapter is about **building communication systems that work when you can't rely on proximity to do any of the work for you.** It is also about being honest about what hybrid work is — which is not the best of both worlds. Done carelessly, it is the worst of both.

What Changes When the Hallway Disappears

The Ambient Information Problem

Ambient information is the category of things you know not because someone told you, but because you were there. You overheard the conversation between your manager and the VP. You noticed three people from operations walked into a conference room looking tense and came out forty minutes later looking relieved.

You caught the project lead at the printer and she mentioned, in passing, that the client call had gone better than expected. None of that was formally communicated to you. None of it would appear in a meeting notes document or a status update. But it shaped your understanding of what was happening — and you used it to calibrate your own work, your own conversations, your own decisions.

When the hallway disappears, ambient information disappears with it. Ambient information is the connective tissue of organizational awareness. It fills the space between formal communication structures with the nuance and context that makes those structures meaningful.

Without it, formal communication has to do everything — and it can't. It's too slow, too structured, and too filtered for the volume of real-time context an organization generates every day.

What you're left with is a constant low-grade information deficit. People don't know what they don't know.

Key Remote Communication Challenges

Challenge	What It Looks Like	Why It Matters
Ambient information loss	Missing context that used to arrive passively	People make decisions on incomplete pictures
"Available on chat" ≠ available	Green status circles that lie about readiness	Senders have false confidence; messages go unengaged
Opt-in vs. opt-out model	Default state is isolation, not awareness	Same habits that worked in-office produce dramatically less information flow
Meeting paradox	More meetings, less actual communication	Packed calendars leave no space to think, write, or process
The hybrid tax	Two-tier information environment	In-room participants consistently have better access than remote ones
Documentation gap	Decisions made in the room don't make it into the shared record	Remote participants operate on outdated or incomplete information
Loneliness as communication barrier	Isolated team members become less likely to reach out, flag problems, or ask for help	The Silent Spiral™ accelerates when isolation drains the energy required to communicate

The False Equivalence of "Available on Chat" and Available

Being logged into a messaging platform is not the same as being available for communication.

Available for communication means:

- I have capacity to receive, process, and respond to what you're sending me.
- I'm not in the middle of complex analysis that requires sustained focus.

- I'm not in back-to-back video calls where I'm technically "online" but reading nothing.
- The message you send me will land in a state of mind that can engage with it.

A green circle next to someone's name *is not a guarantee of any of those things. It is, at best, a signal that their computer is awake.*

In co-located offices, "being available" had texture. You could see that someone was heads-down with headphones on, and you made a judgment: this can wait, or this is urgent enough to tap them on the shoulder. Remote work removed those cues and replaced them with a blinking cursor that carries no information about whether it's a good time.

The fix is not to be online at all times. It is to be **explicit about actual availability** — and to match the channel to the urgency.

From Opt-Out to Opt-In

Model	Environment	Default State	Communication Requires
Opt-out	Co-located	Information flows by default	Active effort to disconnect
Opt-in	Remote	Isolation	Active effort to stay aware

Organizations that moved remote frequently kept their same communication habits — the same level of formality in documentation, the same frequency of deliberate information-sharing, the same norms about when to loop someone in — without realizing those habits were calibrated for an opt-out environment.

In an opt-in environment, the same habits produce dramatically less information flow, because the ambient layer that was doing so much of the work is simply gone.

What fills the gap when it's not deliberately filled? Assumptions. And the Silent Spiral™ begins.

The Meeting Paradox: More Meetings, Less Communication

The shift to remote work was followed, almost universally, by a dramatic increase in meeting volume. The logic was sound: we lost our informal communication channels, so we need to compensate with formal ones. Schedule a check-in. Add a sync. Stand up every morning.

The result, for most organizations, was a calendar crisis that made actual communication worse.

Here's why. Meetings are synchronous — they require everyone present at the same moment. The more meetings on the calendar, the fewer uninterrupted blocks remain for the focused work that generates the information those meetings are supposed to discuss.

- People arrive unprepared because they had meetings before this meeting.
- They half-attend because their minds are on the deliverable that was due before this meeting was scheduled.
- They leave with action items they don't have time to complete because the next meeting is in twenty minutes.

More meetings ≠ more communication. Real communication requires space — space to think, to write, to read, to process. Pack the calendar tight enough and you don't have that space. What you have instead is a constant performance of communication: the appearance of coordination without the substance of it.

The answer is not "fewer meetings" as an abstract principle. It is intentional meeting design — being honest about what a synchronous conversation can accomplish that a written document or asynchronous update cannot, and reserving meeting time for those things.

The Hybrid Tax

Fully remote is harder than co-located. But hybrid — where some team members are in the office and some are remote, sometimes on the same day and sometimes on different days — is harder than both.

Done without deliberate structure, hybrid is the worst of both. It is the two-tier communication problem: two classes of team members, with fundamentally different access to information and influence, operating under the nominal fiction that they are equivalently included.

The In-Room Advantage

Imagine a team of eight. Four are in the conference room. Four are on video call, tiled on the screen at the front of the room.

What the in-room participants experience:

- Direct eye contact and body language
- Ability to read the pause that signals uncertainty, the slight nod that signals agreement
- The rapid glance between two colleagues that signals "are you going to say something, or should I?"
- Full-bandwidth, multi-channel human communication

What the remote participants experience:

- A video feed capturing approximately 60% of the people contributing
- Audio that degrades whenever more than one person speaks at once
- A chat panel where questions may or may not be seen by the person running the meeting
- A document being reviewed on the screen in the room — visible, just barely, if they zoom in

The meeting nominally includes all eight people. In practice, it centers the four in the room. This is not malice. It is physics.

The gap between those two experiences is **the hybrid tax** — the cost that remote participants pay in every interaction where in-person and remote attendance are mixed.

The Documentation Gap

Here is a specific mechanism of hybrid communication failure that is both completely predictable and almost universally under-addressed.

Decisions made in a hybrid meeting — including decisions made in the five minutes before the meeting formally starts, or in the sidebar conversation between two in-room attendees — rarely make it into the shared record with the completeness the decision actually had.

- Meeting notes capture the formal agenda items.
- They don't capture the comment someone made while the screen was still loading.
- They don't capture the conversation between the director and the project lead that happened as people were getting coffee.
- They don't capture the informal agreement reached when someone pointed at the whiteboard and everyone in the room nodded.

The remote participants may not even know what they missed. They know they weren't getting the whole picture — there were whispered conversations at the table edge, movements toward a whiteboard outside camera range, knowing looks between people sharing physical space — but they don't know the specific content.

That gap — between what was said in the room and what made it into the shared record — compounds over time. Each undocumented decision creates a foundation of shared understanding among in-room participants that remote participants don't share, and that no one is keeping track of.

How Hybrid Amplifies Exclusion

Hybrid work does not distribute its communication gaps evenly.

Who tends to attend in person:

- Those who live nearby

- Those without caregiving responsibilities that require scheduling flexibility
- Those with enough political capital that in-office attendance is easy to maintain

Who tends to dial in remotely:

- Those managing caregiving responsibilities
- Those in different geographic locations
- Those with disabilities that make in-person work more difficult
- Newer employees who haven't yet built the relationships that make in-office attendance rewarding

When in-room participants consistently have better access to information, context, and decision-makers than remote participants, **the communication gap and the equity gap align.** The people already working against structural headwinds are the ones paying the hybrid tax.

A colleague in a previous role told me, matter-of-factly: "I'm always on the call. I'm never in the room." She wasn't describing a grievance. She was describing a systematic exclusion from the real communication that ran her organization — not from any meeting's agenda, but from the information environment where her in-room counterparts operated every day. She was right. And the organization paid for it in the quality of decisions that got made without her perspective, and in her eventual decision to leave.

Building hybrid teams that work requires confronting this dynamic directly, not hoping that good intentions will compensate for bad structure.

In the Room (and Not in the Room): The Hybrid Tax in Action

The meeting starts at 9:00. Four people are in the conference room. Three are on video.

The four in-room participants can see each other's faces. They're already mid-conversation when the video call opens.

Facilitator: *"Okay, let's get started. So we're thinking we move the launch date — Sarah and Dev, you were saying before the call that —"*

Priya, on video: *"Sorry, I missed that part. What were Sarah and Dev saying?"*

The facilitator doesn't quite hear Priya. The in-room microphone doesn't pick up video-side voices cleanly. Someone in the room shakes their head slightly at the delay.

The discussion continues. The whiteboard fills up. Priya can see it if she squints and zooms in. She types a question in the chat. Nobody reads the chat.

At the end, the facilitator: *"Any final thoughts before we wrap?"*

Priya unmutes. *"I have a concern about the timeline —"*

"We've kind of decided, but let's take that offline."

The decision is made. Priya's concern is taken offline, which means it disappears.

Priya was in the meeting. She was not in the room. Those are not the same thing — and someone paid for that difference.

Building Communication Systems That Work Across Distance

The challenge in remote and hybrid work is not primarily technical. The tools exist. **The challenge is behavioral and structural: building habits and systems that ensure information flows reliably when proximity can no longer be assumed.**

Default to Writing: If It's Not Written Down, It Didn't Happen

In co-located environments, documentation is valuable but partially optional — the gaps are filled by ambient information and shared memory. **In remote environments, documentation is the only information channel that works for everyone, regardless of time zone, schedule, or whether they happened to be in the office when something was discussed.**

The working assumption for remote and hybrid teams:

- Every significant meeting produces a summary with decisions made, action items assigned, and next steps noted.

- Every decision that affects more than one person is documented in a location everyone can access.
- Every important context — the reasoning behind a decision, the constraints that shaped it, the alternatives that were considered — is captured somewhere, not just assumed to be known.

The practical requirement:

- Someone must be assigned the note-taking function in every meeting that matters. Not "whoever wants to" — that produces no notes. Not "we'll all take notes" — that produces five versions of the same partial information. One person, assigned in advance, whose job is to capture decisions and actions in a shared document that everyone can access before the meeting has been over for an hour.

Think Time: Your Right to Pause

One of the most consequential design decisions in remote and hybrid communication is when to require synchronous communication and when to default to asynchronous.

Communication Type	Best For	Key Advantage
Asynchronous (email, shared docs, documented updates)	Most information sharing; many decisions	Gives recipient time to think, research, and arrive at their actual position
Synchronous video	Complex dialogue; relationship-building; sensitive feedback	Real-time human cues; dynamic iteration
Synchronous phone / audio	Urgent issues; emotional conversations where voice matters	Fast back-and-forth; voice cues without video overhead
In-person	Project kickoffs; conflict resolution; onboarding; celebrations	Full-bandwidth human communication; whiteboard-intensive work

SYNCHRONOUS VS. ASYNCHRONOUS

What they mean — and what they mean for communication.

QUICK RULE

Use synchronous communication when the issue needs live dialogue. Use asynchronous communication when the message needs clarity, flexibility, or documentation.

THREE PRACTICAL REMINDERS

1. Match the channel to the urgency.

2. Set response expectations clearly.

3. Close the loop either way.

Default to async when possible. When is synchronous necessary?

- The issue is genuinely complex enough that real-time dialogue will reach a better answer faster than written exchange.
- Relationship is the point — onboarding, connection-building, celebration — and the real-time human experience is the value.
- The conversation is sensitive — delivering difficult feedback, addressing conflict, discussing performance.
- Speed is genuinely critical and the cost of async delay is higher than the benefit of async quality.

If none of those conditions apply, ask before scheduling: **could this be a document?**

The No Side Conversations Rule

For hybrid meetings specifically, one of the highest-leverage structural rules you can implement: **if you are in a meeting that includes remote participants, all significant conversations happen where the remote participants can hear them.**

- No sidebar discussions at the conference table that bypass the microphone.
- No pre-meeting conversations that produce decisions that get announced as if they were made during the meeting.
- No post-meeting hallway discussions that refine or reverse what was said on camera.

If it matters, it happens on the record. If it happens off the record, it gets documented and shared within twenty-four hours.

This rule requires in-room participants to give up something real: the ease and efficiency of face-to-face communication among co-located colleagues. But when the price of that efficiency is that remote participants are systematically excluded from the real conversation, the price is too high. The requirement is not the elimination of in-person conversation — it's the explicit commitment that in-person conversation affecting shared work gets documented and surfaced.

Hybrid Meeting Best Practices

Before the meeting:

- Assign a dedicated note-taker in advance — one person, explicit responsibility.
- Circulate agenda and pre-reading at least 24 hours prior.
- Confirm technology setup: camera angle captures the full room, microphone picks up all in-room speakers.
- Document any pre-meeting conversations that affect agenda items — in writing, before the call starts.

During the meeting:

- Explicitly invite remote participants to speak — don't wait for them to interrupt.
- Direct in-room side conversations to the microphone: "Let me repeat that for the full group."
- If a whiteboard or document is being used, narrate it verbally for remote participants.
- Assign action items with names attached — not "we should probably…" but "Alex owns this by Thursday."
- Before closing each agenda item, ask: "Anything from the remote participants before we move on?"

After the meeting:

- Post decisions and action items in the shared record within one hour.
- Flag any informal decisions or conversations that happened before the call started.
- Send to all participants — not just those on the call.

Ongoing norms:

- Establish a single source of truth for each category of information — and enforce it.

- Create explicit availability signals (beyond status indicators) so the team knows when you can engage.
- Rotate note-taking so it's not always the same person and always feels lower-status.
- Revisit channel norms at least quarterly — they drift.

Hybrid Meeting Checklist

"Remote Meeting Readiness" Checklist

Before every meeting that includes remote participants — full stop, no exceptions.

- Written agenda sent to all participants at least 24 hours in advance
- All pre-reading materials shared with remote participants with sufficient lead time
- Room camera tested and positioned to show full table, not just one end
- Room microphone tested — all in-room voices audible, no echo
- Screen sharing confirmed visible to remote participants before the meeting starts
- Note-taker assigned by name who will capture decisions and actions in real time
- Remote participants explicitly welcomed by name at the start
- Facilitator has a plan for soliciting remote input at each agenda item — not just "any questions?"
- Any whiteboard content will be narrated verbally and photographed or screenshotted
- Action items will be read back at the end of the meeting with owner names and due dates
- Decisions and actions will be posted to the shared channel within one hour after

- Any pre-meeting conversations that affect the agenda will be captured and shared before the meeting ends

This is the operational version of the best practices above. Use it as a literal checklist before, during, and after every meeting that includes both in-room and remote participants.

Timing	Checklist Item	Owner	Done?
24 hours before	Agenda and pre-reading circulated	Meeting organizer	☐
24 hours before	Note-taker assigned by name	Meeting organizer	☐
24 hours before	Any pre-meeting conversations that affect agenda items captured in writing	Meeting organizer	☐
30 min before	Room camera tested — full table visible	In-room coordinator	☐
30 min before	Room microphone tested — all in-room speakers audible	In-room coordinator	☐
30 min before	Shared screen visible to remote participants	Tech lead / coordinator	☐
At start	Note-taker confirmed out loud to all participants	Facilitator	☐
At start	Remote participants welcomed by name	Facilitator	☐
During	Side conversations redirected to the microphone	Facilitator	☐
During	Whiteboard or screen content narrated verbally	Presenter	☐
During	Remote participants explicitly invited to speak	Facilitator	☐

Timing	Checklist Item	Owner	Done?
	before each agenda item closes		
During	Action items assigned with names — not "someone should"	Facilitator	☐
Within 1 hour after	Decisions and action items posted to shared location	Note-taker	☐
Within 1 hour after	Any hallway or pre-call decisions documented and shared	Meeting organizer	☐
Within 24 hours after	Summary distributed to all stakeholders, including those who did not attend	Note-taker	☐

Camera-On Culture vs. Meaningful Connection

Stop policing cameras. Start designing better interactions.

The instinct behind "cameras on" policies is understandable: non-verbal communication matters, and a screen full of black rectangles does make it harder to gauge engagement. These are real concerns. But enforcement of camera-on policies frequently produces the opposite of what it intends:

- Creates a *performance* of engagement rather than actual engagement.
- Generates resentment among team members with legitimate reasons to keep cameras off — medical conditions, privacy concerns, bandwidth limitations, caregiving circumstances.
- Focuses organizational energy on a face on a screen — rather than actual connection.

A twenty-minute video call where no one speaks except the meeting organizer does not become meaningful because eight cameras are on.

What creates meaningful connection in remote teams:

- Starting meetings with a real check-in question, not a formality.
- Explicitly inviting specific people to respond rather than asking "does anyone have thoughts?"
- Designing agendas that create dialogue rather than broadcast.
- Building relationship infrastructure that makes people willing to show up — not mandating its performance.

Virtual Meeting Do's and Don'ts

The technology works. The habits around the technology are where most virtual meetings fall apart.

Do	Don't
Start with a human question, something real, *not "how is everyone?"*	Open by asking "Can everyone hear me?" for three minutes
Name the note-taker out loud at the start	Assume someone will figure out notes
Invite specific people to respond — "Alex, what's your read on this?"	Ask "Does anyone have thoughts?" and wait
Narrate what's happening on screen: "I'm pulling up the Q3 report"	Share your screen without saying what people are looking at
Assign action items with names and due dates before the meeting ends	Close with "we'll follow up on next steps"
Check in with remote participants before closing each agenda item	Move on when the room has reached consensus
Post notes within one hour of the meeting	Send notes "when I get a chance"
Use the chat panel to capture questions and parking-lot items	Let chat scroll without monitoring it
Design the agenda to create conversation — questions, not just topics	Broadcast one-way information for 45 minutes and call it a meeting

Do	Don't
End five minutes early to give people transition time	Run over and make everyone late to their next meeting

Structured Check-Ins That Replace Hallway Conversations

Hallway conversations maintained relationships, surfaced concerns early, and gave formal communication the human texture that made it feel like a team — not an institution. **In remote environments, that work doesn't happen by default. It has to be designed.**

Structured check-ins are not more meetings. They are intentional rituals that replace the ambient relationship maintenance that proximity provided for free. Done well, they're brief, regular, and useful.

Formats that work:

Format	How It Works	Time Investment	What It Replaces
Weekly async check-in	Shared doc or channel — each person posts: (1) what I'm working on, (2) what I'm stuck on, (3) what I need from others	5 min to write	Morning standup visibility
One-on-one rhythms	Regular individual conversations between managers and team members — protected time for relationship, not just task status	30 min / week	Desk check-ins and hallway reassurances
Informal pairing rotation	Deliberately rotate which team members connect — a 15-min no-agenda coffee chat between two people who don't work closely together	15 min / occurrence	Cross-team relationships that formed organically in shared space

The key design principle for all of these: They must be genuinely informal, or they will not function. The moment a check-in becomes a performance review or a place where people feel evaluated, people stop telling the truth. And the truth is exactly what these rituals are meant to surface.

The Buddy System for Remote Team Members

For anyone joining a remote or hybrid team — especially new employees building their professional understanding of the organization while navigating a distributed environment — the buddy system is one of the most consistently undervalued onboarding tools.

A Buddy is Not:

- A manager
- A formal mentor
- Someone responsible for their performance

A Buddy is:

A peer who has agreed to be the new team member's first call for questions that don't belong anywhere else:

- *"Is this the right channel for this kind of question?"*
- *"How do people usually handle it when you need something from a different team?"*
- *"Am I reading this situation correctly?"*

These are the questions that get answered naturally in co-located environments by the colleague who leans over and says, "Yeah, just text her directly, she prefers that."

In remote environments, they go unanswered — and the new team member spends months building assumptions that may or may not match the team's actual norms.

Buddy System Checklist:

- **Assign every remote new hire a buddy before their first day.**
- Make the buddy relationship explicit: *"Your job is to be their first call for questions that don't fit anywhere else."*

- **Make it time-bound** — the first ninety days, typically.
- Give both parties a light structure (a weekly 15-min check-in) so the **relationship doesn't fade after the first week**.
- **Thank the buddy publicly — this work is real work.**

Tools Are Not the Answer — But the Right Ones Help

Organizations make this mistake in both directions: *believing the right tool will solve communication problems that are behavioral or culture-based,* or *becoming so skeptical of tools that they fail to build any consistent information infrastructure.* **The truth is in the middle.**

Tools are not the answer to communication problems rooted in behavior and culture. But a *chaotic tool environment* makes communication worse, by fragmenting information across platforms in ways that make it practically impossible for anyone to know where anything lives.

The Tool Sprawl Problem

Familiar scenario: You need to find the decision that was made about a vendor three weeks ago.

- Was it in the chat thread?
- The Teams channel?
- The email chain from that Thursday meeting?
- The document linked in the meeting notes?
- The meeting notes themselves — were those in the recording's AI summary, the shared drive, or the project management tool?
- Did someone say it on the call and it was never written down?

This is **tool sprawl**: the proliferation of communication platforms that, instead of creating clarity, creates a fragmented information environment where nobody knows where anything is. Every new tool added without a clear use case and clear norms makes the problem worse.

The result: information lives everywhere and is reliably findable nowhere.

Tool Type	Best For	Avoid When
Teams chat / group messaging	Quick questions; team announcements; informal check-ins; file sharing with context; creating searchable threads	Sensitive feedback; decisions requiring a permanent record; information that needs to reach people who are offline for days
Email	Formal communication; external stakeholders; decisions needing a paper trail; complex information with attachments; communicating with people outside your platform	Urgent matters; rapid back-and-forth dialogue; decisions that need discussion before resolution
Video call	Complex discussions; relationship-building; sensitive conversations; creative collaboration; team rituals (kickoffs, retros, celebrations)	Routine status updates; information that could be a document; any communication that benefits from async response time
Phone / audio call	Urgent issues that can't wait for a written reply; emotionally sensitive conversations where voice matters; quick clarifications where typing is inefficient	Documentation of decisions; complex topics requiring shared reference materials; any conversation more than one party needs to reference later
Shared doc	Collaborative writing; living documents that evolve; decisions requiring context and history; onboarding materials; team norms	Real-time communication; anything time-sensitive; situations where people need to be notified, not just left to find
PM tool	Task tracking; ownership assignment; deadline visibility; workflow sequencing; cross-team coordination	Nuanced discussion; relationship-building; sensitive conversations; anything that requires human tone

Tool Type	Best For	Avoid When
Async video	Walkthroughs, demos, and complex explanations that benefit from visual and vocal tone but don't require real-time response	Simple questions; anything that can be written in three sentences; situations requiring back-and-forth
In-person / offsite	Project kickoffs; conflict resolution; onboarding and culture immersion; celebrations and milestone events; complex whiteboard work	Anything that benefits from an async written record; situations where some team members cannot attend in person

Choosing a Source of Truth

The most important structural communication decision a remote or hybrid organization can make: **designate a single source of truth for each category of information — and enforce it.**

Source of Truth Means:

- **If you want to know the current status of the project, *this is where it lives*.**
- If you find it somewhere else, that information may be out of date.
- Decisions about platform architecture, client commitments, team norms — those live in *one place*, not in three partially-complete versions distributed across four tools.

Enforcement is the hard part. People will continue to send emails when the norm is the shared workspace. They will continue to make decisions verbally when the norm is documented. This is not resistance to be punished — it's habit to be designed around. The source of truth system works only when using it is the path of least resistance — which means the system has to be genuinely better at the task it's assigned than the alternatives.

CHOOSING A SOURCE OF TRUTH

One trusted place for each type of critical information.

- Project status lives in one place.
- If it appears somewhere else, it may be outdated.
- Decisions, commitments, and team norms should not be scattered across tools.

- Reduces confusion and duplicate versions.
- Makes handoffs and updates more reliable.
- Helps teams act from the same information.

- Assign one home for each category of information.
- Use it consistently.
- Make it the easiest place to find the truth.

Rule: One category = one home.

A source of truth only works when using it is the path of least resistance.

When to Use Which Channel

Channel Type	Use For	Do NOT Use For
Async written	Status updates; decisions needing a record; non-urgent questions where a thoughtful answer is better than a fast one; broadly relevant, non-time-sensitive information	Urgent issues requiring immediate action; sensitive feedback
Synchronous video	Complex discussions; relationship-building, onboarding, and connection; sensitive feedback and performance conversations; creative or collaborative work; team rituals — kickoffs, retrospectives, celebrations	Routine status updates; one-way information delivery
Synchronous phone / audio	Urgent issues that can't wait for a written reply; emotional conversations where voice cues matter but video isn't needed; quick clarifications where typing is inefficient	Documentation of decisions; complex issues requiring reference materials

Channel Type	Use For	Do NOT Use For
In-person	Project or relationship kickoffs; conflict resolution when video hasn't been sufficient; onboarding and culture immersion; celebrations and milestones; complex whiteboard-intensive problem-solving	Anything that benefits from an async, written record

Leading Remote Communication

If you lead a remote or hybrid team, the leadership communication challenge in distributed environments is qualitatively different from the co-located version. Not harder because of the tools. Harder because of the invisibility.

You Have to Over-Communicate — and That's Not a Weakness

I've heard leaders describe the deliberate, structured, higher-frequency communication that distributed teams require as "handholding." I want to push back on that framing firmly.

Over-communication in remote teams is not handholding. It is the operational translation of what proximity did for free. When you could see your team, you communicated constantly through presence, through facial expression, through the ten-second reassurance offered at a workstation — and none of that required deliberate action. In remote environments, none of it happens unless you make it happen.

What Over-Communication Looks Like In Practice:

- Send the team a brief context update at the start of a significant week, even when there's nothing urgent to report — especially then, because silence in a distributed environment reads as abandonment.
- Close loops explicitly, even when you're confident the other person knows the outcome: "Just want to confirm this is resolved from your end."
- Narrate your own availability and schedule changes, rather than assuming your team can see your calendar.

- Repeat important information in multiple channels — one message in the wrong channel is often no message at all.

This is not weakness.
This is leadership adapted to the environment.

Making the Invisible Visible

One of the most important things a remote leader can do is narrate the context that, in a co-located environment, would have been ambient.

Your team used to be able to see that you had a tense conversation with the director, that you've been in closed-door meetings all morning, that something is being worked through at the leadership level. They knew to calibrate accordingly. In a remote environment, they see: silence. And silence, in a distributed environment, is almost always interpreted as abandonment, conflict, or bad news.

You don't have to share confidential information. You don't have to narrate every senior conversation. But you can say:

"We're working through some organizational questions right now that I'll share more about when I can. I want you to know I haven't forgotten about the project update I owe you — that's coming by Thursday."

That is twenty-three words that prevents two weeks of anxiety spiraling.

Building Psychological Safety Across Screens

The conditions for psychological safety — framing work as a learning problem, acknowledging fallibility, responding with curiosity rather than criticism, responding productively to failure — apply at least as powerfully in remote environments as in co-located ones. In some ways, more powerfully.

In a co-located environment, a leader who seems distracted in a one-on-one can be read against everything else: the friendly hallway interaction last week, the visible good humor at the team meeting, the wave across the floor. One distracted meeting is contextualized. In a remote one-on-one, that same distracted energy has no context to be read against. It is the entire interaction. The team member leaves the call with far less certainty about where they stand.

What This Means For Remote Leaders:

- Explicit affirmation of good work — specific, not generic.
- Specific language about what's valued.
- The extra pause after someone shares a concern — make sure they feel genuinely heard before you move to problem-solving.
- Model the vulnerability you want to see: acknowledge your own mistakes and limitations openly.

These aren't soft skills. They are the infrastructure of a team that will tell you the truth.

The Loneliness Factor: Isolation as a Communication Barrier

This is rarely named directly in organizational communication frameworks, but any honest account of remote work has to acknowledge it. **Loneliness is a communication barrier.**

When people are genuinely isolated — not just working from home with a functional social life, but cut off from the human contact most people need to function well — their communication degrades:

- Less likely to reach out with concerns
- Less likely to ask for help
- Less likely to flag early warning signs because initiating contact, from a baseline of prolonged isolation, feels disproportionate to the perceived value

The Silent Spiral™ and isolation are co-conspirators. The lonely person tends toward Assumption and Silence because Silence is the path of least emotional resistance. It takes energy to communicate, and isolation drains that energy.

Breaking the Spiral™ Stage 3 — Make It Safe — has a specific application in remote environments: making it safe means actively reducing the energy cost of reaching out. The structured check-ins above, the buddy system, the manager who sends a real question and waits for a real answer — these are not soft management preferences.

They are operational interventions that remove the friction that keeps isolated team members from completing Stage 2 (Break the Silence) when they see something the team needs to know.

Leaders who care about communication performance in remote teams have to care about the human experience of working remotely. That Means:

- Asking real questions and waiting for real answers.
- Noticing when someone who is usually vocal goes quiet and checking in — not with a task-oriented message, but a human one.
- Building team rituals that create genuine connection, not just its performance.

The team that feels genuinely known by its leader will communicate. The team that feels like a grid of names on a screen will eventually stop.

FIELD NOTES: The Decision That Happened in the Room

The distribution center had been running a hybrid coordination model for about eight months — some team members on-site, some working from home, with a standing weekly operations review that mixed both. By most measures, it was working. Attendance was solid, the agenda moved efficiently, and nobody had complained about the format.

The problem became visible on a Friday afternoon, when a team member who had been remote for the previous three weeks sent a message asking about the implementation timeline for a new inventory tracking procedure. She had questions about the handoff process and wanted to make sure her team was prepared.

The response she got back contained information she had never seen. Not just the timeline. The entire approach had changed. The technology had changed. The responsible team had changed. And the decision, she was told, had been made in the operations review two weeks prior.

She had been on that call. She had her notes. Nowhere in her notes — nowhere in any notes that had been distributed — was that decision captured.

What had happened: About six minutes before the video call started, three of the on-site participants had pulled up the proposed approach on one of their laptops and had a quick, efficient conversation about it. By the time the call opened and the remote participants joined, the decision was effectively made. When the agenda item came up, it moved quickly. One in-room participant summarized the approach in a single sentence. Nobody objected. The meeting moved on.

From the remote participants' perspective, a summary had been presented and accepted. From the in-room participants' perspective, a decision had been made and confirmed. Both descriptions were accurate. They were also not the same event.

The consequence: the remote team member, working from what she understood to be the current plan, had briefed her downstream contacts on the original approach. Those contacts had made preparation decisions based on what she told them. When the new approach went into effect, three teams were operating on different assumptions, and the reconciliation process cost more time than the original decision had saved.

When the issue was surfaced in a retrospective, the immediate response from the on-site team was genuine surprise: **"We thought everyone knew." The immediate response from the remote team members was equally genuine: "We had no way to know."**

Both were true. That was the problem.

The fix: Any decision reached — formally or informally — during a meeting or in its immediate vicinity was required to appear in the meeting summary within twenty-four hours, including the context that led to it. Pre-meeting conversations that affected outcomes were either replicated at the start of the call for remote participants, or captured in writing before the call began.

One sentence in a summary document. That's all it would have taken. The hybrid tax doesn't announce itself. It accumulates quietly, in the space between the conference room and the camera, decision by decision, until someone is standing in a Friday afternoon message chain trying to figure out how eight weeks of preparation diverged from the plan that everyone thought they were following.

Key Takeaways

- **Remote work removed the ambient information layer that was quietly compensating for existing communication problems.** Building infrastructure that works without proximity means making visible what used to be invisible — not finding new tools.
- **Hybrid is harder than fully remote because it creates a two-tier information environment.** Without deliberate structure, this gap systematically **excludes remote participants from the real communication that runs the organization.**
- **Default to writing.** If a decision was made in a conversation that produced no written record, **it may as well not have been made for team members who weren't there. Documentation is not bureaucracy in distributed teams — it is equity.**
- **Match the medium to the message.** Async works better than sync for most information sharing and many decisions. Defaulting to meetings for everything is how organizations spend more time communicating and actually communicate less.
- **Leading remote teams requires deliberate over-communication** — sharing context, making the invisible visible, building psychological safety explicitly, and attending to the human experience of working at a distance. **The team that feels genuinely known by its leader will communicate. The team that feels like names on a screen will eventually stop.**

- **Breaking the Spiral™ in distributed environments requires active design.** The five stages — Test the Assumption, Break the Silence, Make It Safe, Close the Loop, Name It — don't happen organically when teams are distributed. **Every one of them must be built into the team's communication infrastructure deliberately**, because the ambient environment that used to prompt them is no longer there.

Reflection Questions

1. **In your current remote or hybrid environment, where is ambient information being lost?** What decisions, directions, or pieces of context are living in informal in-person conversations that never make it into the shared record — and what is the downstream cost of that gap?
2. **Look at your team's communication channels honestly: do you have a source of truth for the information that matters most to your work, and does your team use it?** If the answer to either part of that question is no, what would it take to change that — and what is the cost of not changing it?
3. Think about the team members in your organization who most consistently attend remotely. **What is their actual experience of communication in your hybrid environment?** Not the nominal experience — the actual one. When was the last time you asked?

PART III

SUSTAINING IT

Making Good Communication the Culture

Part I named the problem. Part II handed you the tools. Part III is about whether any of it survives the next quarter.

You can run every framework in this book once and watch the team drift back to the old patterns within ninety days. That isn't a failure of the frameworks. It is the absence of culture.

Culture is what happens when no one is watching. It is the default a team reaches for at 4:45 p.m. on a Friday, in the middle of a crisis, after a leadership change, when the pressure makes the shortcut tempting. The work in Part III is the work of making the right communication behaviors the path of least resistance — embedded into the operating rhythms, modeled by leadership, reinforced when people drift, and rebuilt when something breaks.

The chapters that follow cover both halves of sustainability:

- **How to build a communication culture that holds up under pressure** — the operating rhythms, the modeling, the reinforcement loops, and the systems that turn one good conversation into a team-wide standard.
- **What to do in the moments when it doesn't** — the recovery work after a breakdown: post-mortems that don't blame, hard conversations that rebuild trust, and the discipline of treating every failure as a lesson rather than a verdict.

This is not the part of the book where you learn one more framework. This is the part where you decide whether the work in Part II was a project or a practice. A team that runs Take Five once is following a script. A team that runs Take Five every Friday because that's just how they meet now — that is a culture. **The frameworks in Part II will get you started. The work in Part III is what keeps you from starting over.**

Chapter 16: From Habit to Culture

There is a difference between knowing **what to do** and building a world where **doing it comes naturally.**

I have walked into organizations that had beautiful communication plans. Laminated. Posted. Dated and signed. They had org charts on the walls, escalation paths in the SharePoint folder nobody visited, and a carefully constructed RACI matrix buried in a slide deck from a kickoff meeting eighteen months ago. On paper, they had done the work.

And yet, when I asked a team member a simple question — "Who do you go to when something goes wrong?" — the answer was a pause. Then a shrug. Then, "It depends on the day."

A communication plan is a document. A communication culture is a way of operating. The difference between the two is the difference between a sign that says "Drive Safely" and a road engineered to make driving safely the easiest and most natural choice.

One is aspirational. The other is structural. This chapter is about how you get from the first to the second.

The Plan That Nobody Lives In

The problem is almost never the plan itself. The problem is the gap between the plan and the practice.

A plan is what you intend to do. Culture is what you actually do when no one is watching, when things get hard, when you are short-staffed and overwhelmed and the pressure is on. Culture is what happens at 4:45 on a Friday when something breaks and you have to decide whether to document it now or document it Monday. Culture is what happens in the hallway conversation that never makes it into a meeting note.

A communication culture means that even in those moments — *especially* in those moments — the team defaults to the right behavior. Not because someone is watching. Not because there is a checklist nearby. But because doing it any other way would feel wrong.

Getting there requires more than writing a better plan. It requires embedding communication into the operating system of how the team functions.

FIELD NOTES: The Spreadsheet That Ran the Operation

What I found: The most accurate, most consulted, most operationally relevant tracking document in the building had no official status whatsoever.

How it came to exist:

- The official system for tracking open corrective actions had a response lag that made it functionally useless day-to-day
- Actions had to be entered, routed for approval, and processed through multiple steps before appearing in the visible queue
- In a high-volume environment, that one-week lag wasn't a delay — it was an eternity
- One team member got tired of waiting and built a spreadsheet

What the spreadsheet became:

- **The official tool** got updated because the process required it. **The shadow version** got updated every shift.
- **The official tool existed for compliance and audits. The shadow version existed for actual operational decisions.**
- **The official tool had standard fields in a standard format. The shadow version had extra columns the official system couldn't support — the fields the team actually needed.**
- **The official tool was reviewed in formal reporting cycles. The shadow version was consulted by supervisors who walked over and asked for "the actual list."**
- **The official tool was visible to leadership and auditors. The shadow version** was invisible to anyone outside the team.

Two systems. One real. One performative. The one leadership trusted was the one nobody on the floor used.

By the time I encountered it, the spreadsheet had been running in parallel for over a year. It was the quality tracking system for the operation — entirely invisible to anyone outside the team.

The person who built it wasn't subverting the process. She was solving a real problem. The shadow tool existed because the official tool had failed — failed to provide timely, accessible information in a format that matched how the team worked.

The workaround was rational. It was also a symptom.

What workarounds like this signal:

- Official systems consistently failing the people who depend on them → those people build unofficial ones
- Unofficial systems are invisible to leadership, fragile to turnover, impossible to scale
- When she moved to a different role, her replacement spent weeks trying to understand a tracking process with no documentation, no formal owner, and no connection to the official system

The institutional knowledge was in the spreadsheet. The spreadsheet wasn't institutionalized.

The principle: Building a communication culture means confronting the workarounds — not to eliminate them on principle, but to ask what they're telling you.

Every shadow system is a message: something in the official channel isn't working, and the people closest to the work found a way around it.

That message deserves a genuine response — not a mandate to stop before the root cause is fixed.

FIELD NOTE TAKEAWAY: Before you ask anyone to stop using a workaround, fix what the workaround was built to replace. Shadow systems are rational responses to broken official ones. The person who built the spreadsheet wasn't subverting the process — she was solving a real problem. Honor that by making the official process actually work before you take away the thing that does.

In the Room: The Communication Charter, Six Weeks Later

The all-hands was four months ago. The charter was presented. Everyone clapped. New team member, Layla, three weeks in:

"I'm not sure who to go to when I hit a blocker on cross-functional stuff. Is that the project manager, or my supervisor, or —?"

Colleague: *"Honestly? Depends on the day. There's a chart somewhere."*

Layla: *"The Communication Charter?"*

Colleague: *"Yeah. I don't think anyone's looked at that since the launch."*

Layla: *"What do most people actually do?"*

Colleague: *"Text Marcus. He knows everyone."*

Marcus is not in the charter. Marcus does not even have an official coordination role. Marcus is the communication culture that exists in spite of the document — the workaround that took root because the official system was never actually embedded.

The charter described the culture the team wanted. Marcus is the culture the team built.

Breaking the Spiral™: Stage 4 → Close the Loop

What happens when the leader notices the workaround and uses it as a signal.

Team Lead, to Marcus during a one-on-one: *"I've noticed that people seem to route a lot of coordination questions through you. You're kind of the unofficial hub."*

Marcus: *"Yeah. It's faster than the process."*

Team Lead: *"I believe you. That tells me the process isn't doing what we designed it to do. Instead of asking you to stop, I want to understand what you do that the system doesn't. What does someone get from texting you that they can't get from the escalation chart?"*

Marcus: *"I know who's actually available, who's backed up, and who to go around when someone's not responding."*

Team Lead: *"That's institutional knowledge. It shouldn't live only in your head. Can we figure out how to build that into the system so it survives when you're on PTO?"*

The workaround becomes the blueprint. That is how communication culture gets built — not by posting the charter, but by noticing what people actually do and designing toward it.

Embedding Communication Into the Operating System

The most effective way to build a communication culture is to make communication a non-negotiable feature of every existing rhythm — not an add-on that requires extra effort.

Your team's operating system is the collection of habits, routines, and structures that run in the background every day — the standup, the shift handoff, the weekly report, the way problems get flagged. These rhythms already exist.

The question is whether communication is built into them or bolted on beside them.

The Standup That Actually Works

Most standups become status reports. Someone reads numbers, someone nods, the meeting ends. Information flows in one direction: up. Nothing moves laterally. Nothing prompts questions.

A standup that is part of your communication operating system does three things:

- Surfaces what is going well and what is blocked
- Creates a moment where the team practices saying things out loud to each other

That last part is underrated. The habit of speaking up in a safe, structured context builds the muscle for speaking up in harder contexts. One question that changes everything: **"What's coming that we're not ready**

for?" It makes anticipation a shared responsibility. It makes communication about the future, not just the past.

The Shift Handoff as a Communication Ritual

In operations, the shift handoff is *one of the most critical communication moments that gets the least attention.* "It was fine when I left" is the operational equivalent of "someone else's problem now."

A proper SOS/EOS (Start of Shift / End of Shift) report is more than a form. It is a ritual that communicates respect — respect for the incoming team, respect for the process, and respect for the people downstream who depend on accurate information. When done well, it becomes automatic. It becomes the thing that feels wrong to skip.

Making Communication Visible

One of the most powerful tools for embedding communication into the operating system: make commitments visible. Not in someone's inbox. Not in someone's notebook. Visible — on a shared board, wall, or platform, where everyone on the team can see what was promised, who promised it, and what the status is.

This is not about surveillance. It is about shared accountability:

- When the team can see the loop open, the loop gets closed
- When a commitment lives only in an email thread, it is easy to forget
- When it lives on the team board, it is impossible to ignore

Lean practitioners will recognize this as visual management. Visibility creates shared reality. Shared reality creates shared accountability. Shared accountability creates culture.

Training and Onboarding: Setting the Expectation from Day One

You cannot retroactively install a communication culture in someone who was onboarded into a culture of silence. The moment someone joins your team is the most important communication moment they will have with you.

Most onboarding programs cover the *what*: what the job is, what the tools are, what the rules say. Very few cover the *how* of communication. Build an explicit "Communication Expectations" conversation into every onboarding — a real conversation with the direct supervisor, not a formal presentation, that covers:

Topic	What to Cover
How we communicate here	Which channels we use for what; expected response times; what "urgent" means
Who to go to for what	Not just the org chart — the real answer. The person who knows the system. The person to call at 2 a.m. if something is actually on fire.
How we handle problems	What escalation looks like; what blamelessness means; why "I don't know" is the right answer when it is true
What we expect from you	Including the expectation that they will ask questions, raise concerns, and participate in the team's communication rhythms

This conversation alone — done genuinely, done early — prevents an enormous number of downstream breakdowns. Watch what happens when new employees see that standard modeled by the people around them. Culture is not what leaders say it is. Culture is what new people observe and absorb in their first thirty days.

"New Team Member Communication Onboarding" Checklist

Conduct this conversation in the first week — not as a handout, as a genuine two-way conversation.

- **Channel norms:** Which channel is used for what? What is the expected response time for each?
- **What "urgent" means:** How do we signal urgency? What is the threshold for a phone call vs. a message vs. an email?
- **Escalation path:** Who do you go to when something goes wrong? What is the process for raising a concern above your level?

- **How we run meetings:** What is expected in terms of preparation, participation, and follow-up?
- **How decisions get made:** Who has final say on what? What does the RACI look like for your role?
- **How we handle mistakes:** What does the team's error culture look like? What should you do if you make a mistake?
- **Your voice matters:** Explicit expectation that they will ask questions, raise concerns, and flag problems early
- **Who to actually call:** Not the org chart answer — the real answer for the most common situations they'll face
- **30/60/90 check-in:** Dates set for follow-up conversations about how they are experiencing the team's communication norms
- **Open door is real:** Demonstrate what "bring me problems" actually looks like before they need to test it

Measuring Communication Health

I have a complicated relationship with communication surveys. Not because they are inherently wrong, but because they are almost always lagging indicators.

By the time a survey reveals that 67 percent of employees feel their manager does not communicate effectively, you are already months into a problem that has been quietly leaking value. The patient is sick. The survey told you. Now what?

Surveys diagnose. They rarely prevent. In most organizations, the real damage happens in the gap between knowing and acting. Once the team has told you what is wrong and nothing changes, the silence that follows is louder than the survey ever was.

I have watched teams hit green on engagement surveys one quarter and lose a key employee the next. The survey was not wrong. It was late. By the time the data told us there was a problem, the person who had been signaling it for months had already made a different decision.

LEADING INDICATORS WORTH TRACKING

Early signals that reveal communication health before larger breakdowns appear.

INDICATOR	WHAT TO MEASURE	WHY IT MATTERS
Pulse checks	Weekly or biweekly anonymous check-ins with 3–5 simple questions.	Catches friction early and gives leaders fast signals to act on.
Feedback frequency	How often people give and receive real-time, structured feedback.	No feedback rarely means no problems — it often means people stopped speaking up.
Response time	How long it takes for questions and escalations to receive a response.	Slow responses are a measurable sign of communication drag.
Escalation rate & pattern	How often issues are escalated, where they come from, and how fast they are resolved.	A team that never escalates may have learned that raising issues is not worth it.
Participation breadth	Whether many voices contribute in meetings and shared documentation — or only a few.	Broad participation is a strong indicator of communication health.

What I advocate for instead — or in addition — are **leading indicators of communication health**. Signals that show up before the survey confirms what the team has already been feeling. Indicators a manager, a team lead, or a project owner can watch week to week, without waiting for the annual pulse to tell them what the last six months were like.

Lagging indicators tell you the history. **Leading indicators give you a chance to change it. Here are the signals worth watching — and what they tell you before the survey ever does.**

Communication Health Scorecard

Metric	How to Measure	Target	Red Flag
Pulse check response rate	% of team completing weekly/biweekly check-in	85%+	Below 60% — people have stopped believing it matters
Pulse check score trend	Average score across “Do you have what you need?” items	Improving month-over-month	Two consecutive months of decline

Metric	How to Measure	Target	Red Flag
Escalation response time	Hours between escalation flagged and acknowledgment	Under 4 hours	Consistently over 24 hours
Meeting action item completion rate	% of assigned actions completed by agreed due date	80%+	Below 50% — action items are not being treated as real commitments
Feedback frequency	# of structured feedback conversations per team member per quarter	4+	Zero — silence is not satisfaction
Documentation currency	% of key process docs reviewed/updated in last 90 days	90%+	Docs not reviewed in 6+ months
Participation breadth	# of unique contributors per team meeting (avg)	All members speaking in 3 of 4 meetings	Same 2–3 people dominate every session
Unanswered questions in team channel	# of questions posted that received no response within 24 hours	Zero	More than 2 per week
New hire communication satisfaction	30/60/90-day check-in rating from new employees	4/5 or higher	Below 3/5 at any checkpoint
Post-mortem completion rate	% of significant failures that received a documented root cause review	100%	Any significant failure without a documented AAR

Most teams measure communication after something breaks. This scorecard measures it before — so you catch drift before missed deadlines, repeated errors, and turnover confirm what you were too late to prevent.

Continuous Improvement Applied to Communication: PDCA and DMAIC

The irony of working in continuous improvement environments is ***watching organizations apply rigorous process discipline to everything except their own internal communication.*** A team that runs DMAIC on a defect rate without ever running DMAIC on its meeting effectiveness is leaving improvement on the table.

Communication is a process with inputs, outputs, and variation. It can be mapped, measured, and improved.

DMAIC Applied to a Communication Process

Scenario: Engineers are not receiving updated project status until after they have already done work that needs to be redone.

Phase	Action
Define	Problem = status updates not reaching engineers before work begins. Impact = rework, measured in hours.
Measure	Quantify the lag: hours between a status change and when it is communicated; number of rework incidents traceable to this lag; current process for status updates
Analyze	Where is the breakdown? At the source (update not being created)? In the channel (update exists but engineers aren't receiving it)? In frequency (weekly updates for a daily work cycle)?
Improve	Design a solution: daily status trigger in the project management tool; 5-minute daily standup between two roles; defined handoff protocol with a confirmation step
Control	Standardize the solution. Build it into the operating rhythm. Assign ownership. Measure the rework rate to confirm improvement.

Every communication failure has a root cause. Every root cause can be addressed. The difference between teams that improve and teams that repeat the same breakdowns is whether they ever stop to ask "why did this happen" — and then actually change the system.

The Prosci / Change Management Lens: Communication as a Change Initiative

Building a communication culture is a change initiative. Like any change initiative, it will fail if it is not managed like one. Prosci's ADKAR model — *Awareness, Desire, Knowledge, Ability, Reinforcement* — applies directly. The translation is instructive:

ADKAR Stage	What It Means for Communication Culture Change
Awareness	People need to understand why current communication isn't working and what the cost of that failure is — specific and data-backed, not abstract ("we need to communicate better"). Share the metrics. Share the incidents. Make the cost visible.
Desire	Even when people understand the problem, change requires internal motivation to act differently. This is where leadership modeling matters enormously. If the leader talks about communication culture but continues to respond to emails two weeks late, send meeting-worthy information in a text at 11 p.m., and never close a loop, the team's desire to change will evaporate. Desire is built through demonstration, not declaration.
Knowledge	Once people are aware and willing, they need to know what to do differently. This is the training and tools piece: the templates, the frameworks, the explicit norms established in onboarding. Knowledge without awareness is a lecture nobody shows up for.
Ability	Knowledge and ability are not the same thing. A person can know how to give feedback and still struggle terribly to do it in the moment. Ability is built through practice, coaching, and repetition. Create low-stakes opportunities for teams to practice new communication behaviors before they need them in high-stakes situations.
Reinforcement	This is where most communication improvement efforts die. The training happens. The norms are posted. And then, slowly, the team drifts back to the old pattern — not because they forgot, but because the new behavior was never reinforced and the old behavior was never challenged. Reinforcement means recognizing people who model the standard, addressing people who don't, and continuously returning to the metrics.

A communication culture is not installed. It is cultivated. Tended. Maintained through consistent, intentional reinforcement of the right behaviors and the consistent, courageous correction of the wrong ones.

That is the work. It is not glamorous. The teams that do it have something no plan on a wall can give them: a way of operating that holds up under pressure, through transitions, through crises, and through growth.

90-Day Communication Improvement Plan

Culture does not change in a workshop. It changes in ninety days of deliberate, consistent practice.

Use this plan as a starting structure, not a script. Assign owners, adapt the actions to your context, and hold the review dates. Name one person to own the plan end-to-end, and run checkpoint reviews at Week 4, Week 8, and Week 12 so progress stays visible to the team and to leadership.

The plan is front-loaded by design. The first four weeks focus on diagnosis and structure — the baseline, the priorities, the norms, the paths. The middle four weeks focus on practice — feedback, visibility, handoffs, and reinforcement. The final four weeks focus on learning — review what worked, recognize what should stick, and set the next ninety days. If that cadence feels heavy in the first month, that is expected. The foundation has to be built before the practice can hold.

The Plan

Week	Focus Area	Action	Owner	Success Metric
0	Plan Launch	Communicate the 90-day plan to the team — what it is, why it exists, who owns what, and how progress will be shared	Plan Owner	Team briefed; plan document accessible; questions captured and answered
1	Baseline	Run the Communication Self-Assessment (Appendix A) with the full team	Team Lead	≥90% completion, with non-responses followed up individually; results documented

Week	Focus Area	Action	Owner	Success Metric
1–2	Diagnosis	Identify the three lowest-scoring areas the team can actually influence	Team Lead + PM	Written priority list shared with team
2	Onboarding	Build "Communication Expectations" conversation into the onboarding checklist	HR / Direct Sup.	Confirmed in next new hire's 30-day check-in, or confirmed by supervisor sign-off on the updated checklist
3	Standup	Redesign the standup to include *"What's coming we're not ready for?"*	Team Lead + Rotating Team Member	Question asked at every standup for 4 weeks
3–4	Documenting	Audit shared documentation — identify what is outdated, what is missing, and what should be retired	Document Lead	Audit report completed; gaps assigned with owners and dates
4	Channels	Document channel norms — what goes where, expected response times, and which channel is for urgent vs. non-urgent	Team Lead	Norms posted in shared location; team briefed; checkpoint review held
5	Escalation	Using the Escalation Decision Tree from Part II, map and publish the escalation path with real names and real contact methods	PM / Team Lead	Path document accessible to all team members
5–6	Metrics	Launch pulse check using 3–5 leading indicators from the Measuring Communication Health framework	People Ops Partner	First pulse check completed; results reviewed with team
6	Feedback	Introduce the SIA feedback framework (Situation – Impact –	Manager	Each team member receives

Week	Focus Area	Action	Owner	Success Metric
		Ask); schedule first round of structured feedback		one SIA conversation
7–8	Visual Management	Make commitments visible — shared board, wall, or platform	Team Lead	All open action items visible in one place and updated at least weekly
8	Handoffs	Implement the SOS/EOS template (Start of Shift / End of Shift) for any shift or role transition	Ops Lead	Template in use; incoming party signs acknowledgment; checkpoint review held
9–10	PDCA	Run an A3 on the lowest-scoring item from the pulse check data	Owner closest to the issue	Root cause identified; one improvement implemented
10	Recognition	Publicly recognize one communication behavior worth reinforcing — name the behavior, not just the person	Manager	Specific, named recognition delivered in a team setting
11	Post-Mortem	Run a practice AAR on a recent completed project (even a successful one); close the loop with any Pre-Mortem predictions	Facilitator	AAR completed; predicted vs. actual compared; action items documented
12	Reassess	Rerun the Communication Self-Assessment; compare to Week 1 baseline	Team Lead	Score change documented; next 90-day priorities set; one practice from the first 90 days sunsetted or made standard work

If a Week Slips

Real 90-day plans slip. When a week falls behind, carry the action forward rather than skipping it. Skipping creates gaps in the logic of the plan. Carrying keeps the sequence intact even if the calendar moves. If two or more weeks slip in a row, that is a signal to pause, diagnose why, and adjust — not to push harder. **The plan is the scaffolding, not the scoreboard.**

How This Plan Connects to the Rest of the Manuscript

The 90-day plan is the place where the frameworks from Parts I and II become practice:

- **Week 5 (Escalation)** operationalizes the **Escalation Decision Tree**
- **Week 5–6 (Metrics)** operationalizes the **Measuring Communication Health** framework
- **Week 6 (Feedback)** operationalizes the **SIA feedback framework**
- **Week 8 (Handoffs)** operationalizes the **SOS/EOS** handoff discipline
- **Week 9–10 (PDCA)** operationalizes the **A3** problem-solving framework
- **Week 11 (Post-Mortem)** closes the loop with the **Pre-Mortem** framework

If a team runs this plan in sequence, they will have practiced every core tool in the book by Week 12 — not in theory, but on real work.

Ninety days is long enough to change practice, but *not long enough to change culture on its own.* The purpose of this plan is to build the repetition that makes good communication feel normal — not heroic, not special, just how the team operates.

At the end of ninety days, the goal is not a completed plan. **The goal is a team that no longer needs the plan to do the work it describes.**

Sustainability Checklist

Communication discipline slips the same way it forms — *gradually, through small defaults that no one notices until the pattern is already set*. The items below are **where sustainability actually lives:** in the operating rhythms teams run every day, in the way new people are brought in, in what gets measured, and in what leadership reinforces.

Run through this list quarterly. If an item is no longer true, that is not a failure — it is a signal that the *practice needs to be rebuilt before the drift goes further.*

Operating Rhythms

- Standup includes **"What's coming that we're not ready for?"** — not just status
- Shift handoffs follow a standard SOS/EOS template with **outgoing lead signature**
- Commitments are tracked visibly on a **shared board**, not buried in email threads
- Communication norms are **documented and accessible** — not posted once and forgotten

Onboarding

- Every new team member has an explicit **"Communication Expectations"** conversation with their direct supervisor within the **first week**
- Onboarding covers channel norms, escalation paths, and the **specific person to call** when a specific issue comes up
- New employees are assigned a **buddy** for their **first 90 days**

Measuring

- Pulse checks run **weekly or biweekly** — not quarterly or annually
- **Response time** to questions and escalations is tracked
- Escalation rate and pattern is **reviewed monthly**

- **Participation breadth** in meetings is observed and addressed when imbalanced
- Leading indicators are **reviewed** in PDCA cycles — **not just collected**

ADKAR Reinforcement

Awareness, Desire, Knowledge, Ability, Reinforcement

- Leadership **models** the communication standard **publicly**, not just advocates for it
- When communication failures occur, **root cause** is examined — not just the person closest to the failure
- Positive communication behaviors are recognized **specifically**, not generically

Weekly Communication Health Check

Run this yourself at the end of each week. **It takes five minutes and will tell you more than a quarterly survey can** — which is the whole point of leading indicators.

- Did every meeting this week have a **written agenda** distributed **in advance**?
- Were action items from last week's meetings followed up on — **completed or formally rescheduled**?
- Is there any information my team **needs to know** that they do not have yet?
- Did I give **specific, behavior-based feedback** to at least one person?
- Is there anyone who has gone **quieter than usual** this week?
- Did I **close every communication loop** I opened — or did I communicate a delay with a **new timeline**?
- Were any decisions made in **informal channels** (hallways, side conversations) that should have been **documented**?

- Is the team's action log **current and visible** to everyone who needs it?
- Did I respond to every escalation from my team **within 4 hours**?
- Is there a conversation I have been **putting off** that I need to schedule this week?

Scoring: Missing **one or two** items is normal in a busy week. **Missing four or more** is a pattern, not a fluke. If you answered "no" to more than three, prioritize the items you missed before moving into next week's priorities.

Sustainability is not what you do after the work is done. It is what you do *instead of letting the work quietly come undone*. The 90-day plan gets the team into practice. **These checklists are what keep the team *in* practice** — not because the tools are special, but because **someone is paying attention to whether they are still being used**.

Key Takeaways

- A communication plan is a *document;* a **communication culture is a way of operating**. The goal is to build the latter — and then to keep it from *quietly eroding* once the attention moves on.
- Embed communication into **existing team rhythms** — standups, handoffs, visual boards, shift SOS/EOS — so it becomes part of the operating system, not an add-on that competes with the work.
- Onboarding is your **most important communication culture moment**. Set explicit expectations in the first week, assign a buddy for the first 90 days, and model the standard consistently — because new team members learn the real culture from what they witness, not what is posted.
- Measure **leading indicators** of communication health — pulse checks, response times, escalation rates and patterns, participation breadth, feedback frequency — and *review* them in PDCA cycles. Collecting is not the same as reviewing.

- Apply continuous improvement discipline — **PDCA, DMAIC, ADKAR** — directly to communication processes. They *are* processes. Treat them that way, including root-cause analysis when they fail.
- Sustainability is not what you do after the work is done. It is **what you do instead of letting the work quietly come undone**.

Reflection Questions

1. **If a new team member joined your team tomorrow and simply observed for a week, what *communication culture* would they conclude exists** — based not on what is posted or stated, but on what they **witnessed**? Is that the culture you want them to inherit?
2. **What is one existing team rhythm — a meeting, a report, a handoff — where communication is currently an *afterthought*?** What would it take to make it a **communication-first moment** without adding a new ceremony?
3. **Where are you measuring communication as an outcome** (survey results, satisfaction scores) when you should be measuring it as a **process** (response time, escalation patterns, participation breadth, feedback frequency)?
4. **Looking at the last time a communication breakdown happened on your team, did the review examine the root cause** — or did it stop at the person closest to the failure?
5. **Which item on the Sustainability Checklist is most likely to *drift* first on your team if no one is watching for it — and who owns noticing?**

Chapter 17: When It All Falls Apart — Recovery and Resilience

Every system has failure modes. Every team — no matter how intentional, how skilled, how well-structured — will face a moment when communication breaks down in ways that cause real harm. Projects derail. Trust fractures. People stop talking. Things that should have been said were not, and now you are standing in the aftermath.

This chapter is not a consolation prize. It is not about accepting failure. It is about what you do after the failure — and how you use what happened to become stronger, smarter, and more resilient.

The quality of your recovery is not measured by whether the failure happened. It is measured by what you do in the first hours, the first days, and the first weeks after.

Triage: What to Do When You're in the Middle of the Breakdown

Three Immediate Triage Steps

Step	Action	Key Principle
1. Stop the bleeding	Find out what people think they know that is wrong. Correct the record through a single, authoritative voice as quickly as possible. One message, right channel, right people.	Speed in correcting misinformation is loss prevention. Treat it that way.
2. Establish a single source of truth	Designate one person or one channel as the authoritative source. Communicate that designation explicitly: "All updates on this situation will come from [person / channel]."	Structure creates calm. Calm enables clarity. Borrowed from incident command systems.
3. Communicate status, not just content	"We don't have all the information yet, but here is what we know, here is what we're doing, and here is when you can expect an update."	Stakeholders can tolerate uncertainty far better than they can tolerate silence. Silence communicates either "we don't know" or "you don't deserve to know." Neither is where you want to be.

FIELD NOTES: Green on the Dashboard, Red in the Room

The pattern: a type of project update I have received more than once, in more than one organization, that I now recognize on sight. It arrives as a status report — structured, often color-coded, tracking multiple workstreams — where everything is green or yellow, the language is measured and professional, and the numbers tell a story of reasonable progress. Then you get into the room with the team.

The specific situation: a healthcare-adjacent project with multiple workstreams and a tight delivery timeline. Status reports communicated steady progress. Metrics moved in the right direction. Leadership reviews concluded without alarm.

The report said: workstream updates showing progress.

The reality: a team member who had stopped raising concerns — the last three had gone nowhere.

The report said: vendor dependency on schedule.

The reality: everyone privately suspected the vendor would be late. Nobody escalated because the path felt politically complicated.

The report said: workstream owners updating their sections.

The reality: two leads who had stopped talking to each other, routing every decision through the PM — adding a translation layer to everything.

The dashboard was green. The project was in trouble. Both things were true simultaneously, because the dashboard measured what was reported, and what was reported was the version of reality that felt survivable to say out loud.

When the actual problem surfaced — all at once:

- Vendor missed the delivery
- Dependency became a blocker
- Two workstreams discovered at the integration point that they had been building to different specifications — two leads who had each understood a key decision differently, neither had flagged the discrepancy
- A timeline that looked achievable on paper suddenly wasn't

What triage required: something the status reports had been quietly preventing — telling the actual truth about the state of each component. Without the protective layer of professional framing.

The conversations that happened in the first 48 hours of the crisis contained more useful information than the previous eight weeks of updates combined, because *the crisis had made it safe to say what had been true for much longer.*

What I now raise explicitly at the start of any significant project: *The status report is a tool, not a mirror.*

If it only measures what people are comfortable reporting, you are not measuring the project. You are measuring your team's tolerance for discomfort.

Those are not the same number, and they diverge in exactly the moments when you most need them to match.

FIELD NOTE TAKEAWAY: A green dashboard on a red project isn't a reporting failure — it's a safety failure. The status report reflects what people feel safe saying. If your project updates are consistently optimistic until they suddenly aren't, the problem isn't the reporters. It's the environment that makes honest reporting feel riskier than damage control. Fix that environment, and the data will tell you the truth before the crisis does.

In the Room: What Panic Communication Looks Like

The moment the project manager realizes the launch is broken. Watch how the communication makes it worse.

7:43 AM. The project manager sends an all-caps subject line to a distribution list of fifteen people: **URGENT — DEPLOYMENT BROKEN — DIAL IN NOW.** The body is two sentences. A conference bridge number. No context.

Five people dial in. Three more are in a different time zone and miss it. Two are in other meetings and join late, halfway through someone else's sentence.

Project manager: "Who touched the configuration last? This is bad. We need answers immediately."

Engineer 1: "I updated it Thursday but it should have been —"

Project manager: "What did you change? Why wasn't this flagged?"

Engineer 1 goes quiet. Engineer 2 **has information** *but decides this is not the moment to offer it.*

The next forty minutes produce heat, not light. By the time anyone isolates the actual problem, two of the people who had relevant information have disengaged — not because they didn't want to help, but **because the room taught them that helping looked like being the next person blamed.** The fix takes another six hours. The trust takes longer. For weeks afterward, the team routes information through back channels first, sanitizing it before it reaches the bridge.

Panic doesn't move faster than clarity. It just feels like it does.

Stabilizing Communication in Crisis: Immediate Actions

Once the immediate bleeding is stopped, get the team back into a functional communication pattern.

- **Reassemble the communication architecture.** Which structures broke down? Which channels went dark? Which roles stopped communicating? Identify the specific gaps and reactivate each one deliberately. Do not assume the team will self-organize back to normal — in a crisis, normal patterns often feel impossible. Explicitly restart them.
- **Reduce noise while increasing signal.** Crises generate enormous communication volume — messages, calls, emails, questions — much of it repetitive, adding heat rather than light. Create ruthless simplicity: fewer channels, shorter updates, defined check-in times. You don't want less communication. You want more focused communication.
- **Protect the people doing the work.** Shield the operational team from the full weight of leadership anxiety. When an executive is panicking, every person between that executive and the floor feels the pressure cascading down. This disrupts focus and compounds the problem. The leader's communication role in a crisis: absorb stakeholder pressure and translate it into clear, calm direction — not pass the panic along with a deadline.

The Post-Mortem: Learning Without Blame

If you get nothing else from this chapter, get this: **the post-mortem is a gift.** Used correctly, it is the single most powerful tool you have for preventing the next failure. Used incorrectly — which is how most organizations use it — it is a ritual of blame that teaches everyone present to hide problems more effectively next time.

Set the framing before you begin: "We are here to understand what happened, not to determine who is at fault." This is a prerequisite. If people believe the outcome of the post-mortem is someone getting in trouble, they will not tell you what actually happened.

The Five Whys in Practice

Why #	Answer	What It Reveals
1	Because the project manager didn't tell them	A person — stop here and you have blame
2	Because there was no defined protocol for communicating mid-project scope changes	A process gap
3	Because scope changes were assumed to be rare	An assumption
4	Because the team had no mechanism for tracking them	A missing structure
5 (root cause)	Because scope management was not included in the project charter	A system design failure

Now you have something actionable. **Not a person to blame — a system gap to close.** That gap will cause the same problem again with a different project manager if you do not address it.

End-of-Project Communication Retrospective Checklist

Run this at the close of every significant project. Do not skip it when things went well — *especially then.*

- **Where did information fail to reach people who needed it, and at which stage of the project?**

- **Which handoffs were cleanest, and what made them work?** (Capture this for reuse.)
- **Which handoffs were roughest, and what was the root cause?**
- **Were our escalation paths used appropriately — or did people work around them?**
- **Did the RACI matrix reflect how work actually flowed, or did ownership drift?**
- **What workarounds did people build, and what do they tell us about system gaps?**
- **Were meeting norms followed consistently? If not, what got in the way?**
- **What decisions were made verbally that should have been documented?**
- **What would we build into our communication plan for the next project that we didn't have this time?**
- **Is there anything that someone knew that the team needed to know, but didn't surface until too late?**
- **What made it hard to raise?**

The After-Action Review (AAR)

Borrowed from military practice. Four questions, conducted immediately after the event while memories are fresh:

- **What was supposed to happen?** (Describe the intended plan, objective, success criteria)
- **What actually happened?** (Observable facts, not interpretations)
- **Why was there a difference?** (Apply Five Whys to each significant gap)
- **What do we do differently next time?** (Specific, assigned, with a due date)

The teams that run AARs consistently — and actually implement the changes they surface — are the teams that improve. The teams that skip them because "there's no time" or "nobody wants to dwell on what went wrong" are the teams that repeat the same mistakes under new names.

Rebuilding Credibility After a Communication Failure

There will be moments when the failure is yours. *How you respond will determine how much credibility you retain.*

What Rebuilds Credibility	What to Say / Do
Acknowledge specifically	Not "I'm sorry if anyone was impacted" — the non-apology that communicates you're not quite sure you did anything wrong. Specifically: "I did not communicate the timeline change to the team before the meeting. That left people unprepared, and I own that."
Explain what you understand now	"I thought the email was enough. I understand now that the complexity of the change required a direct conversation." This demonstrates you processed what happened — not just weathered it.
State what you are doing differently	Credibility is rebuilt through changed behavior, not through words. Tell people specifically what you will do differently. Then do it. Then do it again. The second offense after a genuine commitment to change causes damage that is much harder to repair than the first.
Give it time	Trust is built in drops and lost in buckets. People's confidence in you returns when they have enough data points to feel safe relying on you again. You cannot rush that process. You can only feed it.

Conversation Translations: Instead of / Try

The difference between communication that damages and communication that builds is often a single sentence. These are the most common communication moments where the default language undermines the intent — and what to say instead.

Instead of…	Try…	Why It Works Better
"Does that make sense?"	"What questions do you have?"	"Does that make sense?" invites a nod. "What questions do you have?" assumes questions exist and creates space for them.
"I'm sorry if anyone was upset."	"I didn't communicate this clearly. That's on me."	The first is a non-apology. The second owns the gap without requiring others to validate their feelings to receive it.
"We need to communicate better."	"Here's the specific gap I saw and here's what I'm proposing we change."	Abstract problems don't generate concrete solutions. Naming the specific gap does.
"Why didn't you tell me sooner?"	"Help me understand what got in the way of flagging this earlier."	The first is blame. The second is curiosity — and it's far more likely to surface the actual system failure.
"I already sent that in an email."	"Let me make sure this landed — here's the short version."	Sending is not communicating. Delivery without reception is just data transfer.
"That's not my job to communicate."	"I'll make sure the right person has this — do you know who that is?"	Ownership gaps in communication are often discovered by the person who chooses to fill them anyway.

Instead of…	Try…	Why It Works Better
"I assumed you knew."	"I should have confirmed this with you directly. Here's where we are now."	Assumptions are where communication failures are born. Owning the assumption rather than defending it keeps the conversation moving forward.
"We've been over this."	"Let me be clearer about this part specifically — I may not have explained it well the first time."	"We've been over this" closes the conversation and assigns blame. The alternative opens it and assigns responsibility to improving the explanation.
"Everyone knows that."	"Let me make sure everyone has the same information before we move on."	"Everyone knows" is almost never true — and the gap between what you think is common knowledge and what actually is common is where breakdowns live.
"Nobody told me."	"I didn't have this information — let's figure out where the gap is so it doesn't happen again."	The first defends. The second investigates. Only one of them produces a system fix.

When the Best Communication Move Is to Leave

This is the conversation most professional development books are too polite to have. So I will have it.

Not every environment can be fixed. Not every leader will model the standard. Not every organization has the will to address the structural problems producing the communication failures. Sometimes — despite your most skilled, sustained, genuinely committed efforts — the culture simply will not change.

Signals that you may be at that point:

- Leadership has been made aware, repeatedly, and has chosen not to act. Leadership did not forget. **Leadership decided the status quo is acceptable.**
- **You are the primary absorber of every communication failure.** You are compensating for everyone above and around you, and the system has quietly assigned you that role without acknowledging, resourcing, or rewarding it.
- **The culture actively punishes speaking up.** Escalation leads to repercussions. Questions are met with dismissal. Honesty is treated as insubordination.
- **Your own communication is deteriorating.** You are becoming someone you do not want to be — more guarded, more cynical, less willing to engage. That is a signal.

Leaving a broken communication environment is not failure. It is discernment. It is knowing the difference between a problem that can be solved from where you are and a problem that requires a structural intervention not available to you.

Leaving with your integrity intact — documenting what you know, completing your handoffs, being professional in your exit — is itself a communication act. It communicates that you have standards, and that those standards have value.

The Resilience of the Communicator

Communication work is emotionally demanding in ways that rarely get acknowledged. When you are the person building bridges in a culture of silos, following up and closing loops and facilitating the hard conversations nobody else wants to have — that takes something out of you. Resilience for the communicator has nothing to do with toughness. It has to do with practices — the ones that let you sustain your effectiveness over time.

Practices that sustain:

- **Document everything.** Not for protection, though that matters — but for clarity. Writing creates shared reality. It also creates a record that helps you see your own progress, your own patterns, and your own impact.
- **Build your network deliberately.** Find the other people in the organization who share your commitment to clear, accountable, respectful communication. They exist. They may be quiet, because the culture has taught them to be. Invest in those relationships.
- **Know your non-negotiables.** The communication behaviors you will not compromise on regardless of environment. Mine: I will not be the reason someone doesn't have the information they need to do their job. I will not pretend something is fine when I know it isn't. I will not let a breakdown sit unaddressed when I have the ability to address it.
- **Give yourself grace for the failures.** You will miss signals. You will make assumptions. You will have weeks where the communication culture feels like it is moving backward. That is evidence that you are doing something genuinely difficult in an imperfect world — not evidence that you are doing it wrong.

The goal is not perfection. The goal is direction — to be consistently, intentionally moving toward a way of working where people have what they need, where problems surface before they become crises, and where the team functions as something greater than the sum of its parts. That direction is worth everything.

Key Takeaways

- **In a communication crisis, triage first:** stop the spread of misinformation, establish a single authoritative source, and communicate status *even when you don't have all the information yet.*
- **Stabilize by reassembling the communication architecture deliberately — don't assume the team will go back to normal.**

- **The post-mortem is not about blame.** It is about system improvement. Use Five Whys and After-Action Reviews to find **structural causes, not people to blame.**
- **Rebuilding credibility after a failure requires specific acknowledgment, demonstrated learning, and changed behavior — not just an apology.**
- **Know when to leave.** Staying in a communication environment that will not change is a choice — and it has costs. **Leaving with integrity is also a communication act.**

Reflection Questions

1. **Think of the last significant communication failure you experienced.** What would a Five Whys analysis reveal about its root cause — and what system change would have prevented it?
2. **How do you currently take care of your own resilience as a communicator?** What practices sustain you, and what drains you? Is the balance sustainable?
3. **Have you ever stayed in a broken communication environment longer than was healthy?** What kept you there, and what do you know now that you wish you had known then?

Conclusion: The Bridge, Not the Wall

There is a moment I have thought about many times since it happened. Early in my career, I was part of a cross-functional team working on a process improvement initiative. We had a clear objective, strong individual contributors, executive sponsorship, and a reasonable timeline. By every external measure, we had the ingredients for success.

We failed. Not catastrophically, not visibly to the outside world — but we failed to deliver what we set out to deliver, and the project quietly faded into the category of things that used to be priorities. When I looked back at what went wrong, the answer was not resources. It was not skill. It was not the sponsor's commitment or the team's effort.

It was that we stopped talking to each other.

Not all at once. Gradually. The weekly check-in went from thirty minutes to fifteen. Then it became optional. Then the project manager started sending updates by email instead of gathering the team.

Then one department stopped sending their representative because the meetings "weren't relevant to their part." Then decisions started getting made without the full picture. Then the people with the information weren't in the room when the decisions happened. And then, slowly, inevitably, the initiative collapsed under the weight of all the things we assumed other people knew. That experience is why I wrote this book.

What Success Looks Like

I want to paint you a picture. Not an ideal, not a fantasy — a specific and achievable version of what a team that communicates well actually looks like in practice.

The meetings are not perfect. They still run a few minutes long, and the agenda still needs to be tightened on a bad week. But when someone doesn't understand something, they say so. When someone sees a problem forming, they name it before it becomes a crisis. When the meeting ends, everyone in the room knows what was decided, who owns what, and when the next check-in happens. The action items are in writing before people leave the room. The loop is closed as a matter of course, not as a special effort.

The handoffs are not events people dread. When someone transitions off a project or out of a role, the incoming person has the context they need. Not because they got lucky, not because the outgoing person worked late to reconstruct everything at the last minute, but because documentation and knowledge transfer are built into the operating rhythm. The work continues. The institutional knowledge doesn't leave when the person does.

When someone makes a mistake, the response is proportionate and forward-looking. The mistake gets named, the impact gets assessed, the root cause gets examined, and the fix gets documented. Nobody pretends it didn't happen. Nobody catastrophizes it into a referendum on the person's competence. The culture treats honest acknowledgment of error as a sign of professional maturity — because that's what it is.

New team members get onboarded into the communication culture, not just the job. In their first week, someone has a real conversation with them about how the team operates: which channels are used for what, how decisions get made, what to do when they see a problem, who to call when something is urgent. They are not left to figure out the unwritten rules by trial and error. The rules are written. They are shared. They are modeled by the people who have been on the team the longest.

When something goes wrong — and something always goes wrong — the question the team asks first is not "whose fault is this?" It is: "What did we miss, and where in the process can we catch it earlier next time?" The post-mortem is not a blame session. It is a diagnostic. It produces specific changes to specific processes, not vague commitments to "communicate better."

This team is not full of exceptional communicators. It is not blessed with an unusually gifted leader or an unusually self-aware group of individuals. It is a team that decided, deliberately, to build the structures that make good communication the path of least resistance. The norms are clear. The expectations are shared. The tools are actually used. *That team exists. I have been part of it.* I have watched it built from scratch. I have seen it emerge from the wreckage of a team that used to be the other kind.

It is not out of reach. It is a decision, followed by a design, followed by consistent practice. That is what this book is for.

Communication Is the Bridge

I chose the metaphor of the bridge intentionally, because it captures something true about what communication actually is and what it actually does.

A bridge does not exist for its own sake. A bridge exists because there is something worth reaching on the other side — a destination, a person, a resource, a result. The bridge is the mechanism that makes the reaching possible. Without it, you stand on one side and look at what you cannot access. With it, the distance disappears.

Communication is exactly that. It is not the goal. The goal is:

- The project delivered
- The team cohesive
- The patient cared for
- The process improved
- The organization that learns, grows, and adapts

Communication is the mechanism that makes all of those things possible. It is the bridge between good intentions and great results.

I have met leaders with genuinely good intentions whose teams were failing because the bridge did not exist. I have met organizations with extraordinary strategies whose execution was a slow, grinding disaster because the people responsible for implementation were operating on different versions of the strategy, with no shared language, no defined accountability, and no feedback loop to tell leadership that the gap between strategy and reality had become a canyon.

Communication is the bridge. And like any bridge, it requires intentional construction, regular maintenance, and the ongoing commitment of people who understand that getting from here to there does not happen by accident.

Your Role — No Matter Your Title

One of the things I believe most deeply is that communication is not a leadership responsibility. It is a human responsibility. It belongs to everyone on the team, regardless of title, seniority, tenure, or function.

I have seen individual contributors change the entire communication culture of a team through nothing more than the consistent practice of saying "let me make sure I understand" and "I want to make sure you have this information." I have seen frontline supervisors build cultures of psychological safety in their small corner of a large, dysfunctional organization. I have seen administrative professionals become the most important connectors in a siloed environment because they were the only ones willing to pick up the phone and call the other department.

None of these people waited for permission. None of them had a mandate from the executive team. They decided that communication was their responsibility, and they acted on that decision, day after day, until it became the standard.

You have that same power. Wherever you are in the organizational structure, however much authority you hold, however broken the environment around you — you have the ability to choose to communicate more clearly, more consistently, more courageously than the culture currently demands.

That choice does not fix everything. It does not immunize you against the failures of others. But it changes your contribution to the system. And systems are made of individual contributions. Yours matters.

The Porch Light Question

This is the part you don't have a script for.

Think about the person on your team — or in your life — who people keep the porch light on for. The one whose call you answer. The one whose meeting you don't cancel. The one who, when they say "can we talk for a minute," you know it will be worth your time. The one who makes you feel heard, not handled.

Now think about the person people turn the porch light off for. The one whose emails get skimmed. The one whose meetings feel like a performance. The one who talks at you, not with you. The one who makes you feel smaller after every interaction.

Both of those people are communicating. The difference isn't skill. It's intent. It's whether the communication builds connection or erodes it. Whether it opens a door or closes one.

Every framework in this book — every script, every template, every stage of the spiral — comes back to that. Are you the person people keep the porch light on for?

Communication isn't about being the smartest voice in the room. It's about being the one that makes the room work. The one who asks the question nobody else will. The one who follows up. The one who says "I was wrong" before someone has to say it for them. The one who notices the silence and does something about it.

> That person changes teams. That person changes cultures. That person changes outcomes.

I want you to be the one whose call gets answered. The one whose meeting doesn't get cancelled. I want you to be the one they leave the porch light on for.

Two Kinds of Communicator: The Difference Is One Sentence

You've seen both of these people. Maybe you've been both.

The first kind:

The project lead wraps up the all-hands. *"Great. Any questions?"*

Silence.

"Perfect. We'll circle back at the end of the quarter."

Somewhere in that room, three people had questions they didn't ask. Two of them knew something the project lead needed to know. None of that information moved.

The project lead left thinking it went well.

The second kind:

The same meeting. The same silence.

"No questions usually means we're still processing. I'm going to ask one before we close — what's one thing about this plan that you'd want more clarity on before you execute?"

A pause. Then one hand. Then another.

It doesn't take a different personality. It doesn't take a communication degree or a new set of tools. It takes one sentence — a different sentence — that signals: *your information is wanted here.*

That's the bridge.

It's shorter than it looks. And it's worth building every single time.

Twenty Years and One Recurring Theme

In every single organization, across every industry and every role, the story is the same: **the teams that function well are the teams that communicate.** Not perfectly. Not without friction. But consistently, courageously, and with a genuine commitment to shared understanding.

The problems that have consumed the most energy, caused the most damage, and left the most lasting pain in every organization I have ever been part of have all, at their root, been communication failures. Not strategy failures. Not resource failures. Not people failures, in most cases. Communication failures.

Communication is not a soft skill. It is the infrastructure of every team that has ever achieved anything worth achieving. It is the first thing that suffers when stress increases and the first thing that must be rebuilt when the team wants to recover. It is the leading indicator of team health, organizational effectiveness, and project success. It is the thing that turns a group of talented individuals into something that functions as more than the sum of its parts.

A Call to Action

The next time you receive a communication you are responsible for understanding, stop and say seven words:

"Let me repeat what I heard back."

Not "got it." Not a nod. Not the silence that passes for comprehension. Stop and verify. Repeat back what you heard. Ask the question you almost did not ask because you were afraid it would make you seem slow. Close the loop. Confirm the understanding before the assumption has a chance to become the next breakdown.

And the next time you are the one communicating, do not ask, "Does that make sense?" That question invites a nod. Do not rely on "Any questions?" either. That question is too easy to dismiss.

Ask this instead:

"What questions do you have?"

That question assumes questions exist. It creates room for clarification. It tells the room that uncertainty is not a problem to hide — it is part of getting the work right.

These are small actions. Almost embarrassingly small relative to the size of the problem this book addresses. But I have watched small actions, practiced consistently, build communication cultures that produce extraordinary results.

Culture is not built by grand gestures. It is built by ordinary practices, done over and over, until they become the way we do things here.

What to Check	What It Means	Question to Ask	What It Prevents
Meaning	Confirms the message landed the way it was intended.	"Here is what I think this means — am I reading it correctly?"	Misinterpretation, mixed messages, and people acting on different

What to Check	What It Means	Question to Ask	What It Prevents
			versions of the same instruction.
Comprehension	Confirms the person can explain the message back in their own words.	"Can you walk me through how you understand this?"	Nodding without understanding, false agreement, and silent confusion.
Understanding	Confirms the next action, owner, timing, and definition of done are clear.	"What happens next, who owns it, and what does done look like?"	Missed handoffs, unclear accountability, rework, and assumptions about follow-through.

In Closing

At the beginning of this book, we started with a line from a movie.

Not because this is a book about *Cool Hand Luke*. Not because a prison camp in a 1967 film has all the answers for today's project teams, warehouse floors, conference rooms, hospitals, agencies, or operations centers. We started there because that line has lasted for a reason.

"What we have here is a failure to communicate."

In the Captain's mouth, those words were not an invitation to understand. They were not curiosity. They were not accountability. They were power pretending to be communication. They were a wall.

But at the end of the film, when Luke says the line back, something changes. The words no longer belong only to the person in charge. They no longer mean, you failed to listen to me. They become something sharper, sadder, and more honest:

You never intended to listen. That is the turn this entire book has been working toward.

In too many organizations, **communication failure is still treated like a problem with the person on the receiving end.**

- The operator did not follow the instruction.
- The project manager did not escalate soon enough.
- The supervisor did not ask the right question.
- The employee should have spoken up.
- The team should have known.

By now, **you know better.** You have seen The Silent Spiral™. You have seen how it starts with an assumption so small nobody bothers to test it. You have seen how silence gets mistaken for agreement, how frustration gets misread as attitude, how workarounds become the real system, and how failure eventually arrives wearing the costume of surprise.

You have also seen the way out:

- **Test the assumption.**
- **Break the silence.**
- **Make it safe.**
- **Close the loop.**
- **Name it.**

That is Breaking the Spiral™.

Not a slogan. Not a leadership poster. Not a one-time training event that gets forgotten the next time the floor gets busy or the project goes sideways. **A practice. A way of refusing to let communication become something people do to each other instead of something that happens between them.**

That is the difference between the wall and the bridge.

- The wall says, “I told you.”
- The bridge says, “Let me make sure it landed.”
- The wall says, “Nobody said anything.”

- The bridge says, “What are we not saying yet?”
- The wall says, “That is not my job.”
- The bridge says, “Who needs to know this, and how do we make sure they do?”
- The wall says, “We need better communication.”
- The bridge says, “Here is the specific gap, here is the owner, here is the next step, and here is when we will follow up.”

That is how cultures change. Not all at once. Not because one person delivers the perfect speech. Not because an organization suddenly becomes enlightened overnight.

Cultures change when enough people stop walking past the gap.

- They change when one person asks the clarifying question everyone else was afraid to ask.
- They change when one supervisor refuses to treat silence as alignment.
- They change when one manager protects the person who raises the concern instead of punishing the discomfort they created.
- They change when one team decides that sent is not the same as received, received is not the same as understood, and understood is not the same as done.
- They change when the loop gets closed because someone cared enough to close it. That someone can be you.
- Wherever you sit in the structure.
- Whatever your title says.
- However much authority you have or do not have.

You do not need permission to make communication clearer. You do not need a mandate to ask, “What did I miss?” You do not need a reorganization to say, “I want to make sure we are working from the same understanding.” You do not need a senior title to build a bridge in the next conversation you are part of.

You just have to decide that the next time something is unclear, you will not let the silence do the talking.

That is where the spiral breaks. Not in theory. Not someday. Not after the culture gets better.

Here.

Now.

In the next handoff. The next meeting. The next uncomfortable pause. The next moment when someone assumes everyone knows and you are brave enough to ask, “How do we know?”

What we have here does not have to stay a failure to communicate. What we can have here is a team that checks for understanding.

A culture that makes **truth safer than silence.**

A system that **does not wait for failure before it listens.**

A workplace where people have the information they need to do the work well, raise the concern early, recover when something breaks, and trust that their voice has somewhere useful to go.

That is the bridge worth building.

Now go build it.

The next conversation is the one that matters.

— *Ace*

THE COMMUNICATION PLAYBOOK — Frameworks, Scripts, and Use Cases

Playbook

A Reference Guide for Real-World Situations This playbook is designed to live on your desk, not your shelf.

Everything before this section was about understanding why communication breaks down. *This section is about what to do right now, in the situation you are actually standing in.*

Think of it as a field guide. The frameworks here come from crisis communications, public relations, operations leadership, Lean problem-solving, and the kind of practical workplace experience that teaches you very quickly which conversations help and which ones make everything worse. Some were born in boardrooms. Some came from healthcare and aviation. Some were sharpened on warehouse floors — in handoff failures, in bad meetings, and in the moments right before a preventable problem became an expensive one.

This playbook exists to make Breaking the Spiral™ practical. Take Five helps you break the silence with yourself before you break it with someone else. SIA helps you test the assumption by grounding a difficult conversation in observable facts. The Read-Back Technique helps you close the loop. The Pre-Mortem and the A3 help teams name what is actually going wrong before the failure gets blamed on the nearest person. Set the Context helps people understand what they are walking into before they start inventing their own explanation.

That is the point of this entire section — not theory, not communication as performance, but communication as disciplined practice. Use it selectively, practically, and often.

How This Playbook Is Organized

- **Part 1 — Core Messaging Frameworks.** The four foundational tools that shape how you prepare, structure, and deliver communication when clarity matters most. These help you think before you speak. Set the Context, Take Five, SIA, and the Key Message Triangle.
- **Part 2 — Situational Frameworks.** Tactical tools that guide when and how communication should happen. They help you slow down, verify understanding, manage meetings, think before escalating, and solve the right problem before it spreads. The 3-Before-Me Rule, the 24-Hour Rule, the Parking Lot Method, the Read-Back Technique, the Pre-Mortem, and the A3.
- **Part 3 — Diagnosis.** Identify what kind of communication problem you are actually in before you choose a response. Most communication failures are not failures of language. They are failures of diagnosis. This section gives you a faster way to see what is happening and what to reach for next.
- **Part 4 — Use Cases: What to Say in the Moment.** Practical language for real situations. This is where the playbook moves from concept to conversation. Examples for escalation, feedback, capacity, misalignment, and other high-stakes moments where words matter and timing matters just as much.
- **Part 5 — Templates and Working Tools.** Structures that design communication into the way work actually runs. The tools that make communication repeatable, visible, and sustainable across meetings, projects, stakeholder updates, and follow-through. Meeting Agenda, Stakeholder Matrix, Kickoff Communication Plan.
- **Part 6 — Quick Reference.** The condensed prompts you can use in real time — checklists, reminders, and prompts designed for moments when you need speed more than theory.

Master Framework Comparison

Before you dive in, use this table to orient yourself. All frameworks live in this playbook. Each one solves a different problem. Some work alone. Many work better in combination.

Framework	What It Does	Best For	Avoid When	Pairs Well With
Set the Context	Establishes the frame before the message lands	Change announcements, feedback, role shifts, sensitive updates	You need an immediate safety response with no setup time	Key Message Triangle, SIA
Take Five	Converts emotional reaction into a professional response	Triggering emails, public challenge, escalations, criticism	Immediate action is required to contain harm	SIA, 24-Hour Rule
SIA (Situation, Impact, Ask)	Structures difficult conversations around facts, impact, and action	Feedback, escalation, correction, accountability	Facts are still unclear and still unfolding	Set the Context, Read-Back
Key Message Triangle	Keeps communication centered on one message and three proof points	Leadership updates, persuasion, short decision windows	The audience needs a full working session, not a summary	Set the Context
3-Before-Me Rule	Builds self-sufficiency before escalation	Routine problem-solving, manager dependency, team ownership	Safety, legal, compliance, or ethics issues	SIA

Framework	What It Does	Best For	Avoid When	Pairs Well With
24-Hour Rule	Prevents emotional messages from becoming permanent damage	Angry emails, defensive replies, perceived disrespect	Time-sensitive communication truly cannot wait	Take Five
Parking Lot Method	Protects meeting focus without dismissing valid issues	Off-track meetings, side debates, missing decision-makers	The issue is urgent and cannot wait	Set the Context
Read-Back Technique	Confirms understanding by exposing interpretation gaps	Handoffs, feedback, instructions, verbal commitments	Casual low-risk conversations where overprocessing adds friction	SIA
Pre-Mortem	Surfaces likely failure points before launch	Projects, transitions, complex changes, high-risk initiatives	The work is already underway and needs a retrospective instead	Set the Context, A3
A3	Creates one shared cross-functional view of one problem	Recurring failures, multi-team process problems, alignment work	The problem is simple and one person can solve it directly	Pre-Mortem, SIA

PART 1: CORE MESSAGING FRAMEWORKS

These four frameworks are the backbone of the playbook.

They are not complicated. None take long to apply. None require formal communications training. **What they require is the discipline most people skip: pausing before they speak, write, react, or escalate.**

Framework: SET THE CONTEXT

What It Is

The single most common communication mistake in professional life is not saying the wrong thing.

It is saying the right thing without first establishing the ground on which it lands.

You know why the conversation is happening. You know the backstory, the decision process, the constraints, and the stakes. Your audience does not. They are starting cold. When people receive information without context, they do not wait patiently for clarification. They fill in the gaps themselves, usually with the most threatening, frustrating, or self-protective explanation available.

"We need to talk about the project" becomes "I am in trouble" before you say another word.

Set the Context is the discipline of providing the frame before you deliver the picture. Done well, it takes thirty seconds to two minutes and prevents hours of confusion, rumor, and resistance.

When to Use It

- Any email or memo announcing a process, policy, structural, or staffing change.
- A meeting where you need buy-in, not just attendance.
- A feedback conversation where the stakes feel high.
- Any message where the *what* is likely to trigger questions about the *why.*

- Communication across functions where people do not share the same reference points.

The 4-Step Process

Step	What to Do	Key Question
1 — AUDIENCE	Define who is receiving the message, what they know, and what they care about	What is their emotional temperature around this topic?
2 — PURPOSE	State honestly why you are communicating — inform, request, correct, align, or decide	What needs to happen as a result of this message?
3 — BACKGROUND	Brief selectively — three points max	What would they have to not know for this message to make no sense?
4 — MESSAGE	Deliver the core message — short and direct, because the context carries the weight	Is it clear, specific, and actionable?

Without Context vs. With Context

Scenario	Without Context	With Context
New process rollout	"Starting Monday, everyone submits timesheets in the new system."	"Our current timesheet process has been causing payroll delays. Starting Monday, we are switching to a new system that fixes the error at the source. Everyone needs to complete the training by Friday."
Schedule change	"The Tuesday 6am shift is moving to 7am."	"We have had consistent staffing gaps in the first hour on Tuesdays. To address that, the 6am Tuesday shift moves to 7am starting next week."
Role change	"Marcus is going to handle vendor calls."	"We have been stretched thin on vendor coordination, and Marcus is ready for more responsibility. Starting this week, he is taking over vendor calls so those relationships stay consistent."
Performance issue	"I need to talk to you about your numbers."	"I want to have a straightforward conversation about your performance this quarter. Some things have come up in the data that we need to work through together."

Scenario	Without Context	With Context
Project delay	"The launch date has been pushed to Q3."	"A technical dependency surfaced in testing two weeks ago, and the Q2 launch is no longer feasible. We are moving to Q3, and I want to walk you through what changed and what it means for your team."

Framework in the Field: The Rollout Nobody Understood

A regional distribution center rolled out a new quality inspection process in receiving. The updated Standard Operating Procedure (SOP) was emailed to supervisors on Sunday night with a go-live date of Wednesday and a simple instruction to brief their teams.

By Tuesday morning, three different stories were circulating on the floor. One crew thought there had been a quality incident management was hiding. Another thought second shift had caused a problem and everyone was being punished for it. A third assumed it must be tied to a new client requirement. Nobody knew. Because nobody knew, nobody trusted it.

Three days after go-live, the manager called a five-minute huddle and finally did what should have happened on day one. She explained that damaged product had made it through receiving and onto outbound orders three times in the prior month, two had become customer complaints, and the new process existed to catch the issue earlier.

It was not punishment. It was not temporary. It was a quality control change meant to prevent repeat defects. Within forty-eight hours, compliance improved noticeably. The process itself had not changed. The context had.

SET THE CONTEXT

PRE-MESSAGE PLANNER

CLARITY BEFORE CONTENT. CONTEXT BEFORE MESSAGE.

AUDIENCE

Understand who you're talking to.

 Who is receiving this? ____________________

 What do they already know about this topic? ____________________

 What do they care about most? ____________________

 Current emotional temperature around this issue? ____________________

PURPOSE

Be clear on the outcome you need.

 What do I need to happen as a result of this message? ____________________

____

 Am I informing / requesting / correcting / aligning / deciding?

____

BACKGROUND

Set the stage with key facts.

1. ____________________
2. ____________________
3. ____________________

MESSAGE

Make your message clear and actionable.

 Core message in one sentence: ____________________

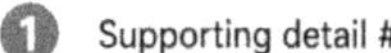

____

Supporting detail #2: ____________________

 Call to action / next step: ____________________

- Have I considered my audience?
- Is my purpose clear and specific?
- Is the background relevant and limited to key facts?
- Is my core message simple and focused?
- Is the next step clear?

GOOD CONTEXT CREATES CLARITY. CLARITY DRIVES ACTION.

Framework: TAKE FIVE

What It Is

Take Five is a structured pause-and-prepare tool for situations where your emotional state is at risk of overriding your professional judgment.

It comes from the same **basic truth that governs good crisis communication:** *the worst possible response is often the first one that feels most satisfying.*

The name is literal. It is not five minutes. It is five mental moves before you open your mouth or hit send.

When to Use It

- You receive criticism that **feels unfair or public.**
- Someone **escalates an issue in a way that implicates your team**.
- You are in a meeting and something is said **that immediately spikes your defensiveness.**
- You receive an email you want to **answer quickly and sharply.**
- A decision was **made without you** and you just found out.

The 5 Steps

Step	What It Means	The Discipline
STOP	Physically pause. Say "Let me take a moment before I respond."	No one has ever lost credibility by pausing to think.
SEPARATE	Separate the trigger (the event) from the actual issue underneath.	Your frustration is real, but it is not the whole problem.
ASSESS	What do you know for certain? What are you assuming? What's the risk of a bad response?	Shift from emotional processing to strategic thinking.

Step	What It Means	The Discipline
DRAFT	Write the response before you deliver it — even if you'll deliver it verbally.	Writing forces clarity that adrenaline does not. Ask: Is there anything here I would regret?
DELIVER	Choose the right channel and timing.	"Now" is not always the right answer.

Example in Practice

Scenario: You are presenting a project update. A senior colleague cuts in and says, in front of everyone, *"This approach has already been tried, and it does not work. I am not sure why we are still talking about this."*

- **Stop:** *"That is a fair challenge. Let me address that directly."*
- **Separate:** The trigger is being challenged publicly. The actual issue is whether the objection is valid.
- **Assess:** You know your proposal. You do not yet know the details of the earlier attempt. The room is watching your reaction.
- **Draft:** *"I would like to understand what was tried before and what the results were. For today, I want to make sure the group has the full picture of what we are proposing and why we believe conditions are different this time."*
- **Deliver:** Calmly, in the room, without turning the moment into a personal fight.

Take Five does not remove pressure.
It keeps pressure from deciding words for you.

TAKE FIVE
RESPONSE PREPARATION

PAUSE. THINK. CHOOSE YOUR RESPONSE.

1

STOP

Pause before you react.

What just happened (one sentence, no editorial)? ____________________

2

SEPARATE

Separate what happened from how you feel about it.

The trigger (the event): ____________________

My emotional response: ____________________

The actual issue underneath: ____________________

3

ASSESS

Get clear on facts, assumptions, needs, and consequences.

What do I know for certain? ____________________

What am I assuming? ____________________

What does the other person need from me right now? ____________________

Risk of a bad response: ____________________

Opportunity in a good response: ____________________

4

DRAFT

Craft your response intentionally.

Opening (acknowledge / set context): ____________________

Core message: ____________________

Call to action or next step: ____________________

Review: Is there anything here I would regret? ____________________

5

DELIVER

Choose how, when, and with whom.

Best channel: ____________________

Best timing: ____________________

Who else needs to be in the room or on the message? ____________________

FIVE MINUTES OF PREPARATION CAN PREVENT FIVE DAYS OF DAMAGE.

Don't react, respond.

Separate fact from feeling.

Get clear before you act.

Intentional beats impulsive.

Right message. Right way.

Framework: SIA — SITUATION, IMPACT, ASK

What It Is

SIA is a three-part structure for conversations where something has gone wrong, something needs to change, or a pattern has to be addressed directly.

Most difficult conversations fail in one of three places:

- The speaker never establishes shared facts **(Situation)**
- They move from problem to personal criticism too quickly **(Impact)**
- They leave the other person guessing what they actually want **(Ask)**

SIA closes all three gaps.

When to Use It

- Performance feedback conversations
- Escalating a cross-functional issue
- Addressing a pattern with a peer or direct report
- Documenting a communication failure in writing
- Any conversation where you need the other person to understand *why* you're raising the issue

The 3 Parts of SIA

Part	What It Is	What It Is NOT
SITUATION	Observable facts — what happened, when, where, who was involved	Your interpretation of those facts
IMPACT	The actual effect on work, team, customer, timeline, or quality — measurable and observable	"You made everyone feel disrespected." Vague emotional accusations.
ASK	Specifically what you need going forward	An implied fix that never gets named — say it explicitly.

Example in Practice

Scenario: A team member from another department keeps sending work directly to your staff, bypassing intake, and your queue is backing up.

- **Situation:** *"Over the past three weeks, our team has received fourteen direct requests through individual messages rather than through the shared intake form."*
- **Impact:** *"We have had to reprioritize work mid-sprint four times, which pushed two deliverables past due and created scheduling conflicts for two team members."*
- **Ask:** *"Going forward, I need all requests to come through the intake form. I can make sure the link is visible in both channels, and I would like to review how it is working in two weeks."*

Clean, factual, and forward-facing.
That is what makes SIA effective.

No blame. No ambiguity. No guessing required.

SIA MESSAGE STRUCTURE

STATE THE SITUATION. EXPLAIN THE IMPACT. MAKE THE ASK.

S — SITUATION (observable facts only)

- On [date/timeframe], [what happened, specifically]: ____________________
- Who was involved: ____________________
- Where / in what context: ____________________

I — IMPACT (the actual effect)

- On the work: ____________________
- On the team / timeline / quality: ____________________
- Measurable or observable outcome: ____________________

A — ASK (specific, actionable)

- What I need going forward is: ____________________
- By when: ____________________
- How I will know it has been addressed: ____________________

TIPS FOR USING SIA

- Stick to facts in the Situation.
- Focus on outcomes, not blame, in the Impact.
- Make a clear, specific request in the Ask.

CLEARER MESSAGE. STRONGER CONVERSATIONS. BETTER RESULTS.

Framework: THE KEY MESSAGE TRIANGLE

What It Is

The **Key Message Triangle** is one of the most useful disciplines in professional communication: one core message, supported by three proof points. Everything you say should trace back to one of those proof points, and each proof point should reinforce the same destination.

The value is not in the shape. The value is in the discipline. It forces prioritization. If something does not support your core message, it probably belongs in a different conversation.

When to Use It

- You have a short window to get a decision from leadership.
- Your audience is skeptical, and you need credibility fast.
- You are delivering bad news and need the takeaway to be action, not anxiety.
- You are at risk of saying so much that no one leaves knowing what mattered.

How to Build It

- Start with the one message your audience needs to remember.
- Build three proof points that make that message credible and specific.
- Keep each proof point distinct.
- Return to the triangle when questions pull the conversation sideways.

Example in Practice

Scenario: You need approval for an additional QA resource.

- **Core Message:** *"We need one additional QA resource to maintain our defect targets next quarter."*
- **Proof Point 1:** *"QA volume has increased 34 percent since Q1 without additional headcount."*
- **Proof Point 2:** *"The defect rate has trended upward for six consecutive weeks."*

- **Proof Point 3:** "Our current inspector-to-volume ratio is below benchmark."
- **Bridge Back To The Triangle:** "That is worth tracking, and what the data comes back to is that we need the resource to protect the target."

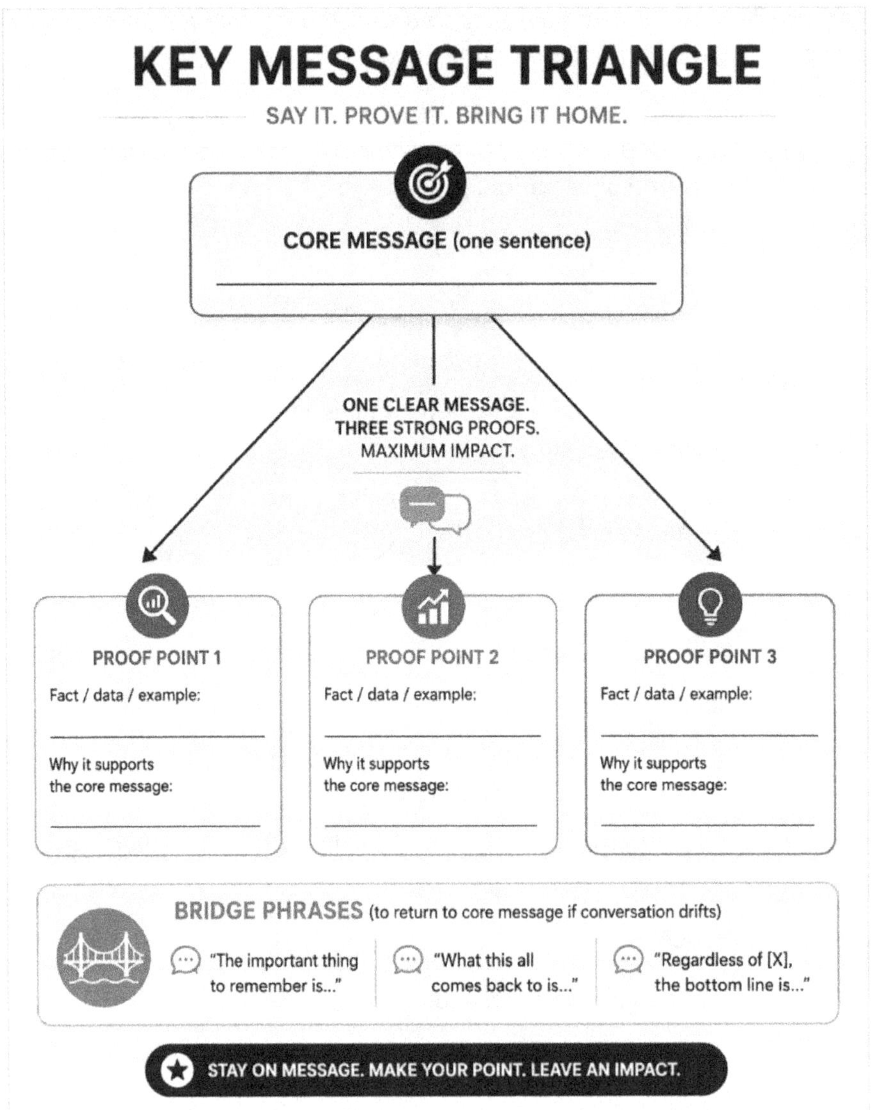

PART 2: SITUATIONAL FRAMEWORKS

These frameworks shape when you pause, when you escalate, how you verify understanding, how you hold the meeting together, and how you keep teams from solving the wrong problem.

Framework: THE 3-BEFORE-ME RULE

What It Is

The 3-Before-Me Rule is a personal discipline for building ownership before escalation.

Before you bring a problem upward, try three genuine resolution paths: use the resources you already have, ask someone at your level or closer to the work, and test a low-risk next step within your authority.

This rule is not about avoiding escalation. Some problems need to be escalated immediately. The point is to escalate responsibly — with facts, context, options, and evidence that you have done what you reasonably could first.

When someone develops the habit of reaching higher on the org chart for every answer, they train others — and themselves — to believe they are not equipped to solve problems independently. That reputation has consequences. The 3-Before-Me Rule helps prevent that pattern by building resourcefulness before handoff.

When to Use It

- You encounter a problem you are not sure how to solve with the tools, authority, or information available to you.
- You are about to ask your manager for guidance on something that may be within your scope.
- You want to build a team culture of ownership, problem-solving, and responsible escalation.

Do Not Use It When

- Safety, compliance, ethics, or legal issues are involved.

- The problem is genuinely above your authority or decision rights.
- A time-sensitive decision requires approval you do not have.
- Waiting would increase risk, cost, harm, or confusion.

Check	The Question	What You're Looking For
1	What resources, information, or tools do I already have access to that could help resolve this?	Documentation, data, process guides, prior decisions, or authority you already have.
2	Who at my level or closer to the work might have the answer, context, or experience I need?	A peer, subject matter expert, cross-functional partner, or team member who has solved this before.
3	What can I try, test, or decide on a provisional basis, with a clear review point?	A low-risk next step you can own, monitor, and adjust if needed.

Framework: THE 24-HOUR RULE

What It Is

The 24-Hour Rule is simple: do not send a message written in anger, frustration, defensiveness, or high emotion without giving it time to cool.

If the message is not urgent, wait. Come back to it later and read it with fresh eyes. **Ask yourself:** *Is this clear? Is it necessary? Is it useful? Does it move the work forward — or does it simply transfer my frustration to someone else?*

This rule is not about avoiding honesty. Hard messages still need to be sent. Concerns still need to be raised. Escalations still need to happen. The rule is about separating the moment you write from the moment you send, because those two moments require different mental states. The first may be reactive. The second needs to be intentional.

In organizational communication, a poorly timed or poorly worded message can damage relationships, credibility, and trust — all of which take far longer to rebuild than they take to harm.

Use the 24-Hour Rule when:

- **You have drafted** an email, message, comment, or **text in response to something that made you angry.**
- **Your draft includes phrases like** "frankly," "I find it hard to believe," "I shouldn't have to," "since no one else is going to say this," or "for the record."
- **You are replying** *late at night, after a bad day,* or while still *emotionally charged.*
- **Someone did something** *that felt disrespectful*, and your main goal is to make them feel the impact.
- **The message is more than two paragraphs** *and spends more time explaining your emotion than clarifying the issue.*
- **You would be uncomfortable if the message were forwarded beyond the person you intended to send it to.**

The Rule in Practice

1. **Write it.** Get it all out. Do not self-edit yet.
2. **Save it as a draft.** Do not hit send. Close the window.
3. **Wait 24 hours.** If the issue is not urgent, sleep on it.
4. **Read it as the recipient.** Not as yourself. Read it as someone receiving it cold, without access to your frustration, history, or intent.
5. **Apply the Edit Test.** Would you be comfortable if your manager, skip-level leader, HR, or the person being discussed saw this message exactly as written?
6. **Revise for purpose.** Keep the facts. Remove the heat. Clarify the ask.
7. **Send the revised version — or decide it does not need to be sent at all.**

The Edit Test Triggers

If any of the following phrases or patterns appear in your draft, **apply a full 24-hour hold before sending.** These are not automatic proof that the message is wrong, but they are warning lights. They often signal that frustration, defensiveness, or self-protection has started driving the message.

Trigger Phrase	What It Usually Signals	Better Move
"I shouldn't have to explain this."	Frustration that will read as condescension.	Explain the gap clearly, without shaming the person for not already knowing.
"For the record…"	You are building a case, not solving a problem.	State the fact, the impact, and the action needed.
"Since no one else is going to say this…"	You are positioning yourself as a martyr, not a collaborator.	Name the concern directly without making yourself the hero of the message.
"I find it hard to believe that…"	An accusation framed as an observation.	Say what you observed and what needs clarification.
"Always" or "never"	Absolute language that invites argument, not conversation.	Use the specific incident, date, pattern, or example.
More than three exclamation points	The emotional temperature is controlling the message.	Remove the punctuation and let the facts carry the weight.
Any paragraph that begins with "I" three times in a row	The message has become about you, not the issue.	Recenter the message on the work, the impact, and the next step.

These triggers do not mean the issue should be ignored. They mean the message needs to cool before it moves. The goal is not to make the message softer. The goal is to make it clearer, more useful, and less likely to create a second problem while trying to address the first one.

Framework: THE PARKING LOT METHOD

What It Is

A facilitation and communication tool for tabling a topic without abandoning it. The "parking lot" is a designated holding space — in a meeting, on a whiteboard, in a shared document — where off-topic items are preserved and addressed later, not ignored or allowed to derail the current conversation.

It respects the person who raised the issue and protects the purpose of the meeting at the same time. That balance matters. Without it, meetings either become rigid and dismissive or so loose that nothing gets finished.

When to Use It

- A meeting is running off-track because a valid, but off-topic issue has been raised
- A conversation is heading toward a decision that requires people or information not currently in the room
- Two people start debating a sub-issue that is important but irrelevant to the group's immediate objective

How to Use It

1. **Name it neutrally**: "That's an important topic — I want to make sure we give it the time it deserves."
2. **Parking lot it explicitly**: "I'm going to put that in the parking lot so we don't lose it."
3. **Record it visibly**: Write it on the whiteboard, in the meeting notes, or in the shared doc where everyone can see it.
4. **Commit to a return**: "We'll come back to this at the end of the meeting / I'll set up a separate conversation for this."
5. **Actually return to it**: The parking lot only works if it's not a place where topics go to die. Follow through.
6. **Do not forget to follow up**. A parking lot that never clears becomes a graveyard and destroys trust in the process.

Framework: THE READ-BACK TECHNIQUE

What It Is

The Read-Back is a communication verification tool. After receiving information, instructions, a decision, or an assignment, you restate what you heard in your own words and give the other person the opportunity to confirm, correct, or add to it.

The technique was developed in aviation and healthcare, where miscommunication is a primary cause of catastrophic error. It is useful in any environment where the cost of misalignment is real — missed deadlines, duplicated work, wrong priorities, broken handoffs, or decisions executed differently than intended.

The Read-Back is not parrot-repetition. It is a synthesis that **reveals your interpretation of what was said.** That distinction matters, because interpretation — not transmission — is where most communication gaps appear. **Two people can hear the same sentence and walk away with different understandings of what it means, who owns it, and what happens next. The Read-Back makes that gap visible before the work begins.**

When to Use It

- Receiving complex instructions, especially those with multiple steps or dependencies
- Coming out of a difficult conversation where both parties may be carrying different takeaways
- After a leadership conversation that includes decisions or commitments you will need to act on
- Receiving verbal feedback you want to make sure you understood correctly
- Ending any conversation where misalignment would cause real downstream cost

Example Language

- "Let me read back what I heard to make sure I have it right."
- "What I am taking from this is..."
- "Here is my understanding of the next steps — correct me where I am off."
- "So what I heard is... Is that what you meant?"

Why It Matters

The Read-Back is one of the simplest ways to close the loop. It takes ten seconds. It costs nothing. It prevents the kind of quiet misalignment that does not surface until the work is already wrong.

It is also one of the least-used tools in most organizations — not because people do not know how, but because the culture has not made it normal to check.

This technique makes checking normal.

READ-BACK STRUCTURE

Let me make sure I heard you right.

What I heard as the core decision / direction: ____________

What I heard as my specific next step: ____________

What I understand the timeline to be: ____________

What I'm less clear on that I want to confirm: ____________

WHY THIS MATTERS

A quick read-back prevents misunderstandings, confirms alignment, and ensures we move forward with clarity and confidence.

Framework: THE PRE-MORTEM

What It Is

The Pre-Mortem is **a structured failure-anticipation exercise used before work begins.**

The team imagines the project has already failed — and then works backward to identify why.

This changes the conversation. Instead of asking people to be cautious in the middle of optimism, it gives them permission to say what they are already worried about.

Developed and popularized by organizational psychologist Gary Klein, the Pre-Mortem works because it removes the social pressure to be optimistic. When you ask, *"What could go wrong?"* early in a project, optimism bias and group conformity suppress honest answers. People do not want to be the one who sounds negative while everyone else is excited.

But when you say, *"Assume it already failed — what happened?"* you change the rules. Now the team is not raising objections. They are diagnosing a failure that has already occurred. That reframe makes it safer to name the risks no one wants to say out loud.

When to Use It

- Starting a project with significant complexity or risk
- Launching a process change that will touch multiple teams
- Entering a partnership, vendor relationship, or operational dependency
- Any initiative where the cost of failure is high and reversibility is low

The Process

1. **Set the frame.** Say to the group: "Assume it is three months from now and this initiative has failed. Not partially — completely. What happened?"

2. **Individual silent writing first.** Each person independently writes down every reason they can think of for the failure. No discussion yet. This prevents anchoring and protects quieter voices.

3. **Round-robin sharing.** Go around the room. Each person reads one item at a time. No debate. No defense. No "that won't happen." Just capture everything.

4. **Cluster and prioritize.** Group similar risks together. Identify the three to five that appear most frequently or carry the highest consequence.

5. **Reverse-engineer prevention.** For each top risk, ask: "What would we need to do now to prevent this from happening?"

6. **Build it into the plan.** Assign an owner and a timeline to each prevention action. If it is not assigned, it will not happen.

What to Watch For

- If the Pre-Mortem produces a risk list that nobody acts on, it was theater — not planning.
- If it turns into a venting session, redirect to prevention. The question is not "what frustrates us" but "what would cause this to fail."
- Do not run this mid-project. That is a retrospective, and it solves a different problem.

Why It Works

The goal of the Pre-Mortem is not to predict the future. It is to surface what people already know but have not said yet — because the room was not designed to make it safe to say it. This tool gives them that room.

PRE-MORTEM TEMPLATE

[Project Name] - [Date]

1 FRAME

Project: ______________________

Timeline: ______________________

Imagined failure date: ______________________

2 INDIVIDUAL FAILURE REASONS

(complete before group discussion)

If this project fails, it will be because:

1. ______________________
2. ______________________
3. ______________________
4. ______________________
5. ______________________

3 GROUP SYNTHESIS

Top risks identified (clustered): ______________________

RISK	OWNER	MITIGATION
Risk 1: ________	________	______________
Risk 2: ________	________	______________
Risk 3: ________	________	______________

4 COMMUNICATION-SPECIFIC RISKS

Who might not receive critical information in time? ______________________

Where are the handoff points that are most likely to fail? ______________________

Which stakeholders are most likely to be surprised by a negative outcome? ______________________

Framework: THE A3 — ONE PAGE, ONE PROBLEM, ONE TEAM

What It Is

A structured one-page problem-solving and alignment format *from Lean/Toyota* **that forces clarity, shared understanding, and follow-through across functions.** The A3 takes its name from the European paper size (roughly 11" × 17") on which it was originally designed to fit. The constraint is intentional: if you can't fit it on one page, you haven't thought clearly enough about the problem yet.

The A3 is not primarily a quality tool. It is a communication tool. Its deepest value is that it forces every person in the room to engage with the same structured picture of the problem before anyone is allowed to propose a solution. The document doesn't tell people what to think — it forces the thinking into the open, where it can be examined, challenged, and agreed upon.

I've used A3s in work products specifically to keep cross-functional projects on the same page. Not metaphorically — literally. When everyone is looking at the same one-page document, the conversation changes. People stop arguing from their separate mental models because the mental model is now shared and visible.

When to Use It

- A recurring problem keeps being discussed but never resolved.
- Two or more functions are in conflict about what's broken and why.
- A project or process keeps failing in the same place, and no one has documented the real causes.
- You want to prevent the next failure without blaming the people nearest to the last one.

#	Section	What It Captures	Your Content
1	Problem Statement	The specific, measurable problem — not a symptom, not a cause	*Late shipments increased __% in Q__; customer complaints up __%*

#	Section	What It Captures	Your Content
2	Background	Why this matters now; who is affected; the business context	*Three shifts, two systems; handoff occurs at __*
3	Current Condition	What is actually happening — data, observation, process map	*__% of orders affected; error occurs at the __ step*
4	Root Cause Analysis	5 Whys or fishbone findings — what's driving the gap between current and target	*Late shipments → mislabeled totes → scanner skips step at shift change → no standard handoff checklist between outbound shifts*
5	Target Condition	What good looks like, specifically and measurably	*__ metric returns to __ baseline by __ date*
6	Countermeasures	Specific actions tied to root causes, with owners and due dates	*Action: __ Owner: __ Due: __*
7	Follow-Up	How you'll verify the countermeasures worked; PDCA loop	*Review at __ weeks; if no improvement, return to Section 4*

When NOT to Use It

- Quick decisions that one person can make with the information already available.
- Individual tasks with no cross-functional dependencies.
- Problems with obvious root causes and obvious solutions — just fix them.
- Emergency or safety situations requiring immediate containment — stabilize first, A3 after.
- Situations where the group is too large or too politically charged to have a productive real-time conversation. Address the group dynamics first; the A3 cannot do that work for you.

Common Mistakes

Mistake	Why It Hurts	Fix
Filling it out alone	One perspective is not shared understanding	Co-create with the team, in the room, in real time
Jumping to countermeasures	Skipping Sections 1–4 makes the wrong problem look official	Spend the time clarifying the problem first
Filing it in a shared drive	Out of sight, out of mind — the A3 is a living document and needs visibility	Post it physically, or pin it in SharePoint/Teams where the team meets daily
Treating it as a paperwork exercise	Complete on paper, empty in practice	Reinforce the norm: the conversation is the output, not the document
Skipping the follow-up	Without Plan-Do-Check-Act (PDCA), you never confirm whether the countermeasures worked	Set the review date before leaving the room

THE A3

One Page. One Problem. One Team.

A structured problem-solving and alignment tool.

1 PROBLEM STATEMENT

What is the specific measurable problem?

2 BACKGROUND

Why does this matter now?
Who is affected?

3 CURRENT CONDITION

What is happening today?
What do we know?

4 ROOT CAUSE ANALYSIS

What is driving the gap?

5 Whys / Fishbone / Notes

5 TARGET CONDITION

What should good look like?

6 COUNTERMEASURES

What actions will we take?

Action	Owner	Due Date

7 FOLLOW-UP

How will we verify results?

Review Date	Metric	Next Step

A3 REMINDERS

- Start with the problem, not the solution.
- Build it with the team.
- Keep it visible.
- Review and update it.

PART 3: DIAGNOSIS

Not every communication breakdown announces itself clearly. Sometimes it shows up as a missed deadline. Sometimes it shows up as a meeting that goes nowhere. Sometimes it shows up as a feeling: something is off, and you do not know what it is. *This section exists for that moment.*

Before you choose what to say, you need to understand what kind of problem you are in. Most communication failures are not failures of language. They are failures of diagnosis. You are solving the wrong problem with the right words.

Part 3 gives you a faster way to see what is actually happening — and what to reach for next. When something feels off, start here. Do not overanalyze it. Do not try to map it perfectly. Find the closest match and move.

If This, Then Start Here

If You're Experiencing...	What's Probably Actually Happening	Start With...	Go Deeper With...
A message that keeps getting misread or misunderstood	The issue is usually the audience, not the wording.	Set the Context — Step 1: Audience	Rework the message around what the audience knows, cares about, and fears.
Decisions are being made without your input	The useful move is to re-enter the conversation with clarity, not just focus on the exclusion.	Take Five	Set the Context to re-establish your place in the conversation.
A team member is not following through	The risk is escalating too early or generalizing the behavior.	SIA	Define the situation, name the impact, and make a specific ask.

If You're Experiencing...	What's Probably Actually Happening	Start With...	Go Deeper With...
A recurring meeting never produces a decision	The problem is the structure of the conversation.	Key Message Triangle	Reset the pattern by anchoring the discussion and clarifying the outcome needed.
You feel like you are always the last to know	This is an information-flow problem, not just frustration.	Take Five	Use SIA to address the gap without turning it into a grievance.
Work keeps landing on your team without a clear owner	You are dealing with a scope and ownership failure.	SIA	Name the ownership gap directly. Do not absorb the work silently.
Communication is breaking down between teams	The actual issue is usually structure and context, not tone.	Set the Context	Pair it with SIA to clarify facts, impact, and next steps.
Escalation has turned into conflict	The emotional layer is now distorting the message.	Take Five	Rebuild the message using SIA before moving forward.
You have bad news to deliver upward	The instinct is to delay, soften, or qualify it.	Key Message Triangle	Pair it with SIA so the message is clear, credible, and actionable.
You recognize a culture of silence	You are dealing with the Silent Spiral™, not just one communication issue.	Set the Context	Expect multiple frameworks to work together; this is a systems problem.
You are avoiding giving feedback	You already know the cost of delay.	Take Five	Move into SIA once you are clear and calm.

If You're Experiencing…	What's Probably Actually Happening	Start With…	Go Deeper With…
A message needs to land with a skeptical audience	Clarity is not enough. Structure matters.	Key Message Triangle	Use proof points and discipline, not more words.
You step into a new role with an unclear mandate	Clarity will not arrive on its own. You have to build it.	Set the Context — all four steps	Define audience, purpose, background, and message early.
A team has stopped trusting each other	You cannot solve this with a single message, but you can reset direction.	Take Five	Pair with Set the Context to name the issue and rebuild the ground under the conversation.
Information is technically shared but never actually received	The issue is message design, not access.	Key Message Triangle	Simplify. Return to one core message.
A process change is meeting resistance	The problem is rarely the change itself. It is the purpose.	Set the Context — Step 2: Purpose	Support it with the Key Message Triangle.
Accountability gaps are showing up	You are dealing with a failure to define ownership.	SIA	Start with the situation and make the ownership gap visible.
Tension is building after a missed deadline or failed deliverable	The urge is to jump straight into correction.	Take Five	Then use SIA to move forward constructively.
You are being labeled difficult for asking	This is likely a mismatch of communication	Take Five	Reframe the question using Set the Context.

If You're Experiencing...	What's Probably Actually Happening	Start With...	Go Deeper With...
clarifying questions	styles or power dynamics.		
A safety, compliance, or quality issue is not being taken seriously	The most important thing is impact.	SIA	Reinforce it with the Key Message Triangle and lead with impact.
Someone consistently talks over others in meetings	This needs to be handled in two layers: in the room and after the room.	Parking Lot Method (in the moment)	Use SIA afterward in a private conversation.
You need to escalate past your direct manager	This requires deliberate structure, not frustration.	SIA	Pair with Key Message Triangle and Set the Context.
A team is about to launch a complex or risky project	Optimism is not a plan.	Pre-Mortem	Surface risks early before assumptions harden into failure.

PART 4: USE CASES — WHAT TO SAY IN THE MOMENT

This section is for the moment you are already in the situation. You do not need theory here. You need a place to start.

The following use cases are ready to adapt. Each includes the situation, the framework to use, a sample message, and a reminder of what not to say. In some cases, it also includes a full example and a short explanation of what made it work.

Edit the language to match your voice, your industry, and your relationship with the other party. What you should not edit out is the structure underneath.

Section A: Escalation and Upward Communication

These are the conversations where something is wrong, unresolved, or at risk, and you need a decision, a resource, or an intervention from above. The risk in these moments is that escalation turns into complaint. When that happens, leadership gets pulled into refereeing instead of solving. *The goal here is to make upward communication actionable, specific, and decision-ready.*

"I Need to Escalate This"

How To Escalate Without Blame
Framework: SIA + Set the Context

When to Use It: Something has gone wrong and you cannot resolve it at your level. The trap here is turning escalation into complaint, which puts leadership in the position of refereeing rather than problem-solving.

The Setup: You have tried to resolve this directly. It has not worked. You need a decision, a resource, or an intervention that only someone above you can provide.

What NOT to Say

- "Nobody is listening to me."

- "I've been dealing with this forever."
- "I'm not sure this is even worth escalating, but..."
- Any version of "It's [name]'s fault."

Full Example: "I Need to Escalate This"

Setting: A quality lead needs to escalate a recurring supplier issue to her operations director. She has attempted to resolve it directly with the supplier twice and once through her peer in procurement, without success.

What Made It Work:

- The speaker led with facts and impact, not frustration, making it easy for leadership to act rather than investigate.
- She came with a specific ask and a concrete next step, turning the conversation from a problem report into a decision conversation.
- She closed by proposing a forward-looking norm so the same question does not require escalation again.

"I Need to Communicate Bad News to Leadership"

How To Deliver Upward Honestly
Framework: Key Message Triangle + SIA

When to Use It: Something went wrong, is at risk, or is off track, and you need to tell leadership before they find out another way. Resist the instinct to soften, qualify, or delay until you have a full solution. Leaders who receive bad news late — especially bad news the messenger already knew — lose trust in the messenger faster than they lose confidence in the outcome.

The Setup: You know the facts. You may not have a full solution yet, but you have something, even if it is simply a clear process for finding one.

What NOT to Say

- Burying the bad news in a paragraph of good news
- "I didn't want to alarm anyone until I had more information."

- Sending bad news in a Friday afternoon email with no call scheduled
- "We're working on it" with no specific details

This script belongs here because upward bad-news communication is a specialized form of escalation: not grievance, not confession, but disciplined, early warning.

"I Need to Go Above My Manager"

How To Escalate To Skip-Level Leadership
Framework: SIA + Key Message Triangle + Set the Context

When to Use It: You have a situation that requires attention from leadership above your direct manager — either because your manager is part of the problem, because the issue is beyond your manager's authority to resolve, or because your manager has been informed and has not acted.

This is a high-stakes communication move. Done wrong, it damages your relationship with your manager and undermines your standing. Done right, it resolves the issue and demonstrates professional maturity.

Before You Go

- Have you addressed it directly with your manager first? If not, do that.
- Does the issue require skip-level authority, or are you escalating because you are impatient?
- Are there safety, compliance, ethics, or legal elements? If so, escalate immediately.
- What is your relationship with the skip-level leader? Cold escalations land differently than warm ones.

The Setup: You have done the direct work first. You are not going around your manager out of frustration. You are going to the right level to get the right outcome.

What NOT to Say

- "My manager isn't handling this."
- "I didn't want to go around [manager's name], but..."
- Surprising your manager afterward, if it was possible to tell them first

This is the highest-stakes version of upward communication in the playbook. That is why it belongs at the end of this section: after ordinary escalation and after upward bad-news delivery.

Section B: Feedback and Accountability

These are the conversations people avoid longest and pay for most. They are not about venting, correcting someone publicly, or finally saying what has been irritating you for months. **They are about naming a specific issue, grounding it in observable facts, and making the path forward unmistakably clear.**

"I Need to Give Tough Feedback"

The Full Conversation Script
Framework: Take Five + SIA

When to Use It: You need to tell someone — a direct report, a peer, or a colleague — that their behavior, work, or communication style is causing a problem. The stakes feel high. You have been putting this off. The longer you wait, the more it will cost.

Before the Conversation

- Run Take Five first — separate the trigger from your accumulated frustration.
- Write your SIA before you walk in the room.
- Know the observable situation, the measurable impact, and the specific ask.
- Ask yourself: "What outcome do I want from this conversation?"

What NOT to Say

- "A lot of people have noticed this."
- "I've been meaning to say this for a while."
- "I'm not criticizing you, but..."
- Anything that sounds like a verdict instead of a conversation

Full Example: "I Need to Give Tough Feedback"

Setting: A team lead needs to address a recurring pattern with a direct report: Marcus has been sending updates to stakeholders before confirming the information with the team lead, resulting in two situations this quarter where incorrect information went out externally.

What Made It Work:

- The speaker used specific dates and situations rather than a generalized pattern.
- She acknowledged Marcus's intent while holding firm on the impact.
- She set a concrete follow-up date, signaling that this was a real accountability conversation, not a one-time venting.

"You Said You'd Have This Done"

How To Follow Up On An Unmet Commitment
Framework: SIA + 3-Before-Me (your own preparation)

When to Use It: Someone committed to a deliverable, a deadline, or an action item and has not followed through. The work is at risk. You need to follow up in a way that gets results without creating an adversarial dynamic.

The Setup: You are clear on what was committed and when. You have checked whether there is a legitimate reason you are not aware of before leading with frustration.

What NOT to Say

- "You said you'd do this."

- "This is unacceptable."
- Escalating before you have had the direct conversation

This script sits naturally after tough feedback because it is often the narrower, more immediate version of the same issue: one missed commitment, one accountability conversation, one chance to correct course before a broader pattern forms.

"You're Talking Over People"

How To Address Someone Who Dominates Meetings
Framework: SIA (private conversation) + Parking Lot Method (in-the-moment)

When to Use It: In a meeting, a colleague consistently talks over others, cuts off contributions, or dominates the conversation in a way that shuts down participation. Address this privately after the meeting, not in front of the group, which would create exactly the kind of public confrontation that damages collaboration.

In the Moment: Use the Parking Lot Method or facilitation language to protect the room without turning the meeting into a power struggle.

Private Conversation After: Use a full SIA structure.

The Setup: You have chosen a private moment — not in the hallway right after the meeting, and not in a written channel where the message lives forever. A brief, direct one-on-one.

What NOT to Say

- "Everyone is afraid to speak up because of you."
- "You always dominate the meeting."
- Saying nothing and then excluding the person from future meetings

This script belongs in feedback and accountability because meeting dominance is not just a facilitation issue. It is a behavior issue with consequences for trust, participation, and decision quality.

"I Have Feedback for You — and You're My Peer"

How To Give Feedback Sideways
Framework: Take Five + SIA

When to Use It: You need to give feedback to a colleague — someone at your level, not a direct report — about their behavior, communication style, or the impact of their work on you or your team. Peer feedback is harder than managerial feedback because you have no formal authority. You are operating entirely on relationship capital and the quality of your communication.

The Setup: You have run Take Five. You have a specific situation in mind, not a general impression. You are raising this because the relationship matters and you want to protect it.

What NOT to Say

- "My team has been frustrated with you."
- "As your colleague, I think you need to..."
- Raising it in a group setting

Full Example: "I Have Feedback for You — and You're My Peer"

Setting: A marketing manager needs to give feedback to her peer in product, whose habit of sending last-minute changes to shared documents before external presentations has twice resulted in the marketing team presenting outdated materials.

What Made It Work:

- The speaker was specific about the impact.
- She invited the peer to explain their perspective before proposing a solution.
- She closed with a concrete, mutual agreement rather than leaving the conversation open-ended.

Section C: Role Clarity, Ownership, and Boundaries

These use cases exist because work rarely breaks down in dramatic ways at first. It breaks down through ambiguity: unclear ownership, informal work absorption, decisions made without the right people, and capacity limits that no one names until quality slips. The goal in this section is not to sound territorial. It is to make accountability visible before confusion hardens into conflict.

"Who Owns This?"

How to establish role clarity mid-project
Framework: Set the Context + SIA

When to Use It: Work is being duplicated, dropped, or disputed because ownership was never clearly established. You are mid-project. You need to stop the bleeding without triggering a turf war.

The Setup: You have noticed specific gaps or overlaps. You have a concrete proposal for how to clarify them.

What NOT to Say

- "That's not my job."
- "I assumed [name] was handling that."
- "Why didn't we figure this out at the start?"

Full Example: "Who Owns This?"

Setting: Two team members — a project manager and a content lead — realize mid-project that three deliverables have no clear owner and that both of them have been partially working on each, creating duplicate effort and version confusion.

What Made It Work:

- The speaker named the gap in concrete, non-accusatory terms.
- She proposed a specific, time-bounded solution.

- She closed with a read-back and a documentation commitment, turning a verbal agreement into a shared record.

"I'm Being Asked to Do Work That Isn't Mine"

How To Redirect Scope Creep Professionally
Framework: SIA

When to Use It: Work that clearly belongs to another team keeps landing on your desk. You need to redirect without burning a relationship.

The Setup: You have identified the specific mismatch between the request and your team's scope. You have a suggestion for where it should go.

What NOT to Say

- "That's not my problem."
- "I don't know why you're asking me."
- Just doing the work and saying nothing

Full Example: "I'm Being Asked to Do Work That Isn't Mine"

Setting: A communications manager receives a request from a department head asking her team to draft and send a compliance training reminder to all staff — a task that has historically belonged to the HR team but has been informally absorbed by communications three times this year.

What Made It Work:

- The speaker named the structural gap rather than just declining the request.
- She offered a specific path forward and took some responsibility for letting the pattern develop.
- She avoided silently absorbing the work one more time.

"I'm at Capacity — I Can't Take This On"

How To Say No To Additional Work When You're Full
Framework: Set the Context + Key Message Triangle

When to Use It: You are at or past your team's capacity. A new request has come in — from your manager, a peer, or another team — and taking it on without removing something else would compromise quality, timelines, or wellbeing. The request is real. So is the capacity problem. Both need to be named.

The Setup: You know what is on your plate. You have done a quick triage of your current commitments and you know specifically what would have to move if you take this on.

What NOT to Say

- "I'm way too busy for this."
- "That's not possible."
- Just saying yes and quietly letting quality slip
- Delegating the ask without telling the requester

Full Example: "I'm at Capacity — I Can't Take This On"

Setting: A team lead receives a request from her director to take on a cross-departmental audit project that would start in two weeks. Her team is currently at full capacity running two active initiatives with hard external deadlines.

What Made It Work:

- The speaker led with the two specific initiatives that established the stakes.
- She named the exact downstream consequence of taking on the new work.
- She came with three options, not just a refusal.

"I'm New and the Communication Culture Is Broken"

How To Navigate Without Authority
Framework: Set the Context + Take Five (for managing your own frustration)

When to Use It: You are new — to the organization, the team, or the role — and you can see clearly that the communication culture is dysfunctional. You are in the frustrating position of having a fresh eye and zero authority to use it.

The Setup: You have been observing long enough to have specific examples, not just impressions. You are raising this with someone who can act on it or help you navigate it.

What NOT to Say

- "At my last company, we did it this way."
- "How does anyone get anything done here?"
- Complaining to peers before you have raised it with anyone who can act
- Fixing things unilaterally without signaling what you are doing and why

Your job in the first ninety days is to understand before you change. Your observations are assets. Protect them by deploying them wisely.

Full Example: "I'm New and the Communication Culture Is Broken"

Setting: A new operations analyst is six weeks into her role and has noticed that decisions are consistently being made by a small group before the broader team is informed.

What Made It Work:

- The speaker used four specific examples.
- She framed the impact in terms of her ability to do her job.
- She left room for the possibility that she was missing something.

Section D: Misalignment, Gaps, and Reset Conversations

These are the scripts for moments when the problem is not one person's behavior so much as a breakdown in shared understanding. Information came too late.

A team keeps repeating the same discussion. A decision happened without the right people. Trust is thinning. In these moments, the job is not to relive the failure. It is to close the gap and reset the conditions under which work happens.

"Nobody Told Me"

How To Address A Communication Gap After The Fact
Framework: Take Five + SIA

When to Use It: You found out something that affected your work after the fact. You are frustrated. You may have made choices based on information you did not know was outdated.

The Setup: You have had a chance to cool down. You are not looking to assign blame. You are looking to close the gap so it does not happen again.

What NOT to Say

- "No one ever tells me anything."
- "I shouldn't have to chase this information."
- "This is a recurring problem."

This script belongs here because it is the classic after-the-fact repair conversation: not about accusation but about closing a gap and establishing a better norm.

"We Keep Having the Same Meeting"

How To Break The Recurring-Problem Cycle
Framework: Key Message Triangle + Set the Context

When to Use It: Your team revisits the same topic in meeting after meeting with no resolution. People are starting to show up disengaged. The conversation always ends with "let's follow up on that," and no follow-up ever happens.

The Setup: You have identified the pattern and you have a specific structural proposal for how to break it.

What NOT to Say

- "We never actually decide anything."

- "I'm not sure why we're even here."
- Sighing audibly or checking your phone

This is a reset conversation disguised as a meeting problem. The real issue is not only inefficiency. It is trust in the value of the room.

"The Decision Was Made Without Me"

How To Re-Enter A Conversation You Were Excluded From
Framework: Take Five + Set the Context

When to Use It: A decision was made that affects your work, your team, or your role, and you were not consulted. You need to re-enter the conversation without seeming territorial and without letting the exclusion quietly define how you are treated going forward.

The Setup: You have used Take Five first. You have separated the sting of being excluded from the substance of the actual decision.

What NOT to Say

- "Why wasn't I invited to that meeting?"
- "I should have been part of this."
- Any version of "I'm just finding out about this now?" delivered as betrayal rather than inquiry

This is one of the most important reset scripts in the playbook because exclusion becomes culture very quickly when it goes unnamed.

"We Need a Reset"

How To Call A Communication Reset With Your Team
Framework: Set the Context + Key Message Triangle

When to Use It: The team's communication has degraded. Whatever the reason — bad project, leadership change, a stretch of constant urgency — people are not talking to each other the right way, or at all. You need to name it and reset without making it a post-mortem or a blame session.

The Setup: You are coming in with ownership of your part first. You have specifics, not generalities. You have a proposed path forward.

What NOT to Say

- "We need to talk about our communication."
- Starting with what others did wrong before naming your own part
- Turning the reset into a retrospective that reopens old wounds

A reset is forward-facing. That is what distinguishes it from complaint, venting, or re-litigation.

Section E: Disagreement, Conflict, and Emotional Moments

This section is for the moments when **emotional temperature is high enough to distort what gets said and what gets heard**. The objective is not to "win" the conversation. It is to keep the exchange from becoming more damaging than the original issue.

These scripts are less about perfect wording than about protecting judgment under pressure.

"I Think This Decision Is Wrong"

How To Push Back On A Bad Decision Respectfully
Framework: Key Message Triangle + Take Five

When to Use It: A decision has been made — by your manager, your team, or leadership — and you believe it is wrong, incomplete, or likely to produce a bad outcome. You have a responsibility to say so. You also have a responsibility to do it in a way that is heard rather than dismissed.

The Setup: You have done Take Five first. You are not reacting to being overruled. You are genuinely concerned about the outcome and you have specific reasoning for it.

What NOT to Say

- "I disagree with this decision."

- "This is going to fail."
- "No one asked me."
- "I told you so," in any form

This script belongs here because disagreement under pressure is often less about logic than about how the objection is framed.

"Things Are Getting Heated"

How To Navigate A Conversation When Emotions Are Running High
Framework: Take Five + Parking Lot Method

When to Use It: A conversation — meeting, one-on-one, or group discussion — has escalated to the point where emotions are visibly running the exchange. Voices have risen, language has sharpened, or someone has withdrawn entirely. The content of the conversation is no longer being heard because the emotional temperature is too high.

The Setup: You are either a participant in the conversation or you are facilitating it. In either case, the most useful thing you can do is slow down the pace.

What NOT to Say

- "Calm down."
- "You're being emotional."
- "I don't know why this is such a big deal."
- Winning the argument

When emotions are high, winning usually makes things worse. Manage for understanding first, resolution second.

"I Just Received Bad News"

How To Respond When You're On The Receiving End
Framework: Take Five (internal processing) + Read-Back Technique

When to Use It: You have just been told something difficult — your role is changing, a project you led is being cancelled, your proposal was rejected, you did not get the promotion, or your team is being restructured. Your emotional response is real and valid. But how you handle the next five minutes will define your professional reputation and your options going forward.

Before You Respond: This is the most important moment to apply Take Five — not as a framework for what to say, but as a framework for what not to say in the first sixty seconds.

- **STOP** — Do not respond immediately.
- **SEPARATE** — The trigger from the emotion.
- **ASSESS** — What do you actually know right now?
- **DRAFT** — What is the one thing you want to communicate right now?
- **DELIVER** — Respond with composure.

What NOT to Say

- "This is unfair."
- "Who decided this?"
- "I can't believe this."
- "Fine."
- Nothing at all

Full Example: "I Just Received Bad News"

Setting: A quality supervisor learns in a one-on-one with her operations director that the department is being restructured.

What Made It Work:

- She paused before responding.
- She used the read-back to confirm the facts and buy processing time.
- She asked specific, forward-looking questions.
- She established a follow-up meeting.

- She closed with genuine gratitude for the direct delivery.

Section F: Clarity, Understanding, and Message Control

Not every breakdown begins with conflict. Many begin with ambiguity, guesswork, or the instinct to fill silence with something that sounds plausible.

This section covers the smaller moments that prevent larger failures: **saying "I don't know" honestly, asking for clarification without sounding lost, and delivering difficult information in a way people can actually absorb.**

"I Don't Know"

How To Say It Without Losing Credibility
Framework: Take Five (internal) + Key Message Triangle

When to Use It: You are asked a question you cannot answer — in a meeting, in front of leadership, in front of a client, or in a high-stakes conversation. **The instinct to fill the silence with something — anything — is strong. Resist it.**

A confident, composed "I don't know" is more credible than a fumbled, hedging non-answer.

The Setup: You have been asked something you do not have the answer to right now. You know that pretending or guessing will cost you more than honesty.

What NOT to Say

- "I'm not sure, but..." followed by speculation presented as fact
- "That's a great question" as filler
- "Someone else probably knows that" without committing to find out who
- Giving a number you are not confident in and hoping no one checks

This script is about information discipline. Credibility rises when uncertainty is handled honestly and specifically.

"Can You Clarify That?"

How To Ask For Clarification Without Sounding Confused
Framework: Read-Back Technique + Set the Context

When to Use It: You received instructions, a decision, or a directive that is not clear enough for you to act on.

You need more information, but you do not want the question to read as incompetence, pushback, or disengagement.

The Setup: You have identified the specific gap — what exactly is unclear and why it matters for your next step.

What NOT to Say

- "I don't understand what you want."
- "That wasn't very clear."
- Proceeding without clarity and hoping you guessed right
- Asking three clarifying questions at once

This is one of the simplest scripts in the playbook and one of the most important. Misalignment compounds fastest when people act before confirming what they actually heard.

"I Have Bad News for the Team"

How To Deliver Difficult Information To A Group
Framework: Set the Context + Key Message Triangle

When to Use It: You need to tell a team — your direct reports, your peers, a cross-functional group — something that will be hard to hear. A project is being cancelled. A deadline is being moved up. A position is being eliminated. A proposal was rejected. The instinct is to soften, bury, or delay. The practice is the opposite.

The Setup: You have prepared your Key Message Triangle. You know what the core message is, what context they need, and what comes next. You are delivering to the group before the rumor gets there first.

What NOT to Say

- Burying the news in fifteen minutes of context before you get to it
- "I can't share much at this point."
- "I know how you're feeling."
- Ending the meeting without opening the floor

Full Example: "I Have Bad News for the Team"

Setting: A project manager needs to inform her team of seven that the product launch they have been building toward for four months has been pushed from Q3 to Q1 of the following year.

What Made It Work:

- The speaker led with the core message in the first sentence.
- She separated what was changing from what was not.
- She handled unanswered questions with a specific commitment rather than deflection.

A Note Before You Leave This Section

Every script in this section was written for a real moment — the kind that makes your chest tighten, your words scramble, or your instinct say not now, not yet, not me.

Here is what twenty years on the floor has taught me: the conversations you avoid don't go away. They compound. The escalation you didn't make becomes the crisis you couldn't prevent. The feedback you swallowed becomes the pattern you can't undo. The clarification you didn't ask for becomes the rework nobody budgeted.

These scripts are not about being perfect. They are about being willing to start. You will not deliver every one of them cleanly. You will stumble over an opening sentence. You will forget your SIA in the middle of a conversation that got emotional faster than you expected. You will walk out of a meeting and think of the thing you should have said. That is not failure. That is practice.

What matters is that you walked into the room at all. Edit these scripts. Mark them up. Cross things out and write your own versions in the margins. The structure underneath — name the situation, ground it in impact, make a specific ask, and follow through — that part stays. The words are yours to change. The discipline is what you keep.

If you are holding this book right now because there is a specific conversation you have been avoiding — the one that's been sitting in the back of your mind since before you opened to this page — then you already know which script to start with.

The next conversation is the one that matters.

PART 5: TEMPLATES AND WORKING TOOLS

The frameworks matter. *But in real work, people also need fast tools.* Sometimes you do not need to study the communication problem. You need to say the thing, frame the meeting, send the follow-up, or keep the issue from getting worse. That is what this section is for.

Section A: Meetings and Shared Decisions

Meetings are where communication is most visible — and most often fails. Not because people are unprepared, but because the meeting itself was never designed to produce an outcome. Most recurring issues in meetings **trace back to one of three problems:**

- No defined purpose
- No structure for decision-making
- No ownership after the conversation ends

These tools exist to fix that.

Meeting Agenda with Communication Checkpoints

A meeting agenda is not a list of topics. It is a decision-making tool. A well-structured agenda forces clarity before the meeting begins:

- Why the meeting is happening and what outcome is expected
- Who is responsible for each part of the discussion

Without this, meetings default to updates, opinions, and circular conversation. **A strong agenda includes:**

- A clearly defined purpose with time-bounded sections
- A distinction between discussion and decision item, with explicit ownership of follow-up actions

When this structure is present, meetings move faster, decisions hold, and fewer follow-up meetings are required.

TEMPLATE 1: MEETING AGENDA WITH COMMUNICATION CHECKPOINTS

Good meeting agendas do more than list topics. They establish purpose, assign decision authority, and create a structure for how information moves.

Use this template for:
Any meeting that involves more than two people and requires either a decision or a meaningful outcome.

1 MEETING BASICS

- Meeting name: ____________
- Date / Time: ____________
- Location / Link: ____________
- Facilitator: ____________
- Note-taker: ____________

2 PRE-MEETING COMMUNICATION CHECKPOINT

- What does each attendee need to have read or prepared before this meeting? (List by person if different) ____________
- Who was invited and why? (Include rationale for each role) ____________
- Who was intentionally NOT invited, and why? ____________
- Is there anyone who should be informed of the outcome but doesn't need to attend? ____________

3 AGENDA

1 CONTEXT-SETTING (5 min)
- Purpose of this meeting: ____________
- What we need to leave with: ____________
- Who has decision authority for each agenda item: ____________

Decision authority for each agenda item: ____________

2 [AGENDA ITEM 1] (___ min)
Topic: ____________
Type: ☐ Decision needed ☐ Discussion ☐ Update
Pre-read required: ____________

Decision authority: ____________

3 [AGENDA ITEM 2] (___ min)
Topic: ____________
Type: ☐ Decision needed ☐ Discussion ☐ Update
Pre-read required: ____________

Decision authority: ____________

4 [AGENDA ITEM 3] (___ min)
Topic: ____________
Type: ☐ Decision needed ☐ Discussion ☐ Update
Pre-read required: ____________

Decision authority: ____________

5 PARKING LOT (5 min)
- Items tabled from earlier in the agenda: ____________
- Owner and follow-up date for each: ____________

Keep the conversation moving. Capture it. Don't lose it.

6 CLOSE + COMMUNICATION CHECKPOINT (5 min)
- Decisions made today: ____________
- Action items: (owner + due date for each) ____________
- Who needs to be informed of these outcomes? ____________
- How / when will they be notified? ____________

Ensure the right people receive the right information at the right time.

4 POST-MEETING COMMUNICATION

- Meeting summary to be sent by: ____________ By when: ____________
- Who receives the summary: ____________
- Are there any items that require a separate follow-up communication to a broader audience? ____________
- If yes, who owns it and by when? ____________

COMMUNICATION TIP: A clear agenda before the meeting leads to clear decisions during the meeting and clear communication after the meeting.

Escalation Decision Tree

Escalation is one of the most misused tools in organizations. Escalate too early, and you create noise. Escalate too late, and you create risk.

Most Teams Do Not Have A Shared Definition of:

- What qualifies as an escalation
- When escalation is appropriate
- Who should be involved

The Result Is Inconsistency:

- Some issues never surface
- Others are escalated prematurely
- Leadership is pulled into problems that should have been resolved lower

An Escalation Decision Tree Provides A Simple Structure

- Is this a blocker, a risk, or a delay?
- Can it be resolved at the current level?
- What is the impact if it is not resolved quickly?
- Who owns the decision at the next level?

This tool removes guesswork and makes escalation a disciplined process rather than a reactive move.

Before You Enter the Tree

An escalation is only useful if the person receiving it can act on it.

Before escalating, confirm you have:

- A clear statement of the issue (what is happening, where, since when)
- What you have already tried and what the result was
- What is blocked or at risk if it is not resolved

- What you are specifically asking the next level to decide, unblock, or authorize

If you cannot answer those four, you are not ready to escalate. You are ready to think.

Define the Trigger

Not every problem is an escalation. Sort the issue into one of three categories before entering the tree:

Category	Definition	Example in a Project Context
Blocker	Work cannot move forward until this is resolved	A required approval is not coming, and the next milestone depends on it
Risk	Work can continue, but a negative outcome is likely if nothing changes	A key stakeholder has gone silent and the decision window is closing
Delay	Work is behind, but the path forward is known and owned	A deliverable slipped a week; the owner has a revised plan

Delays usually do not need escalation. Blockers almost always do. Risks require judgment.

Define the Tiers

Escalation only works if "the next level" is named. A general project communication structure typically looks like this:

Level	Role	Scope of Authority	Expected Response Window
1	Project lead or workstream owner	Day-to-day execution, scope within the workstream	Same day
2	Program manager or functional manager	Cross-workstream coordination, resource reallocation, timeline adjustments	Within 1 business day
3	Sponsor or steering committee	Scope, budget, priority, or stakeholder-level decisions	Within 2–3 business days

Name your tiers before you need them. Escalating into an undefined structure is how messages get lost.

The Tree

1. **Is this a blocker, a risk, or a delay?**
   - Delay with a known path → Do not escalate. Communicate status and continue.
   - Risk → Go to question 2.
   - Blocker → Go to question 2.
2. **Can it be resolved at the current level within the expected response window?**
   - Yes → Resolve it at the current level. Document the decision.
   - No → Go to question 3.
3. **What is the impact if it is not resolved?**
   - Contained to one workstream → Escalate to Level 2.
   - Affects timeline, budget, scope, or another workstream → Escalate to Level 2 with Level 3 notified.
   - Affects the sponsor's commitments, external stakeholders, or the project's viability → Escalate directly to Level 3.
4. **Who owns the decision at the next level?**
   - Named, available, and informed → Escalate with the four-point briefing (issue, tried, impact, ask).
   - Named but unavailable → Escalate to their delegate; copy the primary owner.
   - Not named → Stop. The absence of a named decision owner is itself the escalation. Raise that first.

A Worked Example

Situation: A cross-functional project is three weeks from a go-live milestone. The communications workstream needs final messaging approval from a senior stakeholder who has not responded to three requests over eight business days. The training workstream cannot finalize materials without the approved messaging.

Walking the Tree:

1. **Category:** Blocker. Training cannot proceed and go-live is at risk.
2. **Resolvable at the current level?** No. The project lead does not have authority to approve the messaging on the stakeholder's behalf.
3. **Impact if unresolved?** It affects another workstream (training) and threatens the go-live timeline. That pushes it to Level 2, with Level 3 notified.
4. **Decision owner at the next level?** The program manager is named and available.

The Escalation Message:

- *Issue:* Messaging approval has been pending with [Stakeholder] for 8 business days despite three follow-ups.
- *Tried:* Two email requests, one Teams message, and a calendar hold that was declined without a reschedule.
- *Impact:* Training materials cannot be finalized; go-live in 3 weeks is at risk.
- *Ask:* Request that [Program Manager] engage [Stakeholder] directly by end of week or authorize an interim approval path so training can proceed.

Guardrails

- **Escalate the decision, not the person.** The tree exists to move a decision forward, not to report on who is slow.

- **Do not skip tiers without reason.** Jumping straight to Level 3 when Level 2 was available burns trust and creates noise at the top.
- **Close the loop.** Once the escalation is resolved, communicate the outcome back down the chain so the next similar issue has a precedent.
- **If you escalate the same issue twice, the issue is not the problem — the structure is.** Revisit whether the tiers, owners, or triggers are actually defined.

ESCALATION DECISION TREE

Escalate too early = noise. Escalate too late = risk.

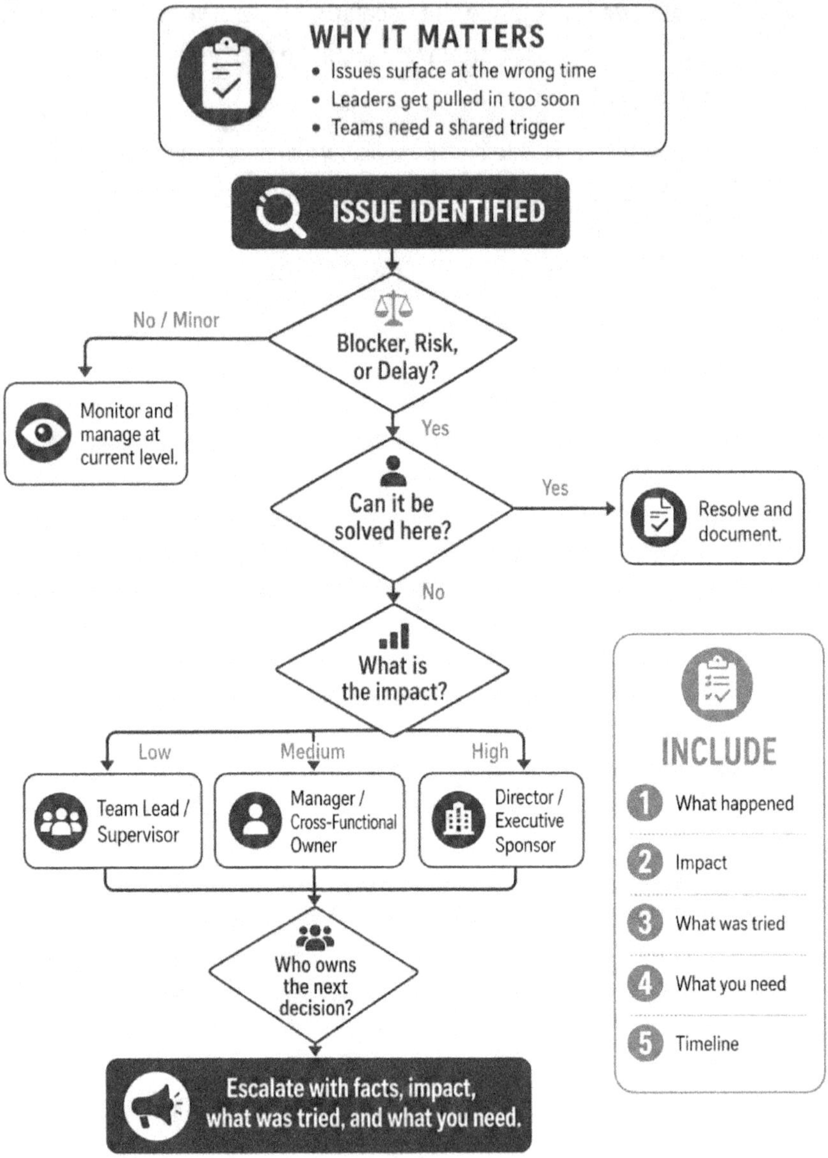

WHY IT MATTERS

- Issues surface at the wrong time
- Leaders get pulled in too soon
- Teams need a shared trigger

ISSUE IDENTIFIED

Blocker, Risk, or Delay?

No / Minor → Monitor and manage at current level.

Yes ↓

Can it be solved here?

Yes → Resolve and document.

No ↓

What is the impact?

Low → Team Lead / Supervisor

Medium → Manager / Cross-Functional Owner

High → Director / Executive Sponsor

Who owns the next decision?

Escalate with facts, impact, what was tried, and what you need.

INCLUDE

1. What happened
2. Impact
3. What was tried
4. What you need
5. Timeline

Section B: Project Communication Infrastructure

Communication does not break down in large, visible moments.

It Breaks Down Slowly, Across Time:

- At Handoffs, Between Teams, During Transitions
- When Assumptions Replace Clarity

This section provides the structures that keep communication intact across the lifecycle of work.

Project Kickoff Communication Plan

Most projects fail before they begin — not because of execution, but because **communication was never aligned at the start.**

A kickoff is not just about introducing the work. It is about defining how information will move.

A Strong Communication Plan Answers Four Questions:

- Who needs to know what?
- When do they need to know it?
- Through what channel will it be shared?
- Who is responsible for making sure it happens?

Without These Answers, Teams Default To:

- Over-communicating to everyone
- Under-communicating to the people who actually need it
- Relying on informal updates that do not scale

The kickoff communication plan creates clarity before confusion has a chance to form.

Stakeholder Communication Matrix

What It Is

As projects grow, so does the number of stakeholders. Not all of them *need the same information and* treating them as if they do is one of the fastest ways to erode trust in project communication.

When everyone gets everything, the important signals get buried in the noise. When communication is scattered, critical people find out late — usually from the wrong source, at the wrong time, and with the wrong framing. Both failures look different on the surface, but they have the same root cause: no one decided, in advance, who needed what.

A Stakeholder Communication Matrix brings discipline to that decision. It answers five questions before the project is in motion:

- Who are the stakeholders?
- What do they care about?
- What level of detail do they need?
- How often should they receive updates?
- Who owns that communication?

Answering those five up front ***prevents the two failure modes* that derail most project communication:**

- Critical stakeholders being surprised by information they should have had early
- Teams spending time communicating to people who do not need the information

Communication becomes targeted instead of scattered. Updates land with the people who can act on them, in the format they can use, at the cadence they expect. That is what separates a project that feels *in control* from one that feels *busy*.

The matrix is not a report. It is a decision. Once it is built, every status update, every escalation, and every change notice has a defined path — and no one has to guess whether to send it, who to send it to, or how much detail to include.

How It Pairs with the Escalation Decision Tree

The Stakeholder Communication Matrix and the Escalation Decision Tree cover two different halves of the same communication surface. The matrix defines **routine communication** — the expected, scheduled, predictable updates that keep stakeholders informed during normal project execution. The Escalation Decision Tree handles **exceptions** — the unexpected blockers, risks, and decisions that require stepping outside the regular cadence.

Together, they form a complete system. The matrix answers *who hears what, when, and from whom* on a normal day. The tree answers *what to do when something is not normal.* A project that has one without the other is either over-communicating in the calm and under-communicating in the storm, or running silent until something breaks. Used together, these two tools give a project team a defined path for every message that needs to move.

The Matrix Itself

The matrix itself is a simple grid — five columns, one row per stakeholder — but the work is in the answers. The grid is easy to draw. The discipline is in refusing to leave any cell vague.

Mistake	Why It Hurts	Fix
Building the matrix once and never updating it	Stakeholders change, interests change, and project phases shift what people need to know	Review the matrix at every major project phase — kickoff, each milestone, and any scope change
Grouping stakeholders who have different needs	Creates the illusion of targeted communication while actually scattering it	One row per stakeholder; group only when the need is truly identical
Filling in "Owner" with the project manager for every row	Concentrates communication load on one person and removes accountability from the	Distribute ownership to the person with the

Mistake	Why It Hurts	Fix
	people closest to the stakeholder	closest working relationship
Defaulting every stakeholder to "weekly"	Cadence becomes a calendar habit instead of a deliberate choice	Match frequency to decision cycles, not to meeting rhythms
Writing the matrix in isolation	The project manager's view of what stakeholders care about is not always correct	Validate at least the top three rows directly with the stakeholders named in them
Treating the matrix as a communications plan document	Plans get filed; decisions get used	Keep the matrix visible in the project workspace alongside the RACI and the risk log

When to Revisit

The matrix should be reviewed at every major point in the project:

- **Kickoff,** to establish the baseline
- **Each milestone,** to confirm cadence and detail still match what stakeholders need
- **Any scope, timeline, or budget change,** because those changes almost always shift stakeholder interest
- **Any stakeholder change** — new sponsor, new site leader, new vendor contact — because the matrix is tied to people, not titles
- **Project closeout,** to define who hears about the outcome and in what form

A matrix that is built once and filed is not a communication tool. It is a *historical artifact*. The discipline is in keeping it current, because the projects where stakeholder communication fails are almost never projects without a matrix — they are projects where the matrix stopped being true.

PROJECT KICKOFF COMMUNICATION PLAN

Define how information will move, who will receive it, when, and how.

PROJECT INFORMATION

Project Name:	Customer Portal Redesign
Project Sponsor:	Maria Sanchez
Project Manager:	James Lee
Kickoff Date:	May 20, 2025
Project Duration:	May 2025 – Dec 2025

COMMUNICATION PLAN PURPOSE

Ensure the right people receive the right information, at the right time, through the right channel so the project stays aligned, informed, and on track.

WHO needs to know what?

WHEN do they need it?

HOW will it be shared?

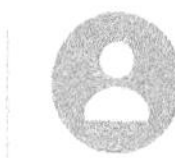

WHO is responsible?

KEY MESSAGES

- Redesigning the portal to improve customer experience, increase efficiency, and support future growth.
- Project success depends on cross-functional collaboration and clear, consistent communication.
- We will communicate proactively, transparently, and at the right level for our audience.

Stakeholder Communication Matrix continues on the next pages.

PROJECT KICKOFF COMMUNICATION PLAN

Stakeholder Communication Matrix

STAKEHOLDER GROUP (WHO)	INFORMATION NEEDS (WHAT)	FREQUENCY / TIMING (WHEN)	CHANNEL (HOW)	OWNER / RESPONSIBLE (WHO)	NOTES
Executive Leadership	• Project status • Key risks & issues • Decisions needed • Major milestones	Monthly (or as needed)	Executive Brief (Email + 30-min Exec Meeting)	Project Manager	High-level view with focus on decisions and impact
Project Team (Core Team)	• Tasks & priorities • Dependencies • Blockers • Progress updates	Weekly (team meeting)	Team Meeting (Weekly) + Slack (#project-updates)	Project Manager	Detailed, working-level information
Extended Team (Contributors)	• Task assignments • Deadlines • Relevant updates	Bi-weekly (or as needed)	Email Update + Project Management Tool (Asana)	Workstream Leads	Need-to-know info that supports their work

Matrix continues on the next page.

PROJECT KICKOFF COMMUNICATION PLAN

Stakeholder Communication Matrix + Governance

STAKEHOLDER GROUP (WHO)	INFORMATION NEEDS (WHAT)	FREQUENCY / TIMING (WHEN)	CHANNEL (HOW)	OWNER / RESPONSIBLE (WHO)	NOTES
Internal Stakeholders (Departments)	• Key milestones • Changes impacting their area • Action needed	Monthly	Email Update + Intranet Post	Project Manager	Focus on what changes mean for them and any action required
External Partners / Vendors	• Scope & requirements • Deliverables • Key deadlines	Bi-weekly (or per contract)	Email + Status Call	Vendor Manager	Align on deliverables and timelines
All Staff (Organization)	• Project purpose • Benefits • Major milestones	Quarterly (or at key milestones)	Company Newsletter + Town Hall	Project Sponsor / Communications	Big picture updates and project impact on the organization

COMMUNICATION GOVERNANCE

- All updates will be accurate, timely, and consistent.
- Owners are responsible for preparing and sending communications on time.
- Escalate communication gaps or risks immediately.
- This plan will be reviewed and adjusted as needed.

Next Review Date: July 15, 2025

ESCALATION PATH FOR COMMUNICATION ISSUES

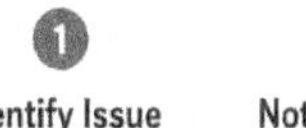

1. **Identify Issue** — Communication not received, unclear, or delayed
2. **Notify Owner** — Contact the owner listed in the matrix
3. **Escalate** — Escalate to Project Manager if not resolved

Goal: Resolve quickly, communicate clearly, keep the project moving.

Remember: Good communication is not about more information. It is about the right information to the right people at the right time.

PART 6: QUICK REFERENCE

Quick Reference: The 5 Questions to Ask Before Any Meeting

QUICK REFERENCE CARD

THE 5 QUESTIONS BEFORE ANY MEETING

Before you send a meeting invite or accept one, run this check.
If you can't answer these five questions, the meeting is not ready.

WHAT IS THE PURPOSE OF THIS MEETING?

If you can't name the purpose, the meeting does not have one.

- **Inform** (someone needs information)
- **Decide** (a decision needs to be made)
- **Align** (shared understanding is needed)
- **Generate** (ideas, options, or solutions)
- **Relationship** (connection, check-in, trust-building)

WHAT DOES SUCCESS LOOK LIKE?

Complete this before you send the invite:

"At the end of this meeting, we will have ___ so that ___."

If you can't complete it, the meeting has no clear outcome.

TIP: A clear outcome creates focus and prevents drift.

WHO ACTUALLY NEEDS TO BE THERE?

For each attendee, ask:

- Decision-maker
- Subject matter expert
- Implementer whose buy-in matters

If none o't these apply, they likely need the summary — not the meeting.

TIP: The best meeting is the smallest one that works.

WHAT INFORMATION NEEDS TO BE IN THE ROOM?

List what must be present (not just available):

- Data
- Pre-reads
- Decisions
- Context

If the required inputs are missing, the meeting will happen twice.

TIP: A meeting held without the right information will have to be held again.

WHAT HAPPENS AFTER THIS MEETING?

Name the owner and timeline for:

- The meeting summary
- Action items
- Follow-up communications

If there is no follow-through plan, there is no accountability.

TIP: Accountability starts before the meeting ends.

PREPARE WELL. MEET LESS. DECIDE FASTER.

Good meetings don't just happen. They are designed.

Quick Reference: Communication Triage

When something needs to be communicated and you're not sure how to approach it, run this triage. It takes three minutes and prevents the most common communication mistakes.

STEP 1 — WHAT IS THE EMOTIONAL TEMPERATURE?

Rate the situation: Low / Medium / High

- *Low* (routine, no strong emotions involved) → Proceed with your message. Use Set the Context if there's any risk of misread.
- *Medium* (some tension, stakes, or history) → Run Take Five before you draft. Use SIA structure.
- *High* (active conflict, significant frustration, or something just went wrong) → Run Take Five fully. Do not draft in the moment. Apply the 24-Hour Rule to any written communication.

STEP 2 — WHO IS THE AUDIENCE?

Question	Yes	No
Does this audience have the same context I do?	→ Proceed	→ Set the Context first
Is this audience likely to be emotionally reactive?	→ Use SIA + Key Message Triangle	→ Proceed with standard structure
Is this audience a decision-maker who needs to act?	→ Lead with the ask	→ Lead with the situation
Does this audience need to share this with others?	→ Design for forward-ability	→ Keep it as-is

STEP 3 — WHAT IS THE RIGHT CHANNEL?

Message Type	Right Channel	Wrong Channel
Urgent, time-sensitive decision	Phone / in-person	Email
Sensitive feedback or difficult conversation	In-person / video	SharePoint / text
Complex information with multiple steps	Email / document with verbal follow-up	Verbal only
Quick status update	SharePoint / async	Meeting
Conflict resolution	In-person / video	Email thread
Bad news to a team	In-person or synchronous video	Async message
Formal record of a decision	Email / documented	Verbal only

STEP 4 — DO THE FINAL CHECK

Before you send, say it, or schedule it:

1. Will this message make sense to the recipient without additional context?
2. Does the recipient know what to do after they receive this?
3. Is there anything in this message I would regret if it were forwarded?
4. Have I separated the facts from my interpretation of them?
5. Is this the right time to deliver this message?

Quick Reference: Red Flags That Communication Is Breaking Down

These patterns are early warning signs. Each one is recoverable — but only if you catch it early. The longer these patterns run, the more entrenched they become.

In Meetings

Red Flag	What It Signals
The same topic recurs without resolution	No decision authority in the room, or someone is blocking a decision outside the room
People stop asking questions	They've learned their questions won't be answered, or the culture punishes surfacing problems
Attendance starts declining	People have decided the meeting isn't worth their time — and they're usually right
Decisions made in the meeting are contradicted or undone by the next meeting	Either alignment wasn't real, or someone with authority wasn't in the room
Side conversations during the meeting are more substantive than the meeting itself	The real work happens in the hallway, not in the room

In Teams

Red Flag	What It Signals
People are working on the same thing without knowing it	Ownership and communication pathways are not clear
Problems surface to leadership before they surface internally	People don't feel safe raising issues to their own team first
The unofficial communication network (the grapevine) is more reliable than official channels	Official communication has lost credibility or is too slow
People say "that's the first I've heard of this" regularly	Information is flowing selectively or getting stuck in channels

Red Flag	What It Signals
Team members solve problems by going around the process rather than through it	The process doesn't work, or people don't trust that it works

In Your Own Communication

Red Flag	What It Signals
You're repeating yourself — same message, different audience, no uptake	The message isn't landing; the issue is usually in Set the Context Steps 1–3
You feel like you're always the last to know	You're either not in the right communication pathways, or someone is choosing not to include you
Your emails are long and your response rate is low	You're writing for completeness, not for the reader — simplify
You're avoiding a conversation you know you need to have	Use Take Five, write the SIA, and have it this week
You feel like your message is being received differently than you intend	Run a Set the Context on your next version; your audience analysis may be off

A Final Note on Using This Playbook

Frameworks are not scripts you read aloud. They are structures that give your thinking a shape before you open your mouth.

The best communicators you've worked with weren't following templates in real time. They had internalized the principles behind them so thoroughly that they could apply them under pressure, without hesitation, without thinking about the steps. That fluency didn't come from talent. It came from repetition.

Use these frameworks deliberately at first — the way you'd use a checklist. Run Take Five before the meeting. Write your SIA on a sticky note. Read your opening sentence out loud before you walk into the room. It will feel mechanical. That's fine. Mechanical is how disciplines start. Instinct is how they finish.

When they become instinct, something shifts. The conversations that used to derail you stop feeling like emergencies. They start feeling like problems you know how to solve. Not because the situations got easier. Because your communication got stronger.

Breaking the Spiral™ is not one perfect conversation. It is the accumulation of small, consistent choices — testing an assumption instead of letting it ride, breaking a silence instead of hoping someone else will, making it safe for the person who's afraid to speak, closing the loop instead of assuming it closed itself, and naming what's actually happening when everyone else is pretending it isn't.

This Playbook is what that practice looks like on a Tuesday morning. In a meeting that's going sideways. In a hallway conversation you didn't plan for. In the five minutes before you deliver news that nobody wants to hear.

***Cool Hand Luke* didn't win every round.**

But he never went quiet.

He never let the system's silence

become his silence.

He used its own language against it —

and he smiled that smile.

Not because things were fine, but because he decided that silence was not the answer.

You have the tools now.

The next conversation is the one that matters.

— Ace

Reader Exercises — Putting It Into Practice

Knowledge without application is shelf decoration. The exercises in this section are designed to move the ideas in this book from your head into your habits. Work through them in order or go directly to the exercise that matches where you are right now.

WHAT YOU'LL BUILD THROUGH THE EXERCISES

These exercises are designed to help you see what's really happening, understand the impact, and take action that creates lasting change.

EXERCISE	WHAT IT REVEALS	WHAT YOU'LL WALK AWAY WITH
SILENT SPIRAL™ SELF-DIAGNOSTIC	Where communication is breaking down—and which stage shows up most.	Clear visibility into your current patterns and where to intervene first.
TEAM COMMUNICATION HEALTH ASSESSMENT	How your team experiences clarity, safety, ownership, and follow-through.	A measurable baseline of communication health.
PERSONAL COMMUNICATION STYLE INVENTORY	How your communication style impacts others—especially under pressure.	Awareness of your tendencies and how they affect clarity and trust.
PRE-PROJECT COMMUNICATION PLAN WORKSHEET	Where breakdowns are likely to occur before work begins.	A structured plan to align expectations, roles, and information flow.
POST-PROJECT COMMUNICATION RETROSPECTIVE	Where communication failed across a real project lifecycle.	A repeatable way to diagnose breakdowns without blame.
THE 30-DAY COMMUNICATION CHALLENGE	The consistency (or inconsistency) of your daily communication behaviors.	Practical habits that build clarity, trust, and follow-through over time.

There is no single right way to build better communication habits — only the next honest step you are willing to take with yourself and your team.

Exercise: The Silent Spiral™ Self-Diagnostic

THE SILENT SPIRAL™ SELF-DIAGNOSTIC

INSTRUCTIONS
Answer each question honestly. For every checkbox you indicate "Yes," note the Spiral Stage™ in parentheses. Add up your total at the end and read your score interpretation.

THIS IS NOT A SURVEY— IT IS A MIRROR.
Answer for right now, in your current environment.

- ☐ 1 I recently sent an important communication and did not confirm it was received or understood. (Stage 1: Assumption)
- ☐ 2 There is a concern I have about a project or process that I have not raised with anyone. (Stage 2: Silence)
- ☐ 3 I have felt frustrated by a decision that was made without my input in the last 30 days. (Stage 2: Silence)
- ☐ 4 I have created or use an unofficial workaround for an official process. (Stage 4: Workaround)
- ☐ 5 A project or initiative I was involved in failed, and the root cause was never fully addressed. (Stage 5: Failure)
- ☐ 6 There is someone on my team whose silence I have noticed but not named. (Stage 2: Silence)
- ☐ 7 I have attended a meeting where the real conversation happened in the hallway afterward. (Stage 3: Frustration)
- ☐ 8 I have assumed someone "got" a message when I have no confirmation they did. (Stage 1: Assumption)
- ☐ 9 I have been the last to learn about a decision that affected my work. (Stage 3: Frustration)
- ☐ 10 I have gone around an official channel because the official channel had stopped working. (Stage 4: Workaround)

THE SILENT SPIRAL™ SELF-DIAGNOSTIC

☐	11	There is a recurring problem on my team that has been discussed in meetings but never structurally resolved.	(Stage 5: Failure)
☐	12	I have softened or withheld feedback because I did not think it would be received well.	(Stage 2: Silence)
☐	13	I have been in a meeting where a concern was raised, parked, and never returned to.	(Stage 3: Frustration)
☐	14	I have done work that was later duplicated by someone who didn't know I had done it.	(Stage 1: Assumption)
☐	15	There is a conversation I know I need to have with someone that I have been putting off for more than two weeks.	(Stage 2/3: Silence/ Frustration)

TALLY

- MY TOTAL YES CHECKBOXES: ____________________
- SPIRAL STAGES REPRESENTED IN MY ANSWERS: ____________________
- THE STAGE THAT APPEARS MOST IN MY ANSWERS: ____________________

SCORE INTERPRETATION

Score	Interpretation
0-3	**Healthy communication environment.** The spiral is not actively at work in your current context. Use this score as a baseline and return to this diagnostic in 90 days. Strong communication environments erode quietly when not maintained.
4-7	**Early spiral indicators present.** You are in the early stages. This is the best possible time to intervene—the patterns are visible but not yet structural. Go back to the chapter that corresponds to your most frequent stage and apply one framework this week.
8-11	**Active spiral in progress.** The spiral is underway in your environment. Use the Breaking the Spiral™ framework and prioritize interruption behaviors designed to interrupt the most common stage you identified.
12-15	**Deep in the spiral.** Start with Chapter 5 (Trust) and work forward. The structural repairs needed at this stage require rebuilding the foundation before the other floors will hold.

REFLECTION: Looking at the specific items you checked, what is the single highest-leverage communication behavior you could change in the next seven days?

____

____

Exercise: Team Communication Health Assessment

TEAM COMMUNICATION HEALTH ASSESSMENT

INSTRUCTIONS FOR LEADERS

Distribute this survey anonymously. Collect responses before a team meeting and review the results together as a communication-culture conversation, not a performance review.

RATING SCALE

All questions use a 1–5 scale.

1 = Never / Strongly Disagree.

5 = Always / Strongly Agree.

 TEAM NAME / DEPARTMENT ____________

 DATE ADMINISTERED ____________

 NUMBER OF RESPONDENTS ____________

QUESTIONS 1–5

QUESTIONS	RATE EACH STATEMENT				
	1	2	3	4	5
1. I have what I need to do my job this week.	○	○	○	○	○
2. When I raise a concern, it is taken seriously and followed up on.	○	○	○	○	○
3. I know who to go to when I need information, a decision, or support.	○	○	○	○	○
4. Our team's meetings result in clear decisions and assigned action items.	○	○	○	○	○
5. I hear about decisions that affect my work before they are implemented, not after.	○	○	○	○	○

→ *Continued on next page*

TEAM COMMUNICATION HEALTH ASSESSMENT

QUESTIONS 6–10

QUESTIONS	RATE EACH STATEMENT				
	1	2	3	4	5
6. Information flows to the people who need it in time for them to act on it.	○	○	○	○	○
7. There is something I know that someone else on this team needs to know, but I haven't said it.	○	○	○	○	○
8. I feel safe raising a problem or asking a question without fear of how it will be received.	○	○	○	○	○
9. When something goes wrong, the team focuses on what broke—not who to blame.	○	○	○	○	○
10. The communication on this team is better today than it was six months ago.	○	○	○	○	○

SCORING RUBRIC

AVERAGE SCORE	INTERPRETATION	RECOMMENDED ACTION
4.5–5.0	High Health	Maintain and measure. Audit leading indicators quarterly.
3.5–4.4	Functional with Friction	Identify the two lowest-scoring questions and treat them as process problems.
2.5–3.4	Significant Gaps	Use the 90-Day Communication Improvement Plan from Chapter 11. Prioritize the lowest two sections.
1.0–2.4	Communication Breakdown	Start with psychological safety (Question 8). Without it, other improvements cannot hold.

LEADER REFLECTION

THE QUESTION THAT REQUIRES THE MOST IMMEDIATE ATTENTION ON MY TEAM:

WHAT IS THIS TELLING ME ABOUT HOW INFORMATION FLOWS?

ONE STRUCTURAL CHANGE I WILL MAKE BASED ON THESE RESULTS:

REVIEW DATE FOR FOLLOW-UP SURVEY:

THIS IS NOT A COMMUNICATION SCORE. IT'S A VISIBILITY SCORE OF YOUR GAPS.

Exercise: The Personal Communication Style Inventory

THE PERSONAL COMMUNICATION STYLE INVENTORY™

Understand how you communicate—especially under pressure.

INSTRUCTIONS

For each question, choose the answer that most accurately describes your default behavior—not your best day, and not your aspirations. Select one response per question.

QUESTIONS 1–5

1 When you need to address a conflict or uncomfortable topic, you typically:

- A ○ Address it directly as soon as possible
- B ○ Think through your position carefully first
- C ○ Talk it through out loud to clarify thinking
- D ○ Wait to see if it resolves itself before raising it

2 In a meeting where you disagree with a decision, you are most likely to:

- A ○ Say so clearly, in the moment, to the group
- B ○ Write a follow-up email with your concerns after
- C ○ Raise it with one or two people informally
- D ○ Mentally note your disagreement but say nothing

3 When you receive complex instructions or feedback, your first instinct is to:

- A ○ Confirm your understanding and act
- B ○ Write it down and review it first
- C ○ Talk through what you heard out loud
- D ○ Nod and figure out later if you're clear

4 When something goes wrong on a project, you tend to:

- A ○ Raise it immediately, even early
- B ○ Gather all the facts and your analysis first
- C ○ Talk to a trusted colleague first
- D ○ Handle it quietly yourself

5 In a high-stakes conversation, your biggest risk is:

- A ○ Coming across as blunt or not open-minded
- B ○ Taking too long to get to the point
- C ○ Talking more than you mean to
- D ○ Agreeing to something you don't agree with

THE PERSONAL COMMUNICATION STYLE INVENTORY™

Understand how you communicate—especially under pressure.

QUESTIONS 6–10

6 Your relationship to written communication (email, messaging) is:

- A A tool for getting decisions made fast ○
- B The mode where you're most precise ○
- C Harder than talking—pick up the phone ○
- D The safer choice when direct talk feels risky ○

7 When you receive feedback on your work, your first response is usually:

- A Ask clarifying questions about what to change ○
- B Ask for time to review before responding ○
- C Talk through your reaction first ○
- D Say "thank you" and decide internally ○

8 You are most effective as a communicator when:

- A The goal and stakes are clear and you act ○
- B You've had time to prepare and have structure ○
- C You're in a trusted, open conversation ○
- D The environment feels safe from punishment ○

9 The phrase that most closely describes your communication instinct is:

- A "Say it clearly, say it once, move forward" ○
- B "Get it right before you say anything" ○
- C "Thinking out loud is how I figure it out" ○
- D "Avoid the friction unless the cost of silence is too high" ○

10 When someone in a meeting is saying something you think is wrong, you:

- A Correct it directly, in the moment ○
- B Wait and address it in writing or one-on-one later ○
- C Ask a clarifying question that surfaces it ○
- D Let it go unless someone asks your opinion ○

SCORING & YOUR COMMUNICATION STYLE

STEP 1: COUNT YOUR ANSWERS

Tally how many A, B, C, and D responses you selected.

A = ____________

B = ____________

C = ____________

D = ____________

TIP:

There are no right or wrong answers. This is about recognizing your natural patterns so you can lead with greater clarity and impact.

STEP 2: IDENTIFY YOUR PRIMARY STYLE

Your primary style is the letter you selected most often.
(If you have a tie, choose the one that feels most "you" in high-stress moments.)

MOSTLY A – DIRECT COMMUNICATOR

You communicate with speed, clarity, and comfidence.

STRENGTHS: Decisiveness, efficiency

RISK: May leave others behind, miss emotional nuance, or close conversations that needed to stay open longer.

FRAMEWORK TO DEVELOP: Take Five

PRACTICE TO BUILD: Ask one more question before you close.

MOSTLY B – PROCESSOR

You communicate with precision and thoroughness.

STRENGTHS: Accuracy, preparation

RISK: Your timing may lag behind the conversation's needs, and others may interpret your silence as disengagement or agreement.

FRAMEWORK TO DEVELOP: Key Message Triangle

PRACTICE TO BUILD: State your core message first, then add the context.

MOSTLY C – VERBAL THINKER

You communicate by talking your way to clarity.

STRENGTHS: Relationship-building, creative problem-solving through dialogue

RISK: You may exhaust your audience before landing the point, or be perceived as less decisive than you are.

FRAMEWORK TO DEVELOP: Set the Context

PRACTICE TO BUILD: Write the core message before you have the conversation.

MOSTLY D – CONFLICT AVOIDER

You communicate carefully, and you read rooms better than most.

STRENGTHS: Empathy, relationship preservation

RISK: The cost of your silence is paid by the team—in assumptions, workarounds, and problems that escalate.

FRAMEWORK TO DEVELOP: SIA

PRACTICE TO BUILD: Identify one concern you are currently sitting on and use the SIA structure to name it this week.

STEP 3: YOUR REFLECTION

My primary style: ____________________________

The communication strength I want to build on: ____________________________

The communication risk I need to actively manage: ____________________________

The one framework I will practice first: ____________________________

YOUR STYLE ISN'T THE PROBLEM. UNMANAGED PATTERNS ARE.

Exercise: The Pre-Project Communication Plan Worksheet

Instructions: Complete this worksheet at the start of any project, initiative, or significant effort. This is not a document to file — it is a working agreement. Share it with your project team, get verbal confirmation, and reference it at every major milestone.

PROJECT NAME: / PROJECT OWNER: / START DATE: / EXPECTED DURATION:

Part A: Stakeholders and Information Flow

Who needs to know what is happening on this project, and at what level of detail?

Stakeholder / Group	What they need to know	How often	Through which channel	Owner of that communication

Who needs to be involved in decisions vs. informed of outcomes?

- **Decision-makers:**
- **Those who must be consulted before decisions are final:**
- **Those who should be informed after decisions are made:**

Part B: Communication Cadence

- **Regular check-in frequency:**
- **Format of check-in (standup, written update, meeting):**
- **Who is responsible for running it:**
- **Where will decisions and action items be documented:**
- **How will the team know if a check-in is cancelled or rescheduled:**

Part C: Escalation Path

- **If a problem arises that I cannot resolve at my level, I escalate to:**
- **The threshold for escalation (what makes it "above my level"):**
- **If I cannot reach my escalation contact, the backup is:**

- **If there is a safety, compliance, or ethics element, the escalation path is:**

The "no surprises" norm for this project: After hours of knowing about a problem that affects the timeline, scope, or another workstream, I will surface it.

Part D: Channel Norms for This Project

Type of Communication	Channel to Use	Expected Response Time
Urgent / time-sensitive		
Status updates and progress		
Decisions and documentation		
Questions and clarifications		
Sensitive conversations		

Part E: Handoff Planning

- **If someone transitions off this project mid-stream, the handoff process will include:**
- **The person responsible for ensuring the handoff happens completely is:**
- **What a new person joining mid-project needs to get up to speed:**
- **This worksheet was reviewed and agreed to by:**
- **Date of agreement:**
- **Next review point (milestone or date):**

Exercise: The Post-Project Communication Retrospective

Instructions: Run this retrospective within two weeks of any significant project closing — whether it succeeded, failed, or landed somewhere in the middle. If you only run it on failures, you will only learn from failures. The teams that improve fastest run it on everything. **Facilitate this as a team**

conversation, not an individual worksheet. One person captures the answers. All voices contribute.

PROJECT NAME: / DATE: / FACILITATOR: / PARTICIPANTS:

Question 1: Where did information flow well on this project — and what made it work?

- What specifically went right (a process, a cadence, a habit, a person's behavior)?
- What would we want to build into the next project's communication plan because of this?

Question 2: Where did information stop flowing — and why?

- At what point in the project did people stop having what they needed to do their jobs?
- Was the blockage a person, a process, a channel, or an assumption?
- What would have needed to be different for that information to reach the right people at the right time?

Question 3: Was there anything that someone knew that the team needed to know, but didn't surface until too late — or never surfaced at all?

- Describe the gap. What made it hard to raise? (Safety concern, no clear channel, fear of reaction, assumed someone else would say it)
- What structural change would make it easier to surface that kind of information next time?

Question 4: Did the communication plan we built at the start reflect how we actually operated?

- What did we plan to do that we didn't actually do?
- What did we actually do that we hadn't planned?
- What does that gap tell us about the realism of our planning or the pressures of execution?

Question 5: If we ran this project again tomorrow with the same team, what is the single most important communication change we would make from day one?

- The change:
- The person who would own implementing it:
- How we would know it was working:

Action Items From This Retrospective:

Action	Owner	By when

- **Will any of these findings change how we build communication plans for future projects?**
- **If yes, who will update the template and by when?**

Exercise 6: The 30-Day Communication Challenge

Instructions: One action per day. Each takes less than ten minutes. None requires permission, a title, or a budget. Check the box when you complete it. After 30 days, look back at what you did and what changed.

Day	Action
1	Ask "what questions do you have?" instead of "any questions?" in your next meeting. Notice the difference in what comes back.
2	Follow up on one outstanding action item from last week that has not been completed. Not a reminder — a direct conversation.
3	Send a brief written summary of a verbal conversation you had today. One paragraph. Send it within two hours.
4	In your next one-on-one, use the read-back technique: "Let me make sure I heard you correctly." Say it out loud.
5	Identify one concern you have been sitting on. Write it down in SIA format. Decide: does it get raised today, or does it need more information first?
6	Find a communication loop you opened recently that you have not closed. Close it today.
7	At the start of your next meeting, state the purpose and what you need to leave with. Before anyone else speaks.

Day	Action
8	When you receive an email or message that requires a non-urgent response, reply with "received, will follow up by [specific date/time]" within the same day.
9	Use the Parking Lot Method in a meeting today. Name it explicitly: "I want to park that and come back to it."
10	Write down one thing you have been assuming a colleague or direct report knows. Confirm whether they actually know it.
11	Give one piece of specific, behavior-based feedback to someone today. Not "great job" — "here is what I saw you do and why it mattered."
12	Identify one communication channel on your team that is being misused (wrong type of content in the wrong channel). Name it in your next team meeting.
13	At the end of a meeting today, state out loud: "Before we close — here is what we decided, here is who owns what, and here is the next check-in." Do this whether or not it is your meeting to run.
14	Apply the Take Five framework to one situation today where your first instinct is to respond immediately. Write the response. Wait two hours. Read it again before you send.
15	Have a five-minute conversation with one team member that has no agenda except: "What's one thing that's harder than it should be right now?" Listen. Take one note.
16	Find a decision that was made informally (in a hallway, a side conversation, a chat message) and document it in writing in the appropriate shared location.
17	Identify one recurring problem on your team that has been discussed but never structurally addressed. Name the root cause. Who could fix it? Is that person aware it needs to be fixed?
18	Before your next stakeholder communication, use the Set the Context framework. Spend five minutes completing it before you write or speak.
19	Ask someone who is newer to your team than you are: "What's something about how we communicate here that still doesn't make sense to you?" Listen without defending.
20	At the close of your workday, answer three questions: (1) Did I close every loop I opened today? (2) Is there anything I know that someone else needs to know? (3) Is there a conversation I'm putting off that I should have this week?
21	Use the Key Message Triangle to prepare for one conversation today where you need to persuade or inform a skeptical audience. Write the triangle before you speak.

Day	Action
22	In your next team meeting, direct a question to someone who has not yet spoken. "What's your read on this?" or "What am I missing?" — directly, by name.
23	Send a note of specific, genuine appreciation to someone who made your work easier in the last two weeks. One concrete example. No generic "thanks for all you do."
24	Audit one team process or meeting that exists because it always has. Ask: does this serve a communication function? Could it be shorter, less frequent, or replaced with a written update?
25	Before you hit "reply all" on your next group email, ask: does every person on this thread need this response? If not, send it to the people who do.
26	Identify the last time you gave someone feedback that turned out to be more about your frustration than their behavior. How would you frame that feedback differently today using SIA?
27	Run a quick personal Communication Audit: (1) Where did information get stuck this week? (2) What did I assume someone knew that they didn't? (3) What loop did I leave open that I should close?
28	Share one "communication win" with your team today — a moment where someone communicated well. Name it specifically and publicly.
29	Write down three communication habits you have built over the last 28 days that you want to keep. Write down one you started but didn't maintain. What would it take to restart it?
30	Return to the Silent Spiral™ Self-Diagnostic from Exercise 1. Take it again. Compare your score to Day 1. What changed? What is still in progress? What do you commit to for the next 30 days?

- **My Day 1 score on the Silent Spiral™ Diagnostic:**
- **My Day 30 score on the Silent Spiral™ Diagnostic:**
- **The communication habit I am most proud of building:**
- **The habit I am committing to for the next 30 days:**

APPENDICES

Appendix A: Communication Assessment

Instructions: Answer each question honestly, selecting the response that most accurately reflects your current reality — not your aspirations or your best day.

For teams, consider having each member complete the assessment independently, then comparing scores as a group discussion exercise.

Scoring:

- **Yes / Always / Strongly Agree: 3 points**
- **Sometimes / Partially: 2 points**
- **Rarely / No / Disagree: 1 point**
- **Never / Strongly Disagree: 0 points**

Section 1: Trust and Psychological Safety (Questions 1–5)

1. Team members can raise concerns or questions without fear of negative consequences (dismissal, ridicule, or retaliation).
2. When someone admits they do not know something or made a mistake, the team's response is constructive rather than critical.
3. I feel comfortable disagreeing with a colleague or supervisor when I believe they are wrong.
4. Team members are honest with each other even when the news is bad or the conversation is uncomfortable.
5. Leadership models vulnerability — they acknowledge their own mistakes and limitations openly.

Section 2: Clarity and Shared Understanding (Questions 6–10)

6. When a decision is made, I understand not just what was decided but why.
7. My role, responsibilities, and the boundaries of my authority are clearly defined and commonly understood by the people I work with.

8. When I receive instructions or direction, I understand them well enough to act without needing to guess.
9. Team members use shared language — terms and definitions that mean the same thing to everyone — rather than assumptions that may differ.
10. At the close of a meeting or project milestone, there is clear documentation of what was decided, who owns what, and what happens next.

Section 3: Communication Cadence and Rhythms (Questions 11–13)

11. The team has defined check-in points (standups, briefings, reports) that occur at predictable intervals and are consistently used.
12. I know when to expect updates and from whom, rather than having to chase information.
13. The team has standard protocols for shift handoffs, project transitions, or role changes that ensure information is not lost.

Section 4: Accountability and Loop-Closing (Questions 14–16)

14. When a commitment is made, there is a reliable system for tracking it so it does not get lost.
15. When someone does not follow through on a commitment, the issue is addressed directly and constructively — not ignored or worked around.
16. I consistently close the loop — confirming receipt, providing status updates, and letting others know when a task is complete.

Section 5: Cross-Functional Communication (Questions 17–19)

17. When my team's work depends on another team, I know who my point of contact is and how to reach them effectively.
18. Information that is relevant to multiple departments actually reaches all of them in a timely way.
19. When cross-functional problems arise, we address them jointly rather than finger-pointing or passing the issue back and forth.

Section 6: Feedback Culture (Questions 20–21)

20. I receive specific, constructive feedback on my work and communication on a regular basis — not just at annual review time.

21. I give specific, constructive feedback to others when it would be helpful, even when the conversation is uncomfortable.

Section 7: Escalation, Channel Selection, and Leadership Communication (Questions 22–25)

22. I know when and how to escalate a problem — and I feel safe doing it without fear of being seen as a complainer or troublemaker.

23. The team uses the right communication channels for the right purposes (e.g., urgent matters are not buried in email; sensitive conversations are not handled publicly).

24. Leadership communicates important decisions, changes, and priorities in a way that reaches everyone who needs to know — not just the people who happen to be nearby.

25. When I have information that someone else needs to do their job, I make sure they have it — even if it is not technically “my job” to tell them.

SELF / TEAM COMMUNICATION ASSESSMENT

Score Sheet

Use this page to document section scores for the assessment in the book.
Complete once as an individual reflection and again as a team comparison if useful.

3 = Yes / Always / Strongly Agree	2 = Sometimes / Partially	1 = Rarely / No / Disagree	0 = Never / Strongly Disagree

SECTION	QUESTION RANGE	MAX POINTS	MY SCORE	TEAM SCORE	NOTES
1 Trust and Psychological Safety	Q1–5	15			
2 Clarity and Shared Understanding	Q6–10	15			
3 Communication Cadence and Rhythms	Q11–13	9			
4 Accountability and Loop-Closing	Q14–16	9			
5 Cross-Functional Communication	Q17–19	9			
6 Feedback Culture	Q20–21	6			
7 Escalation, Channel Selection, and Leadership Communication	Q22–25	12			
TOTAL	**Q1–25**	**75**			

HIGHEST-SCORING STRENGTH: ____________________

LOWEST-SCORING AREA: ____________________

WHAT NEEDS ATTENTION FIRST? ____________________

Use the text in the book for the full questions and interpretation.

Scoring Guide

Add up your points from all 25 questions. Maximum possible score: 75.

60–75 Points: THRIVING

Your team's communication culture is a genuine strength. You have built — or are operating within — an environment where information flows reliably, trust enables honest conversation, and accountability is shared and maintained without blame.

This is not a permanent state; it requires ongoing maintenance. Use your score as a baseline and continue to measure, because communication cultures erode when they are taken for granted.

Recommendations:

- Conduct this assessment every six months to monitor for drift
- Identify your lowest-scoring questions and address them proactively before they become larger issues
- Use your communication strengths as a model — document what's working and share it with other teams
- Focus on resilience: how does your communication hold up under stress? The next time a crisis occurs, treat it as a diagnostic

40–59 Points: AT RISK

Your team has some communication structures in place, but significant gaps exist. These gaps may not be causing acute crises today, but they are creating friction, inefficiency, and a slow erosion of trust that will compound over time.

Recommendations:

- Identify your three lowest-scoring questions and treat each as a process problem with a root cause and a corrective action
- Start with one structural improvement — a defined check-in cadence, a communication norms agreement, or an explicit

escalation protocol — and implement it fully before adding more

- Have a team conversation using this assessment as the catalyst. The discussion itself is a communication intervention.
- Revisit the chapters in Part II that correspond to your lowest-scoring categories and apply the frameworks there

0–39 Points: IN CRISIS

Your communication environment is actively harming your team's performance, morale, and ability to deliver results. Some combination of missing structure, broken trust, unclear accountability, or a culture that punishes honesty is producing the score you see.

This is not irreversible, but it does require immediate, sustained attention — not a workshop and a poster.

Recommendations:

- **Do not try to fix everything at once.** Start with psychological safety (Section 1) — without it, all other improvements will be limited
- **Consider bringing in external support:** a facilitator, coach, or change management resource who can help create the conditions for honest dialogue
- Read Chapter 17 of this book carefully. You may be in the recovery phase, and the triage steps there apply to where you are right now.
- **Leadership must be part of the solution.** If leadership is the source of the communication breakdown, direct reports will not be able to solve it alone.
- **Commit to remeasuring in 60 days.** Progress is possible and often faster than people expect when the commitment is genuine.

Appendix B: Templates and Tools

The following templates are designed to be used immediately. They are starting points — adapt them to your team, your industry, and your specific context. *A template you modify and use is worth infinitely more than one that sits unused.*

Template: Communication Plan

Purpose: To define how information will flow on a project, initiative, or within an ongoing team. Ensures that all stakeholders know what they will receive, when, and from whom.

PROJECT / INITIATIVE NAME: | PLAN VERSION: | DATE: | OWNER:

Section A: Stakeholder Identification

Instructions: List every person or group who needs information about this project. "Communication Need" = what information they need and why. "Level of Detail" = summary, detailed, or data-only. "Preferred Channel" = email, meeting, dashboard, text, etc.

Stakeholder Name / Group	Role	Communication Need	Level of Detail Required	Preferred Channel

Section B: Communication Schedule

Instructions: Add or remove rows as needed. "Owner" is the person responsible for sending/facilitating each communication — not just whoever happens to get to it first.

Comm. Type	Audience	Frequency	Owner	Channel	Format	Purpose
Status Update	Project Team	Weekly	PM	Email	Bullet summary	Track progress
Exe. Briefing	Sponsor	Bi-weekly	PM	Meeting	Slide deck	Decision-making

Comm. Type	Audience	Frequency	Owner	Channel	Format	Purpose
Risk / Issue Alert	Sponsor, Team Leads	As needed	PM	Email + Call	Written + verbal	Escalation

Section C: Channel Guidelines

Channel	Use For	Do NOT Use For	Response Time Expectation
Email	Non-urgent updates, documentation, formal communication	Urgent issues, sensitive feedback	24 hours (business days)
Phone / Text	Urgent, time-sensitive issues	Routine status updates	ASAP / within 1 hour
Team Meeting	Discussion, decisions, alignment	One-way information delivery	N/A
Shared Platform	Documents, reference materials, ongoing project tracking	Private communication	Check daily

Section D: Escalation Protocol

- **Level 1 (Team-level):** Issues resolved within the team → Owner: Team Lead → Timeline: Same day
- **Level 2 (Project-level):** Issues requiring PM decision or resources → Owner: Project Manager → Timeline: Within 24 hours
- **Level 3 (Executive):** Issues requiring sponsor action, scope change, or resource reallocation → Owner: PM escalates to Sponsor → Timeline: Within 48 hours
- **Communication method for escalation:** [Define — e.g., phone call followed by written summary within same day]

Section E: Feedback and Revision

- **This plan will be reviewed at:**
- **Revisions will be communicated by:**
- **Team members can suggest changes by:**

Template: Communication Plan

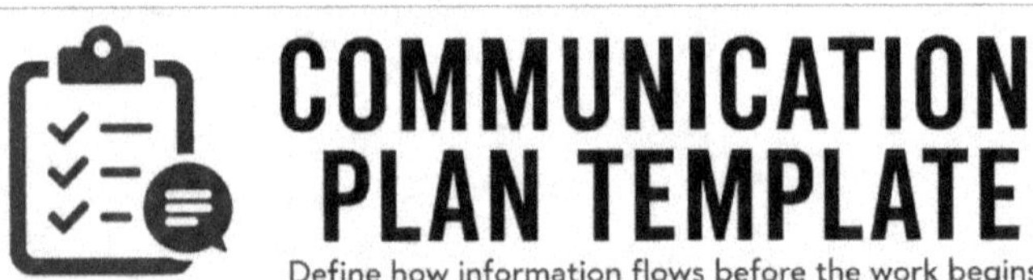

PROJECT / INITIATIVE NAME: ____________________

PLAN VERSION: __________ | DATE: __________ | OWNER: __________

SECTION A: STAKEHOLDER IDENTIFICATION

Stakeholder Name / Group	Role	Communication Need (What + Why)	Level of Detail Required (Summary / Detailed / Data-only)	Preferred Channel (Email, Meeting, Dashboard, Text, etc.)

INSTRUCTIONS:

- List every person or group who needs information.
- Define what they need and why.
- Choose level of detail: Summary, Detailed, or Data-only.

SECTION B: COMMUNICATION SCHEDULE

Communication Type	Audience	Frequency	Owner (Who sends / facilitates)	Channel	Format	Purpose
Status Update	Project Team	Weekly	PM	Email	Bullet summary	Track progress
Executive Briefing	Sponsor	Bi-weekly	PM	Meeting	Slide deck	Decision-making
Risk/Issue Alert	Sponsor, Team Leads	As needed	PM	Email + Call	Written + verbal	Escalation

INSTRUCTIONS:

- Add or remove rows as needed.
- "Owner" is the person responsible for sending/facilitating each communication – not just whoever happens to get to it first.

IF COMMUNICATION ISN'T DEFINED UPFRONT,
it will break down later.

PAGE 1 OF 2

 CLARITY →  ALIGNMENT →  ACTION →  FOLLOW-THROUGH →  RESULTS

SECTION C: CHANNEL GUIDELINES

CHANNEL	USE FOR	DO NOT USE FOR	RESPONSE TIME EXPECTATION
Email	Non-urgent updates, documentation, formal communication	Urgent issues, sensitive feedback	24 hours (business days)
Phone / Text	Urgent, time-sensitive issues	Routine status updates	ASAP / within 1 hour
Team Meeting	Discussion, decisions, alignment	One-way information delivery	N/A
Shared Platform (e.g., Teams, SharePoint)	Documents, reference materials, ongoing project tracking	Private communication	Check daily

SECTION D: ESCALATION PROTOCOL

1 LEVEL 1 TEAM-LEVEL

- Issues resolved within the team
- **Owner:** Team Lead
- **Timeline:** Same day

2 LEVEL 2 PROJECT-LEVEL

- Issues requiring PM decision or resources
- **Owner:** Project Manager
- **Timeline:** Within 24 hours

3 LEVEL 3 EXECUTIVE

- Issues requiring sponsor action, scope change, or resource reallocation
- **Owner:** PM escalates to Sponsor
- **Timeline:** Within 48 hours

COMMUNICATION METHOD FOR ESCALATION: ____________________

(Example: Phone call followed by written summary within same day)

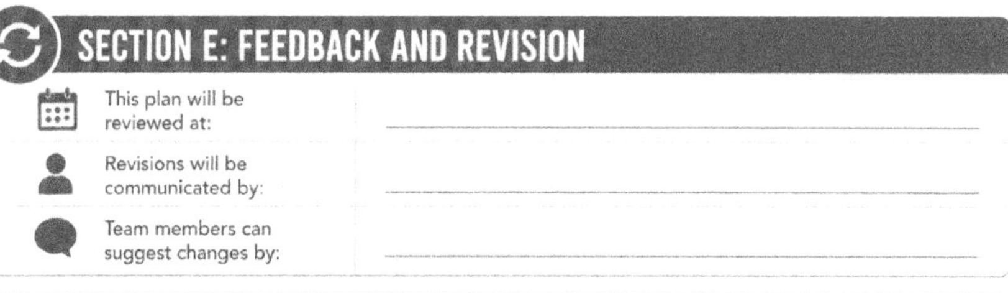

SECTION E: FEEDBACK AND REVISION

This plan will be reviewed at: ____________________

Revisions will be communicated by: ____________________

Team members can suggest changes by: ____________________

CLARITY IS NOT A ONE-TIME EVENT.

It's a system you maintain.

PAGE 2 OF 2

CLARITY → ALIGNMENT → ACTION → FOLLOW-THROUGH → RESULTS

Template: RACI Matrix

Purpose: To define who is **Responsible, Accountable, Consulted,** and **Informed** for every key task or decision. Eliminates ambiguity about ownership before it becomes conflict.

RACI CHART TEMPLATE

Clarify who does the work, who owns the outcome, who must be consulted, and who needs to be informed.

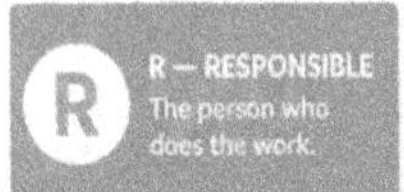

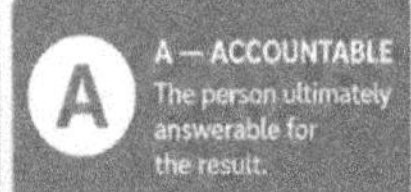

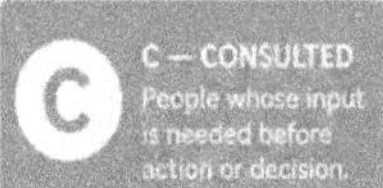

TASK / DECISION / DELIVERABLE	ROLE / FUNCTION 1	ROLE / FUNCTION 2	ROLE / FUNCTION 3	ROLE / FUNCTION 4	ROLE / FUNCTION 5
1.					
2.					
3.					
4.					
5.					
6.					
7.					
8.					

HOW TO USE IT

1. List the major tasks, decisions, or deliverables down the left side.
2. List the key roles or functions across the top.
3. Assign one Accountable owner for each row.
4. Use R, A, C, and I consistently to avoid confusion.

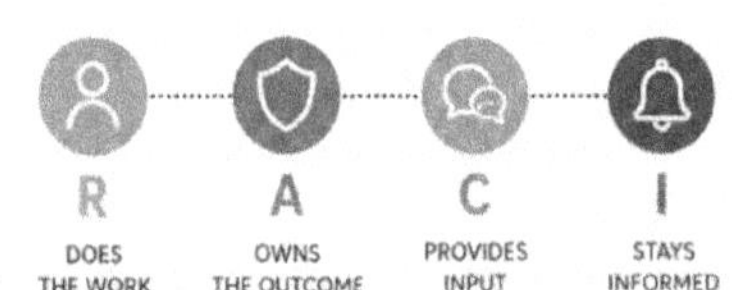

R — DOES THE WORK
A — OWNS THE OUTCOME
C — PROVIDES INPUT
I — STAYS INFORMED

Every row should have one A.

More than one R may be okay.

Too many C's slow decisions.

I means keep them updated—not involved in every step.

Clarity in roles. Alignment in action. Better outcomes together.

Template Meeting Agenda Framework

Purpose: To ensure every meeting has a purpose, a plan, and a productive outcome. **No agenda = no meeting.**

MEETING AGENDA TEMPLATE

A meeting without an agenda is a conversation with overhead.

Meeting Name:	
Date / Time:	
Location / Link:	
Facilitator:	
Note-taker:	
Purpose:	☐ Decision ☐ Discussion ☐ Update ☐ Problem-solving

PRE-READ MATERIALS:

List or link anything participants need beforehand

DECISION(S) TO BE MADE TODAY:

List them clearly

MEETING FLOW (AGENDA ITEMS):

	Agenda Item	Owner	Type
1.			☐ Decision ☐ Discussion ☐ Update
2.			☐ Decision ☐ Discussion ☐ Update
3.			☐ Decision ☐ Discussion ☐ Update
4.			☐ Decision ☐ Discussion ☐ Update

MEETING NORMS REMINDER

- Start and end on time.
- One conversation at a time.
- Phones and laptops closed unless needed for the meeting.
- If you will be late or absent, notify the facilitator in advance.
- Decisions made in this meeting are in effect unless formally revisited.

POST-MEETING

Notes distributed by: ____________ (date/time)

Action log updated by: ____________ (date/time)

WHY THIS MATTERS

If a meeting requires a decision, name the decision in advance. If no decision is needed, be honest that it is an update. A surprising number of bad meetings happen because no one knows what kind of meeting they are in.

Template: Escalation Path Template

Purpose: To define the clear path for raising issues before they become crises. When everyone knows how to escalate, problems surface faster and get resolved faster.

ESCALATION PATH TEMPLATE

Escalate clearly. Escalate early. Escalate with facts.

ESCALATION LEVELS

Level	When to Escalate	Escalate To	Contact Method	Expected Response
1 – Peer / Self-Resolve	Issue can be resolved within your role and authority.	Handle directly; document in log	N/A	Immediate
2 – Supervisor / Team Lead	Needs a decision beyond your authority, extra resources, or team coordination.	[Name / Title]	[Phone / Email / Platform]	Within [X] hours
3 – Manager / Director	Operational impact, cross-functional coordination, or Level 2 could not resolve.	[Name / Title]	[Phone / Email]	Within [X] hours
4 – Executive / Sponsor	Significant organizational impact, resource reallocation, policy exception, or external stakeholder involvement.	[Name / Title]	[Phone / Email]	Within [X] hours
5 – External (if applicable)	Legal, regulatory, safety, or customer-facing issues requiring external involvement.	[Name / Title / Agency]	[Contact]	Per external protocol

ESCALATION DOCUMENTATION REQUIREMENTS

1. **What happened:** Brief, factual description of the issue
2. **Impact:** What is or will be affected
3. **What has already been tried:** Steps taken before escalating
4. **What you need:** Decision, resources, or awareness
5. **Timeline:** Urgency and window for resolution

IMPORTANT PRINCIPLES

Escalating is not failure. It is professional responsibility.

Escalate early — before the issue grows.

Document all escalations in writing.

No response in time? Escalate to the next level.

"I didn't want to bother anyone" is not a valid reason to wait.

Clear escalation protects the work, the timeline, and the people doing it.

Template: Feedback Conversation Script — The SIA Framework

Purpose: To structure a feedback conversation using the SIA framework: **Situation, Impact, Ask.** Use this for both positive feedback (to reinforce) and developmental feedback (to improve).

Script Template (Developmental Feedback)

Opening (set the tone):

"I'd like to talk with you about something I observed recently. I want to share this because I think it's important, and I believe addressing it will help both of us."

Situation: "In [specific situation — meeting, project, interaction, date if relevant], I observed [specific, observable behavior — not judgment, not generalization]."

Example: "In last Tuesday's project update, when the team raised concerns about the timeline, you responded by ending the discussion before all the concerns had been heard."

Impact: "The impact of that was [specific effect on team, work, trust, outcome]."

Example: "Two team members told me afterward that they felt their concerns weren't valued, and I've noticed they've been less engaged in subsequent meetings."

Ask: "What I'd like to ask is [specific, actionable request]."

Example: "Going forward, I'd like us to create space for concerns to be fully heard before closing discussion, even when we're short on time. Would you be willing to try that approach?"

Close (invite response): "I want to hear your perspective on what I've shared. What are your thoughts?"

Script Template (Positive / Reinforcing Feedback)

"I want to take a moment to recognize something specific you did. In [situation], you [behavior]. The impact of that was [result — on the team, the project, the culture]. That's exactly the kind of [quality] I want to see more of. Thank you."

SIA Quick Reference Card

Element	Question to Answer	Common Mistake
S — Situation	What specifically happened? When? Where?	Being vague ("you always..." / "you never...")
I — Impact	What was the actual effect?	Stopping at judgment ("that was unprofessional") without impact
A — Ask	What specifically do you want?	Ending without a clear request for change or acknowledgment

SIA MESSAGE STRUCTURE

STATE THE SITUATION. EXPLAIN THE IMPACT. MAKE THE ASK.

S
SITUATION (observable facts only)

On [date/timeframe], [what happened, specifically]: ____________

Who was involved: ____________

Where / in what context: ____________

I
IMPACT (the actual effect)

On the work: ____________

On the team / timeline / quality: ____________

Measurable or observable outcome: ____________

A
ASK (specific, actionable)

What I need going forward is: ____________

By when: ____________

How I will know it has been addressed: ____________

TIPS FOR USING SIA

- Stick to facts in the Situation.
- Focus on outcomes, not blame, in the Impact.
- Make a clear, specific request in the Ask.

CLEARER MESSAGE. STRONGER CONVERSATIONS. BETTER RESULTS.

Template: Post-Mortem / After-Action Review (AAR) Template

Purpose: To systematically capture lessons from a completed project, incident, or significant event — without blame, with the goal of systemic improvement.

AFTER-ACTION REVIEW

Field	Details
Event / Project Name:	
Date of Event:	
AAR Date:	
Facilitator:	
Participants:	
Document Owner:	

SECTION 1: What Was Supposed to Happen?

Describe the intended plan, objective, or outcome. Be specific: what were the goals, the timeline, the success criteria?

SECTION 2: What Actually Happened?

Describe what actually occurred. Stick to observable facts, not interpretations. Include timeline if relevant.

SECTION 3: What Went Well?

What Went Well	Why It Worked	Should We Standardize This?
		Yes / No
		Yes / No
		Yes / No

SECTION 4: What Did Not Go Well?

What Did Not Go Well	Root Cause (use Five Whys)	System / Process Gap Identified

Five Whys Worksheet (for each significant gap)

Issue:

- Why did it happen? (1):
- Why? (2):
- Why? (3):
- Why? (4):
- Why? (5 — Root Cause):
- Systemic fix:

SECTION 5: Action Items

Action Item	Owner	Due Date	How We'll Know It's Done

SECTION 6: Communication Lessons Specifically

What communication breakdowns contributed to the outcome (positive or negative)? What should change in how we communicate on the next similar initiative?

SECTION 7: Distribution and Follow-Up

- This AAR will be shared with:
- Follow-up review date to assess action item completion:
- Owner of action item tracking:

Facilitator's Note: An After-Action Review is only valuable if its action items are completed and its lessons are shared. A document that sits in a shared drive is not a lesson learned. It is a lesson documented. The learning happens when behavior changes.

AFTER-ACTION REPORT

LEARN. IMPROVE. DO BETTER NEXT TIME.

This is not a blame session. It is an honest reckoning so we capture what we learned and build a stronger foundation for the next change.

INITIATIVE / CHANGE: ______ GO-LIVE DATE: ______

DATE OF REPORT: ______ REPORT DATE: ______

REPORT PREPARED BY: ______ TEAM / STAKEHOLDERS INVOLVED: ______

1 WHAT DID WE PLAN?

What were we trying to achieve and how did we plan to get there?

2 WHAT ACTUALLY HAPPENED?

What occurred during the change? What was different than expected?

3 WHAT DID WE LEARN?

What worked well? What didn't? What were the key takeaways?

4 WHAT WILL WE DO DIFFERENTLY NEXT TIME?

What will we start, stop, or continue? What will we do differently?

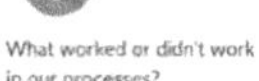

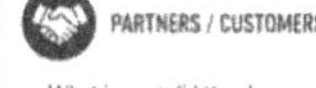

KEY IMPACTS

PEOPLE — What impact did the change have on our people?

PROCESSES — What worked or didn't work in our processes?

TECHNOLOGY — How did systems, tools, and data perform?

PARTNERS / CUSTOMERS — What impact did the change have on our partners and customers?

FINANCIAL — What were the financial impacts (expected vs. actual)?

FEEDBACK HIGHLIGHTS

What did we hear from the front line, partners, and customers?

SOURCE	WHAT WE HEARD	WHAT IT MEANS	ACTIONS TO TAKE

DECISIONS & COMMITMENTS

What decisions are we making based on what we learned?

-
-
-
-

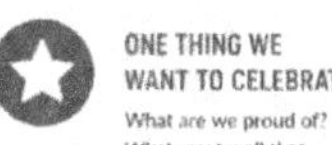

ONE THING WE WANT TO CELEBRATE

What are we proud of? What went well that we should recognize?

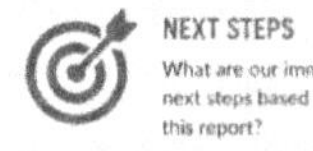

NEXT STEPS

What are our immediate next steps based on this report?

We don't just close the loop—we carry the lessons forward. | Document it. Share it. Use it.

Appendix C: Recommended Reading

The books below represent a curated collection of resources that have shaped the thinking in this book and that I return to regularly. Each is annotated with why it matters for the specific challenge of building communication cultures in teams and organizations.

1. The Five Dysfunctions of a Team

Patrick Lencioni

Jossey-Bass, 2002

The foundational text for understanding why teams fail. Lencioni presents his model as a pyramid: absence of trust → fear of conflict → lack of commitment → avoidance of accountability → inattention to results. Communication is the thread running through every layer. Start here and start with the trust layer.

2. The Fearless Organization: Creating Psychological Safety in the Workplace for Learning, Innovation, and Growth

Amy C. Edmondson

Wiley, 2018

Edmondson's research on psychological safety is the most rigorously evidenced explanation of why people do not speak up — and what you can do about it. Her four-stage model for building psychological safety is directly actionable for team leaders. If I could assign one book to every manager in every organization I have ever worked in, this would be it.

3. Team of Teams: New Rules of Engagement for a Complex World

General Stanley McChrystal with Tantum Collins, David Silverman, and Chris Fussell

Portfolio/Penguin, 2015

McChrystal's account of transforming the Joint Special Operations Command in Iraq is simultaneously a military history, a management masterclass, and the best argument I have encountered for shared consciousness as an organizational strategy. The insight: the problem is not that individual teams are bad at communicating — it's that teams are optimized for internal communication and blind to what is happening outside their unit. Essential for anyone working on cross-functional communication challenges.

4. Radical Candor: Be a Kick-Ass Boss Without Losing Your Humanity

Kim Scott

St. Martin's Press, 2017

Scott's framework — Care Personally, Challenge Directly — is the most practical guidance I have found for the hardest part of leadership communication: giving feedback that is honest without being brutal, and kind without being soft. I have drawn the two-by-two matrix on a whiteboard for teams more times than I can count.

5. Crucial Conversations: Tools for Talking When Stakes Are High

Kerry Patterson, Joseph Grenny, Ron McMillan, and Al Switzler

McGraw-Hill, Third Edition, 2021

The most practical guide to communicating when the conversation is difficult, the emotions are high, and the stakes are real. The STATE framework gives communicators a repeatable structure for high-stakes dialogue. The chapter on Pool of Shared Meaning alone is worth the price of the book.

6. No Ego: How Leaders Can Cut the Cost of Workplace Drama, End Entitlement, and Drive Big Results

Cy Wakeman

St. Martin's Press, 2017

Wakeman is direct in a way that makes some leaders uncomfortable — and that is precisely why this book belongs on this list. Her argument: most "communication problems" are actually accountability problems, and the emotional processing, drama, and defensiveness that consume so much organizational energy are not a management challenge to accommodate but a cultural pattern to change.

7. The Art of Communicating

Thich Nhat Hanh

HarperOne, 2013

This list would be incomplete without a reminder that communication is, at its root, a human practice — and that listening is as much a part of it as speaking. The concept of "deep listening" — listening without preparing your response, without judging, with the genuine intention to understand — is one of the most practical skills a communicator can develop. This book is a recalibration.

8. Switch: How to Change Things When Change Is Hard

Chip Heath and Dan Heath

Broadway Books, 2010

Communication culture change is change management. The Heath brothers' model of the Rider (rational), the Elephant (emotional), and the Path (environment) is one of the most accessible and accurate frameworks I have encountered for understanding why good communication initiatives fail to stick. If your team understands what it should do but doesn't do it, this book explains why.

9. Turn the Ship Around!: A True Story of Turning Followers into Leaders

L. David Marquet

Portfolio/Penguin, 2013

Marquet's account of transforming the USS Santa Fe from the worst-performing submarine in the U.S. Navy fleet to one of the best is, at its core, a story about communication as a leadership philosophy. The shift from "permission to speak freely" to "here is my intention" is a communication transformation with immediate operational applicability.

10. The Culture Code: The Secrets of Highly Successful Groups

Daniel Coyle

Bantam Books, 2018

Coyle's research into the world's most cohesive and effective teams reveals three consistent factors: safety, vulnerability, and purpose. All three are, in practice, communication problems. This book is the most readable account I have found of how great team cultures are actually built — not from values statements, but from thousands of small communication acts accumulated over time.

11. Humble Inquiry: The Gentle Art of Asking Instead of Telling

Edgar H. Schein

Berrett-Koehler Publishers, 2013

Schein's short, dense book makes a deceptively simple argument: most organizational communication is one-directional (telling) when the most valuable organizational communication is two-directional (asking and listening). His concept of humble inquiry — asking questions to which you do not already have the answer, with the genuine intention of understanding — is both a leadership philosophy and a practical communication tool.

12. Leaders Eat Last: Why Some Teams Pull Together and Others Don't

Simon Sinek

Portfolio/Penguin, 2014

Sinek's argument — that the most effective leaders create environments where people feel safe enough to be fully present — is a communication argument at heart. The "Circle of Safety" he describes is built through the communication choices leaders make: what they share, what they withhold, who they include, what questions they ask, and whether they model the vulnerability they ask of others.

About the Author

Adriane "Ace" Crabtree is a Lean Six Sigma Black Belt, a Prosci Certified Change Practitioner, and a Certified Associate in Project Management (CAPM) with twenty years of experience leading teams in environments where communication failures have real, measurable consequences.

Her career spans healthcare, government operations, education, and high-volume warehouse and distribution environments. Across all four, she observed the same pattern: teams with strong technical skills, adequate resources, and genuine commitment to success — failing repeatedly because the communication infrastructure could not support the complexity of the operation.

That pattern is what led her to develop The Silent Spiral™ and Breaking the Spiral™ — diagnostic and intervention frameworks designed to make communication failure visible, measurable, and fixable. Not abstract theory. Operational tools that teams can deploy in the same week they learn them.

She is the developer of the Warehouse Excellence Series, a comprehensive curriculum for operations professionals that includes thirteen training modules, twelve deployment toolkits, and a companion workbook. Her work bridges the gap between academic communication theory and the daily reality of teams that need to move information accurately, quickly, and without assumptions.

Ace holds a Master's degree in Public Relations from Ball State University and a Bachelor's degree in Public Relations and Professional Journalism from Indiana State University — **a background that gave her both her analytical rigor and her belief that clarity is a professional obligation, not a personal preference.** She edits with a purple pen. She writes and teaches from the floor, not the corner office.

Failure to Communicate: The #1 Reason Teams Fail — and How to Fix It

Index

A

B

C

D

E

F

G

H

I

J

K

L

T

U

V

www.ingramcontent.com/pod-product-compliance
Lightning Source LLC
LaVergne TN
LVHW010626110826
845149LV00014B/2788

* 9 7 9 8 9 9 5 6 6 5 9 0 8 *